D0612998

SELLING: THE PERSONAL FORCE IN MARKETING

Wiley Series In Marketing
David A. Aaker, Advisory Editor

SELLING
The Personal Force in Marketing

W. J. E. CRISSY
Michigan State University
WILLIAM H. CUNNINGHAM
ISABELLA C. M. CUNNINGHAM
The University of Texas at Austin

JOHN WILEY & SONS

New York • Chichester • Brisbane • Toronto • Singapore

This book was set in 10 point Times Roman by Techno Logue and printed and bound by Quinn and Boden. The cover was designed by Tri-Arts, Inc. and illustrations were prepared by Judi McCarty. Production was supervised by Chuck Pendergast and Jean Varven.

Library of Congress Cataloging in Publication Data:

Crissy, William Joseph Eliot.
    Selling.

    (Wiley marketing series)
    1. Selling. I. Cunningham, William Hughes, joint author. II. Cunningham, Isabella C. M., joint author. III. Title.
HF5438.25.C742   658.8'1   76-45848

ISBN 0-471-18757-7

Printed in the United States of America.

10 9 8 7 6 5 4

Dedicated to Charlotte and to our parents

About the Authors

W. J. E. Crissy is professor of marketing and of hospitality marketing at Michigan State University. He has well over 100 titles in the psychological, marketing, and management literature. He is coauthor of the internationally recognized *Psychology of Selling* series. For many years he headed a firm of psychologists specializing in sales and marketing consultation and training. He is a diplomate in industrial psychology of the American Board of Examiners in Professional Psychology. His consulting and teaching has taken him to all parts of the United States, Canada, Europe, Asia, Australia and New Zealand. He is a member of many professional organizations including the American Marketing Association, American Psychological Association, and the Academy of Management.

William H. Cunningham is an Associate Professor of Marketing and Associate Dean of Graduate Programs for the College of Business Administration at The University of Texas at Austin. He has published more than twenty articles in journals such as *Sales Management, Journal of Marketing, Journal of Marketing Research, Journal of Business, Journal of Advertising Research, Journal of Social Psychology, Journal of Genetic Psychology, Journal of Experimental Education,* and *Journal of Business Research.* He has taught courses in professional selling at The University of Texas at Austin and Michigan State University. In addition, he has taught Marketing Administration and Selling in numerous advanced management programs for businessmen in the United States, Mexico, Algeria and the Bahamas. He has won three awards for excellence in teaching while at The University of Texas at Austin. He is a member of the American Marketing Association, the Southern Marketing Association, the American Institute for Decision Sciences.

Isabella C. M. Cunningham is an Associate Professor of Advertising at the University of Texas at Austin. She has published articles in several scholarly journals, such as the *Journal of Retailing,* the *Journal of Marketing,* the *Journal of Marketing Research,* the *Journal of Advertising,* and the *Journal of Genetic Psychology.* She has coauthored numerous works including a monograph on the subject of marketing in Brazil and a book of readings on Investment Management. Dr. Cunningham has a J.D. and has received her Ph.D. in Marketing from Michigan State University. She has done consulting work both in the marketing and advertising areas. She is a member of several professional organizations including the American Marketing Association, the Brazilian Bar Association, the Southern Marketing Association and the American Academy of Advertising.

Preface

In view of the quantity and diversity of books on selling, it seems appropriate to describe the kind of book we have written. We claim no "seven secrets of sales success." In fact, we do not think they exist. Our book is neither cookbook nor handbook; rather it is a conceptually oriented treatment in depth of the dynamics of the selling-buying process. We hold that selling in the firm can only be understood as an integral part of the total marketing effort. We see the sales force as the firm's tactical arm in the competitive marketplace and the salesperson as a manager of a business (a territory or a market segment).

The text complements the classroom instructor in forming a learning system. Selling has both knowledge and skill ingredients. Skills are acquired only through practice. This is why we provide an application exercise and cases for each chapter in the book.

The book is organized into six parts. To assist those who have not had a previous marketing course, we begin by discussing selling and how it fits in the marketing effort of the firm. Part 1, "The Role of Selling in the Firm," contains two chapters: "The Professional Salesperson" and "Selling and the Marketing Effort." Here we discuss the various dimensions of sales positions and the interrelationship between selling and the other functions of a marketing department. In order to get insight into what a salesperson does it is important to know something about the company's total marketing team.

Part 2, "Contributions to Selling from the Behavioral Sciences," contains Chapters 3 through 6: "Models of Buyer Behavior," "Interpersonal Communication," "The Salesperson as a Change Agent and Problem Solver," and "The Selling-Buying Process." Today's salesperson must have a firm foundation in the behavioral sciences in order to work effectively with customers, and in this part we attempt to provide this foundation and to relate theory to sales practices as well. It is important to understand fundamental ideas about human behavior in order to appreciate the selling-buying process. Thus we present many economic, psychological, and social factors which influence buying behavior.

In Part 3 of the text we take up "Sales Strategy." This part contains Chapters 7 through 10: "Planning in Selling," "Influencing Individual Behavior," "Influencing Account Behavior," and "Prospecting-Generating New Business." Part 4, "Selling Tactics," contains Chapters 11 through 16: "The Sales Call as a Tactical Situation," "The Approach-Gaining Entree to Sell," "The Presentation-Satisfying Wants Persuasively," "Demonstration-Reinforcing the Presentation," "Objections-Managing Sales Resistance," and "The Close-Satisfying Wants Persuasively." Strategy is antecedent to tactics, refers to the big picture, and is future oriented. It is based on the "knowns." Tactics deal with the "now" and are based on the "unknowns." Selling has both strategic and tactical aspects, but sales tactics are far more complex and diverse, and one's picture of selling would be incomplete indeed if it were treated solely in strategic terms. In fact, the crux of selling is when salesperson and buyer are face to face, and this is when tactics come into play.

Part 5, "Types of Selling," includes Chapters 17 through 20. These chapters examine how the principles, methods, and techniques discussed in the previous portions of the text can be applied in different selling situations. The chapters are entitled: "Selling to the Final Consumer," "Selling to Organizations-Manufacturers," "Selling to Organizations-Government, Nonprofit, and Resellers," and "Selling to Individuals and Organizations by Telephone."

In this part we aim to provide insight into the many situations where selling takes place—in the home, in the community, in various business organizations, in government, in the nonprofit sector, and in reselling firms. We also treat in depth the use of the telephone as an important sales tool.

Part 6, the last portion of the text, is entitled "Building the Sales Force." Here we are concerned with the managerial and legal aspects of personal selling. Part 6 contains Chapters 21 through 23: "Selection and Development of Sales Personnel," "The Financial Aspects of Sales Management," and the "Legal and Ethical Aspects of Selling." We conclude with an epilog on the future trends of selling in an era of mass promotion and distribution and the effects of these on the modern salesperson.

January 1977

W. J. E. Crissy
W. H. Cunningham
I. C. M. Cunningham

Acknowledgments

Special acknowledgment and thanks go to Harold C. Cash, who co-authored *The Psychology of Selling* series with one of us. He has graciously consented to numerous quotations and references from that twelve-volume work. In addition, many of the ideas developed jointly with him have had an impact on this text.

A special debt is also due Professor Robert M. Kaplan who contributed a great deal to an earlier version of this text. Many of his ideas and contributions have stood the test of time and continue in the present book.

We would also like to thank the following individuals who contributed a substantial amount of time and effort to the text: Pam Gordon, Susan Stephens, Carla Williams and Ann McManus worked tirelessly on the production of the manuscript. Roger Holloway, Marketing Editor of Wiley/Hamilton, acted as a constant source of constructive criticism and encouragement. In addition, Alice Keller of the *Journal of Marketing* provided us with invaluable editorial assistance.

Special thanks to David A. Aaker, University of California at Berkeley, John E. Swan, University of Arkansas, Richard M. Durand, University of Alabama, and James E. Littlefield, University of North Carolina at Chapel Hill for their insightful reviews.

A Message for the Student

Your course in selling should be one of the most stimulating and exciting college classroom learning experience. No aspect of business is more creative or challenging than selling. In our competitive enterprise system the customer is "king." Each business, through its marketing and sales effort, seeks to have its products chosen in competition. The personal selling effort is oftentimes the key means of accomplishing this.

The study of selling is useful for a variety of reasons. First, if you are contemplating a rewarding career in sales work, this course is a prime step toward professional preparation. Second, if you are entering the broad field of marketing, the study of selling can be extremely useful in understanding the behavior of others. If you plan to enter the business world in any capacity, it is important to understand as much as possible about the selling-buying process. Effective selling is a critical factor in the very survival of every business. No firm can exist without customers, and only effective selling can create customers.

Several study aids are provided at the end of each chapter, in the form of chapter summaries, problems, and suggested readings. In addition, each chapter has an application exercise which relates your knowledge of selling to actual selling in the real world. These exercises are followed by cases, which enable you to use creative thinking and problem solving in selling situations. A detailed glossary of terms is provided at the end of the book. If you thrive on challenges, enjoy problem solving, have a yen for the new, and want to be "your own man (or woman)" then a selling career may be for you.

Contents

ONE

The Role of Selling in the Firm

Part I is made up of two chapters which provide the background for the entire text. In Chapter 1, "The Professional Salesperson," we examine various dimensions of sales positions and the personal qualities needed for successful sales performance. We also illustrate how a salesperson in any organization plays many roles in the firm's total competitive effort. We conclude this chapter with a discussion of the personal and financial opportunities available in selling, together with some ethical factors that must be considered by a salesperson.

In Chapter 2, "Selling and the Marketing Effort," we interrelate selling with the other functions of a marketing department. Here, we analyze the marketing concept and the factors in the contemporary business environment which influence the competitive effort. We also discuss what comprises marketing in a firm—how selling relates to marketing research, what the channels of distribution are, sales promotion, advertising, pricing, product management, and sales management. Ultimately, the total competitive effort is aimed at creating and sustaining customers in an ongoing mutually profitable relationship.

1. The Professional Salesperson

IN THIS CHAPTER

The Sales Stereotype
The Selling Spectrum
Qualities of a Successful Salesperson
The Salesperson as a Team Leader
Opportunities in Selling
Ethical Considerations

There are few figures in Americana that are more maligned than the sales-person.* He is accused of sins ranging from running off with the farmer's daughter to convincing poor, helpless people that they should buy products they have no need for. In reality, the salesperson has no more fascination for the farmer's daughter than does an accountant, a banker, or a wandering rock star. And, since the salesperson has not mastered the intricacies of the human mind,

*Throughout the text we have used "salesperson" rather than "salesman" to indicate that selling provides opportunities for both men and women. When referring to the salesperson in the third person we have used the pronoun "he" rather than "he/she" for simplicity. Therefore "he" in this sense is a neuter pronoun.

he is therefore, seldom able to impose unwanted products onto the helpless public. This does not mean to imply that there are no aggressive, hard-hitting sales representatives—the drummer of dubious social values such as Willy Loman (in *Death of a Salesman*)[1] is no longer wanted or needed in today's economy. Instead, we are concerned with the contemporary professional salesperson. And, in this regard, we will examine the common stereotype that we have of salespersons, the qualities of the successful salesperson, and the opportunities and rewards that exist for a career in selling.

THE SALES STEREOTYPE

When we think of a salesperson we often stereotype him as a used car salesperson. We will contrast the stereotype of a used car salesperson with the role that a true professional salesperson plays in the selling-buying process.

The Used Car Salesperson

Many people believe that a used car salesperson is selling a product that looks good on the outside, "a cream puff" but has probably been involved in a head-on collision on a figure eight race track. In addition, there is that question that is always in the back of our mind, "How much sawdust has been put in the transmission to keep it from making noise?" We also feel that the used car salesperson will try to use high pressure sales tactics to make us buy the car. He really does not care if it fits our needs, "after all, 'research' has shown that cars with V-12 engines run smoother and are more efficient in some ways than a straight six." Finally we feel the used car salesperson will try lines like, "since this car is such a good value there are several other individuals who are interested in purchasing it. If you act now, it is yours, if you wait I cannot guarantee that it will still be here."

The Professional Salesperson

In contrast to how we perceive the average salesperson, there are a great many sales representatives who act in a very professional manner. As an example, IBM's computer sales representatives begin each sale by trying to determine what the real needs of the customer are. From there, they will try to design a package of computer hardware and software that will solve the customer's problems in the most efficient manner possible. Here, there is never any question that the equipment is not first rate, that the company will not stand behind it, and that the salesperson will not try to take advantage of the customer or use high pressure techniques to make him buy the product.

It is important to make one point clear—there are a great many honest, hard-working used car salespeople, as well as computer salespersons, who want

[1] Carl Rieser, "The Salesman Isn't Dead—He's Different," *Fortune*, Vol. 66 (November 1962), p. 124.

to see that the customer gets a product that is what he really needs and can afford. Yet we tend to stereotype sales representatives in one way, which is not fair to the selling profession and most times is not even accurate.

THE SELLING SPECTRUM

Sales positions must be examined across a variety of dimensions. There is no one dimension that adequately describes sales representatives or their activities. One of the most important factors to be considered, however, is the amount of creative skill that is required for success. To illustrate the relative importance of this factor in the sales function, we will discuss seven types of sales positions— ranging from those that require little or no creativity to those that are highly creative.[2]

Levels of Creativity in Sales Positions

*1. Positions in which the salesperson's job consists primarily of **delivering merchandise**.*   Examples of products that are sold in this manner are bread, heating oil, newspapers, and milk. Although good service and a pleasant manner will increase the amount of sales, the individual's selling responsibilities are of secondary importance. Few new accounts will be obtained by this type of delivery person.

*2. Positions in which the salesperson is largely an **inside ordertaker**.*   This salesperson does not leave his place of business, and his customers have virtually made up their minds as to what they want before they meet with the salesperson. Although a salesperson in this category may offer suggestions at times as to what other individuals have bought, typically he does not try to convince the customer to upgrade the quality of merchandise asked for or to make additional purchases. Examples of salespeople in this category would be clerks in a retail store and those in the parts department in an automobile dealership.

*3. Positions in which the salesperson works in the field but is **primarily an ordertaker**.*   Products sold in this manner are soap or spice. This salesperson visits his regular accounts and takes their orders. No attempt is made to sell the customer anything beyond what he has on the shelves or in his "work." Like the delivery salesperson this individual will be more successful if he has a pleasant personality and offers his customers good service.

4. Positions in which the salesperson is not expected to make a sale but is expected to call on customers to build good will for his firm.   Such a person is

[2]Robert N. McMurry, "The Mystique of Super-Salesmanship," Harvard Business Review, Vol. 39 (March–April 1961), p. 114.

called a *missionary salesperson.* An example would be a salesperson of a major rubber company, who calls on his distributors' accounts. His function is to try to build the confidence of the accounts in the rubber company so that they will purchase rubber products through the distributor. If the missionary salesperson received an order, he would simply turn it over to the distributor. Frequently, the missionary salesperson and the representative of the local distributor will make joint calls, visiting the distributors accounts together.

5. Positions in which the greatest emphasis is placed on **technical knowledge.** This salesperson sells a product that may be used in the manufacturing or research departments of a company. Normally he would have acquired a substantial amount of technical training outside his college or university education. An example would be a computer salesperson. He spends a great deal of his time designing systems that will solve the peculiar problems of his various customers. The salesperson's technical knowledge is vital to the success of his job.

6. Positions that require the **creative selling of tangible products.** Examples would be sales representatives of vacuum cleaners, refrigerators, and aluminum siding. In these situations the salesperson frequently has a dual task. First, he must convince the prospect that he is dissatisfied with his present merchandise, then he must sell the prospect his particular product.

7. Positions that require **creative selling of intangible goods or services** such as insurance, advertising, or education. This type of selling is the most difficult, because the product cannot be readily demonstrated or dramatized.

Reflection on these seven categories reveals that they provide a scale: easy to difficult; routine to creative. The extreme situation is where his clients often may not have heard of the product or understand how it really benefits them. Such selling situations require a great deal of creativity to explain the product and then demonstrate how it will help the prospect. However, we shall see that there are challenging opportunities in all fields of selling, depending on the initiative and talent of the salesperson.

Additional Dimensions of the Sales Position

Although the amount of creativity required is one of the basic elements in classifying a sales position, there are other factors that significantly affect the nature of the sales job.

Types of Accounts.   Selling jobs vary according to the types of accounts being cultivated. At one extreme, the salesperson may call on households as buying units; at the other extreme, he may call only on large manufacturing establishments. The individual company may indicate in very specific terms who its sales representatives are to call on. For example, in the case of a pharmaceutical products manufacturer, the sales representative may be instructed to call on physicians in general practice who have prescription-writing potential above a certain minimum, on all hospitals, and on retail drug stores that exceed a certain annual dollar volume.

Nature of the Product Line. A rough classification for a sales representative's product line might be *consumer* versus *industrial* goods. This can be even further specialized—for instance, a chemicals specialty salesperson. In a diversified company, there might be differentiation of this kind within the sales force. The same company might have a consumer-products sales force and an industrial-products sales force.

Width of the Product Line. This dimension deals with the number of different products a salesperson carries. For instance, the mill-house salesperson might have 5000 catalogue entries to handle, whereas the salesperson for a Coca-Cola bottler would have a relatively narrow and homogeneous product line. This dimension would most likely be reflected in the structure of the field sales force of an individual firm. The company that has a heterogeneous line of products often differentiates the selling jobs by major product groupings. The rationale for this is that it is impossible for one salesperson to understand all the products in sufficient depth to sell them effectively.

Customer Sophistication. The range in level of sophistication of persons called upon comprises a significant dimension. For example, it is not uncommon for an industrial salesperson to have to present his products and services to the man in overalls as well as to the members of the executive suite. In contrast, the salesperson for a clothing manufacturer might call on department and specialty store buyers who are relatively homogeneous in their knowledge and sophistication.

Educational Requirements. Sales positions frequently vary according to the amount and type of education required to perform them. In the case of some selling jobs, a high school education may be sufficient, while in others an advanced degree may be essential. For the individual firm, this is likely to vary according to the amount of technical assistance provided to the salesperson. If relatively little back-up expertise is available, the salesperson must know proportionately more himself. On the other hand, if he has specialists ready to assist him on technical matters, he may not need as much formal education.

Heterogeneity of the Marketplace. This is an important dimension on which to differentiate many selling jobs. One salesperson may be expected to call on small machine shops as well as large manufacturers, whereas another salesperson may have only one major customer as his responsibility. Selling jobs within the same company may vary greatly on this dimension. For example, in a large, dense market considerable specialization by clientele is feasible, while in a smaller, scattered market a salesperson for the same firm may have to call on everyone who is a customer or a prospective customer for any of his firm's products.

Heterogeneity of People.   Related to the dimension of heterogeneity of the marketplace is the heterogeneity of people within the individual account. At one extreme, the salesperson may call only on the purchasing agent. At the other extreme, he may have to call upon purchasing agents, operating personnel, research and development specialists, and other members of management in order to consummate sales.

Specialization by Product.   Selling jobs can often be differentiated by the degree to which specialization by product exists. The salesperson may be responsible for the sale of only a single product from the line (for example, an Ethyl salesperson selling only additives for gasoline to major refineries); or there may be little or no product specialization, in which case the salesperson is responsible for selling the full line. The degree of product specialization is likely to be directly correlated with the extent and complexity of the technical knowledge required to understand and use the product.

Required Service.   Another important dimension involves the ratio of service to products in the product-service mix to be sold. The offering may include the product alone, with a nominal amount of service involved; or the salesperson may have to provide considerable advice and service pre-transactionally to generate the business and post-transactionally as part of what has been purchased. Within the same industry, there may be considerable variance on this dimension. Competitor A may make much of the associated service his salesperson renders as an important part of the selling job. Competitor B may have a separate field service organization, and the salesperson is involved only incidentally in a supportive function.

Degree of Problem Solving.   Sales jobs can be differentiated on the degree of problem solving involved in connection with the use of the products and services. A salesperson for an electronic data-processing equipment firm may have to make a detailed analysis of likely uses of his equipment in order to sell it. In contrast, a salesperson offering expendable office supplies may seldom face problems with the use of his product. In markets where problem solving is an important consideration, firms are likely to provide considerable technical assistance. However, the salesperson must still be sufficiently adept as a problem solver to define the problems and know what talents within his company are needed to solve them.

Size of Order.   Considerable variation exists in the size of the order. One salesperson may sell only capital goods to manufacturers, with each transaction involving five figures or more. Another may sell expendable supplies where the unit order seldom exceeds two digits. This dimension in turn influences the time and investment in each account and the number of customers and prospects comprising a sales territory. The larger the stake in the transaction, the greater is the selling time that must be used and the fewer are the accounts that can be handled.

Nonselling Duties.   Selling jobs vary in the number and complexity of non-selling duties they involve. One salesperson may be furnished clerical and technical support so that he can devote most of his time to making actual calls. Another salesperson, in addition to making calls, may have responsibility for collections, doing preliminary design on proposals, participating in dealers' sales meeting, and helping retailers with displays. There is an obvious correlation between this dimension and the versatility of talent needed in the salesperson. Also, a marketing-oriented company is likely to require more of these nonselling duties than a company that is product or sales oriented.

Segmentation.   Finally, selling jobs vary in the degree to which the market-place is segmented. Generally speaking, the industrial salesperson faces a more segmented marketplace than his counterpart in the consumer sector. However, even in directly competing firms, there may be considerable variation to this dimension. A salesperson may have precisely defined categories of customers and prospects to call on, and his territory may overlap geographically with several other of his firm's territories. As more technical knowledge is required to understand the uses of the firm's products, there is likely to be greater segmentation of the market.

Thus there are many factors affecting the types of sales positions that exist in a highly developed economy. Now, let us examine the difficulties that occur in a selling career and what factors are important for success.

QUALITIES OF A SUCCESSFUL SALESPERSON

Although there are many different types of sales representatives who perform a wide variety of tasks, there are several factors that make for a successful career, regardless of the specific situation. Before we examine these attributes, it is important to realize why selling is a difficult job. While there are great financial and personal rewards apparent in a selling career, it is not an occupation without its share of problems.

Selling Is a Difficult Job

One of the key factors that makes the lives of many sales representatives difficult is that they spend a great portion of their time prospecting for new business—making "cold" calls. This occurs when a salesperson visits a prospective account on whom he has never called before. In many instances, the salesperson does not have enough information to help him know what the prospect's problems are, nor does he have any personal relationship with the buyer. Although some senior sales representatives have such a large group of established accounts that they rarely have to make cold calls, most salespeople are not that fortunate.

Many field sales representatives work alone, sometimes going for days without any personal contact with their supervisors or other employees of the firm. This makes field selling a lonely job. Sales representatives, like most individuals, enjoy the opportunity to discuss their problems and accomplishments with their superiors and their fellow employees. In addition, discussions of this nature are psychologically important, for they offer a chance to let off steam. Yet these contacts are sporadic for field sales representatives because of their schedules.

In addition, the salesperson's work hours are often long and irregular. At times, a salesperson may have to stay up late at night entertaining customers, filling out the reports of his activities to be mailed to his supervisor, or planning his next day's efforts. Since the salesperson must adapt his schedule to those of his customers, he frequently faces early morning appointments with long time gaps between calls. The effective salesperson uses this time wisely, but it is often not easy to do.

Finally, the salesperson may feel he is the perpetual intruder. He is continually interrupting people, many of whom are of higher organizational status than himself, to try to persuade them to purchase his products. And because most individuals have a need for security, love, and certainty, many people find selling a very difficult occupation.[3]

Important Factors for the Salesperson

Occupations in selling range from the retail sales clerk behind the counter to the industrial salesperson with a six-state territory. Formal education requirements may range from high school diploma to advanced degrees, depending on the technical nature of the product line and the sophistication of the market. Historically, field selling jobs have been open only to men, but an increasing number of women are being employed for these jobs today. A wide range of individual differences in age, experience, education, and other factors are evident even among sales personnel of the same firm. There is no set pattern of talents, traits, and motives that spells success. Despite this diversity, however, there are a number of factors that are critical to most successful sales representatives.

Intellectual Endowments.   In general, the more technical the product line and the more sophisticated the persons called upon, the greater is the need for a high level of intelligence in the salesperson. He needs this to master the body of

[3]*Ibid.,* p. 115.

knowledge about the company's products and to cope with the problems involved in their use. In addition, he must be able to match wits with the sophisticated decision makers he encounters. Special aptitudes or flairs may be needed, depending on the nature of the products and the uses and applications associated with them. For example, selling construction equipment requires considerable mechanical aptitude, while selling furniture puts a premium on artistic aptitude and a flair for color and design.

Knowledge.   The amount and kind of education needed, like the level of intelligence, depends on the technical nature of the selling job and the level of sophistication of the customers and prospects. Any salesperson, of course, has to have knowledge beyond that obtained in school. In fact, in some selling fields the body of technical knowledge is changing so rapidly that substantial amounts of time must be devoted each week to merely keeping up with it.

The knowledge needed for any selling job may be thought of as three-dimensional: *general knowledge,* or cultural background; *knowledge of business;* and *technical knowledge,* or expertise. [The amount of general knowledge required is mainly related to the cultural background of those who must be influenced.] It provides the salesperson with something in common with the prospect as he makes his calls. As to knowledge of business, the amount required is related to the nature of the accounts and the commercial significance of the product line from the standpoint of the customers and prospects. For example, the industrial salesperson handling capital outlay items needs more knowledge of finance and accounting than the person selling office supplies. Those calling on resellers need this knowledge to advise their customers. The technical knowledge required varies according to the different market practices adopted. It is not uncommon for a firm to followup on an initial sales presentation with a team of engineers or trained technicians in order to demonstrate the product. In this case, the salesperson's job will be limited to knowing the factors that might make his product desirable for the client.

Skills.   The ability to communicate orally is universally required in all fields of selling. In no other occupational field is this ability as crucial to success. The salesperson's skill in communicating orally depends on his having an adequate vocabulary, selecting the most effective ways of phrasing his ideas, and developing voice qualities that enable him to convey his message with clarity, sincerity, and conviction.

Planning is also essential in all fields of selling. However, several factors influence the amount or level of planning needed and its importance to success. First, the more decentralized the sales organization, the more necessary it is for the salesperson to be a good planner. As he is given increased authority to act on behalf of the company, he must take greater care in planning his actions and commitments. Second, the less supervision provided the salesperson, the more necessary it is for him to be good at self-supervising and, consequently, the more important it is for him to be skillful in planning his work on his own. Third, the more complex the selling-buying relationship, the more need there is for skillful planning. It takes a higher level of planning skill to determine the key decision makers in a large corporation than is needed to influence an individual prospect or customer. Fourth, the more drawn out negotiations are likely to be, the greater is the need for planning. Thus, if the salesperson must conduct several calls to achieve a purchase, careful planning is essential so that each call counts and each one enhances his previous contacts. The salesperson's plans have a wide scope, including territorial coverage, account management, tactics for a specific call, key decision makers to be influenced, and prudent use of personal time.

Character.   Inasmuch as the salesperson must sustain interpersonal relationships over time (i.e., he must wear well in people relationships), his character traits must have both consistency and normality. A salesperson needs to have a well-defined set of life values in order to plan, decide, and act in a consistent manner. In the eyes of many people, his conduct shapes the image and reputation of the firm. This consistency also provides him with the psychological privacy necessary to face harassment, frustration, and disappointment. The salesperson lives in an environment of change, and he must exercise control over situations by persuasion rather than authority. He needs strength of character to adjust successfully under these circumstances. Often things do not go well despite his best efforts; circumstances beyond his control may spoil his carefully made plans. In addition to being consistent, the salesperson must possess life values that at a minimum are defensible and, it is hoped, are worthy of emulation by those he must influence. Each person quickly translates the salesperson's values as he perceives them into those of the company the salesperson represents. As a result, the salesperson will have a much better chance of long-term success if he has both *consistency* and *normality* in his life values.

Personality.   The salesperson must possess a considerable amount of social sensitivity—being "others-conscious," not "self-conscious." This is the ability to pick up the nuances of behavior, the small cues in other persons' reactions.

Coupled with social sensitivity is a need for adjustiveness or flexibility. It would be futile for the salesperson to note cues in the other persons' reactions if he were unable to adjust effectively to them. This does not mean that the salesperson is putting on an act. He is simply flexible enough to adjust to a wide spectrum of reactions in the other person. His behavior must ring true if it is to carry conviction.

Drive.   Another essential personality trait is the salesperson's drive. Typically, the salesperson's work environment is such that he must often keep long, irregular hours. He must eat at odd times and carry on in all kinds of weather. Almost daily, he must adjust to the frustration caused by refusals to buy and unexpected and sometimes unfair competitive behavior. He must cope with factors beyond his control that upset his plans and still have sufficient physical and psychological energy to cope with the challenges of his assignment. He must be able to direct his energy toward worthwhile goals and to reset his goals as need requires. Finally, he must be able to pace himself so that he has as much enthusiasm on the last call in the evening as he had on the first call in the morning.

Motivation.   Motivation refers to the "why" of behavior. There are many ways to interpret human motivation. The effective salesperson has a possessiveness with regard to his territory and the accounts within it. He speaks of "my" territory, "my" customers, not "the company's." He has a strong urge to achieve and to score victories over the competition. Each of his accomplishments sets the stage for seeking new ones. Although he is aware of direct and indirect competition, he sees himself and his previous record as his key competitor.

All of these activities, particularly those conducted face-to-face, must have intrinsic interest for the salesperson if he is to be effective. Only if they are "fun to do" can the salesperson show enthusiasm in doing them. This has a favorable influence on the customer or prospect, since enthusiasm is contagious.

Because the salesperson works in an environment of change, he must find much of his personal security within himself. If he is to be effective in his work, he has to see change as a challenge rather than a problem. The successful salesperson will view each unanticipated event or reaction as a chance to display his tactical skill and his ability to cope with change. Hence, the salesperson must be *inner*-directed and self-reliant rather than *outer*-directed and dependent on the environment for guidance.

Once again it is important to point out that selling is a tough job. Unfortunately, many people enter this profession without a feeling for what is needed to be a successful salesperson. The qualities just listed are not meant to serve as an automatic check list, but individuals who have these qualities or are willing to acquire them will have a good chance of becoming successful sales representatives. We will now examine one additional variable that is critical to successful selling: the ability to organize the efforts of the entire firm to accomplish the sales objectives.

THE SALESPERSON AS A TEAM LEADER

The salesperson is in a rather unusual position. Although as was indicated previously, the field salesperson may find himself separated from his supervisor and fellow employees long enough so that he becomes lonely, he also has at his disposal the resources of his entire company. One of the salesperson's most important functions is to determine *who* in his organization can help him obtain the order and *when* these individuals should be brought into the action to gain maximum impact. The kinds of people the salesperson can use include sales managers, technical specialists, financial officers, and top management officials.

To illustrate, let us assume that a large electrical manufacturer is selling dynamometers (i.e., engine testing devices) to an automobile company. The salesperson probably has been calling on the account for a number of years. He knows who in the automobile company has inputs into the final decision and who is responsible for making the final decision. One dynamometer could cost as much as $70,000, and a typical order could be as much as $400,000.

Once the salesperson becomes aware that an order will be placed in a few months for several dynamometers, he tries to determine where the new equipment will be installed, who will use it, and who will be involved in the buying decision. As a routine matter, the salesperson would notify his sales manager that a large order is likely to be placed within a few months. Through the sales manager, he may bring together an engineer, a finance man, a plant manager, or anyone else needed to map strategy. The sales manager and other executives in the firm may have some contacts at a higher level in the automobile company than the salesperson's contacts. However, since it is the salesperson's account, he is the one who decides which supportive personnel in the company will be brought in to assist with the sale.

In this kind of selling situation, the salesperson is likely to have a considerable amount of technical expertise. However, if the customer is considering new uses for the product or a new product that the salesperson is not fully knowledgeable about, the salesperson may arrange for his company to send a technical specialist to make a joint call in order to augment his own knowledge. The technical specialist would not only meet with the salesperson's usual contacts, but he would also spend a substantial amount of his time with the automobile company's research people. In this way, the technical specialist would be in a good position to understand and formulate responses to the customer's wants and needs. Similarly, if there were other problems, such as financial constraints, the salesperson might ask people from his firm's corporate finance staff to assist him in determining how the product would be paid for.

Finally, if the order is to be quite substantial the salesperson might request that an executive from the firm's management team assist him in the final negotiations. If it is a large order, the decision will likely be made by a top official in the automobile company. Protocol normally requires that a man of approximately equal rank in the selling company should call on the top management of the prospective customer.

The important point is that the salesperson is the conductor—he must orchestrate and synchronize the selling effort, determine whom he needs, when they should arrive on the scene, and whom they will talk to. Although he will receive advice from his sales manager, the sales manager will let the competent salesperson make the key decisions. To dramatize the importance of salespersons, one company listed their salespersons at the top of their organization chart.

OPPORTUNITIES IN SELLING

When a person aspires to have his own business and is unable to do so, employment as a field salesperson is the next best alternative. No other work affords the same opportunity to be independent of direct supervision. To a great extent, the salesperson is master of his own destiny. Related to this is the fact that many sales representatives are compensated proportionately to the results they achieve. Even when compensation is in the form of straight salary, raises are earned on the basis of personal results achieved. Income in sales, initially and in the long run, is higher than in most other occupations.

A Social Contribution

The salesperson has an opportunity to make a genuine social contribution. Effective selling is the key to our private enterprise economy: sales representatives provide the transactions that enable business to flourish. The professional salesperson sees the need for mutual profit in the selling-buying relationship and hence benefits individuals and organizations by helping them to buy profitably. If sales were not being made, business would be at a standstill. In a sense, the salesperson creates jobs for other individuals who make and use the products he sells.

Continuing Education

No other occupational field enables a person to learn as much about all the facets of business. As part of his work, the salesperson is likely to become involved in a multiplicity of problems facing each of his customers and prospects. As he assists them in their solution, he inevitably adds to his own business knowledge. Contrast this with those whose work is done completely within the confines of their own company—and often solely within a single department. No other business occupation affords the individual the same educational opportunity. Furthermore, in no other career does enlightened self-interest benefit more from this kind of learning experience. The salesperson can make direct application of the knowledge he acquires through increased sales.

Success in selling depends in a very major way on the salesperson's continuing improvement of his skills in handling people. In turn, these same skills provide him with a special talent that is useful in all of his interpersonal relationships. Skill in dealing with people has applications in his own home, with his friends and acquaintances, and in such avocational pursuits as lodge work, community organizations, and church groups. These skills are useful wherever there is a need for subtle persuasion. They give the salesperson a competitive edge wherever people are to be understood and influenced. In no other occupational field does the opportunity exist to meet such a wide variety of people in an intimate, interpersonal, persuasive relationship.

Variety has been referred to as the spice of life. Certainly this is provided in abundance in field selling. The unexpected is the expected. No two days are alike. Even the same account varies from call to call. In sustaining favorable selling-buying relations, each day the salesperson faces new problems to solve and new applications for his creativity.

Career Opportunities

An increasing number of companies provide a *Y*-shaped career track for the young person entering the sales force (Figure 1-1). Once the individual has finished his initial sales training and has demonstrated competence as a salesperson, he may pursue a rewarding, lifetime career as a salesperson; alternatively, he may aspire to progress into management. Definite opportunities exist along each path, and there are incentives for achieving excellence in both.

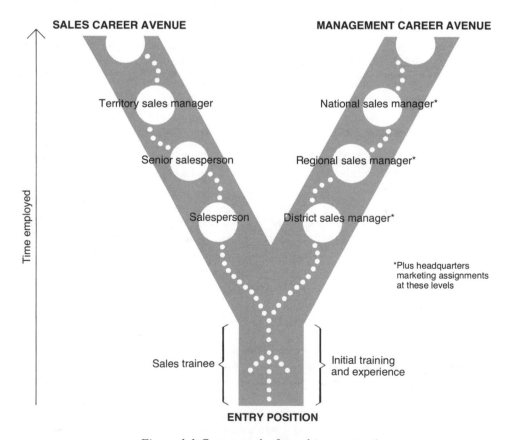

Figure 1-1 Career paths for sales personnel

Sales Career Avenue.   In most firms, there will be a greater number of openings along the sales career avenue than on the management career avenue. One firm differentiates three positions along the sales career avenue: salesperson, senior salesperson, and territory sales manager. An individual may progress through all three steps while selling in the same territory. The differentiation occurs on the basis of competitive position, contribution to profit, amount and share of business in each category of account, and effectiveness in handling accounts. This company provides a higher salary base for each successive step of the sales career avenue as well as other special incentives. For example, as a salesperson moves up each step he is given a better company car. A territory sales manager may designate any mass-produced, U.S. luxury car for his personal use.

Some companies provide advancement in the sales career avenue through transfer to a larger territory. One food processor categorizes territories by volume as *A, B,* and *C.* The salesperson in *A* territory may earn double the average income of those in *C* territories. Other firms accomplish this by moving salespersons to larger and more important accounts. In some situations, advancement comes in the form of increased responsibility for decisions in such matters as commitment of technical resources and pricing. Often, persons who advance to a higher point on the sales career avenue outearn the managers to whom they report. This creates no inequity in view of the salesperson's increased contribution to company well-being.

Management Career Avenue.   The opportunities are numerous and varied for the salesperson who aspires to move up the management career avenue. Initial advancement most often comes in the form of supervisory responsibility over other sales representatives. The position may be designated, depending on the firm, as district manager, branch manager, division manager, or field sales supervisor. To achieve success in such an assignment, the person must be able to communicate his sales knowledge and skills to others in order to achieve results through their efforts. Depending on the organizational structure of the firm, such persons may, in addition to their "people" responsibilities, be responsible for market analysis, sales forecasting, and, in some cases, the management of local inventories: a definite promotional ladder leads from this first-echelon post in field sales management to the position of national or general sales manager.

Less frequently, promotional opportunities occur in various parts of the regional marketing organization. Field sales experience is viewed by some companies as essential for advancement to product planning and management. Such firms reason that a person needs such experience to properly understand products and product groups *through the user's eyes.* If this career avenue is followed, the initial assignment is likely to be that of an assistant in a group handling one of the less important products or product groups of the company. Advancement occurs by increased responsibility in the same group or, alternatively, by movement to a more important product or product group. Another movement on the management career avenue may be to national accounts management or into sales promotion, advertising, or merchandising. In all of these, the sales and marketing intelligence aspects of field selling have direct application. Sales representatives who show talent for quantitative and financial aspects of their work may move into sales analysis and forecasting. Here, field sales experience supplies a person with a feel for the data being analyzed, which is hard to obtain in any other way.

Finally, a person may start out in selling and then advance into some other part of the enterprise. Experience gained in the field may be especially useful in research and development as well as in purchasing. In research and development, the salesperson's knowledge and experience with products in use complements the engineering and design expertise of research personnel. In purchasing, the person with sales expertise has an appreciation for the sales representatives calling on him. He also has a sound basis for evaluating offerings that other purchasing personnel may lack.

Financial Rewards

In addition to the substantial nonmaterial rewards associated with selling, there is an opportunity to make a good living. Table 1-1 illustrates the rise in the average salesperson's total compensation—from $11,004 in 1969 to $14,357 in 1973. During the same period, the average senior salesperson's salary increased to $17,052 and the average sales supervisor's salary climbed to $20,250.

TABLE 1-1 TOTAL COMPENSATION*

	1969	1970	1971	1972	1973	% Change 1969–1973
Sales trainee	$ 8,121	$ 8,455	$ 8,923	$ 9,141	$ 9,495	16.9
Salesperson	11,004	11,569	12,214	12,628	14,357	30.4
Senior salesperson	14,003	14,972	15,119	16,654	17,052	21.7
Sales supervisor	15,378	16,595	17,665	18,667	20,250	31.6

*Source: *Sales Management, The Marketing Magazine* (January 7, 1974), p. 60.

It is interesting to note how sales representatives are paid. A study by the National Conference Board (Table 1-2) found that only 19 percent of the nation's sales representatives are paid on a straight salary, 40 per cent are paid on a salary-plus-bonus scheme, and 22 per cent on a salary-plus-commission scheme. In the salary-plus-bonus system, the salesperson receives additional compensation based on a more subjective evaluation than the commission arrangement. With a bonus system, the firm's management will examine such factors as how hard a man seems to work, how much new business he has created, and how he handles customer complaints. With the salary-plus-commission system, the

TABLE 1-2 TYPE OF SALES REPRESENTATIVES COMPENSATION*

Scheme	Percentage of Respondents
Salary only	19
Salary plus Bonus	40
Salary plus Commission	22
Salary plus Commission and Bonus	8
Straight Commission	11
Total	100

*Source: David Weeks, *Compensating Salesmen and Sales Executives* (New York: The National Conference Board, 1972), p. 41.

salesperson is normally paid his commission strictly on the basis of how many units he sells during a particular time period. The study indicated that only 11 percent of the sales representatives surveyed were paid strictly on commission.

Freedom From Direct Management Control

Many individuals do not like to be closely supervised, and many sales positions offer a unique opportunity to be as independent as possible, while still having the advantages of working for an organization. As an example, many sales representatives plan their own schedules. They may work 13 hours one day and only 4 the next. They do not punch a time clock, and in fact they may go for several weeks without face-to-face contact with their superior. Often when a salesperson is "promoted" to a managerial position, he dislikes the confining routine and returns to the "field." As a result, for the individual who wants to be his own boss, selling comes closer to giving him the independence he needs than most other positions within an organization.

ETHICAL CONSIDERATIONS

The moral standards of salespeople are a great deal like those of the rest of society. Some sales representatives are extremely ethical, whereas others, unfortunately, are just the opposite. While some sales representatives have done things they are not proud of, most sales people try to maintain a set of values worthy of emulation. Table 1-3 presents a list of eight difficult ethical considerations that many sales representatives and sales managers face daily. Before reading on, examine this list and take a stand on each consideration.

If the salesperson or sales manager would take the easy road out and follow the path that would gain the most sales for himself in each situation, he might well be described as unethical. In contrast, however, if he was to take the path of zero temptations, he might not be an effective salesperson for his company.

TABLE 1-3 DIFFICULT ETHICAL CONSIDERATIONS*

1. You are interviewing a former sales manager who has just resigned from your chief competitor company. If you hire him he would be willing to tell you all of the competitor's marketing plans for the next year. What do you do?
2. You have invited a prospective customer out to lunch. Your firm does not permit more than one alcoholic drink per individual to be charged to the company's expense account at lunch. You and the customer have several drinks. You feel that you could hide the extra drinks in another part of your expense account and that you should be fully reimbursed for an expense which you feel is truly part of doing business. What do you do?
3. You have a chance to win a large contract from the army that would mean a great deal to you and your company. The contract officer indicates that he would be positively influenced by a substantial "gift." What do you do?
4. A competitor is planning on announcing a new product feature to a selected set of customers in his suite at a trade show. You feel that it would not be difficult to send a spy to learn what the new feature is. What do you do?
5. You firmly believe that the product that you are selling is a high-quality item. However, at times you find yourself making a claim about the product that might be difficult to substantiate. You are quite sure that the odds that the customer would find out about your stretching the truth are quite slim. What do you do?
6. You are a retail salesperson selling men's suits. A customer has just tried on a suit that obviously does not fit him. However, you feel that if you were to tell him it looks as if it was made for him he would buy it. What do you do?
7. You have just completed interviewing a highly qualified black woman for a position as a salesperson. You know that if you hire this individual your company might lose some business because several of your customers would not want to do business with a black woman. What do you do?

*Several of these have been taken from Philip Kotler, *Marketing Management Analysis, Planning and Control*, Second Edition (Englewood Cliffs, N.J.: Prentice-Hall, 1972), p. 839.

TABLE 1-4 AMERICAN MARKETING ASSOCIATION'S CODE OF ETHICS

As a member of the American Marketing Association, I recognize the significance of my professional conduct and my responsibilities to society and to the other members of my profession:

1. By acknowledging my accountability to society as a whole as well as to the organization for which I work.
2. By pledging my efforts to assure that all presentations of goods, services and concepts be made honestly and clearly.
3. By striving to improve marketing knowledge and practice in order to better serve society.
4. By supporting free consumer choice in circumstances that are legal and are consistent with generally accepted community standards.
5. By pledging to use the highest professional standards in my work and in competitive activity.

6. By acknowledging the right of the American Marketing Association through established procedure, to withdraw my membership if I am found to be in violation of ethical standards of professional conduct.

_____

Signature

_____

Date

The American Marketing Association's Code of Ethics is presented in Table 1-4. It basically states that any individual who is a member of the AMA must recognize that he or she has an obligation to society and to his customers that goes far beyond the responsibility to sell more products. Members of the AMA are expected to make honest and clear presentations, to improve marketing knowledge for the benefit of society, and to support free consumer choice in circumstances that are consistent with local community standards. If all marketing and sales people were to make a real attempt to live up to these standards, the marketplace would be a better place to compete in for all concerned.

SUMMARY

There is no single occupation of selling. Rather there is a vast spectrum of work opportunities that require vastly different skills for success. In this chapter, special attention was given to the creativity dimension in selling. We illustrated that some sales positions (such as inside ordertakers), require little creativity, whereas people who sell intangible goods or services must at times be very creative. Thirteen additional factors that provide insight into sales occupations were also highlighted.

Along with several factors that make selling a difficult career, we also examined the characteristics that make for success in selling. Even though the professional salesperson may feel neglected and lonely at times, he is very much the team captain when it comes to negotiations with prospective customers. If the salesperson needs support from other individuals in the firm, he is the one who determines who should assist him and under what conditions.

We examined the opportunities available in selling, showing how it not only serves as a stepping stone to management, but also provides a good living for the career salesperson. In addition, selling provides a unique opportunity to have the protection of an organization and still be one's own boss.

In discussing ethical considerations, we found that it is easy to talk about ethics in the abstract sense, but difficult to know how an individual will act until he is in a specific situation.

Finally, it is important to realize that everyone is a salesperson, of himself and of his ideas. Thus, the principles that will be discussed in the text will be helpful regardless of one's career pursuits.

PROBLEMS

1. Describe how important you feel creativity is to a career in selling. Would creativity be more or less important to a salesperson than to an accountant or an engineer?
2. The chapter presents thirteen dimensions of the sales position. Which of these do you feel would be most important for the tool and die salesperson calling on the automobile industry? Which would be the least important?
3. How do you feel you would do as a salesperson? Which of the factors that makes selling difficult would disturb you the most? Explain.
4. Drive and motivation would seem to be interrelated. Do you feel both are equally important to a salesperson's chances of success? Do all sales representatives need the same amount of these two characteristics to be successful?
5. Is the salesperson really a team leader? Explain.

Exercise 1.

THE PROFESSIONAL SALESPERSON

Objectives: To increase your understanding of the personal selling function and the great variety of selling jobs.

To gain insight regarding the vocational opportunities in personal selling.

Choose a salesperson to interview. Your instructor may wish to designate a particular interviewee. Otherwise select a salesperson that you know and ask him or her the following questions:

A. Interview with Salesperson

Suggested Questions:
  1. How would you describe your principal duties?
  2. How would you classify your customers and prospects?
  3. What do you sell?
  4. What is your greatest competition?
  5. What do you like most about your job? Least?
  6. What qualifications are needed?

After the interview, using the material presented in the Selling Spectrum portion of this chapter prepare a summary description of the interviewee.

B. Self-Analysis

From your reading of Chapter 1 and the interview with a salesperson, ask yourself the following questions:
  1. What kinds of selling jobs am I most suited for?
  2. What personal qualities do I have which relate to successful sales performance?

Case 1-1 Henderson Electronics

Mike Scott, who is a senior at Southwest Texas University has just completed a trip to Henderson Electronics. In the early spring of this year George Downing, a sales manager for Henderson, interviewed Mike on the campus for a position in the firm's field sales operation. Mr. Downing had been impressed with Mike during the interview and had invited him to Houston to spend two days visiting Henderson's home office.

While at Henderson's, Mike was treated extremely well. He had opportunities to talk with such people as the director of marketing, on down to a sales trainee who had been hired three weeks ago in a position similar to the one Mike was considering. At the end of the second day Mr. Downing offered Mike a job as a junior salesperson at a base salary of $8500. The second year his salary would be adjusted such that his base would be $6000 but he would also have a 3% commission on sales, which should give him an income in the range of $11,000 to $14,000 for the second year.

Henderson Electronics manufactures and sells electrical conduit for buildings. The firm has a good reputation for selling high quality products and for providing good service and technical support. Henderson's products are sold to two types of accounts. Approximately 35% of their sales are made to wholesalers who sell conduit to hardware and electrical supply outlets. The balance of their sales are direct to contractors who are bidding on large jobs. These contractors are particularly interested in obtaining Henderson's technical advice on what types of conduit they should use and on having a "competitive price."

The Henderson salesperson is expected to handle most of the technical advice himself. If he is bidding on a particularly large contract, or if he runs into a problem he cannot deal with, he is encouraged to contact the home office for assistance. If necessary, Henderson can provide practically instantaneous technical back up for its sales representatives.

Over 80% of Henderson's sales force have graduated from a junior college or a four year college or university. However, less than 30% of these individuals have a four-year technical degree. As a result, Henderson runs an extensive technical school for its new salespeople. At the end of the six-week program the Junior Salesperson is expected to be able to deal with most of the technical problems he will run into.

After the individual completes the technical school he spends six months assisting in a sales territory. This is an attempt to give the young person "on-the-job" training in both selling and technical conduit problems. After this six-month period is completed, the new person becomes a full-fledged sales representative and is given a territory of his own. At the beginning he can count on a little extra help from his sales manager in handling his accounts.

Henderson does not promise any new sales trainees a particular territory until they have completed the training program. However, most new salespersons are initially assigned to one of the smaller territories located in the Southwest. The new salesperson will frequently have to spend several days on the road each week before being able to return to his home base. If the salesperson does well he will be promoted by assigning him to a territory with a larger sales potential.

Mike Scott began his college career at Southwest Texas as a mechanical engineering student. After one year, he found himself on scholastic probation. He then transferred to the Business School where his grades steadily improved. His grade point average is now a B- and he has slightly over a B in his marketing classes. Mike told his academic advisor recently that, "I really could have made it in engineering but I guess I just was not interested enough in the subject to study."

Mike has been fairly active socially at college. He rushed a fraternity in his freshman year but could not become active because of his probationary status. Once he was restored to good standing he never went back to the fraternity. He was elected vice president of the Ski Club in his junior year, but was not elected president in his senior year. One of his friends stated "It is too bad about Mike losing the election. Normally the vice president is elevated to the presidency the next year. However, Mike tends to be a little too extroverted at times and he gives people the feeling that he's trying to take over. I think that's what his problem was."

Mike has always been described as highly motivated. He has a definite interest in making money. When he was vice president of the Ski Club he managed the drive for new members, which brought in twice as much revenue as the club had ever had. Mike told his advisor, "I might enjoy working for myself some day. If this doesn't work out, I definitely want to get into a top management position with the firm that I'm working for."

1. Does there seem to be a good match between Henderson and Mike?

2. What qualities does Mike have that would make a valuable employee to Henderson? What qualities might cause him problems?

3. Would you recommend to Mike that he accept this job assuming that he has also been offered a job as a bank trainee in the trust department of a Houston Bank?

Case 1-2 Meadow Brook National Bank

Meadow Brook is a suburban, white-collar, bedroom community near New York City. The National Bank enjoys the largest share of business though there are two other prosperous banks in the community.

Mr. Jack Diamond is the founder and head of National and, to many, *he is the bank*. He is a part of virtually every voluntary group. He avidly supports local high school athletics. He makes good press for he is famous for his quotable quotes. Here are some examples:

"National is a high-class, well-managed hock shop."
"We buy and sell money. Bring yours to us or buy some from us."
"Everyone in National sells; if he doesn't, we don't want him around."
"Customers are the most important people in the world."
"Full service at one stop."

Under his leadership National has flourished although some of the more conservative citizens feel Jack runs a circus rather than a bank. National is always promoting something—new accounts, vacation club membership, certificates of deposits.

Jack insists that all members of the management team devote at least one day a week making calls on customers and prospects among the local businesses. Each person is also required to play an active role in at least one community organization.

1. What do you think about National's policies? What are the hazards?
2. How would you like to work there?

SUGGESTIONS FOR FURTHER READING

Belasco, James A., "The Salesman's Role Revisited," *Journal of Marketing,* Vol. 30 (April 1966), pp. 6–8.

Heddinger, Fred M., "Should Every Employee Be a Salesman?" *Sales Management,* Vol. 101 (Sept. 10, 1968), p. 40.

Mayer, David, and Herbert M. Greenberg, "What Makes a Good Salesman," in *Salesmanship and Sales Force Management,* edited by Edward C. Bursk and G. Scott Hutchinson (Cambridge, Mass: Harvard University Press, 1971), pp. 3–9.

Mayer, Paul J., "Why Salesmen Fail," *Sales/Marketing Today,* Vol. 15 (June, 1969), pp. 15–21.

McMurry, Robert N., "The Mystique of Super-Salesmanship," *Harvard Business Review,* Vol. 39 (March-April, 1961), pp. 113–122.

Peters, Roderic, "Tom Edison's Sales Techniques," *Nation's Business,* Vol. 59 (March, 1971), pp. 52–56.

Pruden, Henry O., and Richard S. Harrigan, "The Salesperson as an Integrator," *Southwest Marketing Association Proceedings* (February 1976).

Rieser, Carl, "The Salesman Isn't Dead—He's Different," *Fortune,* Vol. 66 (November 1962), pp. 124–127, 248, 252, 254, 259.

Rusch, Hugh L., "Qualities of a Good Salesman," *Printer's Ink,* Vol. 293 (Oct. 28, 1966), p. 80.

Sales Management, "Why Salesmen Fail," Vol. 103 (Oct. 1, 1969), pp. 62–76.

2. Selling and the Marketing Effort

IN THIS CHAPTER

Importance of Marketing
The Marketing Concept
The Role of the Marketing-Oriented Sales Representative
Uncontrollable Environmental Factors
The Marketing Mix
Sales Management's Functions and Responsibilities

The salesperson is an integral part of a firm's marketing program, and thus he must coordinate his efforts with the rest of the firm's marketing activities. In this chapter we will examine the importance of marketing and the marketing concept. It is critically important to have a clear understanding of the marketing concept, because the entire firm's sales and marketing efforts are usually based upon it. We shall also examine factors that are beyond the control of the marketing manager that may vitally affect the success of the sales program. In addition, we will analyze the interaction between the tools the marketing manager uses to compete effectively in the marketplace and the firm's personal selling effort. Finally, we will view the functions and responsibilities of sales management.

IMPORTANCE OF MARKETING

What contribution does marketing make to the national well-being? The nation depends on marketing as a key function for the delivery of a high standard of living to its citizens. To the extent that products and services are important elements in peoples' overall well-being, marketing provides the link between the companies that produce the goods and services and the individuals who use them. In addition, individuals involved with marketing and distribution of merchandise represent 30% of the employed population of the United States, and their activities account for 40 cents out of each dollar the final consumer spends.[1]

Marketing is critical to the firm because it is the connection between the firm and its customers. There is an old adage in business that states, "Nothing happens until a sale is made." This does not mean to imply that other functions, such as accounting, finance, production, or personnel are not critically important to the firm's success, but they are all in some way facilitating the marketing operations. If a firm has a fine accounting system and an outstanding production facility, it may be able to produce a quality product at a low cost and keep track of the movement of dollars within the organization. However, unless the firm can sell the products that were so carefully produced and accounted for, all of its previous efforts are wasted. Again, this does not mean that we should downplay the importance of other activities in the firm. Unless all parts of the business operate efficiently as a system, the firm will suffer. Yet, it is important to recognize the vital role that marketing plays in the success or failure of almost any business venture.

THE MARKETING CONCEPT

The marketing concept was first introduced in 1952 by the General Electric Company. It is based on the philosophy that the customer is king, and therefore he or she must be the most important consideration for the company. As a result, the firm which adopts the marketing concept spends a great deal of effort to determine exactly what the market needs and then tries to provide products and services to satisfy those needs.

Before it developed the marketing concept, General Electric felt that its primary responsibilities consisted of raising capital, manufacturing products, and then selling them. Its focus was on its products and not on the needs of consumers. Such a strategy, which focuses on production, may work reasonably well when the firm's merchandise is in very short supply or when it faces very little competition. Under these conditions, the customer may have to accept a product that does not fully satisfy his particular needs.

---

[1]Reavis Cox, *Distribution in a High Level Economy* (Englewood Cliffs, N.J.: Prentice-Hall, 1965), pp. 149–155.

However, in today's economy, most companies are faced with varied and substantial forms of competition. And under such conditions, if a firm does not provide a product that closely satisfies consumer desires, it may not survive.

The Elgin Watch Example

The Elgin Watch Company provides an excellent example of a product-oriented firm.[2] The Elgin Watch Company was founded in 1864. It manufactured high-quality American watches. Its management placed heavy emphasis on making a quality product and selling it through leading jewelry and department stores. In 1957, the firm had a sales force of more than 50 members, its advertising budget exceeded 1 million dollars, and the firm enjoyed sales of approximately 42 million dollars. In 1958, Elgin's sales declined sharply and it lost 2 million dollars.

This dramatic change in Elgin's fortune stemmed from the fact that the company had become so preoccupied with its product that it failed to heed four significant changes that were taking place in its market. First, low-priced, attractively styled pin-lever watches were rapidly gaining popularity in the United States. Second, many consumers no longer felt that a watch had to be extremely accurate, carry a prestigious name, and last indefinitely. Third, large numbers of the new, inexpensive watches were being sold through mass-distribution outlets at relatively low profit margins. Fourth, many of Elgin's traditional competitors had seen the changes in products, customers, and distribution outlets coming and had begun to offer low-priced watches of their own. This insensitivity to shifting market conditions cost Elgin substantial sales and profits.

The New Concept

In contrast to the product-oriented firm, the marketing-oriented business realizes the firm's efforts must begin not with the product but with the market. That is, before the firm decides to manufacture a product, it examines the potential market to determine what its needs are and then decides if it can produce the desired product at a reasonable profit. The marketing-oriented firm also recognizes the need to monitor the post-purchase behavior of its customers by determining who purchased the product, whether the product was satisfactory, and what changes in the firm's market offering would make its products more successful.

Table 2-1 illustrates the differences between the product concept and the marketing concept. Although the end is somewhat similar for both concepts, the focus and means are quite different. The product concept focuses on the product; the means used to achieve success are selling and production. In contrast,

---

[2]Ralph Westfall and Harper W. Boyd, Jr., *Cases in Marketing Management,* (Homewood, Ill.: Irwin, 1961), pp. 16–24.

TABLE 2-1 THE CONTRAST BETWEEN THE SALES AND MARKETING CONCEPTS

	Focus	*Means*	*End*
The Sales Concept	Products	Selling and promoting	Profits through sales volume
The Marketing Concept	Customer needs	Integrated marketing	Profits through customer satisfaction

Adapted from Philip Kotler, *Marketing Management: Analysis Planning and Control*, 3rd ed. (Englewood Cliffs, N.J.: Prentice Hall, 1976), p. 15.

the marketing concept focuses on customer needs and seeks to achieve success through integrated marketing. Integrated marketing involves organizing all of the firm's marketing resources—including advertising, marketing research, product planning, and selling—into a package designed to satisfy the needs of the consumer. The end sought by the product concept is profit through sales volume; for the marketing concept it is profit through consumer satisfaction. The latter strategy helps establish long-run positive relationships between buyer and seller, thus making repeat sales much easier.

Three Key Principles

The marketing concept has three key principles: (1) customer orientation, (2) broad corporate definition of mission, and (3) the determination of target markets.[3] If a firm is to be truly market-oriented, it must embrace each of these principles.

Customer Orientation. This means that the entire firm focuses on the satisfaction of customer needs. This does not imply just taking a customer out for a fancy dinner in the industrial selling world, or smiling and being pleasant in retail sales situations. Rather, it means that through various types of marketing research, including investigative efforts by salespersons, the firm will attempt to determine what it can offer its customers that will meet their needs as closely as possible and will generate a profit for the firm. However, there may be some products that would satisfy a few customers' needs completely that the firm would not be able to supply because they lack the required profit potential.

[3] Philip Kotler, *Marketing Management: Analysis Planning and Control*, 2nd ed. (Englewood Cliffs, N.J.: Prentice-Hall, 1972), p. 18–21.

Broad Corporate Definition of Mission.   In keeping with this principle a firm should determine which broad basic needs it expects to satisfy. Such a broad definition of mission encourages the firm to continually monitor its markets in order to adjust to the current market environment and to take advantage of new opportunities. Charles Revson, the late President of Revlon, provided an excellent example of broad corporate definition in his response to a question about what his firm produced. He stated, "In the factory we make cosmetics, and in the drugstore we sell hope."[4] Mr. Revson's philosophy is that Revlon is not just in the business of making cosmetics, but that it is in the business of providing goods that will satisfy important needs of the consumer. If the consumer changes her mind as to what types of beauty aids are important, Revlon will modify its product offering to fit these new desires. The company's definition of its business is broad enough to permit this type of adjustment.

In the same manner, Theodore Levitt, a Harvard Business School professor, has suggested that the nation's railroads have gotten into substantial problems *not* because the need for their services has declined but because they have failed to meet the need for the service. Levitt states:

They [the railroads] let others take customers away from them because they assumed themselves to be in the railroad business rather than in the transportation business. The reason they defined their industry wrong was because they were railroad oriented instead of transportation oriented; they were product-oriented instead of customer-oriented.[5]

The point is that the transportation market has continued to expand, although the railroads have faltered badly. People and commodities are still being moved by private transportation systems. The problem is that other carriers such as trucks, buses, and planes have taken over jobs the railroads once performed because they more closely meet the needs of that market.

The petroleum companies exemplify firms that are taking on a much broader definition of mission now than they did in the past. Most of the forward-thinking companies in this industry now perceive themselves to be in the energy business rather than in the oil business. As a result, they have diversified into areas such as coal, nuclear power, and solar-energy research. This change in emphasis will put them in a much better position to adjust to the world's future energy needs.

Target Markets.   The third important principle in the marketing concept is the determination of target markets. No one company can satisfy all potential customers and markets at once. This is especially true when it has established a broad-based definition of mission. As a result, at any one point in time, the firm

---

[4] *Ibid.* p. 18.

[5] Theodore Levitt, "Marketing Myopia," *Harvard Business Review*, Vol. 38 (July-August 1960), pp. 45–46.

must strive to serve specific markets and specific customer needs. Examples of firms that try to meet *limited* markets at particular points in time are Southwest Airlines, which flies a commuter service between San Antonio, Dallas, and Houston; Fiat, which primarily produces economy-oriented automobiles; and McDonald's, which sells basically fast-service breakfast, lunch, and dinner foods.

The Role of the Marketing-Oriented Sales Representative

The responsibilities of the salesperson who works for a product-oriented company are very different from those of today's marketing-oriented sales representative. The product-oriented salesperson is responsible for pushing a product or product line on his customer. He is evaluated on the volume he sells relative to his sales quota. (Sales quotas are discussed in Chapter 22). The quota or sales objective is determined by the sales manager primarily on the basis of the salesperson's performance during the preceding year. If a salesperson has a good year and exceeds his quota, he can expect his next year's quota to be increased substantially. As a result of this treadmill situation, there is constant pressure on the product-oriented sales representative to use aggressive sales techniques to try to exceed his inflated quota.

In contrast, the sales quota is not likely to be the dominant tool in a marketing-oriented company. This does not mean that some marketing-oriented firms will not use sales to provide some of the input in the evaluation of the salesperson, but the salesperson will also be held responsible for a broad range of activities which include providing valuable customer and competitor information to management, ensuring customer satisfaction, and aiding in profitability analysis.

Collection and Transmission of Information. One of the most important of the marketing-oriented salesperson's broader responsibilities is to provide information to his company concerning the needs of his customers. Compared with the survey researcher, the salesperson has several substantial advantages in obtaining data about future projects, customers, and competition. First, the additional cost incurred to collect information is relatively low, since the salesperson is meeting with customers anyway. Second, the salesperson can transmit the information he obtains on his regular calls with little extra effort. Third, the sales representative normally has a well-established relationship with his customers and is therefore keenly aware of their needs and wants. Last, a salesperson for a respected company is usually perceived as a potential supplier of problem-solving services and equipment. As a result, prospective customers are normally willing to provide such an individual with information that they might not give to a survey researcher.[6]

[6]Fredrick E. Webster, Jr., "The Industrial Salesman as a Source of Information," *Business Horizons*, Vol. 2 (Spring 1965), pp. 77–82.

Integrated Marketing.   The salesperson is one of the most important individuals involved in integrating the entire firm's efforts to solve a customer's problem. At times the salesperson will have to put together a team of production, research, service, and even accounting or finance people from his company to assist a customer. One of the most common examples of this occurs when a salesperson is bidding on a large industrial contract. He may have to ask his research department to design new plans to fit the exact specifications of the customer. The salesperson will then present the plans to the customer for his approval. Frequently he will be accompanied by a representative of the research department during this crucial stage of the sales process.

Once the sale has been made and the equipment installed the salesperson may become involved in its long-term service requirements. If a problem develops, the customer's first reaction may be to call the salesperson. Although it may not be his formal responsibility, the salesperson who values long-term relationships with his accounts should become personally involved in major service problems.

Finally, a customer who has a problem financing a project may need the assistance of the salesperson's financial organization. They may be able to show the customer how a project can be financed. In some circumstances the salesperson's firm may provide the capital for the project.

Customer Satisfaction.   A second responsibility of the marketing-oriented salesperson is to provide his customers with products that satisfy their real needs. Because of this approach, it will often take the modern salesperson longer to sell his products than it took his product-oriented predecessor. In some cases, it takes months to determine the precise needs of the customer. In industrial selling, this process may require that the seller provide engineering assistance to build new products or modify existing ones to fit the needs of the customer.

The marketing-oriented salesperson also realizes that he will not make every sale, because there will be situations in which the company does not provide a product that would solve the customer's problems. When this occurs, the salesperson should point this out to the customer rather than have him buy the product and then become dissatisfied with it.

The salesperson who takes the required time to actually determine the customer's needs and then recommends his products only if they are capable of meeting such needs will find that he is welcomed and trusted by the prospect when he calls. His recommendations will carry significantly more weight in the purchase decision process than those of the salesperson who tries to push his merchandise regardless of its ability to satisfy the customer's needs.

Profit Constraint.   Finally, the modern salesperson has more of a profit responsibility than a sales volume responsibility. His company will encourage him to sell those products that are profitable rather than just those that might be easy to sell and to call on customers who would seem to have the greatest long-run profit potential for the firm. The marketing-oriented salesperson realizes that there will be accounts where there is not enough potential business to warrant his efforts. The salesperson's compensation plan may reflect these objectives with management offering differential commission based on the relative profitability of particular products and particular types of accounts. We will now examine several criteria that the marketing department should meet in its organization structure to help the salesperson's chances for success.

UNCONTROLLABLE ENVIRONMENTAL FACTORS

Each firm, regardless of products, markets, or management philosophy, faces an array of largely uncontrollable environmental factors—such as culture, technology, legal constraints, economic forces, and limited resources—which interact with the competitive structures. These are uncontrollable in the sense that marketing salespeople have little power over them, and yet they may affect the very survival of the firm. Thus, the firm must monitor these factors closely so that it can adjust its operations as quickly as possible to fit the changing environment.

Figure 2-1 illustrates the interaction that takes place among the largely uncontrollable factors and marketing management. For example, as a result of a recent economic recession (economic environment) the federal government passed laws (legal factors) which were designed to stimulate the construction of new plants and equipment (technology) and consumer spending (culture). Consequently, companies' top managements adjusted their plans for the succeeding year (objectives of the firm). Most marketing executives not only monitored the developments in each of these areas, but they also tried to influence their top management in terms of what plans they felt the firm should adopt (objectives of the firm). In addition, many of these marketing executives also lobbied in Washington either through their corporate offices or through trade associations to try to get laws passed (legal factors) which would be beneficial to their organizations. We shall briefly examine each of these uncontrollable variables from the perspective of the marketing department and the salesperson.

Culture

Culture consists of those values, ideas, attitudes, and other symbols that are created by man to regulate his behavior, and which are passed from one generation to the next.[7] As an example, in Latin America to be 30 minutes late for a sales meeting is not considered to be in bad taste, whereas to be more than 5 or 10 minutes late to a similar meeting in New York City would be. A somewhat different example would be that certain products are consumed by one segment

---

[7]James F. Engel, David T. Kollat, and Roger D. Blackwell, *Consumer Behavior,* 2nd ed. (New York: Holt, Rinehart, and Winston, 1973), p. 72.

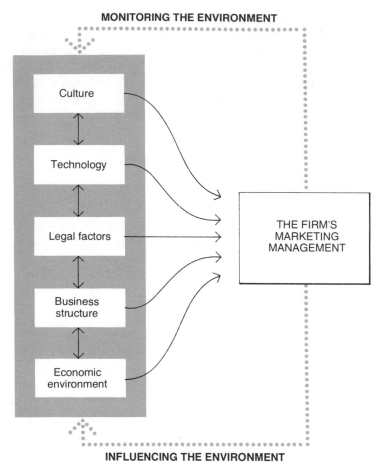

Figure 2-1 Uncontrollable environmental factors

of society and not by others: in many southern states, grits and hushpuppies are very popular; while in the southwest, Mexican food is eaten regularly. In major cities, some newspapers are published in other languages to appeal directly to certain subcultures among the cities' residents. For a salesperson to be successful, he must adjust his behavior to fit the particular cultural situation in which he finds himself.

Technology

New technology is responsible for many of the inventions and innovations that are developed by industry. Manufacturers have learned that products are frequently most profitable in their early stages of production before a great deal of competition exists. Therefore, it is incumbent on the firm to continue to develop and manufacture new products that will satisfy consumer needs. Such products as nylon, television, and the computer have dramatically changed our life styles while producing substantial profits for business. Two of the prime functions of salespeople are to provide the necessary inputs to the technical staff to help them understand what the market is most likely to need and to make those new products of technology available at a reasonable price.

Legal Factors

Many laws regulating the practice of business have been passed by local, state, and national governments. As an example, on the federal level the Sherman Antitrust Act (1890), the Clayton Act (1914), and the Federal Trade Commission Act (1914) make it illegal for two or more firms engaged in interstate commerce to conspire to fix the prices of a product. Only a few years ago, General Electric, Westinghouse, and 29 other corporations were convicted of fixing the prices of electrical-generating equipment.[8] These companies were fined millions of dollars for their involvement in the conspiracy and paid out much larger sums in damages to the utilities that purchased merchandise at inflated prices. Salespersons from each of these firms were intimately involved in establishing the price-fixing arrangements.

The Robinson-Patman Act makes it illegal for the firm or its representatives to provide price discounts or other concessions to one retailer that it does not provide another retailer. Most states have now adopted the Uniform Commercial Code which regulates trade practices within individual states. These state laws directly affect the day-to-day activities of the salesperson. Finally, local municipal and county governments have passed laws dealing with all aspects of selling ranging from the specification of days when certain products can be sold (so-called Blue laws) to the regulation of how and where products can be displayed. (In Chapter 23 we cover in greater detail those pieces of federal legislation and sections of the Uniform Commercial Code that directly affect selling activities.)

Competitive Structure

This factor refers to the type of competition a firm will have. For example, the retail business operates in an environment where there are a great many outlets selling basically the same products as their competitors. In contrast, public utility companies face very little competition and could charge a much higher price for their products if they were not regulated by agencies of the local, state, and federal governments. In this type of situation, the salesperson (frequently called a customer representative) does little more than explain the rate structure and answer customer complaints. Thus, the type of competitive structure used by the firm affects how it sells its products and determines the relative importance of its salespersons.

[8]Richard A. Smith, "The Incredible Electrical Conspiracy," *Fortune*, Vol. 63 (April 1961), pp. 132.

Economic Forces

As the economic environment fluctuates, major changes take place in the level of profitability of various sectors of the economy. As an example, recently the United States experienced a very unusual situation in which a high level of inflation continued during a period of economic recession. This situation hurt the home-building and automobile industries a great deal. Apparently, during periods of economic uncertainty most Americans are unable or unwilling to spend money on products which can be postponed. Although most products sell better during periods of economic prosperity, the firm's marketing management has no control over the basic economic condition of the nation. Yet, salespersons who wish to make the best of a bad situation will try to sell products that are more basic in design and less costly during periods of recession. Then, as the economy turns upward, they can begin to emphasize the more sophisticated and expensive items.

Resources and Objectives of the Firm

Even though the resources and objectives of the firm are somewhat controllable by the firm's top management, they are not within the control of its marketing management. The resources needed to succeed in the marketplace—such as financial strength, physical plant, raw materials, personnel, patents, and the goodwill of the public— are critical to the firm's success. As an example, if a business does not have the required line of credit to borrow enough money at a competitive interest rate, it may not be able to survive. In the same way, if it does not have innovative research and development along with adequate production facilities it may not be able to succeed. Finally, if the firm has developed a reputation for producing poor-quality products it will be very difficult for it to successfully introduce a new product, even if it is of high quality and represents a genuinely good buy.

The objectives determined by the firm's top management will also affect the marketing department's ability to succeed.[9] After World War II, the top officers of Montgomery Ward felt that the nation was heading into a major recession or depression. Therefore, they restrained the firm's natural inclination to follow the nation's migration to the suburbs as Sears did. As history now indicates, there was no major economic downturn at the end of World War II and, as a result, Sears is today a much larger corporation than is Montgomery Ward.

THE MARKETING MIX

Although marketing management does face a series of uncontrollable variables, it also has a set of powerful marketing tools that it can use to compete effectively

[9] E. Jerome McCarthy, *Basic Marketing,* 5th ed. (Homewood, Ill: Irwin, 1976), pp. 99–102.

in the marketplace. The firm can adjust its pricing strategy, increase or decrease its promotional efforts, modify its distribution structure, change the number and types of sales personnel, and develop new products to accomplish its marketing objectives. The marketing and sales managers who are able to structure the best package of marketing tools for each competitive situation will be a great asset to their firm.

The Marketing Tools and the Customer

Figure 2-2 illustrates the relationship between the various marketing tools that are available to the firm and its customers. Area 1 of the figure represents the overall needs and wants of the firm's present and potential customers. Notice that the customer portion of Area 1 is located in the middle to emphasize that the company cannot afford to forget its present customers in its efforts to attract new ones. All too often, a firm begins to take its established accounts for granted and then finds itself in substantial difficulty as these accounts are wooed away by competitors.

Needed marketing information is provided by marketing research and marketing intelligence. This is represented in the far right portion of the Figure 2-2. The two lines commence with the needs and wants in Area 1 and include the other areas of the diagram. The dotted line depicts the efforts of the marketing research staff, and the solid line represents the additional efforts of the sales force and others in collecting useful information. The information flow is continuous and includes data as to what types of products the market wants, what changes should take place in the firm's product offering, and the levels of competitive activity that exist for the firm's various products.

The entire lower half of Figure 2-2 represents the firm's marketing effort. Notice it includes product management, pricing, promotion, and distribution. It is designated Area 2. With the information provided by the marketing research and sales staff, the firm should be in a position to design and then market a product successfully. Product management involves first designing the proper product for the market and then positioning it to meet the needs of specific market segments. (As an example, Virginia Slims was positioned in the market to try to attract female smokers.) Pricing represents a powerful marketing tool, and every firm needs to establish a policy as to how it should price its products—it may build its price up from cost, or work back from demand, or use some combination of both methods. Frequently, the firm will try to use marketing tools other than price to attract its customers, because a shift in the firm's pricing policy can lead to price wars, and also because a reduction in price is easily matched by competition.

Personal selling, advertising, and sales promotion are additional promotional tools presented in Area 2. Advertising themes and strategies developed by the firm are designed to communicate a message to prospective customers. For example, when the firm uses radio, television, or billboards to announce a

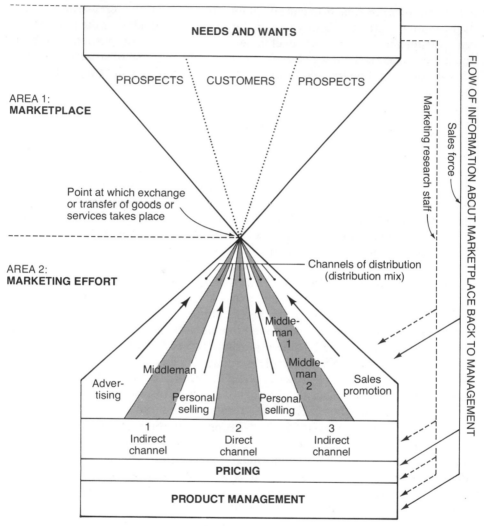

Figure 2-2 The market system

new product or a price reduction it is using advertising. Sales promotions are
those activities other than advertising or selling that stimulate consumer purchasing and dealer effectiveness, such as displays, shows, exhibitions, and
demonstrations.

The firm must decide how its products are to be distributed. This involves
decisions concerning the channels of distribution that the firm will use to move
its merchandise from the plant to the consumer. In Figure 2-2, the middle
channel is pictured as the direct channel, in which there are no intermediaries
from the producer to the consumer. The producer in this case contacts and

sells the product directly to the final consumer. The other channels depict the use of one or more middlemen. The more intermediaries of this kind, the more complicated the distribution effort.

Interaction Among the Marketing Tools

If the firm is to use its marketing and promotional tools effectively, it must recognize that each one interacts with the others. For example, in his efforts to develop a successful promotional program the astute marketing manager will consider the relative emphasis to be placed on selling, advertising, sales promotion, and merchandising in each of the firm's markets. He will also take into account specific plans, decisions, and actions involving choice of media, merchandising aids, and kinds of sales promotional activity. Likewise, when defining the distribution structure, the firm must consider the pros and cons of direct and indirect channels of distribution, criteria for the selection of indirect representation, decisions with regard to warehousing facilities, inventory planning, and management. We will now see how various marketing tools interact with the selling activities of the firm.

Marketing Research.   There are two primary ways that the selling and marketing research functions interact. First, salespersons provide a portion of the input that the marketing research department needs to prepare its reports. At times, the marketing research department may ask the firm's salespersons to ask a specific set of questions and report the finding to the marketing research department. In addition, the marketing research department will analyze the regular data that the salespersons send back to the firm, such as call reports, new sources of competition, and orders to determine if any patterns have developed that may necessitate changes in the company's marketing strategy.

The second source of interaction is that sales representatives use the reports developed by the marketing research staff in their selling activities. As an example, a salesperson for General Electric who is responsible for selling electrical switching gear will want to have information on new sources, types of competitive changes in pricing and service policies, and new uses for the switching gear in order to design the most effective sales approach. If the salesperson knows that a specific firm is his major competitor for a specific contract and that this competition offers primarily low cost items, the salesperson may want to stress that quality, reliability, and service are critical in the long run for a firm which is considering new electrical switching gear.

Channels of Distribution.   The salesperson has a great deal to do with the firm's channels of distribution for the product. If the firm for which the salesperson works sells its merchandise through resellers (wholesalers and/or retailers) then the salesperson is the link between these organizations and the firm. (Resellers are discussed in Chapter 19.) It is the salesperson's responsibility to supply the reseller with the right amount and type of products for his market. In addition, the sales representative frequently works with the reseller's promotion and sales staff providing display material and leading sales clinics for the reseller's staff. These tools give the reseller's salespeople increased product knowledge, thus making them more effective salespersons. Finally, the salesperson may make "missionary" sales calls with the reseller's sales staff. The objective of such a sales call is to contact the reseller's customers to try to get them to place an order for their product through the reseller. This is not an effort on the part of the manufacturer to steal customers from the reseller, rather it is the recognition on the part of the manufacturer that a sale is really not made until his reseller's accounts have purchased the product.

Sales Promotion.   The salesperson is frequently responsible for the implementation of the firm's sales promotion campaign. If a firm that sells packaged foods to grocery stores wants to run a special on cake mixes, it might try to get each local supermarket to carry a special display rack to promote the product. The salesperson who calls on the supermarket frequently would be asked to "sell" the idea to the supermarket. In this same manner, the salesperson can determine if point-of-purchase displays (sent to a reseller by the manufacturer) were set up, the dealers' reactions to them, and how long they were actually used. If the materials were not well received by the dealers, the salesperson can find out why and pass the information back to his management. Other sales promotion activities that would involve the salesperson might include organizing display windows for resellers and providing information and literature at exhibits and trade shows.

Advertising.   In contrast to selling, the main function of advertising occurs prior to an actual transaction. That is, advertising is used to convince the potential customer that he or she should consider the purchase of a product. But only in rare instances does it result in a purchase without being augmented by personal selling. Even at the retail level, many advertising campaigns are designed not to sell one particular product but to attract consumers to the store, where a salesperson can assist them in making a purchase. Advertising does, however, have a secondary, post-transactional function in helping customers rationalize their purchases. For instance, many readers of advertisements are recent purchasers of what is being advertised. It is clear that advertising and selling are interdependent and complementary. References to the firm's advertising and actual samples of it become important selling aids in many situations, particularly when intermediaries are part of the customer-prospect mix. The salesperson, armed with the advertising plans of his company and samples of that advertising, can show how much "pull" his firm is going to exert on the ultimate users who are the customers of the resellers. It may be even more impressive to provide the salesperson with subscriptions to the magazines in which the ads appear. These can then be shown to prospective customers during actual calls.

It is relatively common in the industrial sector to use advertising to generate leads, which are followed up by the field sales organization. This is accomplished by means of coupon returns and, in the case of some industrial trade media, by reader service cards—often referred to as "bingo" cards.

Just as advertising helps the salesperson so does the salesperson help the firm in appraising the impact of its advertising. The salesperson can determine how many of his customers and prospects have actually seen or heard an ad. By questioning them carefully, he can also learn their reactions to the advertisements. This information, along with the salesperson's comments pertaining to the ads, will provide valuable feedback for the firm's marketing management.

Pricing.   Generally, the salesperson has relatively little input into the final pricing decisions for a product. This does not mean that the salesperson might not be asked how a product should be priced; he might even be given some price flexibility when negotiating with his customers. However, the pricing decisions normally are made by executives within the marketing organization. A salesperson does have some direct interaction with the pricing decisions if he finds that his merchandise is continually overpriced compared with competition. This would imply that the salesperson is trying to sell his customers a better grade product than they feel they need, or that the product is simply overpriced. Regardless, the salesperson must try to determine exactly what the problem is if he is to be a successful salesperson.

Product Management.   As with the pricing function, the salesperson is not usually involved with the introduction or "positioning" of new products in the market, relative to the firm's other products and the competition's products. However, the salesperson interacts regularly with the product because he is responsible for selling it. If there is unexpected market resistance to a product, the salesperson will be the first to learn of it, and he will try to determine what the problem is and communicate it back to management.

SALES MANAGEMENT'S FUNCTIONS AND RESPONSIBILITIES

The salesperson interacts regularly with his immediate superior—the field sales manager. We will examine five of the most important functions of the sales manager and how they relate to the salesperson. They include planning, manpower management, communications, selling, and leadership.

Planning

The sales manager frequently participates in the development of the firm's marketing strategy, and very few people will have as good a perspective of market conditions as he does. As a result, he will counsel the firm's marketing and top management in the areas of new product development, price changes on existing products, delivery and production schedules, and advertising activities. In addition, the sales manager is responsible for deploying his own sales force in a way that will generate profitable sales for the firm. This planning function requires the sales manager to perform sales forecasts by district, to determine how often each account should be called on, to ascertain how much time should be spent on each call, and to calculate the travel time from one sales call to another.

Manpower Management

In the area of manpower management, the sales manager is responsible for hiring, training, and promoting his salespeople.

Hiring.   Frequently, members of the personnel staff will do the initial screening of applicants. However, each screened candidate is normally interviewed by a sales manager, who makes the final decision of hiring an individual. This is important, because the experienced sales manager is in the best position to judge an applicant's chances of success in selling. (This will be discussed in more detail in Chapter 21.)

Training.   The sales manager trains his employees in several ways. Individuals who have not sold before frequently begin their career with the firm by spending several weeks in the district sales office. At that time, the sales manager and his staff provide the new employee with the product knowledge he will need and with an understanding of the firm's basic approach to selling. After this introductory period, the new employee frequently is assigned to work with an experienced salesperson for several weeks. Then he is assigned his own territory. Normally, at this time, the sales manager or his training officer will spend several weeks making joint calls with the salesperson to introduce him to his clients and to help him improve his sales tactics.

The sales manager also performs training services for his experienced sales representatives by holding regular sales meetings in which members of the sales staff discuss mutual sales problems; at this time the sales manager also explains any new products and/or marketing programs that the firm is introducing. In addition, most sales managers try to spend several days each month making calls with their sales people. This puts the sales manager in the best possible position to advise the individual salesperson on how to improve his approach to selling. (The design and operation of a sales training program will also be analyzed in more depth in Chapter 21.)

Promotions. The sales manager's manpower development responsibilities also deal with promotions. The general sales manager will select with the aid of his staff those individuals who are to be promoted or transferred. Note that promotion in selling may mean movement to a supervisory position, to a higher level of selling, or to a larger territory.

Communications

The field sales manager is the personal link between each salesperson and headquarters. He insures upward and downward information flow. Sales personnel are a vital source of information to top management. They spend a great percentage of their working day meeting with customers, trying to determine what problems the customer has, and how their firm can best go about solving these problems. The sales personnel are, therefore, in an excellent position to provide management with input for sales forecasts, ideas for new products, problems with existing products, and competitive activity. Such information is of critical importance to the development of the firm's overall marketing strategy.

Selling

A recent survey indicated that sales managers spend approximately 33% of their time on selling activities. Most sales managers have several accounts of their own for two reasons. First, the firm may feel that a particular account is so important that it deserves the best sales representation. If the most qualified individual is the sales manager, he will be given responsibility for selling to this account. Second, most sales managers were salespeople before they were promoted to their current positions. They understand that it is important for them to keep close contact with the marketplace. If a sales manager loses touch with the problems of his customers and the activities of his competitors he will not be an effective counselor to management or to his sales team. Other selling activities in which sales managers participate include handling problem accounts, expediting customer orders, and deciding on customer requests for special sales terms.[10]

There are, however, a number of companies that specifically exclude actual selling from the sales manager responsibilities. These companies argue that this eliminates role conflict for the sales manager and insures that he will do what he is paid to do—manage his salespeople.

Leadership

It is critically important for the firm that the sales manager be a leader. The morale of the sales representatives frequently depends on how effectively the sales manager performs this function. Many sales representatives will not see

---

[10]Rodney Evans and William J. E. Crissy, "The Field Sales Manager—Part I," *Sales Management,* Vol. 103 (October 15, 1969), pp. 51–54.

their manager for several days or weeks. As a result, it is not an authority figure who keeps them working up to standards; rather, it is their own professionalism along with an effective leader who can inspire them to do their job successfully.

SUMMARY

Our objective in this chapter has been to provide an overview of the relationship between selling and marketing. After a discussion of the role of marketing in a free enterprise society, we explored the marketing concept as a way of life for the firm. We pointed out that the most significant difference between the old product concept and the new marketing concept was the realization on the part of the firm that it must focus its efforts on the needs of the consumer rather than on its own products. It is the salesperson's responsibility to determine the needs of his prospective customers and then to sell them a product or service only if it truly meets their needs. Although this process may be time consuming, it generates substantially more long-term business than a strategy that is based on "hard sell" tactics.

A challenge to marketers is that they must accomplish their task despite environmental factors over which they have little or no control. Among these factors are the culture of the society, the laws that govern business activities, and the changing economic environment. In contrast to the uncontrollable factors, the marketing mix contains tools that the marketing manager can use to compete effectively in the marketplace. We illustrated relationships between the firm's customers and marketing research, pricing, promotion, and distribution. In addition, we discussed the relationship between selling and the uncontrollable variables *and* selling and the tools within the marketing mix.

We concluded with a discussion of the basic sales management functions: planning, manpower management, communication, selling, and leadership. In each case the specific function was tied to the salesperson to show how the salesperson interacts with his immediate superior.

PROBLEMS

1. Has the American automobile industry historically been product or marketing oriented? Explain.
2. Describe the different functions a salesperson has if he sells for a marketing- oriented firm rather than a product-oriented firm.
3. Why do you feel that many salespersons are still product-oriented rather than marketing-oriented?
4. What kinds of marketing information might be better obtained through marketing research? Through the field sales force?
5. If you are operating a small real estate agency, which of the uncontrollable factors discussed will have the greatest impact on your sales force?
6. Describe in your own words the interaction that the salesperson has with the rest of the elements in the marketing mix.
7. If you are a sales manager which of the functions that you perform do you feel would be the most important to the prosperity of the firm? How do these functions affect your sales representatives?

Exercise 2

SELLING AND THE MARKETING EFFORT

Objective: To apply marketing concepts to one national advertiser.

Choose a firm that engages in heavy national advertising. Analyze a sample of its ads on radio, TV, newspapers, and magazines, and then answer the questions set forth below:

1. What are the principal appeals used in the ads?
2. Who are the key targets of the ads?
3. What mention is made, if any, of competitors and competitive products?
4. How attention-compelling are the ads?
5. What are your personal reactions to them?
6. What conclusions can you draw regarding the company's marketing strategy?

Case 2-1 Beech Aircraft

Joel Snyder sells for the Beech Aircraft dealership in Las Vegas. He graduated from the Air Force Academy in 1958 and spent the next six years flying jet attack aircraft for the Air Force. When his tour was up, Joel returned to Las Vegas, and began working for a local bank. After three years as an investment officer, he quit the bank and went to work for the local Beech dealer. He stated, "I found banking just too confining. I enjoy meeting people and flying, and now I am doing just what I want to do—what comes naturally to me. In addition, I get to work closely with the most advanced general aviation company in the world—Beech Aircraft.'' Joel is making more than $30,000 a year—consisting of base salary of $13,000 plus commission.

Beech Aircraft manufactures a complete line of general aviation aircraft ranging from the $16,000 Sport Trainer to the $764,000 Super King Air turbo prop. In addition, the company has an ongoing agreement with Hawker Siddelley of Great Britain to produce a Beechcraft Hawker Jet BH 125-600 which is substantially more expensive than the Super King Air turbo prop. Beech Aircraft has always had a reputation for top quality planes— the company is regularly referred to as the ''Rolls Royce of the Air.''

Three companies account for over 75% of all of the general aviation aircraft units sold in the United States. They are Beech, Cessna, and Piper. The general aviation market is segmented: business, commercial, personal, and instructional. Industry-wide business applications amounted to 48% of the total miles flown while commercial represented 16%, instructional 18%, personal 17%, and other 1%. The business category consists of aircrafts used by firms to transport their executives. Commercial includes primarily air-taxi operators. Personal comprises aircraft owned for personal use. Instructional are units used to teach people to fly.

More than 80% of the planes Beech sells are used for business purposes. It is also known that less than 15% of the twin engine planes are purchased by ''Forbes Top 125 Industrialists,'' less than 28% are sold in cities of population greater than 500,000 and more than 63% of the twin-engine planes are sold in cities with a population of less than 250,000.

Until the early 1960s Beech had concentrated its efforts on the high-performance single-engine and twin-engine aircraft. This left Piper and Cessna virtually alone to compete for the lower priced aircraft. However, at about this time Piper and Cessna both began to upgrade the quality of some of their models to compete with the Beech twin. Beech brought out a trainer, called the Musketeer, which was later renamed the Sport-Trainer, to compete with the low-priced Cessnas and Pipers.

Part of Beech's rationale for introducing the Musketeer was that research had shown that there was a high degree of brand loyalty among pilots. As a result, it was felt that an individual was more likely to purchase a plane manufactured by the company that made the plane in which he or she had learned to fly. The Musketeer was initially priced at $13,300 which was almost $5000 higher than its competition. A Beech executive explained the price differential by stating that all of their planes are produced in the ''quality Beech tradition.'' This is accomplished by first manufacturing the plane and then setting a price which reflected the true cost of the airplane. Several Beech executives felt that this approach might not be applicable for the low-priced market.

Beech sells its nonjet aircraft through approximately 150 dealers, while Cessna and Piper each have more than 500 dealers. Beech dealers are primarily interested in selling new planes whereas Cessna and Piper dealers are more oriented toward aircraft maintenance and flying instruction. Most of the Cessna and Piper dealers operate flying schools as a part of their dealer operation.

Joel was asked by his boss to push the Musketeer. But Joel feels that it will not be easy to do, because the plane is too expensive and because the local Piper dealer has traditionally gotten most of the ''trainer market.'' Joel told his boss, ''Listen Fred, my contacts are in the business community. I know what their needs are and I continually work on them to upgrade their aircraft. I have a great following in Nevada which provides me with lots of leads to other businessmen. I just do not feel it makes any sense for us to fool around with this $16,000 airplane." His boss countered by stating, "Joel, I understand your point of view. However, I am getting pressure from Beech to help make the Musketeer sell, and I may want to open a training school of my own."

1. Was Beech Aircraft marketing or product oriented when they introduced the Musketeer?

2. How should Joel handle his boss's request?

Taken in part from Stephen A. Greyser, *Cases in Marketing Management*, (Englewood Cliffs, N.J.: Prentice-Hall, 1972), pp. 39–72.

Case 2-2 Quality Craftsmen Of North Carolina

Florence Escott has been selling furniture for Quality Craftsmen of North Carolina for 11 years. She calls on accounts in Washington, Oregon, and Northern California and is considered to be an above average salesperson by her superiors. She is presently preparing to make a call on Kaplan's Furniture store in Portland.

Quality Craftsmen is an old furniture company with a complete line of solid wood furniture. Most of the units are relatively expensive and compete directly with high quality nationally advertised brands such as Henredon and Heritage.

In the furniture industry most of the buying is done at "market." The various furniture companies display their merchandise in four or five central cities across the United States. Some of the "markets" are permanently set up while others are only in operation during the buying season. As a result the salesperson's role in this industry is unique. It is his responsibility to visit the company's customers to try to keep in touch with what is happening in their territories and to help solve any problems his customers may have with the company. Although the salesperson will try to get the retailer to buy more of his merchandise between trips to the market this sales function is often of secondary importance to the other activities.

Kaplan's furniture store is owned by William J. Kaplan. Mr. Kaplan has been moderately successful over the years. He describes his customers as those in the "value market." Actually, they are mainly lower-middle to middle income families who buy on credit and extended terms. In addition, his customers are younger than average. One of Kaplan's main appeals has always been that it discounts its products 20% off list price. In addition, his sales clerks provide interior decoration suggestions to their customers.

Florence has two objectives to meet on her present swing through the territory. First, she has been asked by Quality's market research department to obtain information concerning what the firm's present competition is at the retail level, and what the dealers estimate future sales will be. This unfortunately will not be easy to obtain from Mr. Kaplan since he is a very guarded person. He feels he is competing as much with his suppliers as he is with other furniture stores. As a result he has not generally been willing to talk about his present sales patterns or what sales growth he projects for the future.

The second objective is to generate participation in a spring sales promotion campaign for Quality's outdoor furniture. Quality is planning to run a series of advertisements on network television and in national magazines to promote its outdoor furniture line. In addition, Quality will provide ad mats to local dealers and it will pay half of the cost of the local advertising. In turn, Quality is asking each of its dealers to carry a floor display and warehouse inventory of at least $25,000.

When Florence finished explaining the program to Mr. Kaplan his reaction was, "Are you kidding? I only stock $60,000 worth of outdoor furniture in the first place, and you want me to tie half of it up in Quality's line. As far as I am concerned you people still want too much money for your product. And, frankly, you are the only furniture company that refuses to give me a price break if I order in volume from you."

1. Have Florence Escott and Quality Craftsmen been marketing or product oriented?

2. How should Ms. Escott respond to Mr. Kaplan's last statement?

3. What sources, other than Mr. Kaplan, can be tapped to secure the information that her marketing research department has requested she obtain?

Case 2-3 Martineau Jewelers (A)

Mr. Jean Martineau is justifiably proud of his firm; after all, he started it over 50 years ago from a very modest beginning. Like many craftsmen and artisans of his generation he learned his trade as an apprentice. He still reminisces about those early days in New York. He likes to point out that most jewelers really don't know very much.

His first efforts on his own were as a watch and jewelry repairman occupying a "hole in the wall" in the jewelry district. His competence and honesty quickly earned him a following among the jewelry retailers who did not choose to handle repairs on their own.

He yearned to have his own store. Every time he visited a retailer it reinforced his ambition. With some trepidation he took the plunge, and the first Martineau's became a reality. Over the years the company grew and now has three locations, two in New York City and one in Miami Beach. It has always maintained a reputation of quality and integrity.

Now the firm faces a crisis in a major part of its business—watches. The store managers strongly recommend that Martineau's stock digital watches, noting the steady growth in market share they are commanding and also noting Martineau's declining sales in watches. Mr. Martineau adamantly refuses to approve such a move. He refers to digitals as gadgets, junk, and a fad. After some heated discussions he agrees to let the store managers make an investigation. The study is to include: (1) sources and brands of digitals with special reference to quality and integrity of the various makes; (2) spot shopping of stores carrying the new watches; and (3) a survey of Martineau's key customers.

The manager of one of the New York stores agrees to pull together a full report on item 1. The manager of the second New York store and the manager of the Miami Beach store agree to make separate reports on items 2 and 3.

How should the store managers carry out their assignments?

SUGGESTIONS FOR FURTHER READING

Cash, Harold C., and William J. E. Crissy, *The Psychology of Selling,* Vol. 12 "The Salesman's Role in Marketing." (Flushing, N.Y.: Personnel Development Associates, 1965).

Kotler, Philip, *Marketing Management: Analysis Planning and Control,* 3rd ed. (Englewood Cliffs, N.J.: Prentice-Hall, 1976), Chapter 1.

Levitt, Theodore, "Marketing Myopia," *Harvard Business Review,* Vol. 38 (July–August, 1960), pp. 45–56.

McCarthy, E. Jerome, *Basic Marketing,* 5th ed. (Homewood, Ill.: Irwin, 1975), Chapters 1, 2, 3 and 5.

Newton, Derek A., "Get the Most Out of Your Sales Force," *Harvard Business Review,* Vol. 47 (September–October, 1969), pp. 130–143.

Webster, Frederick E., Jr., "The Industrial Salesman as a Source of Market Information," *Business Horizons,* Vol. 8 (Spring 1965), pp. 77–82.

TWO

Contributions to Selling from the Behavioral Sciences

Whether people are engaged in acquiring goods for their own consumption or as purchasing agents for organizations or other individuals, their behavior will be affected by a large number of variables—ranging from personality attributes to the influence of formal and informal groups and to the structure of the organization of which the buyer is a member. Several efforts have been made to analyze such patterns of buyer behavior, and in the next four chapters we shall discuss the various contributions the behavioral sciences have made to selling.

In Chapter 3, "Models of Buyer Behavior," we examine buyer behavior from the perspective of the individual. After an introductory discussion of the purchasing process, we analyze the economists' view, motivational theory, and learning theory. In addition, we look at reference group theory and how the salesperson can determine the prospect's motives and intentions. Throughout we try to relate the theory of buyer behavior to selling.

In Chapter 4, "The Communication Process," we examine the ability of people to communicate and the dynamics of the process of communication—in light of the salesperson's task. The selling-buying relationship involves persuasive communication. Several factors related to the ability to persuade and communicate are perception, cognition, and role-relationship. Salespeople are cautioned against some of the most common obstacles to effective communication.

In Chapter 5, "The Salesperson as Change Agent and Problem Solver," we look at the problems that crop up when new products, services, or ideas are introduced in the market. Attention is given to the process of diffusion of innovation, as it is applicable to the sales activity. Salespeople are analyzed in this chapter as to their ability to introduce change and to solve the customers' problems. We conclude with a discussion of how to use logical analysis to solve problems.

"The Selling-Buying Process" is discussed in Chapter 6. The stimulus-response approach, the formula theory, Brewster's approach, and the need-satisfaction theory are four different ways of viewing and explaining the selling-buying activity. Each is discussed in detail along with its advantages and disadvantages. We introduce a conceptual model analyzing the industrial selling-buying process, and conclude with a discussion of pressure in selling.

3. Models of Buyer Behavior

If the salesperson is to be effective, he must have a general understanding of buyer behavior. In this chapter we focus on those theories from the behavioral sciences that relate to the selling-buying process. We try to tie all these theories to the salesperson's activities.

We begin with an example of a simple purchasing decision—our purpose being to illustrate the complex process of buying decisions as well as the numerous components of a purchase. We will then look at different aspects of human behavior that affect the selling-buying process—for example, the Marshallian model, motivation theory, learning theory, and reference group theory. We conclude with a discussion of how the salesperson can discover the prospect's or customer's motives.

THE PURCHASING DECISION PROCESS

The act of buying has become a substantial part of our everyday life. Buying has become such an indispensable activity that we rarely stop to analyze in detail why we have purchased a specific item. The final result of a sales call may be dependent on how well a salesperson has responded to all the explicit and the implied questions of a prospective buyer. A salesperson has to be able to help a customer in his decision, and this cannot be done without a clear knowledge of the purchasing process. Let's examine the purchase decision process involving an automobile, along with the factors that may be influential.

The Purchase Decision Process for an Automobile

Think back to the last time you or your family purchased an automobile. A great number of decisions are involved in the purchase of such a product. First, is the decision of whether or not to buy a car. Why not utilize public transportation? Why not lease the automobile? The answer to these questions would reveal, among other things, whether or not the purchase of an automobile is basically an economic decision, or a choice influenced by such factors as cultural background, education, family influence, or desire for social acceptance.

Another major decision concerns the *model* of automobile you want to purchase. Are you concerned with the mechanical qualities of each model? Are you concerned with other attributes such as comfort, ease of handling, economy, appearance, seating capacity? Are you concerned with *price* as a criterion for choice?

Emotional, social, and rational considerations may determine many purchase decisions. The attractiveness of the exterior design, primarily an emotional factor, could possibly be the major reason for the purchase of a car. Family influence or the desire to be identified with the character used in the advertising appeals may be strong social determinants of buying activities. Rational considerations include economic, practical, and utility factors such as the cost of the product, the gasoline consumption and efficiency, and mechanical qualities.

The final act of purchasing an automobile is, therefore, a complex process in which decisions are made about product, style, size, type, color, channel, and the like. All of these decisions are continuously subject to a multitude of influencing factors. Figure 3-1 illustrates the basic steps in this process.

Once the decision is made to purchase such an item, a series of choices have to follow. The choice of the product type, model, size, outlet, and time of purchase always confront the buyer with a number of alternatives. Consumers' choices at every step in the process may be affected by several factors, and the salespeople can be very important in influencing such decisions.

It seems important here to relate this example with the sales activity. Let us assume that our prospective automobile buyer decides to go to a dealer in order to check on the new car models and to acquire more information on the products available. Although at this point the individual has not yet made the decision to

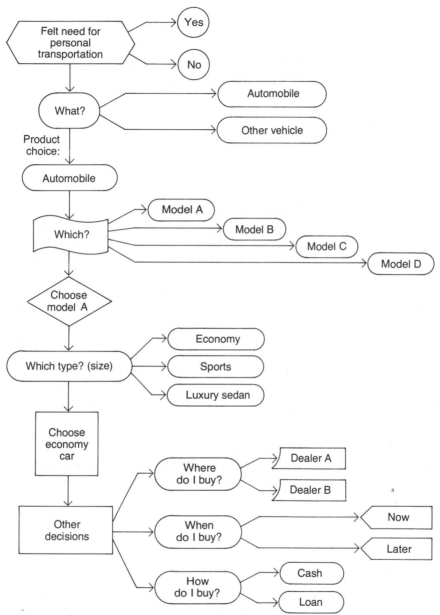

Figure 3-1 An example of the purchasing process

buy, the type of information he will acquire in the marketplace may considerably affect his future performance.

The car salesperson confronted with such a prospective customer must be aware of all the possible considerations involved with the purchase of an automobile. He will, with such knowledge, be careful to respond to the customer's questions and attempt to make suggestions which may influence the final decision. As an example, if the salesperson verifies that economy and mechanical performance are considered to be the most important purchase factors, he will emphasize models which satisfy those conditions, leaving other considerations such as design, interior, and size for later. Conversely, if factors such as design, interior, and size are perceived to be important to the buyer, the salesperson will show automobiles which satisfy those requirements, while reinforcing the advantages of such attributes.

Factors That May Influence Purchase Decisions

If we were to ask observers from various social and behavioral sciences to describe the variables that determine the decision to buy an automobile, we would probably receive several different answers. An economist might argue that the buyer will consider the cost and the value of various models and will finally purchase the car that provides the highest value for the lowest cost. A psychologist might state that emotional reasons very deeply embedded in our subconscious determine the choice. A sociologist might feel that the pressures of social groups and family habits are the most important factors in choosing an automobile. An anthropologist might trace the reasons for the choice of a particular model back to the consumer's cultural background and his ethnic group.

All of these explanations are based on extensive studies and experimentation; however, no one theory—economic, psychological, social, or anthropological—has yet been developed to fully explain consumer buying behavior. The answer can be found only by combining several theories into one dynamic interactive process. Therefore, to understand the consumption activity, one must be acquainted with some major principles derived from a number of the *social sciences*. In the remaining portion of this chapter we will examine those aspects of the behavioral sciences, dealing with buyer behavior, that relate most closely to the selling-buying process.

THE ECONOMISTS' VIEW: THE MARSHALLIAN MODEL

Economists have analyzed human behavior as a process of rational choice.[1] Alfred Marshall, who first consolidated the various economic theories, is the major proponent of modern economic thought. In this section we will examine Marshall's economic man, an example of economic buying behavior, the law of diminishing returns, and the relationship between economic theory and buyer behavior.

---

[1]Adam Smith, *An Inquiry into the Nature and Causes of the Wealth of Nations, 1776* (New York, N.Y.: Modern Library, 1937).

The Economic Man

Marshall's economic man is a rational decision maker who evaluates the consequences of each variable in the purchase decision process, one at a time, in a stepwise manner.[2] He progressively eliminates the less desirable alternatives until he finally selects that alternative which provides him with the highest utility/price ratio.

The measure of utility is determined by the amount of satisfaction earned through the possession of a particular product. Marginal utility is the added satisfaction that can be obtained by purchasing another product. For example, if a particular amount of satisfaction is obtained from the purchase of a $3000 car, the purchase of a $6000 car should provide additional satisfaction proportionate to the additional financial outlay. The economic man is characterized by the following factors:

1. He continually attempts to maximize his economic well-being.
2. He possesses complete information about the market.
3. He is absolutely mobile in that he can reach any market offer that he may need.

An Example of Economic Buying Behavior

The "economic man" is rarely found in everyday buying situations, however we will illustrate the variables affecting this type of purchase behavior. Assume a market situation such as that facing an isolated community which is completely self sufficient. The villagers buy their products at a central market which is held every week in the main square of town. The producers bring their goods to the market and all the villagers come to examine them and the trading begins.

Every villager has immediate and complete information about the quality, appearance, and price of all the products in the market. Furthermore, if conditions change—say, one of the merchants lowers the price of his products—the buyer will have immediate knowledge of it and will be able to adapt to the change. Finally, in order to satisfy the first condition of economic buying behavior, we will have to assume that each buyer's final goal is to obtain maximum value from the transaction. This implies that buyers are capable of objectively comparing the economic value of all the goods available. In this case, each seller's function is that of asking for a price compatible with the relative quality of their product, and of making the product available to buyers.

This example depicts a rather hypothetical situation. With the proliferation and complexity of products available today, it is impossible for the consumer to obtain complete information about the market. Also, because of time and space limitations, buyers are frequently incapable of reaching all existing market

---

[2]Alfred Marshall, *Principles of Economics, 1890* (London: Macmillan, 1927).

offerings. Finally, even though the consumer desires a certain amount of utility from his purchases, this does not mean that he will attempt to maximize his *economic* well-being at all times. Many transactions take place without involving a detailed and careful evaluation of the relative economic value of all existing alternatives. Impulse purchases, purchases motivated by social or emotional reasons, are examples of noneconomic buying behavior.

The Marshallian economic model, despite its limitations, provides very helpful insights into the process of purchase activities—an important one being the law of diminishing returns.

The Law of Diminishing Returns

One of the basic principles of the Marshallian model is the *law of diminishing returns*. According to this principle, the utility of each additional unit of the same product decreases as more and more units are consumed. A somewhat simplistic example of this principle is as follows.

Imagine a situation where, after a very competitive game of tennis on a very hot day, you feel a strong desire for a cold beer. The first glass you drink right after the game will produce a certain amount of satisfaction. As you drink additional glasses of beer at short time intervals, however, the added satisfaction felt is gradually reduced. There is a chance, in fact, that at some point in time an additional glass of beer will actually have no additional utility.

The law of diminishing returns has several selling implications. The fact that people may not derive the same satisfaction from purchasing additional units of the same product suggests that to push a product too hard, or to induce the customer to purchase too many units of the same item, may actually have negative consequences for the salesperson. With a relatively perishable product, for instance, the consumer may be forced to consume it too frequently and, therefore, may desire to switch brands or types of product.

Economic Theory and Buyer Behavior

When a purchasing agent attempts to evaluate the quality of a product with respect to its price, he is acting in an economic manner. It is true that the purchasing agent does not have complete information with respect to all the possible product alternatives; nor is he completely free of all constraints to buy from all sellers. In addition, the purchasing agent has established long-term personal contacts with certain salespeople whom he might personally like to see get an order if the particular salesperson's company is basically competitive on products, service, and price. The point is that although there is no true economic man who is completely objective, much of the behavior of purchasing agents and final consumers is influenced by rational economic considerations.

It is important, therefore, that the salesperson be knowledgeable about the economic advantages that his product has compared to the competitors' offerings. He should be able to emphasize such advantages as well as respond to possible questions on competitive products with regard to performance, efficiency, cost of operation, maintenance requirements, and compatibility with existing equipment so that there will be no misunderstanding as to the economic characteristics of the product he sells.

Many purchasing agents do not mind paying more for a particular product if it gives them substantially more value or utility than the other available alternatives. The salesperson must, therefore, remember that he is not just selling a product, but he is selling an item with a comparative value/cost ratio. The higher this ratio the better chance the salesperson has of completing a profitable sale.

MOTIVATIONAL THEORY

Motivation refers to the "why" of behavior. According to one writer, "motivation refers to the drives, urges, wishes or desires which initiate the sequence of events known as behavior."[3] Human motives are sometimes caused by biological needs. When our physical or emotional state of balance or homeostasis is disturbed, we feel a deprivation or need of some kind. The awareness of such a need is also called a want. When an individual attempts to satisfy that want, he is often experiencing some kind of motivation. Figure 3-2 on page 60 illustrates this concept. In this example, as soon as the individual feels hunger caused by lack of regular food intake, his physical balance is disturbed. This causes a feeling of uneasiness, a desire for food. The individual will then selectively respond to agreeable cues—for instance, a hamburger stand. This simplified example is based on physiological need-want satisfaction.

The needs of men, however, are many and far more complex than those of a physiological nature. In fact, if the tasks of a salesperson were merely to satisfy the hunger or thirst of his customers, he would be concerned primarily with the distribution of his products—so that all such market needs could be promptly matched by his goods.

A number of questions could be asked concerning motivation, such as: Why do people drink alcoholic beverages? Certainly not to satisfy the physiological need of thirst. Women who wear halter dresses do not appear to do so mainly to protect themselves from the cold. The same could be said of those who wear platform shoes; they do not appear to do so in order to protect their feet! It appears, therefore, that other variables are also responsible for motivating people to buy specific products. We will examine many aspects of motivation as they affect buyer behavior, including learned drives, types of motives, hierarchy of needs, value enhancement, and level of aspiration.

[3]Marguerite C. Burk, "Survey of Interpretations of Consumer Behavior by Social Scientists in the Postwar Period," *Journal of Farm Economics,* Vol. 49 (February 1967), p. 2.

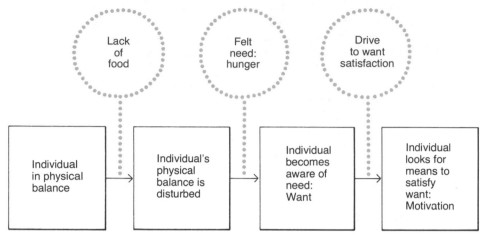

Figure 3-2 The motivation process

Learned Drives

Not all motives are physiological. People also have psychological and social needs, which are related to the environments in which they live. The cultural and educational backgrounds, family life, and personality characteristics of each individual determine the types and intensity of his psychological and social needs. The motivation that stems from these needs will drive the individual toward achieving goals that are acceptable in his environment. These are called *learned* drives.

This theory of learned drives explains many things, one example being why people in different countries consume different products to satiate their hunger. Although the physiological need is the same in any country, the natives have different learned drives. Therefore, an Italian will probably feel a desire for pasta, whereas a Chinese person might wish to have raw fish. Learned drives are very difficult to alter, because they are an integral part of a culture—and as such they resist change. A salesperson should be aware of the nature of these drives so that major consideration can be given to them when approaching customers.

Types of Motives

Buying motives may be classified into two groups: operational and sociopsychological.[4] This classification is based on the idea that some products are purchased because of their intrinsic qualities, whereas others are bought in response to social or psychological needs.

Operational Motives. The motives that are directly related to the anticipated performance of the product are called operational motives. For example, if a

[4]Edward L. Brink and William G. Kelley, *The Management of Promotion: Consumer Behavior and Demand Simulation* (Englewood Cliffs, N.J.: Prentice-Hall, 1962), p. 86.

consumer feels the desire to put a nail into a wall to hang a picture, he may need a hammer. The motive to purchase the hammer would be based on the expectation that it will be an instrument capable of driving the nail into the wall. Most purchases of industrial goods can be classified into this category of motives. As a result, when the salesperson feels that an operational motive is stimulating the buyer to act, he will want to stress the practical and functional aspects of the product.

Sociopsychological motives. These motives imply that the consumer will buy a product because of the social and psychological significance that he associates with the purchase or ownership of the product. The operational performance of the product is only an indirect factor in the purchase. Buyers may be consciously or unconsciously aware of the social and psychological motives that have influenced a particular purchase. For instance, a woman who purchases a mink coat may be doing so because she feels that the garment will convey an image of elegance, distinctiveness, and social prestige, even though she may use the coat only when the weather is cold. The function of protecting her from the bad weather is only indirectly related to the purchase. In this case, the salesperson will want to stress factors such as the coat's "rich and distinctive appearance" rather than its ability to keep the individual warm.

In reality, buying motives should be classified on a continuum ranging from operational motives to sociopsychological motives.[5] The reason for using a continuum is that products usually are purchased to satisfy both operational and sociopsychological motives. For example, a coat is generally purchased for use as protection against cold weather, but the choice of color, length, style, and material will often be made on the basis of a person's likes and dislikes, notion of style requirements, and the like.

Hierarchy of Needs

A. H. Maslow studied human motivation and established a classification of five needs arranged in a hierarchy of importance (Figure 3-3).[6] According to Maslow, the first and most basic needs are physiological—that is, those needs inherent to the biological nature of the individual such as hunger, thirst, and sleep. In the second group are needs for safety which are motivated by physical and psychological threats. The third group is the need for love or a sense of belonging—the need for family affection, for the company of friends, for companionship. In the fourth group of needs are those for esteem, for a high evaluation of one's self, and the respect of others. Finally, in the last category, are those needs for self-actualization. People will be unhappy unless they can accomplish what they are fit to do; there is in each person the desire to become everything he is capable of becoming.

[5]Jon G. Udell, "A New Approach to Consumer Motivation," *Journal of Retailing,* Vol. 40 (Winter 1964–65), pp. 6–10.

[6]A. H. Maslow, "A Theory of Human Motivation," *Psychological Review,* Vol. 60 (1943), pp. 370–396.

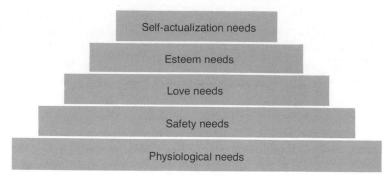

Figure 3-3 Maslow's hierarchy of needs

How Needs are Fulfilled.   Since needs have different degrees of importance, the most important ones (physiological) will have to be satisfied first, then the second most important, and so on, in the hierarchy. According to Maslow, man is a perpetually wanting animal: as he satisfies one need level he will move to the next highest level. However, the average member of our society will only partially satisfy all his needs and wants, and under special conditions individuals may permanently lose interest in the higher wants in the hierarchy.

There is no sharp distinction between each level of need. In addition, it is likely that whatever the items purchased, *needs at various levels* are being satisfied. In a booming and affluent economy, it is doubtful that very many decisions to buy are made solely on the basis of biological needs. In fact, we observe that some people are willing to pay a premium price for foods that are guaranteed to contain little or no nourishment, such as low-calorie soft drinks and dietetic bread.

This view of human motivation is useful in providing general insights into the "why" of behavior. However, it has limited utility in analyzing the motivation of an individual. First, within each category of needs, except the biological, there are almost limitless numbers of needs to be considered. Second, individual differences in intensity exist for each need. As for self-actualization, the highest level of need, one must have insight into the person's life values. In spite of its limitations, Maslow's theory can be useful to salespeople insofar as they can emphasize basic needs when selling a product.

Importance of the Hierarchy of Needs Theory for Selling.   In order to build interest for his product when making a sales presentation to a customer or prospect, the salesperson may want to avail himself of some of the insights provided by the hierarchy of needs theory. It is usually easier to justify basic needs than the more complex higher needs, such as self-actualization. A rationalization of the reasons for the purchase of a product may, therefore, bring quicker and more favorable results.

Let us consider the following example. Jeff Schroeder enters a clothing store to purchase a Fall coat. The salesperson shows him four different lightweight tweed coats, reasonably priced and very traditional. Jeff examines them. The coats are the type of product he needs—not too expensive, long lasting, practical, and with a nonpretentious look.

The salesperson then takes from a rack a luxurious dark brown pigskin coat and shows it to Jeff, saying, "This is one of our newest models, a coat for the times, beautifully tailored." After trying it on, Jeff decides that the coat is magnificent. Of course, it costs about four times as much as the tweed coats. The decision is very hard. The salesperson, noticing Jeff's preference, stresses the elegance, the durability, and the general appearance of the coat. He adds that although the coat is considerably more expensive than other models, it is a more fashionable item, and it would also be appropriate for more formal occasions. The purchase is finalized.

In this example, the salesperson has shown sensitivity to the customer's felt needs. Although some of the determining factors of the purchase were rational in nature, Jeff also felt some sociopsychological desires. The salesperson was able to point out clearly how the product might satisfy Jeff's rational and sociopsychological needs, therefore supplying him with a suitable solution for his problem—the purchase of the coat.

It is important that the salesperson be aware of these factors. Had he stressed the coat's capability of fulfilling status needs only, he might have failed to make a sale. Although Jeff felt the desire for social status, other more basic needs had to be satisfied first, such as durability and versatility.

Level of Aspiration

David McClelland has interpreted the motivations of individuals, as well as whole societies, in terms of their wishes, hopes, dreams, and aspirations.[7] He postulates that the critically important factor in motivation is the fact that much of what an individual does is done to provide himself with a sense of achievement. Actual achievement relative to characteristics of a person's aspirations is especially important. We will look at four considerations that are useful in determining the intensity of an individual's motivations and the influence of achievement motivation on purchasing decisions.

Four Basic Considerations.   First and most important, is the level of aspired achievement relative to the actual achievement of the individual. The well-motivated person is constantly seeking to do more and to do it better. The less-motivated person either has "pie in the sky" aspirations (goals that are unrealistically high in terms of his talents and opportunities) or, at the other extreme, his aspirations are at or beneath the level of achievement. He has no desire to improve.

Second, the aspirations of the well-motivated person are self-generating; that is, each goal achieved begets other goals. In contrast, the less-motivated person depends on others to set the goals; he lacks initiative.

[7]David C. McClelland, *The Achieving Society* (Princeton, N.J.: Van Nostrand, 1961).

Third, the well-motivated person has flexibility in his goals. He knows when to persist as well as when to quit. The less-motivated person, in contrast, either lacks definite goals or adheres rigidly to goals even when they have become obsolete or inappropriate.

Fourth, in the case of the well-motivated individual, the aspirations tend to form a mutually enhancing relationship. There is relative freedom from conflict among the goals for which he is striving. What the individual seeks on the job is not in opposition to his off-the-job aspirations. His personal goals are congruent with those he has for his family. Table 3-1 illustrates the differences between individuals with different levels of aspirations.

In summary, then, analysis of a person's motivations from this viewpoint is provided by the answers to four questions:

1. How realistic are the person's aspirations relative to his talents and opportunities?
2. To what extent are his aspirations self-generating?
3. How flexible are his aspirations?
4. To what extent are his aspirations mutually enhancing and free of conflict?

Influence of Achievement Motivation on Purchase Decisions.   Achievement motivation may influence buying behavior in various ways. For instance, it is possible that achievement-motivated consumers will use different criteria for selecting and purchasing goods than nonachievement-motivated consumers.

Consider two customers who enter a specialized photography equipment store to buy a good quality camera. They are both interested in taking pictures as a hobby, but while the first individual does not quite know what he needs to purchase, the second wants equipment which will allow him to take photographs of a quasi-professional level. One of the customers is nonachievement-motivated, while the other is a very achievement-motivated individual. The salesperson approaching the first individual will have to concentrate on orienting the customer toward specific products which will produce satisfactory results by asking questions, and sometimes making decisions for him. An automatic, unsophisticated camera may be the final purchase decision of this individual.

The situation facing the second customer is very different. In this case, the achievement-motivated individual will inform the salesperson very specifically of his needs, and he may even have considerable knowledge about the existing products which may interest him.

The salesperson's job here is somewhat simpler. His primary task is to respond clearly to the customer's requests. His role in this individual's purchase decision will be primarily that of a technical counselor.

Motivation Theory and Buyer Behavior

The more one studies motivation, the more evident it becomes that there simply is no one theory that fully accounts for this extremely complicated phenomenon.

TABLE 3-1 A COMPARISON OF INDIVIDUALS WITH DIFFERENT LEVELS OF ASPIRATION

Achievement-Motivated Individuals	*Non-Achievement-Motivated Individuals*
1. Level of aspired achievement: always try to do more and better	1. Level of aspired achievement: a. unrealistic, or b. beneath the level of achievement
2. Self-generating aspirations	2. Dependence on others for goal setting
3. Goals are flexible	3. No definite goals, or rigid goals
4. Goals are mutually enhancing	4. Goals may be conflicting

Rather, there are a number of theories, each of which explains a portion of what motivates buyers to act in particular ways under very specific circumstances. As an example, many people who join a fancy private club do so not because they will use the facilities but because they are searching for the "esteem need" or feeling of self-respect. The fact that they can now afford to join the club indicates to themselves and to others that they have arrived at a particular social plane in life. Each of the motivational models has implications for buyer behavior under certain circumstances. Throughout the text, we will analyze situations which involve the knowledge of motivation theory on the part of the salesperson. The handling of customers' objections, the sales presentation, and the close are all activities in which motivation plays an important role.

LEARNING THEORY – PAVLOV

Ivan Pavlov, a Russian psychologist, developed a learning model based on his experiments with the behavior of dogs. Every time he fed the dogs, Pavlov rang a bell. After some time, the dogs would salivate whenever the bell was rung, whether or not they received food. The conclusion Pavlov drew was that behavior can be conditioned through a process of association.[8] Later, other investigations extended conditioning research to human subjects. We have selected four central concepts of learning theory to show the importance of this aspect of behavior in understanding the buying-selling process.

Four Central Concepts

Learning theory can be described in terms of four central concepts—drive, cues, response, and reinforcement. Each is discussed below.

Drive.   This is represented by the needs, the motives, that are felt by the individual and that stimulate his action. There are two kinds of drive—phys-

[8]Ivan P. Pavlov, *Conditioned Reflexes,* Transl. by G. V. Anrep (London: Oxford University Press, 1927).

iological (those of a biological nature) and learned or conditioned (those acquired through social influences). Examples would be the drive to eat (physiological) and the drive to achieve success in a professional career (learned).

Cues.   These are stimuli that exist in the environment which suggest to an individual ways to satisfy his drives. The cues determine when and where people respond to drives. For instance, an ice cream advertisement could be the cue that stimulates a person to satisfy his drive for a cool, sweet dessert.

Response.   This is the reaction to the cues. Responses to the same cues may differ from individual to individual. An example might be the case of two individuals feeling drives for a dessert who see the same ice cream advertisements. While one of them may respond by driving to the nearest Baskin-Robbins store to purchase an ice cream cone, the other may completely disregard the cue because of personal taste, because he is on a diet, or for a number of other reasons.

Reinforcement.   The response will be reinforced whenever the individual finds it rewarding. This means that if a similar need is felt and the same cues are perceived, the individual will tend to respond as he did the first time. Going back to our previous example, this means that under similar circumstances, the individual who bought the ice cream cone to satisfy his dessert drive and was pleased with the results, may do the same thing when the need is felt again. This concept emphasizes the importance of cues in the formation of purchasing habits and brand loyalty.

Learning Theory and Buyer Behavior

The learning model is important to the understanding of buyer behavior, because it emphasizes the value of repetitive appeals as strong cues to customers—an essential part of the effort to penetrate the individual's conscious awareness. This is especially important in a very competitive market where products are relatively similar.

Learning theory also implies that sales appeals must be able to arouse strong drives in the customer. Product-related appeals must emphasize as much as possible the needs for the product as well as the satisfaction that it will provide. For instance, an insurance salesperson appealing to the sense of responsibility that the head of the family feels for his loved ones will be stimulating strong drives while furnishing a means of satisfying such needs through the purchase of insurance. In this case, the drive to buy insurance would be reinforced according to the amount of satisfaction obtained by the buyer. Let's look at concepts of learning theory as they influence selling activities.

Habit Formation.   Learning is the first step in habit formation, a very significant aspect of an individual's personality. Once certain reactions become a matter of habit, an individual resists interference with them. This happens in part because habits (things that are being done without conscious effort or thought) must be pondered if they are to be changed. Habit patterns provide the individual with a feeling of stability within his environment. Thus the effective salesperson learns as much as he can about the habits of any prospect or customer so that, in adapting his appeal to that person, he causes minimal change or interference.

When purchase decisions are relatively simple and frequent, it is likely that the buyer will tend to form habits of purchase. A salesperson can be instrumental in gaining the customer's loyalty to his product and his firm by making sure that no delivery problems occur, and that the quality of the product is uniform and satisfactory to the customer. Salespeople handling industrial supplies, for example, should make an effort to keep each account trouble-free, thus preventing competitors from invading their accounts. The prompt services provided to such customers, as well as the ability to resolve complaints, are vital in maintaining this type of relationship.

Drive.   A second generalization which can be derived from the learning model and is very important for selling is the concept of drives. Primary and learned drives are motivating factors which can trigger a sale. The salesperson should be aware of the existence of drives when approaching prospects, so that his efforts can better be concentrated on those who are more likely to become customers.

Also, the knowledge of customers' learned drives can provide a salesperson with vital information about the product variables which may best fit the individual needs. The sales presentation can thus be prepared more efficiently and possibly yield better results.

Cues.   In a personal sales situation, the sales representative provides the cues to the buyer. If he performs well, he will convince the buyer to choose a rewarding solution for his problems. For example, consider a situation in which a purchasing agent of a large company has had successful experiences with firms that have a very strong technological know-how. The salesperson who is aware of the existence of such a learned drive would employ this knowledge as a useful cue in his sales presentation, thus stressing his company's research and development programs as well as their technological experience. When properly stressed, a valuable cue may be an important factor in the completion of a sale.

Reinforcement.   This is the last concept generated by learning theory which is very helpful to sales. Rewarding experiences strengthen a favorable attitude toward a product or firm. The salesperson, as a representative of his company, has the very important role of making a good impression on his customers. By maintaining a pleasant attitude and providing good quality and responsive service, the firm will benefit through increased goodwill.

Continued positive reinforcement builds association between the firm and perceived values of the customers. Through reinforcement the firm might be considered more reliable, more responsive, and more flexible than its competitors. This attitude is essential to gain entry with additional product lines and to achieve confidence in product innovations, as well as to keep the customers' loyalty.

REFERENCE GROUPS – THE VEBLENIAN MODEL

Thorstein Veblen, an economist, was a major advocate of the theory that social groups have a major influence on the behavior of individuals. Veblen believed that man is a social animal, and as such his actions are influenced by the environment in which he lives. The individual's cultural background, his family, and his friends are instrumental in shaping his aspirations and desires.[9] Let us consider the types of reference groups found in society and how they affect buyer behavior.

Types of Reference Groups

Sociologists today define any group that affects a person's behavior as a reference group. An example would be a purchasing agent who asked three colleagues to form a committee to give him advice on the procurement of a new product. If the committee's advice affected his decision as to the purchase of the product it would be a reference group for him. However, if the group's advice did not affect his decision in anyway, it would be merely a collection of three people and not a reference group.

There are three types of reference groups. One type a person belongs to because of birth, occupation, or any other formal affiliation. Such groups would be family, business associates, political party, and the like. There are also groups to which an individual belongs because of certain demographic characteristics, such as age, sex, level of education, marital status, and the like. Finally, there are reference groups to which an individual aspires to belong. As an example, an individual who wants to join a private club but has not yet been accepted for membership may still try to conform to what he believes is the proper behavior for club members. Because they wish to be identified with those who actually belong to these groups, individuals will imitate their behavior.[10]

Relative Influence of Various Reference Groups

An individual will be influenced by a number of different reference groups at any point in time. This means that different purchases might be motivated by the

---

[9]Thorstein Veblen, *The Theory of the Leisure Class* (New York, N.Y.: Macmillan, 1899).

[10]James F. Engel, David T. Kollat, and Roger D. Blackwell, *Consumer Behavior* (New York, N.Y.: Holt, Rinehart, and Winston, 1973), pp. 162–164.

desire to be identified with different groups. For instance, the purchase of a suit might be a consequence of the dressing style of the informal social group to which an individual belongs, whereas the type of car he purchases might be influenced by the cars his work associates drive.

It is important to note that while a reference group may be influential on a specific purchase decision, it may not affect other types of activities. For instance, a businessman might buy conservative suits because he feels he should dress in the same basic style as other men in his work position. On the other hand, his political decisions may not necessarily be influenced by the people he works with; rather, they may be a consequence of party affiliation and informal groups. Thus his business associates act as a reference group with respect to the type of clothing he purchases but not with respect to his political decisions.

Reference Groups and Buyer Behavior

It is important for the salesperson to find out which reference groups are most influential in determining an individual's demand for the products he sells. The extent to which a person conforms to a reference group's rules is a function of several factors. Reference groups in which members relate closely to each other, often have greater influence on the behavior of their members. Also, individuals who belong to groups with formal organizational structures and rules, such as fraternities and social clubs, tend to follow the norms of behavior of the group more closely than those who belong to less structured reference groups, such as a neighborhood association.

A person's attitudes and personality will also determine how deeply his behavior is affected by reference groups. For example, an individual displaying strong personality and independent attitudes will be less likely to conform to group behavior than a more dependent individual. Now let's examine a consumer goods example of reference group appeal and sales strategy.

A Consumer Goods Example

Assume that a real estate salesperson is approached by a prospective house buyer. Although some indication of the buyer's preferences can be reached by establishing an acceptable price range for the home, this information is still not sufficient. The salesperson will do a better job of selecting homes that please his customer if he knows his occupation, social status, hobbies, education, and life style. In this manner, it is easier to identify the symbolic values of the customer and search for homes that best fit such values.

Let's take Mr. Peter Tennisworth as an example. He has been hired by Mid-Michigan College as an Associate Professor with a salary of $19,000. He has three children who enjoy playing tennis. Their ages are 9, 13, and 17. Mr. Tennisworth and his wife are active golfers. Mr. Tennisworth told the salesperson they want to live in a "professional section of the city that need not be dominated by university types."

This information gives the salesperson a great deal to work with beyond the economic situation of the Tennisworths. Evidently, the family is quite interested in sports and might like to consider a home in the Country Club Estates. However, the salesperson also realizes that the club is located eight miles out of the city, and this might present transportation problems for the two younger children if they plan to participate in extra curricular activities.

Thus by learning of the Tennisworth's reference groups the salesperson is better able to find the best house for their needs.

HOW TO DISCOVER BUYER'S MOTIVES AND INTENTIONS

It is critical for a salesperson to discern what the buyer's motives are. To achieve this, he must have a basic understanding of the various behavioral sciences—including marketing, selling, communications, psychology, and sociology. There are three simple methods the salesperson can utilize to obtain a good understanding of what motivates a particular individual. These are (1) listen and observe, (2) utilize past records and experience, and (3) read and study.[11]

Listen and Observe

It is very important to hear what a prospect is saying, and the ability to do this may be critical to a salesperson's success. If a salesperson asks the right questions, most prospects will tell him what they want in a product or what motivates them.

As an example, if the prospect asks such questions as "What mileage does this car get on the highway and in town? How often does the car need service? Is the car designed to permit the amateur mechanic to repair it?" the salesperson might logically conclude that this individual is interested in an economical automobile. In the same manner, if a purchasing agent asked such questions as "How long is the service policy on the equipment? Can the service policy be extended by a fee? How long does it take to get parts? Where is the service center located?" the salesperson can reasonably conclude that the purchasing agent is concerned about service.

The most important points for the salesperson to remember are that the prospect will generally not purchase because of one motive alone, but some motives will be not as important as others. The salesperson must therefore learn to ask questions that will unveil the motives of the individual.

[11]Carlton A. Pederson and Milburn Wright, *Salesmanship Principles and Methods*, Sixth edition (Homewood, Ill.: Irwin, 1976), pp. 89–90.

Utilize Past Records and Experience

The good salesperson will make full use of his prior experience. After dealing with a customer for a period of time, the salesperson learns his behavior patterns.

As an example, an industrial salesperson may be selling the identical products to three different accounts. One account may be interested in service, another in delivery speed, and the third in price. Although, the product is the same, the salesperson will want to stress different aspects of the product and features of the company when he calls on each of the three accounts.

However, most organizations operate in a very dynamic world, and as a result the salesperson must be aware of shifting motives on the part of the buyer. Still, the salesperson's past experience will be a very good indicator as to how an account should be approached.

Read and Study

Finally, the salesperson should continually monitor trade magazines and other applied journals so as to keep up with the latest theories about individual behavior. Through proper use of published studies, a salesperson can improve his selling techniques and obtain a significant advantage over his competitors.

SUMMARY

In this chapter we focused on the key variables that affect buyer behavior. First we discussed the complexity of the purchasing decision process. Then we studied the motives of the Marshallian economic man. Although the "economic man" may live only in theory, many purchasing agents attempt to make decisions based on economic concerns. Thus, the salesperson must be aware of the economic advantages of his product.

We discussed several theories of motivation, and stressed the hierarchy of needs for motives. That is, individuals first attempt to satisfy basic biological needs, and then they move up, eventually trying to satisfy needs of self-actualization. Finally, we examined McClelland's interpretation of motivation— here, the critically important variable in motivation being the achievement motive. Although motivation theory is quite complex, the salesperson must have an understanding of it, because so much of what he does involves human motivation.

We also discussed the central concepts in learning theory: drive, cues, response, and reinforcement. Each concept was discussed from the perspective of selling. The last behavioral concept we examined was reference group theory. Here, we found that buyers, like all other individuals, are affected by social as well as individual variables.

We concluded with a discussion of how to discover a buyer's motives and intentions.

PROBLEMS

1. Analyze in detail all possible decision steps you went through the last time you purchased a shirt.
2. In which way is economic theory useful to explain buyer behavior?
3. Explain the advantages and disadvantages of using Maslow's hierarchy of needs to explain buyer behavior.
4. Examine your level of aspirations, and compare yourself with McClelland's model. Would you be considered an achievement-motivated individual?
5. How can learning theory be used to develop brand loyalty by customers?

Exercise 3

MODELS OF BUYER BEHAVIOR

Objective: To obtain a first-hand knowledge of the applicability of the purchasing influences and factors discussed in the text.

A. Inferential Evidence from Advertising

Go to the library and select two volumes of a magazine (e.g., Fortune, Time, Mademoiselle, Esquire) which are at least 10 years apart. Analyze the ads for a common product, (e.g., clothing, automobiles) noting and comparing the appeals used in the two different time periods.

Magazine selected: _____

19 ___ volume (old)   *19 ___ volume (recent)*

Economic

Motivational

"Learning"

B. Inferential Evidence from Interviews

Use the questions furnished below and interview at least ten students who are not in your sales class.

1. What was your last purchase of five dollars or more?
2. Where did you make the purchase? What factors influenced your choice of store?
3. What do you like best about what you purchased?
4. Do you consider it a good buy? On what basis?
5. How would you describe yourself as a customer?

Case 3-1 Martineau Jewelers (B)*

Sunday afternoon following the heated store managers' meeting on digital watches, Mr. Martineau's attention is drawn to the cover story of a business magazine on the very subject:

> **The Angry U.S. Watchmakers.** The established companies say that the semi-conductor makers are going after market share at the expense of profits, as if they were in another calculator price war. They worry that digital profits will disappear just as calculator profits did this year. Says Jerome Clarke, president of Clarke Corp. (an Alpha Corp. division) and a major watch company: "I told Mitron (currently the price leader) that by cutting their digital watch by $10, they just threw $5 million in the garbage pail this year."
>
> **The Frightened Jewelers.** The digital watches are scaring the daylights out of jewelers and other retailers with high selling expenses. Digital watchmakers are putting the squeeze on retailers; they are not financing inventories and are dropping margins from the traditional 50% or "keystone" level. Jewelers will also have less service to offer customers because the watchmakers themselves will handle what little service or repair is needed on digitals. But jewelers worry most about what they see as a lack of quality and price stability. "If manufacturers take the calculator approach to the digital watch, it could kill the watch market for quality jewelry stores," says Thomas Martin, Stack's group vice-president in charge of the jewelry store division.

In the meanwhile King, Peters, and Wilson, the store managers, are finding it difficult to draw any firm conclusions. We find them chatting on a conference call to Ms. Wilson.

King: It's hard to pin down the best brands. However, I'm inclined to recommend only those firms whose names and labels are associated with watches. It's a shame none of our present suppliers are in the field. I think customers would be wary of a timepiece made by a computer house.

*Be certain you read Case 2-3, Martineau Jewelers (A), before analyzing this case.

Peters: That makes sense. What do you think, Jeanne?

Wilson: I agree. There doesn't seem to be any pattern among my competitors. Price lining** seems to be the only consideration. Their customers don't seem to ask for any special brand. Buyers of digitals seem to be young people. At least that's the way it looked when I visited local stores.

King: What about your own clientele, Jeanne?

Wilson: Well, I was pretty low key in my inquiries since I didn't want to generate too much interest in an item I can't deliver. I'd say that there wasn't much interest.

Peters: I have a gut feel that digitals are a status symbol. If someone in a group buys one, others will keep up.

1. What comments do you have?
2. Are there any social dimensions to such a watch purchase?
3. How would you analyze Mr. Martineau's stand on the issue?

Case 3-2 The Brown-Talleyrand Encyclopedia

The Murphys are a young couple living in the suburbs of Phoenix, Arizona. They are both highly educated. John Murphy has a Ph.D. and teaches at the local university. Liz, his wife, has a Master's Degree and works as a consultant for a local firm. They have two children, Peter and Gregory aged 9 and 7, respectively. The Murphys are very concerned about their children's education and make sure the best schools and programs in the city are available to them.

In October, Liz decided that the children were old enough to make use of encyclopedias. While reading a magazine, Liz noticed an advertisement for encyclopedias and called the local representative for an appointment.

Two weeks later, Mr. Rudolf Schick, the encyclopedia salesman, called on her. Liz explained that she wanted him to show her all the advantages of owning such a collection. The resulting dialogue went as follows:

Mr. Schick: Very well, first of all let me show you one of our sample volumes. As you can see, the binding is all in genuine leather with gold-leaf engraving. All fifty volumes are bound in this same way and they look marvelous in the showcase.

Liz: I see. Can you tell me something about the books?

Mr. Schick: Certainly. The books are organized in alphabetical order, so that it becomes easy to find information on a specific item. The pictures and illustrations are all in beautiful color. As you can see, this is the picture of all the flags of South America; look at the sharp colors!

Liz: I can see that, but I am more interested . . .

**Price lining is the act of setting a few price levels for a line of merchandise and then pricing all of the products in the line at one of the prescribed prices.

Mr. Schick: I know what you mean! The books are concerned with many different aspects of knowledge. For instance, you have here a beautiful Atlas, with detailed geographical charts. It is really a very useful source of knowledge for adults.

Liz: I am really concerned about my children!

Mr. Schick: Sure! I can understand that! Bless their hearts, if they decide to play with the books and scratch them with crayons or paste peanut butter all over them! This is why our company makes this special bookcase with glass doors and key lock, so that the little angels will not ruin your marvelous investment.

You know, of course, this is a very valuable investment. This collection has a high resale value. It becomes more valuable as time goes by. It is also a beautiful decoration piece. We hardly get back the money we spent in having the cabinet made. May I write up your order?

Liz: Well, Mr. Schick, I really would like to think it over. Maybe you could leave me some literature about the collection, so that I could learn more about it.

Mr. Schick: I really do not have any supplementary literature with me. Also, I would like to mention that we are offering a special easy payment plan this week only, and I would suggest that you take advantage of it.

Liz: I am afraid that I am not really ready to purchase the product now. I should think about it a little further . . .

Mr. Schick: Shall I call you tomorrow? It would be a very nice gift to your husband . . .

Liz: Well, no, not really. I don't think we are interested right now. Thank you so much.

Mr. Schick: Thank you, and good bye. Please give me a call if you change your mind.

Liz: Good bye.

1. What did Mr. Schick do wrong?
2. What would have been a motive for Liz to buy the encyclopedia?
3. What would you have done if you had made this sales call?

Case 3-3 Nudesign Furniture Co.

Nudesign is a small manufacturer of office furniture. It was founded three years ago by three graduates in commercial design. The firm produced modern furniture of very luxurious design and materials. They built some reputation with decorators in town who worked with very wealthy professionals and corporate officers of major companies.

The three associates felt that they should expand their activities. An informal market research done three months earlier had shown that there was a large market for office furniture within a more modest income bracket. This market was composed primarily of young doctors, lawyers, and businessmen who were willing to spend $1000 to $5000 to furnish their office.

Presently, this market had a somewhat limited choice of office furniture—primarily restricted to traditional designs and materials. Nudesign felt that more innovative and sophisticated furniture would appeal to the young, fast-growing market.

By designing furniture for a larger and less expensive bracket, Nudesign had to start an aggressive sales policy, so that the increased volume would make possible a drop in prices. In order to do this, Mr. Gettem was hired to select and train a force of twelve salespersons who would call on stores, decorators, and final customers.

Mr. Gettem decided first of all to verify the actual demand structure, so that he could establish what sales appeals would be most effective. The results showed that the market was very concerned with such factors as price, durability, and design of the furniture. New graduates from law and medical schools were very anxious to establish their reputation. They were very ambitious and very hard workers. They tried to identify very closely with well-known, established practitioners. They were, however, more liberal, less pragmatic, and more cosmopolitan than their older counterparts.

Nudesign offered four lines of their less expensive office furniture to this market—all modern and elegant. It was Mr. Gettem's task to develop a direct mailpiece which would appeal to this market and thus would generate leads for the company's salespersons. He also would develop a structured sales presentation for Nudesign sales representatives. All new graduates would receive a direct mailing and, if interested, would receive a visit from a Nudesign representative.

1. Make a list of the most important appeals which should be used by Nudesign.

2. Assume you have Mr. Gettem's job; prepare a prototype of a sales presentation for your product.

SUGGESTIONS FOR FURTHER READING

Britt, Steuart H., (ed.) *Consumer Behavior and the Behavioral Sciences,* (New York, N.Y.: John Wiley, 1966).

Cardozo, Richard N., and James W. Cagley, "Experimental Study of Industrial Buyer Behavior," *Journal of Marketing Research,* Vol. 8 (August 1971), pp. 329–334.

Engel, James F, David T. Kollat, and Roger D. Blackwell, *Consumer Behavior,* 2nd ed. (New York, N.Y.: Holt, Rinehart, and Winston, 1973).

Grubb, Edward L., and Harrison L. Grathwohl, "Consumer Self-Concept, Symbolism and Market Behavior: A Theoretical Approach," *Journal of Marketing,* Vol. 31 (October 1967), pp. 22–27.

Kassarjian, Harold J., and Thomas S. Robertson (eds.), *Perspectives in Consumer Behavior* (Glenview, Ill.: Scott, Foresman, 1968).

Kirkpatrick, Charles A., *Salesmanship,* 5th ed. (Cincinnati: South-Western Publishing, 1971), Chapters 1 and 2.

Kotler, Philip, "Behavioral Models for Analyzing Buyers," *Journal of Marketing,* Vol. 29 (October 1965), pp. 37–45.

Markim, Rom J., *The Psychology of Consumer Behavior* (Englewood Cliffs, N.J.: Prentice-Hall, 1969).

Sheth, Jagdish, *Models of Buyer Behavior: Conceptual, Quantitative and Empirical* (New York, N.Y.: Harper & Row, 1974).

Tucker, W. Thomas, *Foundations for a Theory of Consumer Behavior,* (New York, N.Y.: Holt, Rinehart, and Winston, 1968).

Witt, Robert E., and Grady D. Bruce, "Purchase Decisions and Group Influence," *Journal of Marketing Research,* Vol. 7 (November 1970), pp. 533–535.

4. The Communication Process

The success of a firm's selling efforts hinges on its ability to communicate with everyone who affects the firm's relationship with its customers and prospects. The firm may have excellent products and an abundance of physical, financial, and human resources behind it, but if it cannot convey the scope of its offerings in a favorable way it will not survive. Ralph Waldo Emerson's statement that, "If a man can write a better book, preach a better sermon, or make a better mousetrap than his neighbor, though he builds his house in the woods, the world will make a beaten path to his door," is not aligned with the facts of business life.

Although mass communication has become increasingly important in our economy, the salesperson still remains the single most important communicator in the entire marketing organization. He provides the personal link between the marketplace and the firm. He is the one who brings about the actual selling-buying transaction. This accounts for the adage that, "Nothing really happens in a business until a sale is made." The salesperson has the task of personalizing and individualizing the firm's offerings to each individual and to each account. To do this he must be an able communicator.

In this chapter we will analyze the process of communication as it applies to the salesperson by examining the definition of communication and discussing its components. In addition, we shall describe several types of communication, the factors which influence sending and receiving a message, persuasive communication, and some obstacles to communication.

COMMUNICATION – A DEFINITION

There are many definitions of communication. It has been described as "an exchange of meaning," as "the process or form of behavior by which any living organism affects the behavior of another living organism" or as "a system for sending and receiving messages."[1] We will examine a general model of communication, and explore the importance of the salesperson as a source of communication.

A General Model of Communication

Interpersonal communication in its simplest form is the transmission of a message from a source to a receiver (Figure 4-1). All forms of communication require a source, a signal, a channel, and a receiver. In interpersonal communication, the source is a person, the signal is the spoken language, and the channel is the air between the two individuals that conveys the signal in the form of sound waves. The receiver is also a person. The signal is made up of message and noise. The *message* is the information to be conveyed. Filtering, blocking, or distortion of the signal is the *noise* ingredient. A key objective of communication is to maximize the message and minimize the noise. The source unwittingly adds noise to the extent that the words, numbers, and symbols employed only approximate the message he wishes to convey. The receiver adds more noise to the degree that his background, purpose, and setting differ from those of the source.

In a sales presentation, the salesperson must be as clear as possible so as not to confuse the prospect with useless remarks and complex terms. If too many products are demonstrated at the same time, for instance, the prospect may not be able to retain and comprehend those which are most useful to him. This "noise" in the sales presentation may jeopardize the closing of an order.

The salesperson's responsibility often goes beyond the sales presentation, as such. His appearance, personality, and professional capability are key elements in the communication process.

[1]*Webster's New Twentieth Century Dictionary of the English Language–Unabridged,* 2nd edition (Springfield, Mass.: World, 1968), p. 367.

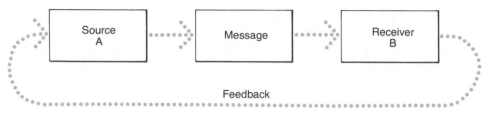

Figure 4-1 Two-way communication

The Importance of the Salesperson as a Source of Communication

Although the source of a communication is often thought to be an individual or a corporation, communication research has shown that audiences frequently perceive the source of a promotional message to be the sponsoring company and the medium. This phenomenon is known as the source effect.[2] Theodore Levitt investigated the importance of salespersons as opposed to their firm's reputation as a source of information for industrial purchases.[3] The following conclusions were drawn by Levitt, as a result of this study.

Securing the Interview.   Levitt found that a company's reputation is valuable as far as enabling the salesperson to secure interviews with prospects and also as a means of securing early adoption of a new product. This appears to be true primarily in the case of complex industrial products. Here, the implications for sales is that it will be harder for a salesperson representing a relatively unknown firm to introduce technologically complex new products in the market. The salesperson may want to avail himself of referrals from well-known persons in the industry, in order to gain entrance to his prospective companies.

More is Expected From Well-Known Companies.   Although salespersons of well-known companies appear to have an edge on other salespeople, more is expected from them by their customers, because they are perceived to have some advantages over the salespeople of lesser known firms. This finding implies the need for a well-prepared and well-executed sales presentation by all salespersons, because this is a very important factor in the buying decision. A salesperson cannot rely solely on the effectiveness of his company's name, reputation, or promotional campaigns. His customers will expect from him a performance commensurate with the firm he represents.

Technically Complex Products.   The study revealed that the sales presentation of a technically complex product will affect how the product itself is perceived by

[2]Carl I. Hovland and Walter Weiss, "The Influence of Source Credibility on Communication Effectiveness," *Public Opinion Quarterly,* Vol. 15 (Winter 1951–1952), pp. 635–650.

[3]Theodore Levitt, "Communications and Industrial Selling," *Journal of Marketing,* Vol. 31 (April 1967), pp. 15–21.

the prospect. Thus if the salesperson of a relatively unknown company is selling a complex piece of machinery, he may obtain an edge over a well-known competitor if he delivers a sales presentation of better quality. As a result, companies marketing industrial products should concentrate their efforts in selecting and training their salespeople.

Perceived Risk.   Levitt's next finding concerned measuring the source with regard to the risk involved in industrial purchase decisions. The firm's reputation has a greater effect on perceived risk than the sales presentation. In other words, although a good salesperson is more effective in reaching the purchasing agent and in demonstrating the product, his efforts alone may not be able to give the buyer enough confidence in the product's reliability, if he represents a relatively unknown company. In order to decrease the amount of risk perceived by the buyer, the company may concentrate its efforts on promotional activities and utilize testimonials by well-known industrialists or respected technicians and scientists. This sales tactic should also be used by salespeople in their presentations of new, highly technical items.

The Buyer's Competence.   The study found that in lower-risk decision situations the competent technical personnel were more influenced by the quality of the sales presentation than were the purchasing agents. On the other hand, in high-risk decisions purchasing agents were more influenced by good sales presentations than were the technical personnel. This finding has several implications for salespeople, as to the choice of their audience and the quality of their presentation. They must be aware of the knowledge of their audience when preparing the sales presentation, and when presenting a complex new product to technical personnel they should rely on the ability of engineers or other qualified production people in their company.

Levitt drew some very important conclusions from his study:

All this suggests that in making his adoption decisions the customer is influenced by more than what the salesman specifically says about the product or even how effectively he communicates product facts. It seems very probably that the communicator's personality and what he says about things other than the product in question play a vital role in influencing his audience. The effective transmission of product facts seems to be more important in the long run than in the short run.[4]

Thus there is evidence that in a personal sales situation both the salesperson's character and ability and the company's reputation affect the perception of a message and the decision to purchase a product. This dual-source effect will vary with the complexity of the product, the buyer's technical competence, and the span of time between the sales presentation and the actual decision to buy the

[4]*Ibid., p. 21.*

product. We will now present an analysis of different types of communications as they apply to sales.

TYPES OF COMMUNICATION

Communication can be classified as verbal or nonverbal depending on the code used to send the message. Another way of classifying communication is by the existence or lack of feedback to the sender. Accordingly, communication can be divided into one-way or two-way communication.

Nonverbal Communication

Nonverbal communication uses actions, gestures, facial expressions, and other nonspoken forms to signify human emotions. Nonverbal communication may occur simultaneously with verbal communication. It expresses the feelings of the sender and/or the receiver, which may not be easily described with words. It is difficult to state just how important nonverbal communication is to the total communication process, but it does play an important role in interpersonal communication.

Three Segments of Sign Language.   In their book, *Nonverbal Communication,*[5] Jurgen Ruesch and Welden Kees divide the world of nonverbal communication into three segments: sign language, action language, and object language. Sign language uses gestures to communicate, (e.g., a football official raising both arms to indicate a score has been made). Action language includes all bodily movements which communicate ideas that are not primarily intended for communication (e.g., a boy who eats his dinner unusually rapidly may communicate something about how hungry he is). Object language involves the display of material things (e.g., an expensive imported sports car may communicate something about the driver's personality, his financial status, and his overall life style).

　　In personal selling an example of sign language on the part of the customer might be that he repeats a word during a sales presentation. This possibly indicates that he understands what the salesperson is saying. An example of action language might be when a buyer puts his feet up on his desk and leans back in his chair. This indicates that he is not rushed and is willing to give the salesperson a reasonable amount of time to complete the sale. Finally, an example of object language might be that this buyer has a very fancy office which indicates his importance to the firm.

[5]Jurgen Ruesch and Welden Kees, *Nonverbal Communication* (Berkley, Ca.: University of California Press, 1959).

"Time Talks" and *"Space Speaks."* Edward Hall in his text, *The Silent Language*,[6] examines nonverbal communication from another perspective: time talks and space speaks. For example, in the United States it is polite to be on time to a party, whereas in South America one is expected to arrive as much as one hour after the formal time of the invitation. Again, in the United States, people find business transactions more comfortable if they are separated from each other by an arm's length. In other parts of the world, such a distance is considered to be in poor taste and a sign that the individual who insists on the distance is a cold-hearted person who cannot be trusted.

Source Credibility. The information provided by a salesperson can be an important factor in diminishing the risk perceived by the buyer. The response of the buyer is considerably influenced by his attitude toward the source of the communication. The believability of the source depends on how the receiver perceives it: it is not an objective evaluation, in that it usually represents the subjective feelings of the receiver.

The salesperson's credibility is transferred to the product he sells, the company he represents, and the services he is offering. It is very important, therefore, to verify the variables that influence source credibility. The level of expertise displayed by a salesperson determines his credibility. It is important for the receiver to feel that the sender of the message is knowledgeable about the subject matter. Does the salesperson have sufficient expertise about the product he is trying to sell? Does he know the most efficient use for the product?

The external characteristics of the seller are also instrumental in conveying an image of credibility. Mannerisms, appearance, language, dressing standards, and age all provide bases for inferences about source credibility. Based on this knowledge, firms may establish dress codes for their salespeople, so as to avoid negative inferences which may be derived from appearance.

Another determinant of source credibility is the extent to which the source is able to give an unbiased opinion. If the buyer perceives that the seller intends to change his attitudes toward a product, the buyer may develop a defensive attitude. A salesperson should be able to show a balanced attitude toward the products and services he offers. He should show the advantages of his products over the competitors', but he should not push for a sale when his product is not appropriate to satisfy the buyer's needs.

The image of prestige conveyed by the source is also positively related to its credibility. Respected members of the community are perceived to be more trustworthy than other sources, and therefore can become useful tools in obtaining the confidence of prospective buyers. Thus, a salesperson's local activities are important to his credibility, and he should avoid any attitude which may jeopardize this value as perceived by buyers.

[6]Edward Hall, *The Silent Language* (Garden City, N.Y.: Doubleday, 1959).

Verbal Communications

Verbal communication occurs through the use of language. It can be written or oral. It uses words, expressions, and phrases that have been incorporated into a specific culture and have some conventional meaning. Verbal communication is limited to the extent that the source and the receiver interpret the meanings of words in the same way. For example, some black people use the word "ride" to describe an automobile. The use of this word may not contribute an effective message, however, because not all receivers understand that "ride" and automobile designate the same object. Another way of classifying communication is by the existence or nonexistence of feedback to the sender. According to this criterion, communication can be one way or two way.

One-Way Communication

One-way communication is typical of most forms of mass communication. It implies that the message flows from the sender to the receiver, and no feedback is received by the sender. When a department store uses a television station to act as a medium to promote a forthcoming sale, it is impossible for the store to adjust its signal individually to fit the reference frames of its multiple receivers. Even if the store examined the socioeconomic, demographic, and sociopsychological characteristics of its target market so that it could adapt its promotional message, the store still would not be able to answer any individual questions or elaborate on items of particular interest to specific individuals through this medium.

Only in very rare circumstances does the salesperson have to rely on one-way communication. Even if the salesperson is very rushed and is not permitted to give the receiver sufficient time to ask questions, the sender will be able to observe his facial expressions which will help him determine if his message got through to the receiver.

Two-Way Communication

In contrast to one-way communication, two-way communication is ongoing and interactive. Look again at Figure 4-1. Here, source A sends a message to source B, who in turn transmits a response signal to source A. This process continues as long as A and B are engaged in a dialogue. The return signal is called feedback.

The sales presentation is a good example of two-way communication. As the salesperson starts to explain the advantages of his products, the customer's reactions, questions, gestures and other nonverbal messages are an indication of how interested he is in the sales presentation.

In a personal selling context, the salesperson's ability to make effective use of the ongoing interpersonal interaction is largely dependent on his "empathic" ability. Empathy, in this context, is defined as the ability to make accurate inferences about a potential customer during face-to-face interaction and to modify behavior in response to these inferences. In addition to being able to exploit one's own empathic ability, there are four distinct advantages to using two-way communication: (1) continuous feedback, (2) an opportunity for the customer to talk, (3) less likelihood that the salesperson will engage in projection, and (4) opportunity for the customer to take action.

Continuous Feedback.   Two-way communication provides an opportunity for continuous feedback, which lets the salesperson know what progress he is making and which points in his presentation need amplification or amendment. As a result, this communication process is more accurate because the sender realizes when he is getting his message across to the receiver.

An Opportunity To Talk.   In two-way communication, the other person has an opportunity to talk. An important psychological principle applies here, in that the more a person participates in a discussion the more likely he is to become convinced about what is discussed. Another advantage is that active participation tends to be ego-gratifying. As a result, if the salesperson asks the right questions, many times he can get the customer to sell the product to himself.[7]

In two-way communication important points can be reinforced through two or more sensory channels. Examples of this in the selling-buying process would be the effective use of visual and audiovisual aids by the salesperson.

Projection.   Through continuous feedback, there is less danger that the salesperson will engage in projection—that is, talk about things of interest to him rather than those that meet the customer's needs. The verbal and nonverbal signals that the receiver is sending to the salesperson will let him know if he is wandering into areas that do not interest the receiver.

An Opportunity For The Customer.   Two-way communication makes it easy for the buyer to take action. All he has to do is say "yes." The salesperson does the rest. Many sales are lost with mass media advertising because the individual who has been sold by the ad has no immediate way to close the sale, and when he is finally given this opportunity he may have changed his mind. However, when the salesperson is present and the customer has agreed to buy, then the transaction can be immediately finalized, before the customer changes his mind.

The effectiveness of personal communication versus mass media communication has been studied extensively. One famous study by Katz and Lazarsfeld[8] analyzed the differences in persuasive influence between various types of communication. Their results showed that personal influence had a greater effect on opinion changes than did mass media. In fact, relatives, friends, and

[7]James Campbell and Hal Helper (eds.), *Discussions in Communications*, (Belmont, Ca.: Wadsworth, 1964), pp. 1–3.

[8]Elihu Katz and Paul Lazarsfeld, *Personal Influence: The Part Played by People in the Flow of Mass Communication* (New York, N.Y.: Free Press, 1955).

acquaintances were more frequently identified as the persuasive cause for buying certain food products, for decisions about fashion, and for other items.

From this study it could be inferred that two-way communication is most effective when a personal buying commitment is desired and a certain amount of persuasive effort is necessary; one-way or mass communication is not as effective in changing strong attitudes and beliefs, and may not secure personal purchasing commitments from the customers.

FACTORS THAT INFLUENCE SENDING AND RECEIVING OF MESSAGES

For two individuals to communicate with one another they must have enough background in common so that they are able to understand each other. Each person is unique in that his background is made up of a set of past experiences, observations, and knowledge that differentiates him from other human beings. The individual uses this set of past experiences to form his own particular framework of values, attitudes, and beliefs (i.e., his frame of reference) with which he interprets the events that occur in his environment. If there is no overlap between two individuals' past experience, communication will be impossible.[9] In addition, several human factors affect the communication process. Among these, three deserve special mention: perception, cognition, and role relationship. Each of these factors is related in turn to the individual's background and his ever-changing set of values, beliefs, and attitudes.

Perception

Perception is subjective, selective, and summative in nature. It is influenced by personal factors or present needs. Let's look at each of these characteristics of perception.

Subjective Perception.   Perception is subjective because no two individuals perceive the same object or event in the same way. If a Republican and a Democrat attended a political rally to hear a Republican Senator discuss a clean-air bill he introduced into Congress, it is likely that each of them would perceive the presentation differently. The Republican might very likely perceive the bill to be "far-reaching" and certain to help cure the nation's air pollution problems. In contrast, the Democrat might perceive the proposal as limited in scope and nothing more than political propaganda.

Why would the two views vary so dramatically? Although it is possible that both men see themselves as having an objective opinion concerning the proposed legislation, it is likely that their past political biases influence what they perceive the actual message to be. As a result, each would walk away from the

[9]Wilbur Schramm, *The Process of Mass Communication* (Urbana, Ill.: University of Illinois Press, 1960), p. 6.

meeting wondering how the other could be so ignorant as not to understand the true meaning of the Senator's speech.

This same situation occurs in selling. The salesperson can feel that he has made a logical sales presentation of a product that really does represent a good value for the customer. However, the customer's past background including such factors as what he thinks about the salesperson's company will influence his perception of the entire presentation. As an example, if the customer feels he has been "burned" by the company in the past, there may be no way to secure an order from this particular account.

Selective Perception.   Only a few of the signals we receive each day are converted into messages. We receive approximately 10,000 advertising signals per day through exposure to billboards, store signs, and other forms of mass media. Since it is impossible to deal with 10,000 advertising messages, our minds only perceive a few such messages selectively.

In personal selling, selective perception occurs when the prospect or customer only perceives some of the appeals and reasons for buying the product from the sales presentation. This phenomenon occurs for a variety of reasons. The receiver of the message may have some psychological reason for not wanting to perceive some of the sales appeals. Or he may be preoccupied and not want to listen to a particular sales presentation.

Whatever the reason for selective perception on the part of the prospect or customer, the salesperson must detect it and make sure that his presentation is fully accepted and heard by the prospect. He may want to reschedule his appointment for a more convenient time, when the customer or prospect may be able to give him full attention.

Another useful recommendation based on this phenomenon is to limit the number of products or models shown during any single presentation. Excessive information which cannot be easily handled by a receiver will cause him to selectively perceive only parts of the total message. The salesperson should therefore concentrate on those items which appear to be most relevant and desirable to the prospect or customer to whom he is making the presentation.

Summative Perception.   Perception is summative because the reception of a signal frequently depends on the cumulative effects of the signal. The more often the signal is received, the greater is the likelihood that the receiver will decode and interpret it. Also, the probability that a receiver will correctly interpret a signal is enhanced if it is sent through two or more channels. As an example, a salesperson who wants to make sure a customer is aware of the qualities and availability of a new product may send him a direct-mail promotion, but he will also pay him a personal visit and demonstrate the uses of the product. This concept is referred to as redundancy in communication. The salesperson should not be upset if he has to make several calls to convey his message. In the same way, if the customer is able to see a demonstration of the product in question, it may increase the chances of this communication being received.

Personal Factors.   Personal factors which influence perception include the individual's image of himself, his needs, and his past experience.[10] The manner in which an individual perceives himself will influence how he perceives an object—a person who sees himself as a playboy is more likely to notice a sports car than a four-door sedan. A person's needs also determine his perceptual selectivity. An advertisement for a new home is less likely to be perceived by an individual who is extremely happy in his present home than by an individual who has been transferred to a new location and is expecting his wife and six children to join him the following week.

Cognition

Cognition derives from past experience (memory) and present experience (perception). It relates to a person's past store of knowledge. The more the receiver knows about the subject of the source's message, the easier it will be for the receiver to comprehend the message. For example, in the university setting, certain courses are prerequisites for other courses. For a student to have a reasonable chance of success in a particular course, he must know the type of material that is taught in the prerequisite course.

In a buying-selling situation, the salesperson must aim his message at the correct level for each individuals he talks to. As an example, a salesperson may begin his call with a purchasing agent who has very little technical expertise with the product. As a result the message must be kept on a rather nontechnical basis. The same salesperson may then call on an engineer in the firm's production facility. Here, the salesperson must switch gears and be prepared to talk in very technical terms about his product in order to communicate effectively with the engineer.

Role and Status Relationships

Role and status relationships also tend to influence the communication process. This relates to the idea that the more related peoples' roles and attitudes are, the more likely they will be successful in communicating with one another. Related to this concept are the ideas of homophily and heterophily. *Homophily* concerns the degree of similarity displayed by two subjects, while *heterophily* concerns the degree to which two subjects are different in their physical and psychological attributes. Research by Rogers and Bhowmik, experts in communication theory, found that:

In a free choice situation, when a source can interact with any one of a number of different receivers, there is a strong tendency for him to select a receiver who is like himself. Empirical evidence of the homophily principle is available from studies of a great variety of communication situations: Political influence patterns in a presidential election were homophilous in age and social status,

[10]Thomas Robertson, *Consumer Behavior* (Glenview, Ill.: Scott, Foresman, 1970), p. 15.

interactions among members of a legislature were between those of equal age, partisanship, and prestige; Iowa farmers talked about agricultural innovations with those of similar attitudinal disposition; communication patterns in formal organizations are mostly horizontal (that is, between individuals of similar hierarchical status) rather than vertical; Chicago ghetto dwellers share family planning ideas with others of like social status, age, marital status, and family size; and Indian peasants interact mostly with other villagers of similar caste ranking, education, and farm size. We could go on and on. In summary, we suggest *communication patterns frequently tend to be homophilous.*[11]

However, they hypothesize that, "For maximum communication effectiveness, a source and a receiver should be homophilous on certain variables and heterophilous on some variables relevant to the situation."[12] We will discuss some of the research which tested this hypothesis along with the implications of role and status relationships in selling.

Homophilous on Some Variables.   Rogers and Bhowmik's hypothesis is supported by the work of Alpert and Anderson.[13] They showed slides of three individuals to 192 male undergraduate business students. After examining the first slide, the students were asked to indicate their perceptions on 21 attributes of personality and behavior of that person. The subjects then read a statement attributed to the person in the slide. Next they were asked to indicate the extent to which they agreed or disagreed with the statement. The same procedure was used on the remaining two slides. Finally, the subjects were asked to rate themselves on the same 21 personality attributes.

Alpert and Anderson found that "maximally effective communication occurs when the source is perceived as neither totally homophilous nor totally heterophilous but somewhere in between."[14] That is, subjects found that they agreed more with individuals who were slightly different from themselves than with individuals whom they perceived to be very much like themselves or very different from themselves. If these findings are confirmed in future research, it may be possible for communicators to develop the required "optimal heterophily" and thus be able to communicate more effectively with their audiences.

Implications for Selling.   The implication here is that it might be possible to choose and train salespeople to be and behave in a very similar way to their customers or prospects. If perceived by their customers or prospects as being "one of them," salespeople may be more effective at selling their products. For

[11]Everett M. Rogers and Dilip Bhowmik, "Homophily-Heterophily: Relational Concepts for Communication Research," *Public Opinion Quarterly,* Vol. 23 (Winter 1970), p. 528.

[12]*Ibid.*

[13]Mark Alpert and W. T. Anderson Jr., "Optimal Heterophily and Communication Effectiveness," 1971 unpublished working paper, The University of Texas, Austin, p. 15.

[14]*Ibid.*

example, Cadillac salespeople will tend to dress conservatively and to behave in a sedate and traditional manner. The same is not true of compact or sports car salespeople, who tend to behave more like the customers they cater to—young, sporty, carefree.

PERSUASIVE COMMUNICATION

The action of selling involves a certain amount of persuasion, in that the salesperson attempts to provoke a specific response behavior from the buyer. Persuasive communication involves an overt attempt by an individual to change the behavior of another individual or group of individuals.[15] We will examine why all communication is not persuasive, the fact that attitude change leads to opinion change, and the importance of persuasive communications in personal selling.

Not All Communication Is Persuasive

Although the objective of persuasive communication is to affect people's behavior, not all communication that modifies behavior can be considered persuasive in nature. The receiver may modify his behavior for other reasons: a subordinate might comply with an order without examining the reasons behind it. Persuasive communication exists only when changes in the receiver's behavior are understood and accepted by him.

The amount of success a salesperson has is partly a function of how well he can persuade his customers to purchase his products. However, the effects of persuasive communication are not always immediate. Therefore, a salesperson's performance cannot be judged solely on the outcome of each sales call; any evaluation must include a total view of his overall efforts.

In addition, there are several degrees of success to persuasive communication. A Coca-Cola advertisement may cause some receivers to buy *any* soft drink, whereas others will buy Coca-Cola. Here, two results describe two degrees of persuasion achieved by the same message. A salesperson's objective is to persuade a client to buy his specific product and not a similar product produced by another manufacturer.

Attitude Change Leads to Opinion Change

Attitudes are mental states or emotions related to specific situations and beliefs. Opinions are evaluations made of a situation or an individual based on a series of impressions or attitudes. Opinions are more stable than attitudes and, therefore, more difficult to change.

Changes in behavior are preceded by other changes. In a recent study these steps were identified. Attitude changes lead to opinion changes, then to percep-

[15]Erwin P. Bettinghaus, *Persuasive Communication* (New York, N.Y.: Holt, Rinehart, and Winston, 1968), p. 9.

tion changes, then to affect changes, and finally to action changes.[16] For this reason, the salesperson may require a considerable amount of communication effort before he finally obtains an order from a customer.

It is important to note that persuasion is affected primarily by the way the message is perceived by the receiver. Four factors are central to persuasive communication from the receiver's point of view: the variations within the source, the variations within the message, the differences in the channels used, and the variations in the situation.[17] The credibility of the source, the nature of the arguments used, the fact that the message is delivered personally or in a written communication, and the physical environment in which it is delivered are examples of different factors that may considerably affect the results of a salesperson's efforts.

The Importance of Persuasive Communication

The sales presentation must be persuasive in order to achieve the desired results. A salesperson should be aware of all tools available to him in order to achieve such a goal. He must make sure that he is personally accepted by the prospect as a trustworthy, competent representative of his firm. His message must be coherent, internally consistent, and logical. In addition, he should never contradict himself when talking about the product and its capabilities.

Many factors can increase the persuasive power of a sales presentation such as the use of visual aids, demonstrations, and testimonial letters from satisfied customers. These are all effective tools in helping the salesperson prove the authenticity of his arguments, and they should be included in a sales presentation.

It is important to be aware of the difference between high pressure sales and persuasive communication. A customer must never feel he has "been sold" some product; rather he must consider the decision to buy as his own personal free choice. Persuasive communication must therefore be tactful, and above all it must be convincing and logical.

Persuasion is the most important type of communication within the selling function. Its nature and effects will be discussed at greater length in Chapter 13.

OBSTACLES TO COMMUNICATION

Although it is not feasible to examine all possible obstacles to the communication process, there are four areas that cause a large percentage of the difficulties in communications: (1) lack of receiver orientation, (2) low interest level on the part of the receiver, (3) the receiver's limited knowledge of the

[16]Carl I. Hovland and I. Janis (eds.), *Personality and Persuasibility* (New Haven, Conn.: Yale University Press, 1969), pp. 1–28.

[17]Bettinghaus, *op. cit.,* pp. 23–24.

proposition, and (4) the failure on the part of the sender to make his intention clear.

Lack of Receiver Orientation

The major problem in communication is that the communicator fails to empathize with the receiver; that is, he does not look at the world from the perspective of the receiver. All the other problems in the communication process are secondary in importance to the failure of the source to be receiver-oriented. When the salesperson thinks about his own problems and the attributes of his products in an abstract sense, he not only violates the basic principles of the marketing concept, but he is also not likely to be an effective communicator.

Low Interest Level on the Part of the Receiver

Often the receiver is contacted when he is preoccupied with something else, and is therefore not open to receive the message. Furthermore, he is contented with his present state or situation and sees no reason to change. Unless his complacency is disturbed, he is unlikely to receive the message. In selling, one approach to overcoming this obstacle is for the salesperson to ask questions that show the customer that the status quo is not as attractive as he thought it was.

The Receiver Has Limited Knowledge of the Proposition

The source must make a conscious effort to determine how much knowledge the intended receiver of the message has concerning the subject of the discussion. If the receiver has a limited background in the sender's area of expertise, the receiver may choose not to admit his ignorance by asking questions. As a result, the source may think he is doing a fine job of communicating when, in reality, the receiver does not understand him. In selling, the salesperson must continually be on guard so that he does not talk over the customer's head. If the customer really does not understand what is going on, the chances are very slim that he will purchase the product.

Failure to Make Intent Clear

We have all had conversation with individuals who were either unwilling or unable to make us aware of the precise subject of the discussion. Although it may be an unpleasant task at times, the source must make the subject clear to the receiver. This not only improves the likelihood that effective communication will take place, but it also puts the receiver in a position to make appropriate responses. As a result, the salesperson should not be afraid to come to the point of his visit, so that the buyer is in a position to respond either positively or negatively.

SUMMARY

In order to be successful, firms must learn to communicate effectively with their customers. For many firms the primary way to accomplish this is through their sales force. We discussed a general model of communication, and showed that all forms of communication require an encoder, a signal, a channel, a medium, a decoder, and a receiver.

We examined the importance of the salesperson as a source of communication. A salesperson's character and ability, along with the company's reputation, can affect the perception of the sales message.

We discussed four types of communication: nonverbal, verbal, one-way, and two-way. We pointed out that while verbal communication is an important aspect of the sales presentation, the salesperson must also be aware of the nonverbal communication that takes place. The advantages of two-way communication were discussed in detail.

We then analyzed the key factors which influence the sending and receiving of a message: perception, cognition, and role and status relationships.

We examined persuasive communication and saw that not all communication is persuasive and that attitude change leads to opinion change. We concluded by describing four obstacles to communication.

PROBLEMS

1. Is the salesperson always perceived as the only source in the sales communication process? Explain.
2. After describing the qualities of your product to a prospect, he informs you that he is not sure his firm has the financial ability to acquire your product. Describe what your response would be, assuming you are capable of empathizing with the prospect's problem.
3. How can a salesperson engage in two-way communication?
4. Describe some important types of nonverbal communication which could be effectively used by an encyclopedia door-to-door salesperson.

Exercise 4

THE COMMUNICATION PROCESS

Objectives: To increase our understanding of the communication process.
To see the application of communication principles and techniques to the buying-selling interaction.

A. Contrast Advertising and Selling from a Communication Standpoint

Indicate at least five ways in which advertising and selling differ.

	Advertising	Selling
1.		
2.		
3.		
4.		
5.		

B. Analyze full page ads in a current magazine.

communications standpoint and justify your evaluation.

Magazine: _____   _____
                     name   issue

Best ad: _____   _____
                     page   subject

Why:

Poorest ad: _____   _____
                        page   subject

Why:

C. Go to a New Car Showroom or a Used Car Lot

Question a salesperson about a particular car. Evaluate his effectiveness as a communicator.

Case 4-1 Ross Brothers Sporting Goods

Ross Brothers is a wholesaler serving a three-state area. The firm carries a full line of athletic and outdoor recreational equipment. Most of its customers are retail stores but it does sell goods to the athletic departments of high schools and colleges. It relies mainly on direct mail and personal selling to cultivate and sustain demand for its products. The field sales force consists of five sales representatives. Jim Ross, one of the brothers, is in charge of all promotional activity.

We find Jim conducting a sales meeting with his five sales representatives. He says: "I think all of us agree that our personal selling efforts must be closely coordinated with our direct mail. As you know our new catalog is in; you've each received a quantity for use in your territory. I'm planning to mail each of our accounts a copy along with a cover letter. Here are drafts of two letters, A and B. Letter A is for our store accounts; B will go to the other customers. I want each of you to review the drafts carefully and give me your suggestions for improving them by Monday."

LETTER A: TO STORE ACCOUNTS

Dear Mr. _____:

Enclosed is our new catalog. As you can see it is bigger and better than ever.

We have added several items to the line which you, our retailers, have suggested: shuffle board, imported felt-top sports shoes, archery sets, and pee-wee hockey equipment. As always, if we don't stock an item we can get it for you on special order.

May I take this occasion to thank you for your past patronage. Working together, we can be "partners in profit."

Sincerely,

James Ross
Marketing Manager

LETTER B: TO INSTITUTIONAL ACCOUNTS

Dear Mr. _____:

Enclosed is our new catalog. Should you need extra copies for others in the organization we will be glad to supply them.

You'll be pleased to learn of our new policy regarding sales to schools, colleges, and other institutions. We recognize that you establish an annual budget for your athletic program. If you place your full year order at once we are prepared to offer you an additional 5% discount on top of your normal professional discount. As far as we know, Ross Brothers is the only sports equipment house offering such an incentive for contract purchasing on an annual basis.

May I take this occasion to thank you for your past patronage. We want to continue to serve you in the future.

Sincerely,

James Ross
Marketing Manager

1. What are your suggestions for improvement for Letters A and B?
2. How might the sales representatives be tied in with the other promotional efforts?

Case 4-2 The Strategy Of Ms. Green

Julia Green had just received her MBA degree from the University of South Carolina. She was very excited about her new career. Her father was a modest blue collar worker, and she was the first one in her family to obtain a graduate degree.

There were considerable opportunities in the market for women graduates that year, due to pressures from the Department of Health Education and Welfare to hire more women and minorities. Ms. Green knew, however, that she had to be successful in order to keep her job and to be promoted. She was aware of the fact that her performance had to be as good or better than that of her male counterparts.

Ms. Green felt that a sales job would give her a better opportunity to be promoted and to acquire "real world" experience. She accepted the offer of a well-known chemical firm which sold fertilizers to large farm cooperatives in the midwest. The firm offered a three-month course on the products they sold and after that two months of field training with a senior salesperson. The candidates, however, were given the opportunity to start field sales immediately after the course, provided that they had shown adequate proficiency with company products.

Julia Green studied very hard during the initial three months and was offered the opportunity to start field sales immediately on her own. She considered the two alternatives and decided that she would rather start alone. She did not believe the two months of field training would help her very much, especially considering the fact that most of the senior salespeople were older men, without graduate degrees, and they may be prejudiced against her.

Ms. Green knew that one of her major problems was to sound knowledgeable and credible to her prospective buyers. The purchasing agents of farm cooperatives were usually very conservative, hard working men who were not used to trading with young well-educated women. Julia felt that many of them would try to test her competence by asking her difficult and unusual questions, possibly not always relevant to the products she was selling.

After thinking very carefully about her problem, Ms. Green developed a well-structured sales presentation which covered all possible aspects of her products and offered a thorough description of their use. Her strategy would be to initiate the sales presentation and to continue on with it without giving the respondent a chance to interrupt her. In this way, she would eliminate the possibility of being put in an embarrassing position by her prospective buyers.

1. Considering the characteristics of the source and of the receiver in this specific communication situation, do you agree with Ms. Green's strategy?

2. Is feedback needed in this sales relationship? If so, what kind?

3. Do you think Ms. Green will succeed in her new career? Why?

4. What advice would you give Ms. Green as an expert in communications?

SUGGESTIONS FOR FURTHER READING

Beckman, M. Dale, "Are Your Messages Getting Through?" *Journal of Marketing*, Vol. 31 (July 1967), pp. 32–38.

Crane, Edgar, *Marketing Communication, A Behavioral Approach to Men, Messages and Media*, 2nd ed. (New York, N.Y.: John Wiley, 1972).

Delozier, M. Wayne, *The Marketing Communication Process* (New York, N.Y.: McGraw-Hill, 1976).

Khera, Inder P., and James D. Benson, "Communication and Industrial Purchasing Behavior," *Journal of Purchasing*, Vol. 6 (May 1970), pp. 5–21.

Levitt, Theodore, "Communications and Industrial Selling," *Journal of Marketing*, Vol. 31 (April 1967), pp. 15–21.

Richardson, Lee (ed.), *Dimensions of Communication*, (New York, N.Y.: Appleton-Century-Crofts, 1970).

Selivitz, R., "Communications: Key to Survival," *Industrial Distribution* (August 1975), pp. 29–32.

Stidsen, Ben T., "Interpersonal Communication and Personal Selling," *Marketing for Tomorrow-Today, American Marketing Association* (June 1967), pp. 111–116.

Watzlawich, Paul, and Janet Beavin, "Some Formal Aspects of Communication," *American Behavioral Scientist*, Vol. 10 (April 1967), pp. 4–8.

Webster, Frederick E., Jr., "Interpersonal Communication and Salesman Effectiveness," *Journal of Marketing*, Vol. 32 (July 1968), pp. 7–13.

Webster, Frederick E., Jr., "Informal Communication in Industrial Markets," *Journal of Marketing Research*, Vol. 7 (May 1970), pp. 186–189.

Wilding, John, and Raymond A. Bauer, "Consumer Goals and Reactions to a Communication Source," *Journal of Marketing Research*, Vol. 5 (February 1968), pp. 73–77.

5. The Salesperson as Change Agent and Problem Solver

IN THIS CHAPTER

Diffusion of Innovation
The Salesperson As A Change Agent
Innovations and Their Characteristics
Logical Analysis

The accelerated rate of growth and the keen competition found in virtually all industries in the United States point to the important role the salesperson must play as change agent and problem solver. Consider the flow of new and improved products and services, all of which must be sold. Each company's stake in such innovation is high, and the risks are large. One study found that 33 percent of the products introduced into the market fail.[1] Although the reasons for failure of new products are not always clear, much of the responsibility can be attributed to shortcomings in the marketing and sales strategy.

[1]John T. O'Meara, Jr., "Selecting Profitable Products," *Harvard Business Review,* Vol. 39 (January–February 1961), p. 83.

Salespeople play an important role in gaining acceptance for new products. At the same time, the salesperson is always seeking new customers for existing products. In both cases, he is engaged in the task of suggesting new solutions for existing problems. To accomplish this, salespeople must be aware of the variables that may affect their performance of such a task. In this chapter, we are concerned with the knowledge the salesperson must possess to play the dual, interrelated role of change agent and problem solver to bring about acceptance of new products and services. In this regard, we will examine the process of diffusion of innovation, the salesperson as a change agent, innovations and their characteristics, and logical analysis.

DIFFUSION OF INNOVATION

The roles and characteristics of change agents have been analyzed in detail as part of the study of the process of diffusion of innovation. It is important, therefore, that salespeople be aware of the main concepts involved in the diffusion and adoption of a new product. Significant parallels can be drawn between the role of salespeople when approaching new prospects or introducing new products and the role of change agents as analyzed within the process of diffusion of innovation.

The diffusion of innovation has been studied in depth. One of the investigators, Everett Rogers, developed a comprehensive analysis of this process. He describes the diffusion process as the way in which, "new ideas are communicated to the members of a social system."[2] We will apply this definition to new products and services. Attention will be given first to the adoption process. Then we will examine the five adopter categories and how they bear on the time it takes an individual to purchase a product.

The Adoption Process

The study of the diffusion process provides valuable information about the product life cycle and its relationship to the marketing strategy of the firm. The adoption process, however, is more important for understanding the behavior of customers when faced with a *new* product. The adoption process describes the decisions made by an individual at each stage of adoption. As such, it provides salespeople with insightful information that can be used to select a strategy for approaching customers when selling new products.

When an individual is confronted with an innovation, his decision to adopt the new product can be broken down into five different steps or stages: (1) awareness, (2) interest, (3) evaluation, (4) trial, and (5) adoption.[3] At each stage, different variables influence his decision.

[2]Everett M. Rogers and F. Floyd Shoemaker, *Communications of Innovations–A Cross-Cultural Approach* (New York, N.Y.: Free Press, 1971), p. 7.

[3]*Ibid.*, p. 100.

The Awareness Stage.   At this stage, the individual becomes aware of the existence of the innovation—either through conscious effort or by accidental circumstances. As an example let's take an individual who, after several years, needs to replace his watch. As he shops for a watch, he becomes aware of new products introduced in the market, such as digital watches. Usually, the awareness of innovation does not occur through intentional effort of the adopter, but by accident—as, for instance, when he sees an advertisement in a magazine.

The Interest Stage.   At the awareness stage, the customer's interest in a product is usually of a casual nature; as he becomes more interested in it, he will voluntarily seek additional and more detailed information. This action is definitely purposive in nature. As an example, if a person becomes aware that he wants to purchase a new typewriter, he might telephone several typewriter dealers to obtain information about their products. Here, as in the preceding example, the electric typewriter is considered an innovation. In an attempt to gain information from sources unrelated to any one company, he might check the ratings of different typewriters in such publications as *Consumer Reports*. An important point to remember, however, is that a great deal of the information available to our prospective typewriter purchaser emanates from the companies which sell this equipment. Their salespeople play a large role in the interest stage, because they frequently serve as the conduit from the firm to the prospective customer.

The Evaluation Stage.   The individual, at this stage, analyzes the advantages and disadvantages of trying an innovation. It is critical that the customer be informed about all key variables of the product. The customer perceives the innovation as a risky venture, since he is not sure about the benefits that it might yield for him. Our prospective typewriter customer, for instance, might seek information from his friends who own an electric typewriter.

   Mass communication will be too general to provide the reinforcement that the individual seeks at the evaluation stage. The salesperson who has made an effort to learn what the prospective customer really needs is in an excellent position to provide the proper supportive material as to why his product will meet the real needs of that individual.

The Trial Stage.   The innovator decides to use the new product on a small scale, to assess by experience whether or not it is worth adopting. The most important variable at this stage is the interpretation of the results of the trial. If the results are not interpreted correctly, the innovation will be rejected, regardless of its actual value. Although many individuals adopt or reject a product without going through a trial stage, many others do not. To help assure that our prospective customer gives the product a fair analysis, the salesperson may suggest that the customer take the typewriter home—either on a rental or a free-trial basis—to determine if it really is what he wants. This type of action is likely to move the customer out of his state of homeostasis and convince him to try the product.

The salesperson's duty is to eliminate any dissonance in his customer's evaluation of the new product after the initial trial.

The Adoption Stage. At this stage, the individual is satisfied with the results of the trial and decides to adopt the innovation on a full-scale basis. Continuous service and assistance are still important, however, so that regular use of the new product is as satisfactory to the innovator as was the trial phase. The salesperson's job does not end at the closing of the sale, because he needs to establish a long-term relationship with his customers. If this customer bought the typewriter for his personal use, the salesperson would be wise to contact him after a few weeks to make sure the machine is acting properly. In this way the salesperson (1) demonstrates his concern for the customer; (2) he assures the customer that his company will provide maintenance for the machine over the years, which could amount to a substantial sum of money; and (3) he might get some new prospects from his satisfied customer.

In an industrial setting, where the customer was a purchasing agent who bought only one typewriter, the salesperson would need to develop an ongoing relationship so that he could sell more new typewriters as they became needed in the organization.

Adopter Categories

Not all individuals adopt new products and ideas in the same quantity and at the same rate. Research evidence indicates that it is possible to group people into different classifications according to their degree of innovativeness. We will examine the five adopter categories and the role of "early adopters" in the diffusion process, as well as a market strategy built on diffusion theory.

Five adopter categories. The five adopter categories consist of innovators, early adopters, early majority, late majority, and laggards.[4] Table 5-1 illustrates the percentage of the adopters population in each category, along with a profile of the different characteristics for each category. As an example, the early majority represent approximately 34 percent of the population. They tend to be "deliberate" and above average in social status. In addition, they have considerable contact with change agents, and they possess some opinion leadership in society. Change agents are individuals who try to influence change in a specific direction. (The salesperson as a change agent will be examined later in this chapter.)

It is important for the firm to realize that there are various types of individuals in society who differ in the degree that they are willing to try new products. This helps marketing management identify its initial target market for new products. In this way, the firm can adjust its advertising message and sales appeals to fit the people who would be most likely to adopt the product. In addition, there is a clear implication that once a product has shown some staying power in the market, the firm's sales force should direct its attention toward the

[4]*Ibid.,* pp. 175–195.

TABLE 5-1 A COMPOSITE PICTURE OF ADOPTER CATEGORIES

Adopter Category	Percent of Population	Salient Values	Personal Characteristics	Communication Behavior	Social Relationships
Innovators	2½%	"Venturesome"; willing to accept risks	Youngest age; highest social status; largest and most specialized operations; wealthy	Closest contact with scientific information sources; interaction with other innovators; relatively greatest use of impersonal sources	Some opinion leadership; very cosmopolitan
Early adopters	13½%	"Respected." Regarded by many others in the social system as a role-model	High social status; large and specialized operations	Greatest contact with local change agents	Greatest opinion leadership of any category in most social systems; very locally oriented.
Early majority	34%	"Deliberate." Willing to consider innovations only after peers have adopted	Above-average social status; average-sized operations	Considerable contact with change agents and early adopters	Some opinion leadership
Late majority	34%	"Skeptical." Overwhelming pressure from peers needed before adoption occurs	Below-average social status; small operation; little specialization; small income	Secure ideas from peers who are mainly late majority or early majority; less use of mass media	Little opinion leadership
Laggards	16%	"Traditional." Oriented to the past	Little specialization; lowest social status; smallest operation; lowest income; oldest	Neighbors, friends and relatives with similar values are main information source	Very little opinion leadership; semi-isolated

Source: Thomas W. Anderson, adapted from Everett M. Rogers, *Diffusion of Innovations* (New York, N.Y.: Free Press of Glencoe, 1962), pp. 169–189.

"early adopters" who are more likely to adopt the product in large numbers and whose actions will be imitated by others in the community.

The role of early adopters. The early adopters are considered the most influential group within the diffusion process. They are individuals who are well integrated into the community or the trade, and their behavior usually can exert some kind of social pressure on other members of their group. Early adopters will add credibility to a new product when they adopt it.[5]

A practical case analysis of the influence of early adopters on their peers was described in a study of the adoption of a new drug by physicians.[6] The findings revealed that the early adopters relied upon professionals, media, or community leaders to learn about new products and services. The early majority, late majority, and laggards, (or followers) appeared to rely primarily on social interaction with family, friends, and peers to obtain information about innovations.

Most important, then, is for the salesperson to reach the early adopter group, which has a great impact on the behavior of the remaining potential market. An illustration of the interactive relationship between the promotion function, opinion leaders, and followers is given in Figure 5-1.

Market Strategy.   In terms of the type of strategy to be used by salespersons, behavioral theory indicates that the "early adopters" respond to different types of information about the new product than do the followers. The early adopters are more interested in technical details, scientific information, and statistical data regarding tests of performance of the innovation, whereas the followers will look for the opinion of others who have tried the innovation as a means of verifying its feasibility. Testimonials and referrals from opinion leaders are more valuable tools to use with these prospects than would scientific and technical information be.

Although a salesperson cannot control the flow and effects of interpersonal influence within his potential market, his knowledge of the product and of his customers will be very valuable in his interaction with every prospect. He will have to examine the market and identify the opinion leaders, and then approach them with relevant and thorough information about the product. His influence can be enhanced by special promotions of the firm, such as the sponsoring of professional meetings—this would increase the prestige of the firm and the credibility of the information source.

The salesperson's approach to followers will concentrate on information about successful applications of the product by opinion leaders, so as to apply the social pressure needed to stimulate emulative action by them. Although technical knowledge of the product is still important, "case histories" are more likely to trigger action within this group.

[5]Elihu Katz, "The Diffusion of New Ideas and Practices," in Wilbur Schramm (ed.), *The Science of Human Communication* (New York, N.Y.: Basic Books, 1963), p. 82.

[6]James Coleman, Elihu Katz, and Herbert Menzel, "The Diffusion of an Innovation Among Physicians," *Sociometry*, Vol. 20 (December 1957), pp. 253–270.

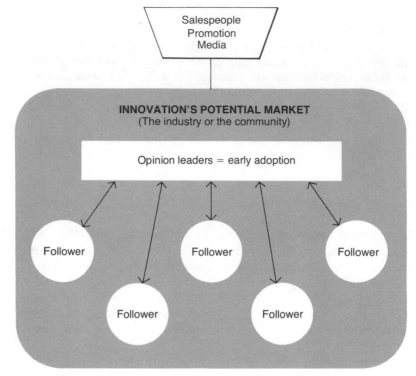

Figure 5-1 The interaction of opinion leaders and followers in the adoption of innovations

THE SALESPERSON AS A CHANGE AGENT

Salespeople have a very important role in the process of diffusion of innovation. They perform the functions of a change agent, which is defined as "a professional person who attempts to influence adoption decisions in a direction that he feels is desirable."[7] Salespeople are commercial change agents because much of their effort is directed toward influencing people to buy *their* products and services rather than other available alternatives.

The role of the commercial change agent has been subject of several studies.[8] Their primary areas of influence are summarized in two major generalizations:

[7]Rogers and Shoemaker, *op. cit.*, p. 227.

[8]See: E. M. Rogers and M. D. Yost, *Communication Behavior of County Extension Agents,* Wooster, Ohio Experiment Station Research Bulletin 850, 1960; Bryce Ryan and Neal C. Gross, "The Diffusion of Hybrid Seed Corn in Two Iowa Communities," *Rural Sociology,* Vol. 8 (1943), pp. 15–24; George M. Beal and Everett M. Rogers, "Informational Sources in the Adoption Process of New Fabrics," *Journal of Home Economics,* Vol. 48 (1957), pp. 630–634; James H. Copp et al., "The Function of Information Sources in the Farm Practice Adoption Process," *Rural Sociology,* Vol. 23 (1958), pp. 136–157.

1. Commercial change agents are more important at the trial stage than at any other stage in the adoption process.
2. Commercial change agents are more important for early adopters than for late adopters.

Change Agents and the Trial Stage

The salesperson is instrumental in inducing adopters to try new products. Through his actions, customers become aware of the existence of the innovation. His sales presentations contribute to their interest, and through their personal interaction with him, they become motivated to try the new product. The trial stage is crucial in the adoption process. The product, in small quantities, is subjected to the usage test. The salesperson should assist his customers with technical information during the trial stage. He should make sure that the results are correctly interpreted by the customer in order to eliminate dissonance regarding the product.

Change Agents and Early Adopters

Inasmuch as the commercial change agent is more important to early adopters than to followers, the salesperson should dedicate the greater amount of his time and efforts toward them. He should make sure that his customers perceive him to be a credible and reliable source of information, and he should concentrate on communicating the product's relative advantages to them.

Once the commercial change agent has sold the new product to the early adopters, they, in turn, will help his future sales. The other members of the same social group will try to imitate the early adopters' behavior. As a result, future sales of the product will be a simpler task.

INNOVATIONS AND THEIR CHARACTERISTICS

One of the major factors in selling is that the salesperson have knowledge of the products he sells. This knowledge is particularly important when attempting to introduce new products into the marketplace.

The rate of adoption differs substantially among new products. Some innovations are readily accepted, whereas others require a substantial time period to be adopted. Several characteristics are responsible for the speed with which a new product is adopted. These crucial factors can be classified as: *relative advantage, compatibility, complexity, divisibility,* and *communicability*.[9]

Relative Advantage

An innovation must be perceived as an improvement over existing products in order to be adopted. Relative advantage is the degree to which the new product is superior to competing products.

[9]Rogers and Shoemaker, *op. cit.,* pp. 137–157.

The relative advantage may range from evident dollar savings to esthetic appeal. The challenge to the salesperson is to communicate the one or more ways in which the new product has an edge over those presently in the market. If he is unable to do this either because there are no real advantages to his product or because he is not an effective communicator, the salesperson will have a difficult time getting the sale.

Compatibility

The degree to which an innovation is compatible with existing norms and products will increase its chances of rapid adoption. When a new product is introduced, the firm should carefully consider existing products and services. If major changes are needed because of the innovation itself, education and training programs and materials should be provided to the customer to facilitate the transition. One example of this is the computer. Although it represented a somewhat drastic change from existing information and accounting systems, its adoption was facilitated by educating the customers about its use. The more the innovation is in conflict with existing norms, the harder the salesperson must work to eliminate this conflict between the new product and the values of prospective customers.

Complexity

The complexity of a product acts as a deterrent of adoption. Product design and development, promotional materials, and sales presentations are tools which can aid the customer in understanding the use the product. The salesperson must at all times be aware that he is talking with someone who is not as informed about the product as himself. His objective at all times should be to make the customer understand the concept of the product—not make it more difficult.

Divisibility

The degree to which a new product can be used on a small scale for trial purposes, will facilitate its adoption by the innovator. Promotions which utilize small samples of food products or drugs will usually produce satisfactory trial results. Since risk is one of the major considerations within the adoption process, divisibility is a very important factor of innovation. As a result, the salesperson should not discourage trial orders. If the product is good and the customer tries it on a short-term basis, he will then purchase a large order of it—assuming the trial use was successful.

Communicability

Word-of-mouth communication is very effective in motivating other customers to follow the innovators in the trial and usage of a new product. Sales personnel should be aware of this and capitalize on each other's successful results to increase the sales of the innovation.

LOGICAL ANALYSIS

When competing products, services, and companies approach equality, one source of differential competitive advantage remains: the *problem-solving ability* and *creative thinking* of the salesperson. As we mentioned in earlier chapters, marketing goals are the satisfaction of consumer needs at a profit. This means that the salesperson's task goes far beyond presenting market offerings to potential customers. Rather, his major function is to solve the customer's immediate or long-range problems. The solution of a customer's problems may in some instances even curtail the sale of a product, but this sale is only a means and not an end in itself. Each salesperson is seeking a continuous and mutually profitable relationship with his clients, and this is achieved by his role as idea man, problem solver, counselor, and consultant. In order to help his customers in the solution of problems a salesperson may use logical analysis as a form of communication. We shall examine the need to differentiate between facts and opinions, the restrictions that influence the problem-solving process, and the steps that take place in logical analysis.

Facts Versus Opinions

Figure 5-2 depicts the elements and steps involved in logical analysis. Notice that the stimulus which triggers logical analysis is the problem as it is thought about or stated. Seldom, however, is the initially formulated problem amenable to solution. Thus, the problem solver is faced with the need to assemble two kinds of background information—facts and opinions.

The definitions of *fact* and *opinion* are important in that the existence of one or the other will influence the logical analysis process differently. The following distinction is helpful in this regard:

A *fact* is any information, the reality of which is independent from the reporting source. Facts are, by their very nature, objective and reliable. Thus, other things being equal, the person with the relevant facts at his command can expect to be more adept at problem solving than the person who is less informed.

An *opinion* is any information, the worth of which is dependent on the reporting source. The value of an opinion is no better nor worse than the person giving it! Thus, the effectiveness of the problem solver often depends on his knowing trustworthy sources.[10]

Obviously, the more precedent there is for the problem, the greater is the number of facts that are likely to be available. Conversely, when solving problems without precedent, opinions become the prime input.

---

[10] William J. E. Crissy and Harold Cash, *The Psychology of Selling, Vol. 8.* "Logic and Creativity in Selling" (Flushing, NY: Personnel Development Associates, 1963), p. 21.

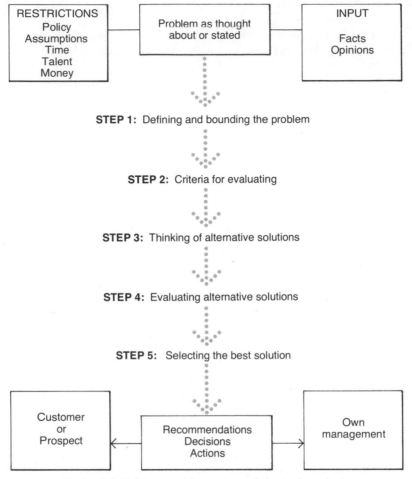

RESTRICTIONS
Policy
Assumptions
Time
Talent
Money

Problem as thought
about or stated

INPUT

Facts
Opinions

STEP 1: Defining and bounding the problem

STEP 2: Criteria for evaluating

STEP 3: Thinking of alternative solutions

STEP 4: Evaluating alternative solutions

STEP 5: Selecting the best solution

Customer
or
Prospect

Recommendations
Decisions
Actions

Own
management

Figure 5-2 Solving problems through logical analysis

Restrictions on the Problem-Solving Process

Again referring to Figure 5-2, note that almost inevitable restrictions exist which influence the problem-solving process, particularly the choice among alternative solutions. First, the person must do his problem solving within the restraints of company policy. Another restriction involves time. The problem solver must use judgment in committing time proportionate to the commercial worth of the problem. The salesperson often operates under the duress of deadlines, and it may be better for him to devise a workable solution that meets the time restraints than arrive at the "perfect solution" the day after his competitor has obtained the sale.

A third restraint is talent commitment. The salesperson, if he is to be an effective problem solver, must use good judgment in committing his own talents and those of supportive personnel to the problems he faces in his accounts.

Money also constitutes a restriction. The problem solver must be aware of hidden and indirect costs. These might include use of free samples, commitment of technical help without charge, and call frequency relative to the potential payoff.

The Five Steps in Logical Analysis

Once the problem is defined, a series of logical steps follows (Figure 5-2). Additional inputs and new restrictions often become evident as the logical process evolves.

Step 1: Defining and Bounding the Problem.   The problem as initially posed must be broken down into *subproblems.* Each of these in turn breaks into still smaller problems until no further division is possible. An analogy might be drawn from chemistry. A molecule represents the problem as initially thought about or stated. The atoms comprising the molecule are the first group of subproblems. Each atom in turn contains still smaller particles, which are the still smaller problems. Each particle may be made up of subparticles. So it is with each problem. In summary, problem definition consists largely of breaking down the big problem into smaller segments.

As this process develops, there is interaction with both inputs and restrictions. For example, in the course of problem definition, it is common to find the need for more facts, for additional opinions. Also, as problems involve specific policy, time, or money questions, restrictions may arise that were not anticipated.

Let us assume that a salesperson of duplicating machines visits the department of a growing university. The department is engaged in modernizing and updating the existing facilities and is interested in considering all available alternatives of duplicating and copying machines.

In order to set up a sales presentation, the salesperson must first identify and define the needs of the department, so that the appropriate products will be offered. From the general problem of "modernizing existing copying and duplicating equipment," a number of subproblems must be defined, such as, "What kind of mimeographing machine is needed to satisfy the department's needs for students' handouts, course schedules, etc?" "What types of duplicating jobs are most often required by the faculty and students of the department?"

Once the problem has been defined in this manner, each smaller problem is taken in turn through the next step. When each of these small problems is solved, the big problem is solved.

Step 2: Establishing Criteria for Evaluating Alternative Solutions.   Before the salesperson attempts to solve a problem, he must consider how alternative solutions are to be evaluated. This is especially true if others are to be involved in the task. Failure to do this may result in a poor solution if working alone, or disagreement if other people are concerned.

Certain of the restrictions become criteria. Thus, time and money expenditures may impose limits. Good commercial judgment dictates that the investment of time, effort, and money must not exceed the commercial worth of the problem's solution. Often the engineer has to guard against solving a problem with a tool or component that is more precise or versatile than is warranted.

It is good policy to choose a solution that minimizes the chances of losing an account in case results are not as expected. For example, in helping a customer solve a problem, a salesperson would rarely want to place an account in jeopardy if his proposed solution were not successful. Loss is another consideration. Failure to cope with some problems may be more costly than to attempt almost any reasonable solution.

Let's consider again the salesperson who has specifically defined the problems faced by the duplicating department of the university. He must now determine the criteria for selecting suitable alternatives. Several possible criteria should be considered, one of which is the budget capabilities of the department. The amount of money available would determine whether purchase or lease of equipment is more suitable.

Another criterion to be considered is the compatibility of the duplicating equipment with the other equipment already acquired by the department. As an example, if most of the existing production is made by machines which use legal size paper, the new duplicating equipment should be capable of handling the same type of paper.

Finally, there may be specific criteria peculiar to each problem which should be identified before proceeding to the next step.

Step 3: Thinking of Alternative Solutions.   This step is largely the domain of creative thinking. It challenges the ingenuity of the problem solver. It is tempting, once the first potential solution is reached, to settle on it. If the problem solver is to be effective, however, he continues to think of other possibilities. If there is time, ideas should be permitted to gel. Often a second or third attempt at a solution reveals new alternatives. Once an exhaustive list of alternatives is formulated, the next step can be undertaken.

Going back to our example of the duplicating and copying equipment, this step is concerned with careful and thorough consideration by the salesperson of all suitable alternatives to be offered to the department. The salesperson should make a detailed evaluation of *all* products which may fit the needs and purchase criteria of the client. It is not sufficient to develop a small number of suitable alternatives; in this way, possibilities may be overlooked, and competitors may take advantage of this weakness in the sales presentation.

Step 4: Evaluation of Alternatives. Each alternative in turn is weighed against the criteria. As evaluation proceeds, additional criteria may suggest themselves. Also, in applying the criteria, modifications may occur in the relative weight given each one. Some criteria are rigid and admit of no exception (e.g., policy), whereas others encompass only desirable, but not mandatory, factors. It is helpful to indicate for each alternative how it fares with each criterion and thus arrive at a "score" for each potential solution.

A salesperson must be prepared to handle objections and all possible questions about a product, therefore, he must be aware of how well his products fit the customer's needs and his purchase criteria.

In our example of the university department, the salesperson might check all the requirements for the equipment, so that he can efficiently demonstrate the advantages of his products. He might establish parameters for evaluation of all proposed solutions, so as to facilitate the buying decision of the department.

Step 5: Selecting the "Best" Solution. The "best" solution is that alternative among those considered that best meets the differentially weighted criteria. We use quotation marks with "best," because there is always the possibility that a solution was overlooked that might have been superior to any of those considered.

Note that this analysis produces three types of outputs: recommendations, decisions, and actions. Depending on the setting for the problem, these outputs are directed to either a prospect or customer account or to the salesperson's own management. With recommendations, the way they are expressed may influence their acceptance. Decisions have to be weighed against the initial restrictions, particularly company policy. An important criterion to use in evaluating a decision is whether it can stand the test of time. Each time a decision is countermanded it detracts from the confidence the other person has in the decision maker. If the output takes the form of actions, they are usually commitments to be performed within a prescribed timetable. Here, too, confidence is lost when actions are not taken.

Although our duplicating and copying equipment salesperson is not responsible for making the final purchase decision, he may be very helpful to those who will actually make the purchase. His assistance in answering technical questions, a good demonstration, and the use of testimonials from other satisfied customers may be very important factors in reaching final consensus as to the solution of the department's equipment problem.

Caution in Using Logical Analysis

The problem-solving process is not as orderly, clear, and neat as Figure 5-2 suggests. For instance, in Step 1, as the problem is being defined, other related problems may emerge. As solutions are being considered, new criteria may be discovered. Problems may pop up as the outputs are implemented.

Such interacting and sidetracking often occur when two or more persons become involved in the process. For instance, the salesperson may have to call upon a technical specialist to help him with a problem. Participants in the process are likely to have different opinions and approaches. The problem solver must draw out the ideas of each person who is helping with the problem without at the same time becoming diverted from the orderly problem-solving task. When another person's aid is enlisted, it is important to brief him on the background and restrictions within which the solution must occur.

Here are seven factors which facilitate problem solving:

[First]Perhaps the most important influence on logical analysis is an attitude of open-mindedness. Pre-judgments or prejudices prevent a fresh approach. Second, the problem solver must have a positive viewpoint. This is illustrated by a sign in an office which reads "The difficult we do immediately; the impossible takes a little longer." Third, as mentioned earlier, the problem solver must be a "knower" and aware of who the other "knowers" are. Fourth, the problem solver must be able to fail successfully. This does not mean that he condones failure in himself or others. Rather, he learns from his failures and tries not to make the same mistake twice. Fifth, he is not so tied to precedent that he is unwilling to try the new. The effective problem solver takes a calculated risk in innovating. Sixth, he provides himself enough psychological privacy to think in an unhurried, orderly fashion. Problem solving under duress often results in half-baked thinking. Seventh, he maintains a commercial perspective in terms of time, talent, and money investment.[11]

SUMMARY

In this chapter we examined the difficult task of selling new products and services. The adoption process an individual goes through when confronted with an innovation can be broken down into five stages: awareness, interest, evaluation, trial and adoption. An understanding of these stages provides the salesperson with valuable insight into his prospects when selling new products.

We examined the five adopter categories. We saw that the early adopters are the key figures in selling most new products, because once they are "sold" on the product's value they will help sell the product to the followers.

We then discussed the salesperson as a change agent, and saw how he plays a key role in the trial stage of the adoption process. The salesperson must be certain that his customers have the correct information to permit them to make an informed decision on his products.

We concluded with an analysis of the characteristics that tend to make a product more easily adopted by society and a discussion of logical analysis.

[11]*Ibid.*, p. 36.

PROBLEMS

1. What are the different stages of the adoption process and how can they influence an introductory sales strategy?
2. The Mass Transit Corporation recently developed a new three-wheeled electric car for urban transportation with three-passenger capacity. This new car is operated by batteries and its operating costs are one-tenth those of a normal automobile. Examine the relevant characteristics of this product, and, based on them, try to predict the rate of adoption of this new car.
3. Color television sets have now penetrated the early adopters category in South America. Explain your sales and market strategy to reach the early majority and the late majority as efficiently as possible.
4. Describe how the salesperson can act as a change agent.
5. Explain how logical analysis can be used to solve a customer's problem by an effective salesperson.

Exercise 5

THE SALESPERSON AS CHANGE AGENT AND PROBLEM SOLVER

Objectives: To understand the nature of the diffusion process and its application in marketing and sales.

To understand how logical analysis can be used in problem solving.

A. Self-Analysis

Reflect on your own buying behavior. How would you categorize yourself—innovator, early adopter, early majority, late majority, laggard? Cite your evidence.

B. New Product

A well-known manufacturer and marketer of dental and mouth-care products—toothbrushes, toothpaste, and mouthwash—is considering the promotion of a small package containing a "throw-away" toothbrush impregnated with toothpaste and a plastic vial with enough mouthwash for a single use.

1. What would be a good name for the product?
2. Who are the potential users?
3. How can the company gain acceptance for this new offering?

Case 5-1 Sterling Tools, Inc.

Sterling is a nationally known company engaged in the manufacturing and marketing of power-driven fastening and drilling tools. Its products are likely to be found wherever holes and nut-bolt fasteners are part of the production process, such as automobile companies and farm-equipment manufacturers.

Conventional fastening tools, including Sterling's, are set to a constant torque (i.e., each nut is tightened to a preset force or twist):

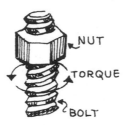

Inasmuch as nuts and bolts show variations in machining control on torque means some nuts are loose, some tight, and some to specifications.

Sterling has now remedied this with a technological breakthrough! Their new models can be set for a constant tensor, as shown below:

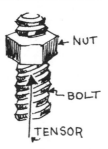

This means that every fastening will be exactly to specifications.

The Sterling sales force has been briefed on the new line and each sales representative has been furnished brochures describing the unique advantages of tensor-controlled fastener tools in a variety of production situations.

1. What difficulties do you anticipate in selling the new line?

2. What strategies do you suggest that Sterling's salespersons adopt for its new product?

Case 5-2 The Fafco Solar Heating Co.

Fafco is a small California company which, in 1972, introduced the first mass-produced solar heating system for swimming pools. Although much has been said about solar energy since the oil embargo of 1974, solar heating units are still very new products. Most consumers are not familiar with solar systems at all, and little product promotion has been made.

Fafco feels it has a very good product which offers significant comparative advantages over traditional heating systems. The firm has a large working capital and is expanding its operations nationwide. To reach such a large distribution, thirty salespeople were hired. Their major task is to reach distributors and to try to secure their cooperation in selling Fafco products to final users.

Fafco's major product is the swimming pool Solar Panels. These are modular panels which are usually placed on the roof of a home, facing South. They are used to heat the pool water. The operation is very simple. The water flowing from the filter back to the pool is diverted to the solar panels by the auto-control valve. In the panels, the water is heated by the sun, and then circulated back to the pool. The panels are built in such a way as to insure an even flow of water throughout, so that every square foot of area exposed to the sun is contacted by the water passing through.

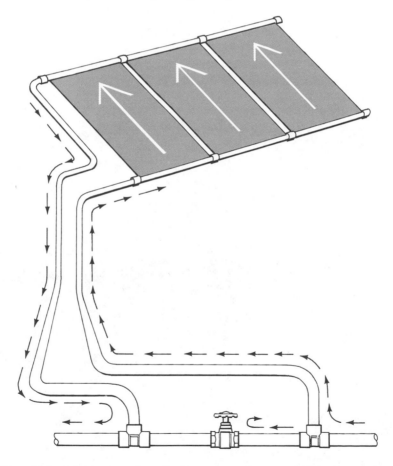

The solar heater is easy to install, this can even be accomplished by the homeowner without help from outside technicians. It is very economical, because it utilizes the existing filtration pump of the pool. The management of Fafco estimates that at current energy prices, the investment for a solar heater will be completely recovered in energy savings within two years of operation. The direct cost of the product to the user would vary depending on the size and the location of the pool to be heated, but on the average the price would be approximately $1500.00.

It is very important that the new salespeople be aware of the advantages of the product so that this introduction effort will secure prompt and good results. Fafco feels that this product could be easily imitated by competitors, once its popularity were assured. Mr. Fox is in charge of training the new salespeople and he is trying to develop a reference chart with all the valuable points about the product which should be stressed in the sales presentation. He is concerned with training the salespeople to respond to the most common objections that could be found by prospective customers and distributors. He is also supplying the salespeople with pictures of systems already installed and working for a reference to introduce their product:

1. Assume you are Mr. Fox. Prepare a checklist of advantages and disadvantages of the Fafco Solar Heater for your salespeople.

2. Assume you were asked to single out the target market for Solar Heaters in the United States at this point in time. What would be the main characteristics of your target customers?

3. What difficulties would face a salesperson trying to introduce this product in the market?

SUGGESTIONS FOR FURTHER READING

Blackwell, Roger D., James F. Engel, and Robert J. Kegerreis, "Word-of-Mouth Communication by the Innovator," *Journal of Marketing,* Vol. 33 (July 1969), pp. 15–19.

Boone, Louis E., "The Search for the Consumer Innovator," *Journal of Business,* Vol. 43 (April 1970), pp. 135–140.

Donnelly, James H., Jr., "Social Character and Acceptance of New Products," *Journal of Marketing Research,* Vol. 7 (February 1970), pp. 111–113.

Greif, Edwin C., *Personal Salesmanship: New Concepts and Directions* (Reston, Va: Reston Publishing, 1974), Chapter 3.

Rogers, Everett M., and F. Floyd Shoemaker, *Communications of Innovations–A Cross-Cultural Approach* (New York, N.Y.: Free Press, 1971).

Wasson, Chester R., *Dynamic Competitive Strategy and Product Life Cycle* (St. Charles, Ill.: Challenge Books, 1974).

6. The Selling-Buying Process

If a salesperson were asked, "What is the selling-buying process?" he might very well answer with another question, "What do you mean *selling-buying?*" Or he might instead answer the question, "What does a salesperson do?" He might tell about his company, the products he sells, and the activities that make up his day's work. He might mention the kinds of customers and prospective customers he calls on. It is doubtful, though, that he would make any reference to the buying part of the selling-buying process. In fact, most books and articles on selling treat the subject almost exclusively in terms of what the salesperson says and does and how he says and does it. Yet, there can be no selling without buying. Indeed, the two comprise a single, interactive, interpersonal relationship—whether the process occurs at home, in a retail store, or in the executive suite of a large business. Buying is fully as active and participative as selling. We cannot consider one without the other.

The interaction of buyer and seller and the influence of environmental factors on their decisions are the main elements of the selling-buying process. Personal selling is concerned with the communication that occurs during the process, because the knowledge gained from such interchange is essential to the selling-buying purpose. We will examine four general selling-buying approaches: the stimulus-response model, the formula approach, Brewster's formula, and the need-satisfaction model.[1] In addition, we will describe a general model of the industrial selling-buying process, and discuss the use of pressure tactics in selling.

THE STIMULUS-RESPONSE MODEL

The stimulus-response model is the simplest of the four selling-buying approaches presented in this chapter. It has its psychological origin in early experiments with animals. Investigators found that a given stimulus would cause a given response and that subjects could be conditioned to respond to a substitute stimulus (Figure 6-1). We will analyze the application of this model to selling along with its limitations.

Figure 6-1 The stimulus-response model

Application of the Stimulus-Response Model to Selling

The sales application of this theory postulates that if the salesperson says and does the right things, (i.e., provides the appropriate stimuli), the prospect or customer will buy (i.e., respond to the stimuli). This relationship is illustrated in Figure 6-2.

This method of selling is used in situations where a salesperson has a few key approaches that are good or that have worked in other situations. As an example, take a wholesale clothing salesperson trying to sell to a retail store buyer. He may say, "This is our most popular item, and all the stores in your city will be showing it next season." He hopes that the prospect's response to this stimulus (a "popular item," "all of prospect's competitors will be showing it next season") will be a purchase of some quantity of that item.

[1]W. J. E. Crissy and H. C. Cash, *Psychology of Selling,* Vol. 1 "A Point of View for Salesmen" (Flushing, N.Y.: Personnel Development Associates, 1958).

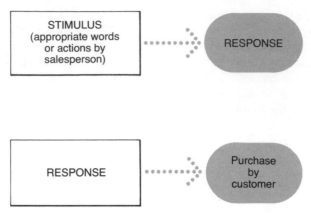

Figure 6-2 The stimulus-response model applied to sales

Limitations of the Stimulus-Response Model

This approach to selling is useful in situations where the unit sale is low and the time devoted to the sales effort is very brief. However, there are a number of weaknesses in the use of such a standardized stimulus. In our example of the clothing salesperson, if he did not analyze the prospect and his wants, he may find that he said exactly the *wrong* thing. This buyer may not want to carry merchandise that all the other stores have; instead, he may wish to carry distinctive merchandise for his customers. Therefore, his response to such a stimulus would probably be one of disinterest, if not dislike, and the desired sale would be lost. There are five specific limitations of the application of his model to the selling-buying process.

First, the stimulus-response model runs counter to what is known about individual differences among customers and prospects. According to the stimulus-response model, a given word, phrase, or action should invariably elicit the same response from a prospect or customer, regardless of who the respondent is. The second shortcoming, which is closely related to the first, is that this viewpoint implies that a given stimulus will elicit its particular response with the same person under varying circumstances. Yet every salesperson knows that a person might behave quite differently at lunch than he would at his desk or when colleagues are present in a conference room. The third weakness of this theory is the implication that the salesperson is in control of the situation in the same way that a psychologist is when he experiments with white rats in the laboratory. A fourth limitation is the fact that this theory does not take into account what is going on inside the customer's or prospect's mind; it merely deals with his overt behavior. It ignores motivational factors and eliminates choice as a consideration. The fifth limitation is that the salesperson who relies on this model really has no way of improving his performance on the basis of his experience. Instead, he continues searching for the magic words and phrases that he assumes will guarantee success.

THE FORMULA APPROACH

Like the stimulus-response model, the formula approach implies that all customers react alike. This theory assumes that to make a sale, the salesperson must take the customer through a series of steps which are the same for all customers and for all selling-buying situations. The *formula* view of selling most frequently cited is AIDA, which stands for *attention, interest, desire,* and *action.* This approach postulates that the customer or prospect must be taken through successive reaction stages, namely, paying attention to the presentation, becoming interested in it, desiring what is being presented, and acting by purchasing what the salesperson is promoting. Sometimes the additional steps of satisfaction and conviction are included. We will examine the primary method used by proponents of this approach—the "canned" sales talk—and its limitations.

The "Canned" Sales Talk

The salesperson using the AIDA approach will develop a standard presentation, or "canned" sales talk, if he has not already been supplied one by his management. He will, in each sales presentation, make statements designed to attract attention, arouse interest, create desire, and obtain action (Figure 6-3).

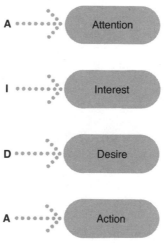

Figure 6-3 The AIDA model

The salesperson tends to ignore the thoughts of the customer as he tries to develop these mental states in sequence. Through this method, proponents claim that all important product information is presented to each customer, and that it elicits the reactions for the salesperson to make a sale. This method is valuable whenever prospective customers have identical, or at least similar, needs and where the salesperson lacks the ability to develop a sales approach based on each customer's individual needs.

Limitations of the Formula Approach

The chief weakness of this method is that a particular customer is not likely to move smoothly from step to step, despite the best efforts of the salesperson. Second, this approach, like the stimulus-response model, assumes a similarity of reaction among people that does not exist. The salesperson, therefore, could convince himself that he is some sort of an engineer who, by following a standard procedure, can induce the customer to make a purchase. The method, then, is an analysis of the situation from the salesperson's point of view rather than the customer's.

This approach runs into further difficulty when the customer wants an answer to a specific question. If the salesperson fails to perceive this, and continues to make the presentation, he may literally talk himself out of a sale. Alternatively, with this approach, when a salesperson is interrupted by a prospect he may find it difficult to get started again, because the presentation does not prepare him to interact with the customer. As a result, salespeople who use the formula approach frequently fear questions and discourage the prospect from asking them.

BREWSTER'S FORMULA

Ray Brewster[2] proposed a somewhat more comprehensive technique to the formula approach. The major difference in his formula is that it permits the salesperson to better adjust to and fit the individual prospect. We shall analyze the four steps that comprise Brewster's formula (Table 6-1).

The Four Key Steps

Step 1:   This is the beginning of the sales interview. The salesperson's objective is to describe the benefits of the product to the buyer during his presentation. The salesperson will emphasize general benefits that are congruent with most customers' needs so as to avoid any kind of negative reaction and gain time to develop more specific adjustments.

Step 2:   No matter how good a salesperson is at opening a sale, he still has a big job to do. The prospect is still skeptical: "What has all this, interesting as it is, to do with me?," he thinks. "What are you leading up to?" Therefore, the objective of the salesperson during this second step is to allay suspicion in the prospect's mind and to consolidate the "mental accord" established by his opening statements. He must offer the prospect the dignity of choice. While the

---

[2]Ray C. Brewster, "More Psychology in Selling," *Harvard Business Review,* Vol. 31, (July–August 1953), pp. 91–99.

TABLE 6-1 BREWSTER'S FORMULA FOR PERSUASIVE PRESENTATION

Step	Generic Term	Explanation
Step 1	Show openers	Make openers something customers surely want. Relax conscious defense mechanism. Keep openers logical, possible, provable.
	Establish mental accord	Be able to relate openers to your product naturally, in presentation. Build integrity in presentation
Step 2	Declare your hand	Tie in openers to your proposition. Establish "I want what you propose—prove it" attitude.
	Tie in product	Fortify psychological position by leaving decisions to prospect.
Step 3	Prove openers	Prove only each point in openers—no variation. Summarize when points are proved—with brevity—tersely. Relate proven points to original agreement. Keep prospect's mind on track. Blend Steps 3 and 4 into one close.
Step 4	Showdown	Refer to original accord. Refer to proof. Suggest affirmative action.
	Pay me—Close!	Repeat customer's need. Give choice and alternative for affirmative action.

prospect may be willing to buy, he does not want anybody to make decisions for him. At this time the salesperson might say, "I mention this because I have a product that may do these things." He must make more specific suggestions directly related to the product offered. Two important aspects of a sale are thus accomplished: (1) the salesperson tries to anticipate what the prospect is thinking, and (2) he avoids making such statements as, "I will prove that I have what you want," which may be perceived as coercive.

Step 3:   During Step 3, the salesperson's objective is to prove that what he said in the first two stages is correct. He should not introduce any new points. By summarizing only the key points for the customer, the sales presentation remains uncomplicated, emphasizes the most important objectives, and saves time.

Step 4:   The salesperson's objective during this step is to complete the sale. Brewster feels that if his approach is used correctly to this point, the salesperson will have developed the degree of agreement and cooperation needed between himself and the prospect to close the sale. After building a rapport with the prospect there is no subconscious reason for hesitancy during the closing of the sale.

Brewster's formula for selling, like AIDA, puts the burden on the salesperson to ensure that an orderly sequence of reactions occurs on the part of the prospect. This viewpoint tends to spell out in detail what the salesperson should say and do in order to achieve orderly behavior in the prospect. Taken to the extreme, this formula, like the AIDA formula, results in a completely structured, or "canned," sales presentation.

Applications of Brewster's Formula

There are three circumstances that suggest the use of this approach. First, if those called upon have a relatively homogeneous set of needs that the product or service satisfies, and if they are relatively homogeneous in their sophistication with respect to the offering, the Brewster formula may save time in working up the content and format of the sales presentation. Second, from a managerial viewpoint, this may be an effective approach when a salesperson is relatively unseasoned and lacks sophistication with regard to the uses of products or services. An insurance company of international reputation provides the beginning salesperson with a fully structured sales presentation that he learns and practices at the company school. This enables him to become productive quickly. However, as he gains experience, he is encouraged to do more questioning of customers and prospects and to individualize his presentations to each person. Third, this predetermined presentation may be used when a known time limitation exists for the presentation. Some pharmaceutical firms use this approach and require their salespeople to make a verbatim presentation or detail to the physicians. Typically, these pharmaceutical salespeople may expect only from three to seven minutes per call.

Limitations of Brewster's Formula

There are several limitations to Brewster's formula for selling. First, it implies an orderliness of behavior on the part of the salesperson and supposes a relatively passive and complying customer or prospect. Also, when carried to an extreme, it will not permit the salesperson to meet the unique needs of his various customers. Finally, if interruptions occur, the salesperson has the awkward problem of deciding whether to start again or to continue from the point of interruption. If he starts again, he may be viewed as an automaton without flexibility. On the other hand, if he continues from where he left off, the customer or prospect may have lost track of the presentation up to that point.

THE NEED-SATISFACTION MODEL

The need-satisfaction model was first postulated by Edward Strong.[3] Of the four general approaches to the selling-buying process, only the need-satisfaction model accounts for selling and buying as an interactive, unified process. As a result, the need-satisfaction model, has broader applicability and fewer limitations than the other approaches just discussed.

The Five-Stage Interactive Process

Figure 6-4 depicts the dynamics of the selling-buying process as described by the need-satisfaction model. There are five primary stages: needs, want-satisfiers, sales presentation, action, and satisfaction.

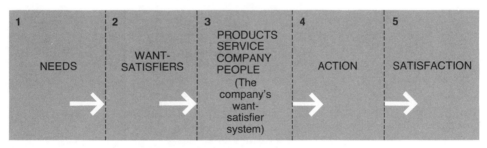

Figure 6-4 The five-stage interactive process of the need-satisfaction model

Needs.   The selling-buying process, according to Strong's model, begins with determining the needs of the customer or prospect. Unfortunately, needs are sometimes vague or generalized and difficult to think about or verbalize. And as a result they tend to create a state of dynamic balance, or *homeostasis.* Because of this, the salesperson frequently hears such statements as: "I don't need any." "I'm satisfied with my present sources of supply." "I have all I need right now." Unless the salesperson can disturb this homeostasis, he cannot reach the second step (want-satisfier analysis). The best way to break through is with questions. For example, a salesperson for a food manufacturer might say to a food retailer, "Would you like to learn how you can increase your profit 10 percent on the frozen foods you sell?" An office equipment salesperson might say to a purchasing agent, "Would a reduction in clerical payroll of 25 percent be of interest to your management?" A recurrent advertising strategy is to disturb homeostasis by using "scare ads." Think, for example, about the ads for deodorants or breath fresheners.

[3]Edward K. Strong, Jr., *The Psychology of Selling and Advertising,* (New York, N.Y.: McGraw-Hill, 1925).

Want satisfiers.   After homeostasis is disturbed, the second step is to establish want satisfiers. Here, the salesperson questions the prospect to determine how his wants are now being satisfied. He can then determine how to satisfy them better with his products and services (his company's want-satisfier system). The salesperson can present his firm's wants satisfiers (Stage 3 in Figure 6-4), individualized to the wants of the prospect. Table 6-2 lists questions used by the Sylvania salespeople to stimulate their thinking about customers' needs.

The salesperson thus learns the wants of the other person through inquiry and observation. In a larger context, this step can be thought of as the marketing-intelligence function of the salesperson. As an example, the salesperson calling on a food store might inspect the frozen-food stock on display prior to his interview with the prospect. Much of what he learns may be useful to his company in addition to providing him with a basis for a personalized presentation.

TABLE 6-2 SYLVANIA ELECTRIC PRODUCTS QUESTIONS USED TO DETERMINE A CUSTOMER'S NEEDS

(These are some cue questions that you as a salesperson can ask that may produce leads to the real needs of individual customers.)
1.   What is the account's total annual production?
2.   What percentage of total production was made with our competitor's machines? With ours?
3.   What acceptance does the customer's product line have in the market?
4.   What equipment does he use—both Sylvania and competition? The *why* of each?
5.   Is production off in any of his product lines? Why?
6.   Is he ahead of or behind his last year's production? Why?
7.   Are his standard manufacturing costs in line?
8.   Does he have any control figures on down time, reject rates, maintenance cost?
9.   Is the company strong on new product innovation?
10.   Is the company entering new markets?
11.   Does he have adequate and competent production personnel?
12.   Is the firm losing customers? Why?
13.   Do employees have a positive attitude toward the employer's business and Sylvania?
14.   Are they adequately informed and trained to use our equipment?
15.   What is his credit or financial condition? If in a tight position, is he reluctant to mention it? How can we help him without embarrassing him?
16.   Is the man you deal with progressive?
17.   What is the position of the company's marketing department on packaging?

18. What is the customer's attitude toward Sylvania's competition. Why?
19. Who is his competition—what are their strengths and weaknesses?
20. What is his attitude toward *his* competition?
21. What are the relationships between members of your competitors' organizations and your customer or his people?
22. What poor experiences has your customer had with competitors' equipment or services? How about yours? How does he feel now?
23. What is his rate of growth? Prospects for future growth? Market potential? How can we help him grow?
24. Has he budgeted for new equipment purchases?
25. Specifically, who makes the buying decisions in the customer's firm (R & D, Plant Manager, Product Design, General Manager, P.A., etc.)? What are their basic motives in making a buying decision?
26. Are expense requisitions required? Who must approve?
27. Who are the key influencers on the decision maker? What needs do they have as individuals for recognition, credit, or other psychic (status) satisfactions? How can you supply them?
28. What is the customer's relationship with our headquarters personnel? Can they help you?
29. Does the customer have a habit of spreading his purchases among manufacturers? If so, what is his real reason for doing so?
30. If he is manufacturing private label products, what is the reaction of his customers toward current packaging?
31. What special projects is the customer working on or does he anticipate?
32. What business losses has he suffered? How recently? How have these affected his philosophy of operation or relationship with us—or with the competition?
33. If the individual with whom you must do business must in turn sell others in his organization, what information, help, or support does he require from you?
34. Does he have any problems in the following areas that you (with or without help from others in the company) can help him solve: Space facilities? Packaging materials? Packaging design? His location? Production methods or costs? Financial inexperience? Disposing of used equipment? Can you (or the company) help him in these areas?
35. Will he welcome help in any of these areas or will it antagonize or embarrass him if offered?
36. Does his long-range buying potential justify the time it will require to get the answers, or does it justify any compromise he asks you to make in your work schedule?
37. Have you lost any previous orders? Why? . . . be honest now!
38. When he asks for a quote, is he ready to do business or is he looking for ball park figures?
39. Have you recorded key information in your customer file for future reference in your sales planning?

Sales Presentation.   The third step is the presentation of the company's want-satisfier system. This includes the firm's products, services, image, and people (including the salesperson, himself). Based on what he learned in Step 2, the salesperson presents his offering in a way designed to meet the wants of the customer or prospect *differently* from and *better* than the want satisfiers now in use. Thus, he must make the customer or prospect perceive, think, and feel that his want satisfiers are superior to alternative offerings. Unless he accomplishes this, he will not make a sale. Because of the selective nature of perception (discussed in Chapter 4), it is imperative for the salesperson to single out a relatively small but important number of benefits that make his products better than what are now being used. An acid test for this selection is to pick those characteristics on which his firm's offering has greatest *differential competitive advantage.* (This concept will be discussed in greater detail in Chapter 9.)

Action.   The fourth step in the need-satisfaction model (Figure 6-4) is action by the prospect or customer. This represents a *purchase, not a sale.* The good salesperson doesn't sell—he induces people to buy. In a competitive economy the purchaser resents being coerced. He wants to make his own decisions. This does not mean that the salesperson should not ask for an order. It implies only that he should be subtle and tactful when cultivating business. Also there are many selling-buying situations in which the salesperson does not expect to come out with an order as such. For instance, in the case of the pharmaceutical salesperson, the action he seeks is that the physician understand and accept information about his firm's products and offer to prescribe them for his patients when the occasion arises.

Satisfaction.   The fifth step in our model is satisfaction. The selling-buying process does not terminate at the point of transaction, but continues with the satisfaction the purchaser derives from the action he takes. This step is critically important, because in most selling-buying relationships the firm desires to cultivate ongoing accounts rather than one-time purchases. It should be evident that the more satisfaction a person derives from the action he has taken, the more likely he is to continue with the same means of satisfaction. This suggests that the strategy followed with a *customer* is quite different from that followed with a *prospect.* With a customer, the salesperson is seeking to establish homeostasis, with his offerings as the need and want satisfiers. His task is to make the account as invulnerable as possible to the inroads of competitors. In his presentation he stresses the benefits the customer is gaining from the selling-buying relationship. He follows through on each purchase to ensure that continuing satisfaction exists. He provides the customer reassurance that he is doing the right thing by buying from him. He helps the customer rationalize (i.e., justify things as they are).

In contrast, with the prospect (someone else's customer), the salesperson has the task of disturbing the homeostasis. Unless he can find some way to upset the status quo, he will not make an inroad. This means that through observation and inquiry, he must show that his offering is different and better than what is now in use or of alternative offerings.

Advantages of the Need-Satisfaction Model

Because this approach to selling is more comprehensive than the other three approaches, it has unique advantages. First, it encompasses both the selling and buying ingredients of the selling-buying process. It emphasizes the viewpoint of the customer or prospect by accounting for his needs, perceptions, thoughts, and feelings. Second, both parties are active participants, and thus the salesperson is an attentive observer and an astute questioner. Third, this theory accounts for individual differences and the need to personalize the presentation. The key to personalization is using what has been learned about the other person's needs and wants. Fourth, it provides a basis for determining what the salesperson should say and do and how he should say and do it. Fifth, there is an implicit caution against coercing the other person. The action sought is a purchase, not a sale. You could do a little experiment to demonstrate this point. Ask one of your friends, "Where did you get those shoes?" The likelihood is that he or she will reply, "I bought them at such and such a store." Indeed, if by chance the reply is, "I was sold them," the next question you are likely to ask is, "What is wrong with them?" Sixth, this viewpoint indicates that the selling-buying process does not terminate with the action of purchase but also encompasses the satisfaction derived from the buying decision. It emphasizes the need to follow up on purchases to see that satisfaction is being derived.

Limitations of the Need-Satisfaction Model

The need-satisfaction model does have some limitations. Inasmuch as it places far more responsibility and freedom of action in the hands of the salesperson than do other selling approaches, its effective use requires relatively sophisticated sales personnel. It also implies that the stake in the potential transaction is sufficiently high for both buyer and seller to invest significant time and effort in the proposition. Use of the need-satisfaction approach is likely to take more time than the other three approaches.

Need satisfaction is the most appropriate approach when (1) there are marked individual differences among customers and prospects; (2) there is great diversity of needs to be met; (3) the products and services are complex and technical; (4) the level of knowledge and skill of sales personnel is high; (5) the unit transaction is large; and (6) the likelihood of a continuing selling-buying relationship warrants the effort.

AN INDUSTRIAL SELLING-BUYING MODEL

The four models of the selling-buying process presented so far are general models—that is, they are applicable to either the industrial or the consumer sectors of our economy. We will examine a selling-buying model that deals solely with the industrial market. This model is of interest because it illustrates those elements that differentiate the industrial from the consumer sectors.

Industrial buying behavior is more complex than consumer buyer behavior, because additional elements intervene and interact. Industrial purchases involve individuals as such and also as elements of an organization. This means that the human factors and the organizational objectives both have to be considered by the salesperson when attempting to make a sale to a business firm.

In order to better understand the industrial buying process, we will use a conceptual model.[4] This model divides the buying activity for an industrial organization into four basic steps, as shown in Figure 6-5.

PROBLEM RECOGNITION ••••••••> BUYING RESPONSI-BILITY ••••••••> SEARCH PROCESS ••••••••> CHOICE PROCESS

Figure 6-5 Analytical structure of the industrial buying process

Problem Recognition

The purchase of products by industrial organizations is usually a response to a particular need or problem. This need may be directly related to the firm's overall objective of making a profit while satisfying its own customers, or it may be the consequence of other extraordinary factors such as a product innovation, invasion of a new market or, modification of facilities.

More commonly, a problem is perceived when a discrepancy exists between several existing goals of the firm and its actual performance. Equilibrium can be reestablished by two means—either by reformulating the firm's objectives and goals, or by adapting performance to the desired objectives. These decisions are influenced by organizational factors and by the character, personality, and attitudes of the people involved in the decision.

A salesperson should be aware of the firm's philosophy and objectives, and knowledgeable on the traits and characteristics of the people involved in such decisions. This information can be very helpful in shaping his sales strategy.

Buying Responsibility

A specific buying decision for an industrial organization is frequently assigned to one individual in the firm. The criteria used to assign such responsibility are many. The choice could be influenced by the organizational structure of the firm, by the type of competitors the firm has, by the product or market structure, or even by personal factors.

It is important to know exactly who is responsible in the business firm for the buying decision, and this may involve accurate research on the part of the

[4]Webster, Frederick E. Jr., "Modeling the Industrial Buying Process," *Journal of Marketing Research,* Vol. 2 (November 1965), pp. 370–377.

salesperson. The sales approach should be made only to those people who can either influence or make the purchase decision.

The Search Process

Once the responsibility of making the purchase is determined, the buyer initiates the process by gathering information on all available alternative solutions for the firm's needs. In order to evaluate the alternatives, the purchaser will establish desired criteria or standards of performance for the product or service being examined.

In some cases, when it is verified that existing products and services do not satisfy the desired standards, the criteria of selection may be modified or goals may be changed according to the existing supply.

Two elements are very important at this stage: the cost of gathering search information, and the the time needed for the search. As this process can be very lengthy and costly, a good salesperson may achieve differential competitive advantage by being alert to the industrial customer's needs and by providing prompt and clear information to his inquiries.

The Choice Process

The choice of supplier is directly related to the search criteria used for alternative evaluation. Variables such as product characteristics, price, delivery time, availability, and service are the important factors in establishing priorities for the final decision. At this stage of the buying process, one or more suppliers will be chosen based on their offerings.

In very competitive situations, it is possible that several product and service offerings will be judged equally feasible and acceptable by the industrial buyer. It is in these cases that the ability and personal behavior of a salesperson are important to the final outcome. A good salesperson will analyze the situation and be flexible to any additional needs of the buyer. The salesperson's personal interaction with the purchasing agent may be the decisive variable affecting the sale.

This industrial buying model is a generalized approach to the purchasing activity of organizations. Each situation has special characteristics and influencing factors which should be considered by the salesperson. The advantage of this model is that it clearly points out the crucial decision steps in the process as well as the main decision factors to be considered. (Additional aspects of industrial buying are discussed in Chapter 18.)

PRESSURE IN SELLING

Whatever general approach to selling is used, it is imperative that the customer or prospect not feel coerced. In fact, the universal tactical objective in selling is *to be in control without seeming to be.*

Writers and practitioners frequently use the term *sales pressure* to refer to the salesperson's behavior vis-a-vis the other person. A high-pressure salesperson is seen as pushy and aggressive. Yet, relating pressure to the salesperson's behavior has the same weakness as the basic premises of the *stimulus-response* and *formula* theories of selling—it fails to encompass what is going on with the customer or prospect.

Pressure is more appropriately considered in terms of the other person's perceiving, thinking, and feeling at the termination of the sales call. If, at this time, the customer or prospect perceives, thinks, and feels, "We (the salesperson and I) decided; we solved the problem together," this represents *no pressure*. In contrast, if his reaction is, "I was sold; I was pushed into ordering," this is *high pressure*. *Low pressure* exists when the reaction is, "I bought." No salesperson can afford to create a high-pressure state in the other person. The order may be cancelled. At a minimum, continued business is unlikely.

SUMMARY

In this chapter we analyzed four general models of the selling-buying process and a specific model of the industrial selling-buying process. The stimulus-response model is based on the theory that if the salesperson says and does the right things, the prospect will purchase the product. One of the most significant limitations of this model is that it does not recognize individual differences.

The second model, the formula approach to selling, is based on the assumption that to complete a sale the salesperson must take the customer through a series of steps which are the same for all individuals. The chief weakness of this "canned" approach to selling is that a particular customer is not likely to move smoothly from step to step.

The third model, Brewster's formula is more comprehensive and useful than is the traditional formula approach. It requires that the salesperson go through four distinct steps to complete the sale. One of the more severe limitations to this approach is that it assumes an orderliness on the part of the salesperson and a relatively passive customer neither of which exists in many selling situations.

The need-satisfaction model was the fourth general model of the selling-buying process we examined. It is the most comprehensive of the models discussed. Although it encompasses both the selling and buying ingredients of selling, it approaches the process from the viewpoint of the prospect or customer. Although it has several limitations, its advantages far outweigh its disadvantages for many selling situations.

The last model we examined was the industrial selling-buying process. It divides the buying activity of an industrial firm into four basic steps: problem recognition, buying responsibility, the search process, and the choice process.

PROBLEMS

1. What are the major advantages and disadvantages of using the stimulus-response model in the selling-buying process?
2. You are a door-to-door salesperson for a manufacturer of home-care products. You want to develop a sales presentation applying the formula approach to the selling-buying relationship. Describe your plan and illustrate your tactics in order to gain your customer's attention, interest, desire, and finally action.
3. Compare and contrast the AIDA approach and Brewster's formula. In which circumstances would Brewster's formula be preferred to the AIDA approach?
4. Define in your own words the need-satisfaction model.
5. Your firm has just developed a new energy-generating instrument that uses solar energy to supply single housing units with the electricity necessary for normal living conditions. Explain how the need-satisfaction approach could be used to sell such a product to individual homeowners.
6. Apply the same principles used in Question 5, but this time tailor your sales appeal to housing construction firms.

Exercise 6

THE SELLING-BUYING PROCESS

Objective: To understand the selling-buying process along with the advantages and disadvantages of the stimulus-response model, the formula approach, Brewster's formula and the need-satisfaction model.

Below is a segment of a sales interview. Indicate for each statement by the salesperson what viewpoint(s) of selling is (are) illustrated and, where possible, what phase of the viewpoint(s).

Salesperson: Good morning, Mr. Black, I represent Cresco and I want to tell you how we can make money for you.

Black: Well, I'm never too busy to hear how to make money. What's your proposition?

Salesperson: I'm sure you have a lot of "do-it-yourselfers" coming in to buy tools. We sell our tools singly and in various kit combinations.

Black: Hold on. I wish we did have a big demand like you describe. I think most of our tool sales are for fixing things around the house.

Salesperson: Well, Cresco tools are great for that, too. However, I think our window display material and cooperative advertising will flush out more "do-it-yourselfers" than you think are around. Besides, wives will buy tool kits as gifts for their husbands.

Black: I don't know how I'd squeeze another thing in our windows. I've noticed, too, that both the local discount houses carry your line. How can I compete with them if I do stock Cresco?

Salesperson: Don't you carry other items which are available in the discount stores? How do they sell?

Black: Well, some move pretty well; some don't.

Salesperson: The big edge you have is that you give your customers personal treatment. We have a retailer's guide from which you can get a lot of ideas for helping people use tools.

1. Indicate what you might have said had you been the salesperson.
2. Do you think Black will buy? Defend your answer.

Case 6-1 Fleur De Lis Jewelry

Fleur de Lis Jewelry manufactures and markets a fine line of costume and semiprecious jewelry which it sells direct to consumers. It advertises heavily in women's magazines, and the brand name is well known and highly regarded. It has a large nationwide sales force of part-time and full-time representatives who work on a straight commission basis. Incomes range from $3000 to $30,000 a year.

Actual sales are made at "parties" hosted by former purchasers of the jewelry who are also induced to stimulate future "parties." Thus the sales representative has two kinds of selling to accomplish: first, to sell as much jewelry as possible at each party; and second, to line up future hostesses at each "party." Each hostess receives "free goods" as an incentive, the amount depending on how many sales are made.

Their market consists of two segments—young married housewives who find the morning coffee or the afternoon tea a relief from the humdrum of the home; young working women, single and married, who enjoy a social evening. The firm's prime source of salespeople are former hostesses who find the selling job a pleasant way to earn either a primary or supplemental income.

1. Which theory or viewpoint of selling would seem to be most applicable in selling jewelry at a party and convincing a party guest to be a hostess at a future party?
2. What should Fleur de Lis look for in selecting hostesses?
3. What should Fleur de Lis look for in recruiting salespeople?

Case 6-2 Institutional Foods, Inc.

Manufacturers of kitchen equipment for commercial operations (such as restaurants, hotels, cafeterias) or for institutions (such as hospitals and schools) produce all types of machinery and accessories for large food operations. Although there is little differentiation as to the types of products offered, the quality of service performed by such equipment and its durability and reliability are very important considerations for the purchase.

There are several manufacturers of kitchen equipment for commercial or institutional organizations, and the prices of their products are very comparable. Two of them, however, The Kitchen Co., and Institutional Foods, Inc., price their equipment at about 10% above the other competitors in the market. The two organizations rationalize the price difference by stating that their products are more durable and more reliable than those of competitors.

The management of Institutional Foods, Inc., is aware that institutional buyers are very cost-oriented when purchasing equipment for their operation. They also know that the durability and reliability of the equipment are advantages hard to prove because the average life of such goods is eight-to-ten years.

It was clear that to achieve differential competitive advantage, an additional effort had to be made by Institutional Foods, Inc. They decided to train their sales representatives so that they could quickly diagnose each customer's equipment needs, based on their estimated production needs and time constraints. For three months, each salesperson attended a highly specialized course in Food Management at the University of Houston Hotel and Restaurant Management School.

In May, 1976, the sales manager of Institutional Foods, Inc., received a memo from the president indicating that once the specialized training of salespeople has been completed, the management expects its representatives to concentrate all their efforts into using such knowledge. This means that the sales representatives are expected to use their skills and sell equipment to potential customers by acting almost as consultants to them.

The sales manager likes the idea of using the problem-solving approach to sales in order to build a unique image for his firm in the market. He is faced, however, with the task of developing a semi-structured sales presentation in order to make the best use of their skills—planning forms, information leaflets, and slide presentations have all been prepared to aid in the sales task. It is a matter now of putting it all together in the best possible form.

1. Assume that you are the sales manager. How will you proceed?

2. How can commercial kitchen equipment be differentiated? Explain.

3. If you were the president of Institutional Foods Inc., would you have taken another approach at differentiating your products?

SUGGESTIONS FOR FURTHER READING

Cash, Harold C., and William J. E. Crissy, *The Psychology of Selling,* Vol. 1 "A Point of View for Salesmen," (Flushing, N.Y.: Personnel Development Associates, 1965).

Greif, Edwin C., *Personal Salesmanship: New Concepts and Directions* (Reston, Va.: Reston Publishing, 1974), Chapter 10.

Sheth, Jagdish N., "A Model of Industrial Buyer Behavior," *Journal of Marketing,* Vol. 37 (October 1973), pp. 50–56.

Webster, Frederick E., Jr., "Modeling the Industrial Buying Process," *Journal of Marketing Research,* Vol. 2 (November 1965), pp. 370–376.

Willets, W. E., "Buying Decisions: Early Stage to Final Stage," *Purchasing,* Vol. 69 (December 1970), pp. 61–63.

THREE

Sales Strategy

Part III consists of four chapters dealing with sales strategy. Strategy is differentiated from tactics (which are examined in Part IV) in that strategy consists of the development of an overall plan of action, whereas tactics are the adjustments that must be made in the strategy at the time it is implemented. Therefore, a salesperson may have carefully designed a strategy for use with an account, but factors that he could not foresee will force him to make tactical adjustments at the time of the sales call.

In Chapter 7, "Planning in Selling," we discuss management's role in this process and the four key elements in planning: objectives, program, contemplated execution, and contemplated evaluation. We describe the planning that should take place before the salesperson calls on current customers, on prospective customers, or makes joint calls with other members of his firm.

In Chapter 8, "Influencing Individual Behavior," we deal with the strategy of influencing an individual's behavior. We point out that the universal objective in dealing with people is to accord them uniqueness—that is, the salesperson must make each of his customers and prospects feel that they are unique, important individuals. We also deal with trait analysis, which is designed to permit the salesperson to develop his strategy for an individual based on a series of personality dimensions.

Chapter 9 is entitled "Influencing Account Behavior." Here we focus on how the salesperson can influence account behavior. The salesperson must be aware of who the key decision makers are in the procurement process. We discuss several specific strategies for dealing with prospective accounts including trial orders, free samples, plant visits, and testimonials. We conclude by analyzing several of the more important outside influences that can affect the decision-making process.

In Chapter 10, "Prospecting—Generating New Business," we describe how the salesperson should prospect for new business. One excellent source for new business is existing accounts which can either buy more of what the salesperson has been selling them or can purchase products from the salesperson that they have not bought from him in the past. We also discuss eight ways in which the salesperson can generate new accounts. We conclude by analyzing various methods for routing sales representatives.

7. Planning in Selling

Ed Matthews, who sells greeting cards, was developing a strategy for his visit to Burton's Book Store in Denver. He wanted them to carry a line of greeting cards. He spent the first four days of the week visiting stores in the suburbs of Denver, and he planned to spend most of next week in Chicago at a trade show. If he was to achieve his objective of getting Burton's to place at least a trial order with him he must be able to convince Cynthia Carr, a hard-nosed aggressive buyer, and her boss, Mr. Burton, that they should place an order today for his greeting cards.

A salesperson must plan on a continual basis. He must determine which accounts he will visit each day, who are the key decision makers in the respective accounts, and how he will deal with each decision maker as an individual. Before we examine each of these specific applications of planning, it is important to understand management's role in planning and the nature of the planning process itself. We shall briefly examine these two topics and then concentrate on the procedure a salesperson should use for planning each call, and the cost-benefit tradeoff in planning.

MANAGEMENT'S ROLE IN THE PLANNING PROCESS

It is the exclusive prerogative of top management to define and set short-term, intermediate, and long-term goals that must be achieved if the firm's mission is to be accomplished. Top management alone (the chief marketing officer is normally a member) has access to all relevant information from within and outside the firm. Thus it is in the best possible position to determine the overall direction of the firm. Top management must account to the owners or shareholders for the quality of the firm's performance. However, top management must have inputs from the marketing department before it sets the firm's final goals. Invariably there is a two-way flow of communication before the planning process can occur. In our greeting card example, top management would probably make the final decision to develop a line of greeting cards to be sold through bookstores.

Marketing Management's Role

Middle and lower-level marketing executives play a role in top-level decision making by providing information to top management with regard to market and product opportunities and the activities of competition. In addition, these marketing executives must insure that the marketing effort is supportive of corporate objectives. An acid test of a firm's marketing plan is its congruency with and contribution to the firm's mission. If it does not meet this test, then the marketing department is out of line with the rest of the organization, and it must quickly readjust its efforts to comply with the overall objectives of the firm. In the greeting card example, the firm's marketing management would decide how the cards would be sold to bookstores, what markets the cards would be designed to appeal to, and how much advertising would be used to support the sales of cards to bookstores.

Sales Management's Role

Sales management provides critical information to marketing management concerning the sales implications and feasibility of marketing plans. However, once marketing management has determined its overall goals and plans, sales management must align its plans and strategies to insure achievement of the marketing objectives. Finally, each salesperson sets his plans for his market segment or territory so that they are congruent with the total sales plan of the firm. The more experienced and successful the salesperson is, the more he will be permitted to plan and operate in the manner he sees best for his specific sales territory. Most salespersons, although asked to submit their plans for regular examination and approval, have considerable freedom of action as long as their objectives contribute to the achievement of the total sales objectives, and ultimately to the corporate objectives of the firm. In our example, the sales manager would be responsible for planning such activities as how to allocate the sales force to the territory, how to hire and train salespersons to sell the greeting cards to bookstores, and how to compensate the salespersons for selling to bookstores. The salesperson would be responsible for planning the actual sales call.

The important point is that the planning process takes place at several levels within the organization. At each level, people from a lower level give their advice on how the firm should operate. However, once a decision is made at a particular level, the people on the lower level are expected to design plans that will accomplish the objectives of the next higher level. In the remaining portions of this chapter we will examine the planning process from the salesperson's perspective.

THE PLANNING PROCESS

The planning process consists of four interactive elements: *objectives, program, contemplated execution,* and *contemplated evaluation.* This process and the relationships between its elements are depicted in Figure 7-1. Although they are interrelated, we will examine each element individually.

Objectives

The first step in planning is to decide what is being sought. Let us assume that our greeting card salesperson, Mr. Matthews, has been calling on Burton's regularly for a year. Although the store personnel have expressed interest in his merchandise, Burton's has never been willing to stock it. Mr. Matthews' objective today is "to obtain a trial order for his merchandise."

If the salesperson's objectives are to be effective, they must meet five basic criteria. They must be (1) commercially worthwhile, (2) congruent with other objectives, (3) potentially achievable, (4) definite and concrete, and (5) have a reasonable timetable for achievement. Using our greeting card example, we shall apply each of these criteria to the objective of receiving a trial order to show how they apply to the planning process.

Commercially Worthwhile Objectives. The commercial venture for which objectives are being set must be potentially profitable. A trial order, though usually not profitable in itself, paves the way for additional orders and an ongoing profitable account. If, after analyzing factors such as the prospect's current

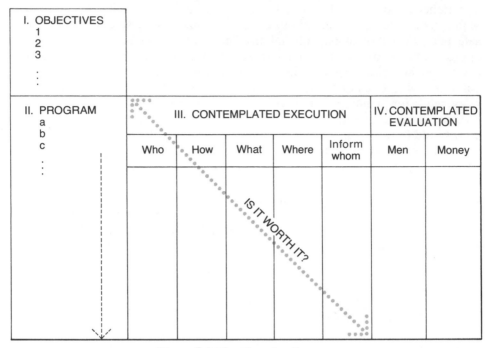

Figure 7-1 The Planning Process

needs and potential growth, Ed Matthews comes to the conclusion that Burton's will never be able to purchase enough of his greeting cards to provide a profit, he should not seek a trial order; and if the firm tries to purchase his products he should turn them down.

Although it is very difficult to say no to a prospective customer, a great many firms each year lose large sums of money by serving accounts that are not profitable and probably never will be profitable.

Congruent with Other Objectives.   This particular objective must fit in with the objectives the salesperson has set for the account. In turn, his objectives for the account must be aligned with his objectives for the territory, which also must be acceptable to the sales manager. In the case of a trial order, Mr. Matthews began his relationship with Burton's Book Store by providing them with information about his company and his product line. Once this information had been provided and the customer had developed some level of confidence in him, Mr. Matthews felt it was appropriate for him to ask for a trial order. The rest of the objectives that Mr. Matthews set for this account hinge on his getting a trial order on this particular call.

Potentially Achievable Objectives.   The salesperson must use his knowledge of the prospective account, of competitive conditions, and of the time, talent, and money resources available to determine if he has a reasonable chance of meeting his objective. All too often, a salesperson will continually push to get a trial order from an account when there is very little chance that he will obtain the business. In a situation such as this, the sales representative would be wiser to devote his time to other new accounts in which he has a reasonable chance of success. In our example, Ed Matthews has made four previous visits to Burton's over the last year. Three of these visits were made in conjunction with other calls in the Denver area, and thus did not take much of his time. However, Ed Matthews has decided that if he does not get at least a trial order this time he will quit calling on Burton's.

Definite and Concrete Objectives.   The objective must be precisely stated. When it is expressed in vague terms, there is little likelihood that it will be achieved. Continuing the example, notice that Ed has set his objective: to obtain at least a trial order for the greeting cards. This is far more definite than if the objective had been to obtain whatever business is available.

Timetable for Achievement.   There should be a definite timetable for achievement of each objective. This becomes increasingly important when the objective as set extends fairly far into the future. In varying degrees, all human beings suffer from procrastination. If a timetable is not set, there is a temptation to postpone action. Again using the same example, Ed Matthews set this call as the time to achieve his objective. He might also have as an objective to sell $5,000 worth of greeting cards to Burton's over the next six months, and $30,000 over the next twelve months.

Program

For each objective, the planner must think through the steps or events that must take place down the timetable into the future if that objective is to be achieved. These steps or events comprise the program, which to be effective must be *definite* and *understandable*. All individuals who will be assisting the salesperson must be aware of exactly what is to take place.

In addition, each step in the program should be allocated a definite amount of time; this is extremely important for long-term plans. In such situations, each step or event in the program becomes a subobjective to be achieved. Unless the timetable is adhered to, the total plan will not be completed on schedule.

Finally, the steps must meet the test of *sequentiality*. Each step as it is completed leads into the next one with a minimum amount of backtracking or overlap.

As the program is thought through, it may become necessary to modify the objective as originally spelled out. The planner may discover that too much effort or time would be required to achieve it. He then must change the objective or improve his program. Thus, interaction almost inevitably occurs between the objective as set and the program designed to achieve it.

Let us continue our example of Mr. Matthews. He designed a five-step program which he feels will permit him to get a trial order (see Table 7-1). It consists of (1) providing sales promotion literature to Burton's in advance of his call, (2) making a call appointment (3) explaining the advantages of his merchandise to Burton's key decision makers, (4) emphasizing to the key decision makers that the sale is an experiment and if it does not go as anticipated they have very little to lose, and (5) attempting to close the sale for a trial order.

Contemplated Execution

For each step in the program, it is necessary to think through *in advance* the best way of executing it. An important criterion here is that the planner must be anticipatory and farsighted with regard to eventualities that may arise and the alternative courses of action available to him. More specifically, contemplated execution involves thinking through the answers to the five questions presented below.

Who is the best person to do this?   The planner must answer this question for each step in the program. While the salesperson does most of his work on his own, there are occasions when he needs help from other people in his firm. For example, as Table 7-1 indicates, Mr. Matthews ask his sales-support personnel to provide Burton's with the appropriate promotion literature that will introduce this season's greeting cards. In addition, either he or his secretary will call Burton's to make an appointment. Normally, Mr. Matthews would want to do this himself since it adds a personal touch to the relationship. The last three steps in the program are performed by Mr. Matthews. Yet, there are situations where this would not be true—for example, Mr. Matthews' sales manager might accompany him on the call or he might arrange for Mr. Burton to visit his company's headquarters to talk with the firm's technical staff.

How should each step in the program be accomplished?   The effective planner takes advantage of successful past experience but also shows a willingness to innovate. Continuing the example of Mr. Matthews in Table 7-1, he accomplishes the first two steps in his program by mail and telephone, respectively. In the third step, which has been divided into four substeps, he accomplishes quick delivery by showing the proximity of his company warehouse to Burton's and providing references of customers who document that he has always provided quick delivery. Mr. Matthews demonstrates the proven stability of his merchandise by providing industry studies, which talk about his firm's sales growth, and by providing references and letters of recommendation. Mr. Matthews also discusses company policy of free display material and ninety-day credit.

What will be needed?   This is a question that every good administrator considers. The planner needs to think through the information, facilities, and resources required to accomplish each step in the program. In our example, Ed Matthews

TABLE 7-1 BURTON'S BOOK STORE

Program	Proposed Execution				
	Who	How	What	Where	Inform Whom
Provide literature in advance of call	Corporate sales-support staff	Mail	Well-documented current literature	From company headquarters	Schwartz
Make call appointment	Mr. Matthews or his secretary	Telephone	Names of key decision makers	From company headquarters	Williams
Relate advantages of products					
(a) Quick delivery	Mr. Matthews	References, location of warehouse	Letters of recommendation Map showing warehouses	At Burton's	Witt
(b) Proven salability	Mr. Matthews	Industry studies, references	Reprints of industry studies Letters of recommendation	At Burton's	Witt
(c) Free display rack	Mr. Matthews	Company policy	Pictures of display rack	At Burton's	Witt
(d) Ninety day credit	Mr. Matthews	Company policy	Copy of contract	At Burton's	Witt
Experiment for six months	Mr. Matthews	No long-term contract	Copy of contract	At Burton's	Witt
Close	Mr. Matthews	Logical close (discussed in Chapter 17)		At Burton's	Witt

needs well-documented and current sales promotion literature to accomplish his first step. The second step can be accomplished only if Matthews knows who the key decision makers are; his previous visits to the store have provided him with this information. In terms of the advantages of his merchandise, he will have letters of recommendation and a map showing the warehouses to prove he can provide quick delivery. For proven stability he will again supply letters of recommendation and reprints of industry studies. For the display rack and ninety-day credit, Mr. Matthews will show pictures of the display rack and a copy of the contract, respectively.

Where is the best place to accomplish it?   The salesperson often faces this question in deciding whether to pursue the objective on the customer's premises, his company's headquarters, or perhaps in some other place. In the trial-order example, the call is normally sought at the prospect's place of business; although, sometimes a visit to the firm's headquarters is most effective. Table 7-1 indicates that except for the first two steps, each of the remaining steps is carried out at the prospect's place of business

Who needs to know?   This is the final question that the planner must answer. In a business enterprise, individual plans tend to be interrelated. Each one is part of a larger plan. Thus, the planner must anticipate who needs to be informed as each step in the program is carried out. Continuing the trial order example, Matthews needs to get Mr. Schwartz's help in sending out the sales promotion literature and Ms. Williams's help to make the appointment for him. In addition, Matthews feels that Mr. Witt, his supervisor, should know what he is trying to accomplish and where he can be reached.

As the contemplated execution is completed for each step in the program, there are likely to be modifications of the actual steps and, in the extreme case, the objectives themselves may have to be modified. Thus, a second interaction exists in the planning process—that is, between programming and contemplated execution.

Contemplated Evaluation

This is the ingredient in planning that is most often omitted or treated too superficially. The planner needs to weigh the cost of each step in the program in terms of the talent and money required. Analytical and evaluative thinking of this kind insures against waste and increases the likelihood of profitable payoff. As the cost of each step is determined, it may be necessary to modify it, to change its execution, or, in the extreme case, to omit it altogether. Hidden costs exist in the use of talent; loss occurs if a greater level of talent is used than is required for successful execution of a particular step. Thus, the field salesperson must be evaluative in committing technical and managerial resources to problems with his accounts. Once the time and talent costs are aggregated for all the steps in the program and a conversion is made to dollars, the good planner asks,

"Is it worth it?" In other words, with one eye on his objective and the other eye on costs, he decides if the price is worth the commitment.

When a customer is asked to visit a plant, the talent commitments are a particularly important consideration. The salesperson's management team and the technical staff play a role in entertaining the prospect. If there are too many plant visits, the firm's personnel will find it difficult to accomplish their regular jobs. In the case of a sales call, the presumption is that the account's potential warrants the visit.

Reflection on this discussion of planning reveals that certain human qualities are essential in a planner. He must certainly possess *analytical* and *evaluative thinking*. This enables him to weigh the present situation and to set forth in orderly fashion a plan of action for the future. He must also have the *foresight* in order to anticipate eventualities. In a very real sense, a good planner is a good *forecaster*. Inasmuch as his plans are rarely completed without modification, the planner must have sufficient *flexibility* and *adjustability* to replan as necessary. Finally, the planner in a business setting needs *commercial judgment*. He must be able to weigh outcomes in terms of inputs to ensure that there is a profit.

PLANNING EACH CALL

The sales call is the keystone of effective selling. A salesperson may perform all of his other duties in superlative fashion; yet, if he is unable to conduct successful calls, he fails miserably. Also, each call represents a step in a larger plan that the salesperson has for the particular customer or prospective account. The sales call consists of three phases: *before*, or planning and strategy; *during*, or face-to-face tactics; *after*, or evaluation and followup. Obviously, a key input for the *before*-phase of planning a call is the *after*-phase of the last call to that individual. This information and experience enables the sales representative to make his next visit more effective. In the *during*-phase, replanning occurs as the salesperson adjusts to the unforeseen and the unanticipated. In the *after*-phase, the salesperson determines lessons learned and, in reality, begins planning his next call on the account even though it may be weeks or months away.

Planning Calls to Current Customers

In planning calls to current customers, the salesperson has many things in his favor. Certainly the most important of these is that he knows what the customer's problems are and how his products can be effectively used to help solve them. The salesperson also knows who his major sources of competition are and how much of the customer's business he is getting relative to the competition. The sales representative realizes that the only way to improve his position is to sell a larger quantity of what he is currently selling or to sell additional items in the line that the customer is not presently purchasing.

Before making the actual sales call, the salesperson should check over his last call report to determine if there were any unanswered questions, commitments made, or unfinished items that should be part of the present visit. In addition, he should review what he knows about each individual with whom he will be talking; this includes the individual's motivational patterns, outstanding characteristics, idiosyncrasies, position in the firm, and likely influence on purchasing decisions. The sales representative realizes that every person wants to be treated as a unique individual and that nothing is likely to turn the person off faster than a lack of personal interest and attention. Good recordkeeping enables the salesperson to be aware of the unique characteristics of each of his customers.

Planning Calls to Prospective Customers

In making a call to a prospective account, the salesperson's problem is incomplete information. He may not even know whom to see. Often his only insights are derived from secondary sources. He might not know what role the various members of management play in purchasing decisions, or who the company is currently doing business with, or what the firm likes about its current suppliers, or what problems the prospective customer has that he might be able to solve.

There are, however, several sources of information available to the salesperson before he calls on a prospective account. Such services as *Moody's, Standard and Poor,* and *Dun and Bradstreet* provide analyses on most of the firms that operate in the United States, and industry directories supply similar information for particular industries throughout the country. These data usually include the firm's financial status, its primary operating location, its major product line, and the name of the chief executive officer. If the salesperson's company does not have this reference material, it is available in most public libraries. In addition, the salesperson may know sales representatives of noncompeting companies who call on the prospective account. There is nothing unethical about the sales representatives exchanging ideas about a firm, including information about current problems and key developments.

The important point is that the salesperson who calls on a prospective account may not hope to accomplish more on his initial visit than to obtain information about the firm. However, it is still important for him to plan his call carefully so that he will ask the right questions to obtain the pertinent information and to appear knowledgeable and interested in helping the prospective customer.

Face-to-Face Tactics

To the extent that the salesperson has carefully planned his sales call, the face-to-face interaction of salesperson and customer is likely to go quite smoothly. There are, however, two factors—*people* and *competition*—that frequently upset even the best laid plans and force the salesperson to make adjustments during the sales call. Some of the common people factors include (1) finding the customer in an unanticipated mood, (2) not being able to visit with the customer, (3) being asked to make the sales presentation in front of several additional and unexpected individuals, (4) finding the customer interested in an aspect of the product for which he was not prepared, and (5) finding shifts in the firm's organizational structure that affect purchasing decisions.

Competitive factors that may force a shift in the sales representative's strategy include (1) unanticipated price changes, (2) new product break-throughs, and (3) changes in inventory policies, such as a willingness to take back all unsold or unused merchandise. The salesperson must tactically adjust to these changes within the constraints of his firm's policy and his own authority to act. In many situations, the salesperson will not have the authority to make adjustments in such factors as pricing policies. As a result, he will have to rely on the goodwill he has developed over the years to obtain a postponement in the purchase decision until he can check with the appropriate corporate officer. (In Part IV we treat sales tactics in considerable detail.)

Joint Calls

While the salesperson plans and conducts most sales on his own, occasionally he must plan for a joint call. This occurs either because the salesperson's supervisor schedules a "work with" period in his territory or because it is appropriate to bring additional personnel from his firm.

Supervisor-initiated Joint Calls.   When this occurs, the sales representative sometimes faces a difficult problem of preventing his boss from taking over during a face-to-face meeting with a customer. If the salesperson handles the call effectively on his own, the supervisor is likely to be impressed both by the knowledge the salesperson displays of the account and the care with which he plans his calls. It is the salesperson's responsibility to brief the supervisor so that the during-phase of each joint call goes smoothly. The salesperson may have more tolerance for joint calls if he recognizes that his boss has a responsiblity to observe his work and to evaluate it.

Salesperson-initiated Joint Calls.   Sometimes the sales representative initiates joint calls. This is usually to achieve some combination of the following objec-tives: (1) to reinforce his own personal selling effort, (2) to provide the account with technical information beyond the scope of his own knowledge, (3) to have someone in his own firm gain information on the customer's application of the company's product line, and (4) to help in the training of other sales representa-tives. In each instance, it is important for the salesperson to keep in mind that he is the account manager and that it is his responsibility to plan such calls. He must brief the other person sufficiently so that he can obtain the impact desired from the joint effort.

If the call objective is to reinforce his own selling effort, the salesperson is likely to bring in a member of his firm's management. To get maximum benefit from this, he should arrange, within the account, specific appointments with key decision makers. Then, as part of the before-phase, the salesperson can brief his associate on each person to be seen and what he hopes to accomplish with them.

If the objective of the joint call is to provide technical information, it is critically important in the planning stage to brief the technical person on the "people" as well as the "thing" side of the account. It is particularly important for the technical person to know the level of sophistication of each person with whom he comes in contact—otherwise, he may talk over the heads of the decision makers.

If the objective is to help someone within his own firm to get information, the sales representative should be judicious in which accounts he calls on—since the customer is providing a favor. The sales representative certainly does not want to upset a favorable selling-buying relationship with such a call. In addition, he must be sure to brief his colleague on the customer, and fill him in on the buying history of the account and the specific applications the account is making of the company's product line. It may also be pertinent for the salesperson to inform his colleagues about any directly competing products being used by the account. By doing this, tactful questions regarding these products can be raised, and comparative evaluations can be developed from the customer's point of view.

If training is the objective of the call, it should never be attempted at the expense of maintaining a favorable account relationship. The salesperson should brief the sales trainee fully before the face-to-face meeting. If the trainee is sufficiently advanced in his knowledge and skill to make presentations, they may be arranged in selected accounts in advance. The constructive criticism and suggestions of the customer may be solicited. Alternatively, such practice may be used on prospective accounts of low potential.

PLANNING TO INFLUENCE EACH ACCOUNT

With few exceptions such as normal order solicitation activities, every salesperson seeks to cultivate ongoing selling-buying relationships in his accounts. Therefore, the salesperson must formulate an account plan for each customer and each prospect.

With customers, the key objectives are to increase the share of business and to thwart competitive inroads. With prospective accounts, the objective is to initiate a mutually profitable selling-buying relationship. Each firm's growth objectives influence what mix of old and new business will be sought. Also, there is bound to be some account mortality. This is an additional incentive to generate new accounts.

The first step in customer account planning is for the salesperson to determine how much total business has existed there, not only for himself but for all competitors. He then relates what his own business has been in the account. The ratio of these two items tells him what his share of that market has been. Next, he must answer the question, "What does the future look like in this account?" This involves his forecast of the total business available in the time period for which he is now formulating plans and his prediction of what his business will be in the account. The ratio of these two figures will give him his projected share of business. Finally, he asks himself, "What is the trend?" For example, is the total business available increasing, declining, or holding steady? If there promises to be a sharp increase in business, he may have to allocate proportionately more effort to the account. In contrast, if the account's business appears to be decreasing he may lessen his efforts; in the extreme case, he may drop the account altogether. He notes the business he now has relative to his potential sales and the potential business in that account. If his projected share of the business in the account is greater than his current share, it means that he hopes for additional penetration of the account. If his projected share is less than his current share of the account, it means that he is gradually being displaced. Figure 7-2 provides a matrix which illustrates the relationship of the required information for individual account planning.

	Past	*Future*	*Trend*
Industry sales	Market ($)	Potential market ($)	Increase, decrease, no change
Company sales	Sales ($)	Potential sales ($)	Increase, decrease, no change
Company share of market	Market share (%)	Potential market share (%)	Increase, decrease, no change

Figure 7-2 Account Planning

This kind of thinking must also be applied to prospective accounts, although the salesperson has a less detailed basis on which to formulate his plans in such instances. He can, however, make a "guesstimate" of how much business currently exists in a given prospective account, what the future potential appears to be, and what the trends are. If he knows which competitors are now getting the business, he can also forecast the amount of business he hopes to cultivate during the period ahead. (Chapter 9 contains additional information on account planning.)

THE COST-BENEFIT TRADEOFF IN PLANNING

Planning is not without substantial costs to the salesperson and his firm. The planning process is indeed very complex and requires a substantial amount of time. This will become more evident in subsequent chapters.

As a result of the time pressure a salesperson is under, the total amount of planning he will do for any one situation will be a function of how much potential business he feels the prospect has to offer. As an example, an individual who sells paper and office supplies to a large department store will spend more time planning this call than he would for a call on a small neighborhood store in the suburbs.

SUMMARY

In this chapter we examined the role of planning in professional selling. We began with a discussion of top management's role in determining overall corporate objectives and how the marketing and selling plans must be interrelated with these objectives. We saw that while all levels take an active part in the planning process, once a decision is made, these levels are expected to design plans to accomplish the stated goals of higher management.

We described a successful planning process, which includes four key elements: *objectives, program, contemplated execution* and *contemplated evaluation.* Each of these elements interacts with the others.

We noted the differences that should be allowed for in planning calls on current versus prospective customers. We also provided a plan for analyzing the potential of accounts to determine the amount of resources to commit to each one.

We concluded by examining the cost-benefit tradeoff in planning each call. Some calls warrant a great deal of planning, and others do not.

PROBLEMS

1. What are the roles of top management, marketing management, and sales management in the firm's planning process? What role, if any, does the salesperson play in this process?
2. Explain in your own words what the key elements are in the planning process. In what ways do these elements interact?
3. What are the differences in planning calls on current customers in contrast to prospective customers?
4. Why might a salesperson initiate a joint call? What steps should he take prior to the joint call?
5. Why is it important for the salesperson to know his market share for each of his accounts?

Exercise 7

PLANNING IN SELLING

Objectives: To increase our understanding of the planning process.

                 To apply our knowledge of planning to the sales call.

A. Personal Application

What is the most important thing you hope to achieve tomorrow? Outline your plan, noting:

1. Your objectives:

2. Your program:

3. Your contemplated execution:

4. Your contemplated evaluation:

B. Call Planning

There are three phases to each call—*before, during,* and *after*. Indicate at least five considerations that are relevant to a *customer* call.

Before	*During*	*After*

C. Call Objectives

The following are statements of possible call objectives. Select the one you think best meets the criteria discussed in the text and develop a plan to achieve it.

1. To obtain more business.

2. To introduce one or more of our products.

3. To seek information about the account.

4. To convince the purchasing agent to test a sample of our product X compound.

5. To sell at least a trial order of our product Y compound.

Case 7-1 Mr. Richard Rogers

Mr. Richard Rogers is an independent insurance agent who owns his own agency in Schenectady, New York. He represents three of the nation's largest insurance companies. Each company writes a full range of insurance coverages including health, life, automobile, and home. Mr. Rogers is a highly ethical and successful insurance man who tries to put together the best package of insurance protection to cover his client's real needs.

Mr. Rogers has been a long-time member of the Schenectady Country Club. He was recently paired with Dr. Richard Cox, a casual acquaintance, in a Club golf tournament. The golf tournament took place over a three-day weekend. Although Rogers and Cox did not win the tournament they did place third, which was considerably higher than they expected. They enjoyed each other's company. They had several drinks together on Friday, and on Saturday their families had dinner at the Club together. After the victory banquet was over on Sunday night, Cox told Rogers, "Someday let's get together and pull some teeth and talk about my insurance needs."

Rogers learned quite a bit about Dr. Cox through their conversations and by talking with mutual friends. Cox had talked at length of his second love—hunting. He and two other dentists had purchased a lodge in Colorado several years before. As Cox described it, "The lodge really is not too lavish. It has five bedrooms, three baths, and a beautiful study. In addition, it has an unending view of the mountains. We rent the lodge out when we are not using it, and it's tax deductible."

Rogers also knows that Cox lives in one of the better sections of the city, and that he has three children, aged 3, 5, and 8. Rogers knows that Cox takes great pride in the kids. Several times during the tournament he mentioned their accomplishments and showed photos of his family.

Rogers knows that Cox owns only a small amount of life insurance. Cox told him that his parents gave him a paid up life policy for $24,000 when he graduated from dental school. Because his expenses were so high when he opened his practice he just did not have the extra money to buy any more life insurance. He also told Rogers, "Dick, speaking very frankly, I feel that many people buy more insurance than they really need. The rate of return on a whole-life policy is just too low to justify the expenditures involved."

Rogers has not yet decided on how, if at all, to approach Cox as a prospect. He knows in his own mind that Cox has a need for additional life insurance. He also knows that Cox surely has substantial home and automobile insurance needs. Too, Cox is a highly respected dentist in Schenectady who might be able to provide him with valuable contacts.

1. How should Rogers respond to Cox's statement concerning his insurance needs?
2. What planning should take place before Rogers calls on Cox?

Case 7-2 Joseph Shanks Of Austin

Mr. John Murphy, a sales representative for Joseph Shanks of Austin, is preparing for a very important sales call to Lake Travis West—a resort community located in the Texas hill country. Mr. Murphy has worked for Shanks for five years, and his familiarity with the Austin area has helped him become one of the store's more successful salespeople.

Joseph Shanks is a large furniture store which sells middle to upper quality furniture. Most of its business is with private individuals who purchase furniture for their homes. However, Shanks always bids on institutional orders such as banks, state office buildings, and large apartment complexes if the management feels they "have a reasonable chance of winning a profitable bid."

Lake Travis West is a resort complex being built on Lake Travis. When the first section is completed there will be eighty apartment units for rent. The developer plans to eventually develop two additional areas on Lake Travis West which will have 75 apartment units each. When the resort complex is finished it will have a full array of water sports facilities along with tennis, golf (an eighteen-hole course is currently under construction), and horseback riding. The complex is designed to cater primarily to wealthy families in Houston and Dallas.

Murphy had never made an institutional bid for Shanks before. He became involved in Lake Travis West because a fraternity brother of his, Jerry Jones, is handling the decoration and furniture selection for the complex. When Murphy told his boss, William Sinclair, that he had been invited to submit a bid for the furnishings of the apartments, Sinclair had told him to go ahead and that he would be pleased to help him with negotiations if necessary. Sinclair would have to approve the final bid before Murphy could submit it to Lake Travis West.

Murphy provided a great deal of technical assistance to his friend Jones. He spent countless hours working on room designs and furniture layouts. In addition, he investigated practically all the nation's major furniture manufacturers so that he would be able to get Lake Travis West the most furniture for their money. He presented four room "concepts," which included all the furniture, draperies, carpeting, and wall decorations. In order to give the complex some variety he suggested they adopt all four concepts, rather than just one room design for each of the apartments.

Murphy thought everything was going well until he got a call from Jones explaining that he had presented the four concepts and the total price to his boss, Mr. Caskey, whose initial reaction was: "the price is too high" and, "I just do not like the concepts Shanks has come up with."

Jones thought that it would be desirable to have a joint meeting between Mr. Caskey, Murphy, and himself. After Murphy related these developments to his boss, Sinclair suggested that it would be best for Shanks to be represented by Murphy, himself, and Bob Taylor—Shanks' number-one designer. (Taylor had worked on the concepts behind the scenes with Murphy so he was aware of them.)

Murphy was a little nervous about Sinclair going with him. He felt that Sinclair did not trust him with such a big order and this would give Sinclair a chance to observe him in action.

1. What role should each of the people from Shanks's play?

2. Should Murphy alert Jones of his fear of Sinclair?

3. What types of planning should go into this call on the part of the Shanks employees?

SUGGESTIONS FOR FURTHER READING

Christopher, William F., "Marketing Planning that Gets Things Done," *Harvard Business Review,* Vol. 48 (September–October 1970), pp. 56–64.

Else, Robert A., "Sales Planning: Selling by Measurable Objectives," *Sales Management,* Vol. 110 (May 14, 1973), pp. 22–24.

Gwinner, Robert F., "Base Theory in the Formulation of Sales Strategy," *Business Topics,* Vol. 16 (Autumn 1968), pp. 37–44.

Gwinner, Robert F., "Coordinating Strategy and Tactics in Sales Administration," *Business Topics,* Vol. 18 (Summer 1970), pp. 56–62.

Katzenbach, Jon R., and R. Champion, "Linking Top-Level Planning to Salesman Performance," *Business Horizons,* Vol. 9 (Fall 1966), pp. 91–100.

Kurtz, David., H. Robert Dodge, and Jay E. Klompmaker, *Professional Selling* (Dallas: Business Publications, 1976), Chapter 3.

Stern, Mark E., *Marketing Planning: A Systems Approach* (New York, N.Y.: McGraw-Hill, 1966).

8. Influencing Individual Behavior

The word *strategy* originated with the military, but today it has widespread usage. Political commentators often refer to the strategies of opponents in an election; sportswriters talk about the strategy used by a particular team. It has also become a part of the businessman's vocabulary; executives often speak of corporate strategy. We shall see that it is an invaluable concept to apply to the selling-buying process. But what does it really mean?

Strategy is the overall plan of action. It relates to the total plan being executed, as well as to key steps in the program. It is future oriented, although past events become an important input. A very successful corporate strategy occurred when the Ford Motor Company introduced the Mustang. The strategy was to provide a vehicle for those individuals who were "young at heart," regardless of age. The car was designed to be a sporty yet relatively inexpensive car that would appeal to the mass market.

In contrast, tactics are the adjustments and modifications to strategy that must be made when the unforeseen and the unexpected occur. In the example of the Mustang, if a customer asks for special wheel covers and an FM radio which are not original equipment on the car, the Ford dealer is able to tactically adjust and install the equipment himself. In selling, as in corporate planning, things seldom go exactly as planned.

In this chapter, we will examine the strategic planning that a salesperson must use to be in the best position to successfully influence the behavior of the *decision makers* or *influencers* within the account. While the next chapter focuses on the strategic implications of the *total account,* in this chapter we center on developing a *strategy* to deal with the *individual* apart from his product-related needs. We emphasize the universal objective in all interpersonal relations of according uniqueness; typecasting and trait analysis as alternate ways of analyzing people; persons who are difficult to understand; factors that influence a salesperson's effectiveness; and the interaction that takes place between the customer and the salesperson.

THE UNIVERSAL OBJECTIVE

The universal objective in all interpersonal relations is to *accord uniqueness.* The reason for this is that each person has a strong quest for individuality. As a result, those who are able to accord this individuality are likely to exert influence. Thus, the sales representative's primary strategic task is to realize and appreciate the uniqueness of each person he calls upon. To see the significance of this objective, reflect on a situation in which you were the prospect or customer.

To respond to this drive for uniqueness, many successful salespeople maintain a file on each individual they visit. Figure 8-1 illustrates an example of a customer file. This file usually includes such background variables as age, position, hobbies, buying habits, education, and unusual or particularly strong personality traits. It also might include dominant motives of purchase. This information is refined and amended as new insights are gained. If other personnel in the salesperson's company contact this person, their observations are added. With the number of people a salesperson meets and with the diverse characteristics each displays, it is foolhardy to try to remember such details. Therefore, before a visit, a good salesperson will review the customer's file, and afterward he will add any new information he might have learned.

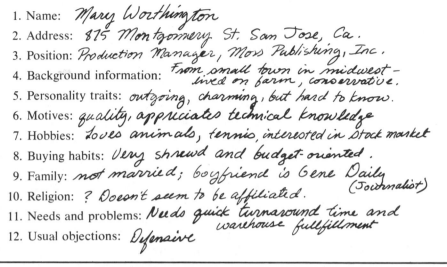

1. Name: *Mary Worthington*
2. Address: *875 Montgomery St. San Jose, Ca.*
3. Position: *Production Manager, Moss Publishing, Inc.*
4. Background information: *From small town in midwest – lived on farm, conservative.*
5. Personality traits: *outgoing, charming, but hard to know.*
6. Motives: *quality, appreciates technical knowledge*
7. Hobbies: *loves animals, tennis, interested in stock market*
8. Buying habits: *Very shrewd and budget-oriented.*
9. Family: *not married; boyfriend is Gene Daily (Journalist)*
10. Religion: *? Doesn't seem to be affiliated.*
11. Needs and problems: *Needs quick turnaround time and warehouse fullfillment*
12. Usual objections: *Defensive*

Figure 8-1 Example of a Customer File

TYPECASTING

When asked to describe an individual, all too often we respond by making a comment such as "He is an extrovert," or "He is shy." This is typecasting the person. We are trying to place him in some *a priori* system. Although this approach is of some use in comparing one individual with another, it is of little help in planning a campaign to influence a particular person. The task is to learn *what makes that person different,* not what he has in common with other people.

There are several important reasons why typecasting fails.[1] First, it tends to mask rather than highlight the variety of characteristics of an individual. When an individual is classified as an extrovert, all of one's attention tends to focus on this characteristic rather than on the many other facets of the individual's personality. In addition, there are vast differences in the gradations of characteristics. To use the example of extrovert-introvert once again, there are few people who truly represent one extreme or the other; most people fall somewhere in between. Finally, typecasting permits the person making the statement to change the basis of classification from one individual to another. The same person might describe one acquaintance in terms of physical features, another by his mannerisms, and still another by his attitudes. This results in describing one person as tall, another as reactionary, and a third egotistical. Such a nebulous

[1]H. C. Cash and W. J. E. Crissy, *Psychology of Selling,* Vol. 4 "Personality and Sales Strategy" (Flushing, N.Y.: Personnel Development Associates, 1965), pp. 27–31.

system cannot be very useful in developing principles for dealing with prospective customers when the objective is the same in all cases—to influence the person to buy!

TRAIT ANALYSIS

An alternative to typecasting is trait analysis. This approach recognizes that people have multifaceted personalities. Although all human beings have personality and behavioral traits in common, no two people are alike, because they differ in the amounts they possess of these traits. In using trait analysis, the first task is to identify those traits that the other person possesses in an extreme amount, as compared to people generally. These are the traits that set him apart as a unique individual.

Three categories of traits are of primary concern: (1) those that describe the person's intellect, knowledge, and background—the "what" of his behavior; (2) those that describe his personality—the "how" of his behavior; (3) those that describe his motivations—the "why" of his behavior. To the extent that these traits can be identified in the customer, the salesperson has a basis for his strategy in dealing with him. From another standpoint, it would be impossible for a sales representative to accord a person uniqueness if he did not know what characteristics made the individual unique. Table 8-1 presents 96 traits which help to evaluate an individual. We will examine the various inputs for trait analysis, relating traits to strategy, grouping traits into patterns of behavior, and mapping strategy on the basis of behavior patterns.

Inputs for Trait Analysis

Many factors influence the accuracy with which traits are identified. The most important factor is the sheer amount of evidence on which the analysis is based. Everytime the salesperson calls upon a person, he increases his knowledge about that person. In fact, as he completes the call he should ask himself, "What have I learned about this person that I didn't know before I saw him today?" Some traits are manifest almost immediately, whereas others do not become evident until later.

Factors that Influence the Inputs to Trait Analysis.   Seeing a person under a variety of circumstances may bring out traits that otherwise would not be manifest. For example, light talk over lunch may reveal avocations and interests that would never come to the surface in a more formal atmosphere. Likewise, a prospect may behave far differently at an industry meeting than he does behind his own desk. Thus, it is important to observe a person under varying conditions to get as full a trait picture of him as possible.

TABLE 8-1 COMMON TRAITS TERMS TO HELP SIZE UP PEOPLE

1. adaptable / inflexible	25. depressing / stimulating	49. imaginative / plodding	73. progressive / reactionary
2. affected / natural	26. derogatory / complimentary	50. imitative / original	74. rash / cautious
3. alert / sluggish	27. distant / friendly	51. inexperienced / sophisticated	75. realistic / self-deceiving
4. apathetic / enthusiastic	28. estranged / sociable	52. industrious / indolent	76. reliable / undependable
5. argumentative / agreeable	29. evasive / frank	53. interests-wide / interests-narrow	77. remorseful / conscienceless
6. ascetic / sensuous	30. excitable / calm	54. intuitive / logical	78. rude / courteous
7. autocratic / democratic	31. extravagant / thrifty	55. irreverent / pious	79. sarcastic / gentle
8. benevolent / malevolent	32. extreme / temperate	56. jealous / well-wishing	80. satisfied / displeased
9. blundering / tactful	33. fatalistic / self-controlling	57. leisurely / hurried	81. self-pitying / Spartan
10. boastful / self-effacing	34. feminine / masculine	58. light-eater / gluttonous	82. self-respecting / shameless
11. bold / retiring	35. fluent / inarticulate	59. loyal / unfaithful	83. self-sufficient / dependent
12. bungling / clever	36. forbearing / complaining	60. mature / childish	84. sensitive / callous
13. charming / repugnant	37. foresighted / hindsighted	61. modest / conceited	85. sincere / hypocritical
14. cheerful / gloomy	38. formal / informal	62. moody / stable	86. strong-willed / suggestible
15. complacent / ambitious	39. forgetful / retentive	63. naive / shrewd	87. talkative / close-mouthed
16. confused / clear-thinking	40. frigid / amorous	64. negativistic / agreeable	88. teetotaler / alcoholic
17. considerate / selfish	41. gay / serious	65. open-minded / opinionated	89. treacherous / trustworthy
18. conventional / non-conforming	42. generous / stingy	66. opportunistic / non-exploiting	90. trusting / suspicious
19. co-operative / obstructive	43. grateful / ungrateful	67. optimistic / pessimistic	91. unconcerned / curious
20. courageous / cowardly	44. habit-bound / venturesome	68. persuasive / yes-man	92. unrestrained / inhibited
21. crude / polished	45. harsh / mild	69. pliant / stubborn	93. unsure / self-confident
22. cruel / affectionate	46. honest / deceitful	70. practical / theoretical	94. vacillating / decisive
23. defiant / obedient	47. humble / overbearing	71. practical joker / considerate	95. vindictive / forgiving
24. deliberate / impulsive	48. humorous / somber	72. price-minded / quality-minded	96. worrying / indifferent

Source: Harold C. Cash and William J. E. Crissy, *The Psychology of Selling Series*, Vol. 4, "Personality and Sales Strategy." (Flushing, N.Y.: Personnel Development Associates, 1965), pp. 56–58.

Another factor that is bound to influence the accuracy with which traits are noted is the degree of attentiveness toward the other person. The salesperson is likely to arrive at a more accurate assessment of the customer if he goes into the call well prepared and with a conscious objective of learning all he can. If the salesperson has to direct too much of his attention inwardly to think about what to say or do next, he cannot give full attention to the other person; and hence he misses cues concerning that person's behavior.

Because of these factors, it is important when making a trait analysis of a person to ask the question, "What evidence do I have for each of the traits I have identified?" The evidence for each trait is likely to be a combination of *manner cues* (style of behavior) obtained by observation as well as *matter cues* (information generated by inquiry). Generally speaking, manner cues are much more important than matter cues in arriving at an accurate assessment of the other person's personality and motivational characteristics. These nuances of reactions are usually not within that person's conscious awareness.

Evidence is important because it lessens the tendency to "type" the other person. Also, as evidence accumulates, refinements and changes can be made in assessing traits.

The Role of the Third Party.   Depending on circumstances, the sales representative may learn some things about the customer by questioning other people who have had contact with that person. Of course, caution must be exercised in using this source of information, because a third party's opinion may bias the salesperson's own judgment favorably or unfavorably and lessen the likelihood that he can approach the customer with an open mind. More often than not, however, another person's viewpoint is useful. Inasmuch as perception is both subjective and selective, the third party might observe some aspects of the customer's behavior that the salesperson might miss. Therefore, it is probably sound practice for the salesperson to check with other people in his own firm who have had contact with those he is seeking to influence.

Relating Traits to Strategy

The salesperson's next task is to consider each prominent trait he has identified and then ask himself, "Knowing this, what should I do or avoid doing?" It is important to remember that the salesperson will have examined a large set of traits, but he is only interested in those that help identify the particular individual as a unique human being.

Figure 8-2 lists the dominant traits of a customer, Mr. Quickslip. How would you deal with him? Write down how you would react to each of his traits, and then compare your responses with those set forth below.

---

1. Intelligent
2. Technically Competent
3. Intrinsic Interest in Technical Aspects
4. Dominant
5. Bold
6. Impulsive

Figure 8-2 Characteristics of Mr. Quickslip

Intelligent. If the customer possesses a superior amount of intelligence, the salesperson may reason on the basis of this trait that he does not need to go into great detail in making his presentation. If he hits the highlights, Mr. Quickslip, being very intelligent, will fill in the specifics. The salesperson may also reason that he had better be prepared for searching questions. In fact, part of his preparation for the call may very well include trying to anticipate difficult questions that are likely to be asked so that he can have answers ready.

Technically Competent. If Mr. Quickslip is also very knowledgeable concerning the technical aspects of the salesperson's product, the salesperson might use technical jargon peculiar to the products and services. It also forewarns the salesperson that he had better be extremely well prepared himself on the technical aspects of the presentation. He certainly should not attempt to give glib answers to any technical questions.

Intrinsic Interest in Technical Aspects. In addition, if Mr. Quickslip is extremely interested in the technical aspects of the product, the salesperson could explore the proposition in depth without losing his attention. Knowing his great interest and superior knowledge and experience, the salesperson may question Mr. Quickslip on his views about the technical side of the product and related services rather than attempt to give him information with which he is probably already familiar.

Dominance. If Mr. Quickslip has an outstanding amount of dominance in his personality, he would react adversely if the salesperson cited favorable experiences that other customers had with the product. Instead, the salesperson might well capitalize on this trait by seeking the prospect's opinion about the product and by encouraging him to be the first to use it. This strategy would certainly be sound if, as an additional characteristic, the salesperson sensed that Mr. Quickslip was striving for status in his industry and prided himself on scoring firsts.

Bold.   If Mr. Quickslip is a bold individual, there is every reason to believe not only that he is confident in his actions but that he will be willing to try new things that many prospective customers would feel were too risky. As a result, when the salesperson has a truly new product with substantial promise, Mr. Quickslip would be a good prospect for it.

Impulsive.   Finally, if Mr. Quickslip can be described as impulsive, the salesperson should be able to close the sale more quickly than he might with a more deliberative customer. This does not mean that the salesperson should push Mr. Quickslip too fast. However, when it becomes apparent he has thought over the proposition and is favorably disposed to it, the salesperson should try to complete the sale.

The salesperson thus has the task of thinking through his best course of action relative to each distinguishing characteristic he has identified in the customer. However, the salesperson must also recognize that this is an analytical procedure and that he is dealing with a whole person—not with an aggregate of separate traits. His next task is to synthesize his knowledge about the person into a description of him as a unique individual.

Grouping Traits into Patterns of Behavior

The salesperson must now go back to his inputs—those dominant traits that describe the "what," "how" and "why" characteristics that give the prospect his uniqueness. The salesperson must ask himself, "Which of these traits interact with one another?" "Which ones suggest a common strategy?" Looking at Mr. Quickslip again, superior intelligence plus in-depth knowledge of the technical aspects of the product and an intrinsic interest in such matters constitute an interactive pattern of traits. In addition, the traits of dominance, boldness, and impulsiveness constitute a second interactive pattern. Once these patterns are identified, the salesperson is ready for the next step: mapping his strategy.

Mapping Strategy on the Basis of Behavior Patterns

The salesperson plans his strategy on the basis of *patterns* of behavior. By reviewing each *individual trait,* he knows what to do and what to avoid. Referring again to Mr. Quickslip, the combination of superior intelligence, an unusual amount of technical expertise, and an intrinsic interest in the technical aspects of the product might call for the strategy of a high-level, carefully conceived, technical presentation. The combination of dominance, boldness, and impulsiveness might suggest that the salesperson give Mr. Quickslip an ample amount of time to participate in the sales presentation. If the salesperson does more listening than talking, the customer may easily sell himself the product. Finally, this combination of dominance, boldness, and impulsiveness suggests that Mr. Quickslip might be interested in purchasing products that provide new ways of solving old problems. He probably has confidence in his own decision-making ability, and may be willing to purchase the product without a great deal of fanfare on the part of the salesperson.

PERSONS WHO ARE DIFFICULT TO UNDERSTAND

The method suggested above for mapping strategy and influencing the prospect or customer may seem thorough and straightforward, but in actual practice these principles are sometimes difficult to apply. There are three basic reasons for this: lack of psychological maturity on the part of the customer, the customer's reluctance to actively participate, and individual differences from one customer to another.

Psychological Maturity

A lack of psychological maturity usually manifests itself in inconsistencies of behavior. In such a situation, the customer's reactions are highly unpredictable. It is difficult to know where he stands because he does not know himself. His thought processes are not orderly. Instead, he jumps from idea to idea. Frequently, there is a lack of emotional control; hence, behavior is impulsive and based on feelings of the moment. Going back to our distinction between strategy and tactics, it is clear that such a person presents a tactical rather than a strategic challenge.

Active Participation

Another factor that influences the effectiveness with which strategy can be formulated is the extent to which the customer participates. It is difficult to plan strategy for dealing with the unreactive person. As you enter the selling situation you cannot really tell how you are progressing in your relationship with the unresponsive individual. If such a person is encountered, it is important in mapping strategy to ask, "Why is this person unreactive?" A cosmetics salesperson cites this example of drawing out the unreactive person: When the cosmetics buyer failed to react, the salesperson asked, "What have I done to cause you to dislike talking with me?" The other person pointed out that the salesperson parked his car directly in front of the store on each visit. The buyer had mentally reserved the spot for customers.

Individual Differences

The salesperson must recognize that there will be individual differences in the degree to which there is personal acceptance by the people with whom he is dealing. Whereas the salesperson will generally be able to maintain a comfortable, productive, and well-informed relationship with those individuals with whom he has established good rapport, it is difficult for him to obtain in-depth insight into a person with whom mutual confidence and respect have not been established. It is not easy to make headway when the prospect does not particularly like the individual who seeks to influence him.

Just as individual differences in traits exist among people, so each person shows internal differences in the amount he possesses of various human qualities. There are some persons who have no readily apparent outstanding traits. Inasmuch as the key inputs for individual sales strategy are the outstanding traits of the customer or prospect, when none is apparent it is difficult to plan a strategy. If a salesperson encounters such a person in his territory, he faces a real challenge in trying to acquire inputs for his strategy. He must establish a wide variety of situations in which such a person can be observed. Eventually, circumstances will be discovered that draw the other person out and make manifest heretofore hidden qualities.

FACTORS INFLUENCING EFFECTIVENESS

How effective a salesperson will be in planning strategy to influence a particular individual depends on many factors. The most important one is that he be sufficiently attentive to the other person's behavior to observe subtle differences in reactions. Failure to do this means that he is likely to miss cues and hence misjudge the prospect or customer.

Similarly, projection can bias one's assessment. An individual is prone to see his own traits, especially those he considers desirable, in each person with whom he interacts, whether they are there or not. Furthermore, when such traits are actually present, they may bias his judgment about other characteristics of the individual. This is why we emphasize the importance of having adequate evidence for the trait analysis and remaining objective and open-minded about the person being analyzed.

Friendliness on the part of the salesperson increases the likelihood of establishing rapport with the other person. In turn, this creates a climate in which there is mutual confidence and interaction. Again, caution must be used.

A broad cultural and social background can also help in understanding the prospect or customer and planning strategy to influence him. The broader the salesperson's background, the more likely it is that he will share experiences in common with the other person. This common ground creates a favorable climate in which interaction can occur. Also, breadth of background provides him with an appreciation of the great diversity of reactions that are encountered with the people he contacts.

Finally, there is a natural tendency for the salesperson to engage in *type* thinking rather than *trait* thinking in analyzing the customer. This comes from the tendency to aggregate specific information into a generalized concept or type of individual. For instance, it is more difficult to remember that a customer has four specific traits, such as clever, stingy, formal, and alert, than simply to recall that the customer is economy minded. Each of us desires a definitive, simple answer with regard to human behavior—including our own. Conscious effort is required to remain open-minded about each person to be influenced.

CUSTOMER – SALESPERSON INTERACTION

Once the salesperson examines the customer or prospect from the perspective of trait analysis, he should direct most of his efforts to those with whom he has the best chance of interacting in a positive manner. Although this evidence is not completely conclusive, a number of studies have indicated that the more similar the salesperson and the customer are, the more likely it is that a sale will result from the meeting. Four of these studies are discussed in detail below.

Initial Research

Research in this area began with two sociological studies. The first study[2] found (1) that salesclerks perceived customers who rejected the store's merchandise as rejecting them personally, and vice versa; (2) that customers who were in a hurry felt that the salesclerks were not interested in them; and (3) that salesclerks who felt secure about themselves were more likely to feel that the customer really needed their help. The second study[3] examined the relationship between waitresses, their customers, and the cook. This study found that the higher the social class of the customer, the less personal and friendly was the waitress. In addition, if the waitress and the cook had an argument, she frequently would take out her feelings on the customer by being discourteous and providing poor service.

Life Insurance Salespersons and Their Customers

Selling life insurance is considered to be one of the more creative types of professional selling. Research suggests that the life insurance agent is likely to be perceived as better trained, more honest, less agressive, and less high pressure than the automobile salesperson or the real estate sales agent. One study by Franklin Evans[4] found that most consumers believe there are relatively few differences between the policies of the major life insurance companies. Therefore, the particular insurance agent who calls on a given person is very important in determining whether or not a sale will be made.

The main hypothesis of Evans' study was that the more similar the life insurance salesperson and his customer were, the more likely it was that a sale would result from their meeting. The areas studied by Evans included social, economic, physical, personality, and communicative characteristics of both individuals.

[2]George F. Lombard, *Behavior in a Selling Group* (Boston: Harvard University Press, 1955).

[3]William F. Whyte, *Human Relations in the Restaurant Industry* (New York: McGraw-Hill, 1948).

[4]Franklin B. Evans, "Selling as a Dyadic Relationship—A New Approach," *American Behavioral Scientist,* Vol. 6 (May 1963), pp. 76–79.

TABLE 8-2 INTERNAL PAIR SIMILARITY OF SUCCESSFUL AND UNSUCCESSFUL SALES
REPRESENTATIVES AND THEIR PROSPECTS

Characteristic	Successful Sales Representatives (Percentage)	Unsuccessful Sales Representatives (Percentage)	Total (Percentage)
Salesperson same height or taller than Prospect	32	68	100
Salesperson shorter than Prospect	28	72	100
Salesperson same or better educated than Prospect	35	65	100
Salesperson less educated than Prospect	23	77	100
Salesperson and Prospect less than nine years apart in age	33	67	100
Salesperson and Prospect more than nine years apart in age	25	75	100
Salesperson earns same or more than Prospect	33	67	100
Salesperson earns less than Prospect	20	80	100
Salesperson and Prospect either both smokers or both non-smokers	32	68	100
Salesperson and Prospect have different smoking habits	26	74	100
Salesperson and Prospect have same religion	32	68	100
Salesperson and Prospect have different religions	28	72	100
Salesperson and Prospect have same political party	35	65	100
Salesperson and Prospect have different political parties	27	73	100
Prospect perceives Salesperson's religion the same as his own	36	64	100
Prospect perceives Salesperson's religion different from his own	28	72	100
Prospect perceives Salesperson's political party the same as his own	48	52	100
Prospect perceives Salesperson's political party different from his own	20	80	100
Total Dyads	30 (45)	70 (104)	100 (149)

Source: Franklin B. Evans, "Selling as a Dyadic Relationship—A New Approach," *American Behavioral Scientist,* Vol. 6 (May 1963), p. 77.

Table 8-2 indicates that the successful sales representatives were, indeed, closer to their clients than were the unsuccessful sales representative. This is true in terms of physical characteristics (age, height), of other objective factors (income, religion, education), and of personality-related variables (politics and smoking). It is also interesting to note that the perceived similarity of religion and politics was much higher and of seemingly more importance to the sale than was the actual similarity.

Role Consensus between Buyer and Seller

Another study, By Tosi,[5] examined the effect of buyer-seller role consensus and the success of the salesperson. Role consensus is the degree of agreement between two individuals regarding behavior in a particular situation. One would anticipate that when two people agree on the normative behavior for a particular situation, they will find it much easier to get along with each other. In the selling situation, it would seem reasonable to hypothesize that if the buyer and seller agreed on the role of the salesperson, the seller would find it easier to make a profitable sale. As an example, if both parties to the transaction feel the salesperson should provide and set up promotional displays for the retailer, agreement is more likely to be reached on other aspects of the sale as well. Tosi determined that when the buyer perceives that the salesperson's performance matches his own concept of what the "ideal" salesperson's performance should be, the customer will maintain contact and limit his purchases to a relatively small number of sources whose sales representatives meet these criteria. On the other hand, if the customer does not feel that the salesperson's behavior is close to what an "ideal" salesperson's should be, he will look to a large number of sources to buy the product.

Tosi concluded by stating that the "customer's level of expectation seems to be a necessary but not sufficient condition for effective selling performance. That is, the more similar the customer and the salesperson are in terms of expectation the more likely a sale will result."[6] These findings complement those of Evans regarding the similarity of physical and objective factors with respect to the customer and the salesperson. This, of course, does not mean to imply that a salesperson should only call on prospects that are similar to himself. Many sales result from calls made on customers who are very much unlike the salesperson. However, a good salesperson will attempt to minimize the differences between himself and the customers in the areas that he has some control over. As an example, if he is a smoker and the customer is not, he should not smoke while calling on the customer. In addition, if he has different political views than the customer, he should keep them to himself. Almost always there are some areas, such as hobbies or children, where both people have enough in common that the salesperson can emphasize the communality between himself and the customer rather than their differences.

---

[5]Henry L. Tosi, "The Effects of Expectation Levels and Role Consensus on the Buyer-Seller Dyad," *Journal of Business*, Vol. 39 (October 1966), pp. 516–529.

[6]*Ibid.*, p. 529.

SUMMARY

In this chapter we differentiated between strategy and tactics in relating to other people. Strategy is the overall plan of action, whereas tactics are modifications in strategy (tactics are discussed in detail in Part IV).

We pointed out that the universal objective in dealing with people is to accord them uniqueness. Each person has a need to feel he is a unique individual. To the extent that the salesperson can make each of his customers feel this way, he will find it much easier to accomplish his sales objectives.

We outlined four steps for dealing with each potential customer. They are (1) to identify his outstanding traits, and to document each with evidence, (2) to decide what to do or avoid doing, (3) to group traits into patterns, and (4) to develop the appropriate sales strategy.

We discussed certain characteristics that make some individuals difficult to understand or influence. As an example, customers who are psychologically immature or unresponsive to the salesperson's inquiries make it almost impossible for the salesperson to develop a strategy to effectively influence them. In addition, we examined several factors that positively influence the salesperson's effectiveness.

Finally, we cited several studies which indicate that the more similar the salesperson and the customer are in terms of background, personality, and motivation, the more likely it is that a sale will result. This knowledge supplements the salesperson's knowledge of the customer's traits and makes it easier for him to successfully complete the sale.

PROBLEMS

1. Differentiate between the concepts of strategy and tactics.
2. How do typecasting and trait analysis differ?
3. Assume that you are a life insurance salesperson and that you are planning a strategy to influence a friend of yours to buy insurance. Select this friend and do a complete trait analysis of him. How does this vary from how you might have typecast him?
4. Referring to your answer to Problem 3, was the person you selected difficult to understand for any of the three reasons stated in the text? If so, how did you overcome the problem?
5. What are the implications of the studies by Evans and Tosi?

Exercise 8

INFLUENCING INDIVIDUAL BEHAVIOR

Objective: To illustrate trait analysis and sales strategy.

A salesperson notes that a key decision-maker on one of his accounts possesses each of the traits in Column 1, in extreme amount. In Column 2 indicate for each listed trait the evidence that might underlie it. In Column 3 indicate for each listed trait what the salesman ought to do or avoid doing.

Trait	*Evidence*	*What to Do or Not to Do*
Intelligent		
Quantitative thinker		
Widely read		
Able conversationalist		
Honest		
Religious		
Charitable		
Mature		
Self-possessed		

Trait	Evidence	*What to Do or Not to Do*
Sincere		
Sociable		
Friendly		
Sensitive		
Empathic		
Industrious		
Open-minded		

Now indicate the traits that form *patterns* of behavior and what the salesperson's strategy ought to be.

Patterns	Strategy

Case 8-1 The Madison Glove Company (A)

The Madison Glove Company manufactures high quality industrial gloves. Its products are used by many firms to protect their employee's hands from harsh objects or high temperatures. In addition to its standard line of gloves, the company regularly designs special-order gloves to fit a customer's unique problem. The firm's gloves range in price from $1.50 per pair for its regular workgloves to $65.00 per pair for its thermal insulated gloves. The company always felt it should have a complete line of products, but that it had the most to offer over competition in the high price, high quality lines.

Joseph Baker has worked for Madison as a salesperson for twenty-one years. He calls on a number of accounts, including Claymore Steel, Inc., which is a steel service center located in Houston, Texas. Steel service centers handle about 20% of the nation's total mill output. They in turn sell to firms that require smaller quantities than can be furnished directly by the manufacturer.

Mr. Baker has done business with Claymore for five years, yet he has never had more than 25% of their glove business. The purchasing agent, Mr. Waxley, has resisted Mr. Baker's efforts to obtain a larger proportion of their business.

Mr. Baker decided that he must obtain more business soon from Claymore or he will have to discontinue selling to the firm. His cost of calling on Claymore is too high to continue his present sales efforts. Baker has done a trait analysis on Mr. Waxley, and feels that Waxley's outstanding traits are the following: estranged, impulsive, agreeable, alcoholic, frigid, narrow interest, special interest in family, serious, evasive, self-sufficient, unconcerned, and low mechanical ability.

1. How do you suggest that Mr. Baker deal with each of these traits?
2. Develop a strategy for dealing with Mr. Waxley.

Case 8-2 Victor Publishing Company

Victor Publishing Company is a small firm located in Madison, Wisconsin. It specializes in texts for the college or university social science market. Victor has been quite strong in psychology and sociology for the past decade. Four years ago the company published two texts in economics which were aimed at the senior level undergraduate courses. These were marginally successful and are currently under revision.

Two years ago, Victor contracted for a principles of economics manuscript written by two professors at the University of Tennessee. The book is now available in page proof forms and the final text will be published in two months. Although the "principles" market is very competitive, Victor feels it needs to have such a text to begin rounding out its economics offering, and the company's economics editor is hopeful the text will do quite well. The text is somewhat shorter than those of the competition, but the editor feels it is tightly written. In addition, there are several short cases at the end of each chapter, which is unusual for economics books. Finally, the book is very current and devotes more content to socioeconomic issues rather than the standard topics found in economics texts (e.g., national income accounts and price theory).

Selling books to professors is a very unusual type of selling. First, professors are frequently given complementary books with the hope that they will adopt them for their own classes. Very few books are ever sold directly to faculty members. In addition, the selling activity must be very low key. Each professor must feel that he is deciding for himself what he will use in his courses. As a result, the textbook salesperson spends a great deal of his time just trying to make each of his accounts aware of what the firm has. In addition, he tries to point out the key points that make that particular book different and better than any others.

Janice Spence has been employed as a salesperson for Victor Publishing for eight years; she has called on her current accounts for the past five years. Ms. Spence is preparing to call on Dr. Robert Gibson, who teaches a night class in Principles of Economics to 450 undergraduates at Detroit University.

Ms. Spence has been calling on Dr. Gibson for two years and feels she knows him rather well, yet she has never been able to get him to adopt any of Victor's economics books. She has just completed an in-depth trait analysis of Dr. Gibson, and feels he has the following characteristics: strong willed, deliberate, rude, self-confident, distant, cautious, hard-working, derogatory, repugnant, autocratic, formal, conceited, argumentative, and industrious.

1. What advice would you give Ms. Spence on how to approach Dr. Gibson?

2. Do a complete trait analysis of Dr. Gibson.

3. What do you feel are the chances that Ms. Spence will get Dr. Gibson to adopt Victor's new book? Explain.

SUGGESTIONS FOR FURTHER READING

Cash, Harold C., and William J. E. Crissy, *The Psychology of Selling,* Vol. 4 "Personality and Sales Strategy," (Flushing, N.Y.: Personnel Development Associates, 1966).

Evans, Franklin B., "Selling as a Dyadic Relationship—A New Approach," *American Behavioral Scientist,* Vol. 6 (May 1963), pp. 76–79.

Garman, Ronald H., "Role Conception and Purchasing Behavior," *Journal of Purchasing,* Vol. 7 (February 1971), pp. 57–71.

Hanan, Mack, "Manpower Management: Getting to Know the Customer Better than He Knows Himself," *Sales Management,* Vol. 106 (May 1, 1971), pp. 58–60.

Tosi, Henry L., "The Effects of Expectation Levels and Role Consensus on the Buyer-Seller Dyad," *Journal of Business,* Vol. 39 (October 1966), pp. 516–529.

9. Influencing Account Behavior

Most field salespersons have businesses and organizations as customers and prospects rather than individuals. Even the salesperson calling in the home should view the family as a buying unit or "account." Consequently, the salesperson's strategic objective is to accord *uniqueness to the account*. This begins with the salesperson's strategically sound treatment of each individual decision maker in the account (see Chapter 8), but it encompasses more than that. The salesperson must be aware of each decision maker's role in the organization and learn from him not only what his personal needs are but what the needs of the firm are *as he pictures them*. We will focus on the types of information a salesperson should have before he calls on his accounts and the strategic implications of calls on current and prospective accounts.

IMPORTANT INFORMATION FOR THE SALESPERSON

Account strategy is often difficult to determine because the salesperson lacks information in two vital areas: the account's procurement policies, and the degree of competition that he faces. The successful salesperson will make every effort, within the bounds of professional ethics, to obtain these types of information.

Procurement policies

Account strategy is often complicated by the fact that the formal organizational structure of the company does not necessarily reflect the decision-making process within the organization nor is it apparent who has ultimate authority to purchase. One question that is useful in determining this information is: "Who, besides yourself, must approve this type of a purchase?" Notice that the question is not aimed directly at the current purchase under discussion. This permits the customer or prospect to avoid the question if he wishes. However, most customers who have some rapport built up with the salesperson will answer the question by stating specifically who in the firm must approve the purchase under consideration. In this way, the salesperson will not seem pushy, and yet he will learn a great deal about who, under what conditions, has the authority to make the purchase decision.

It is also necessary to learn as much as possible about the operation of the company. The salesperson needs in-depth knowledge of the account's procurement policies and procedures, as well as of the departments that are likely to use his product. He has to see how his offering fits in with the firm's mission. If the prospective account is a manufacturer, the salesperson must discover how his products and services fit in as ingredients or components of the company's products and services. He may be able to demonstrate that using the products he offers gives the firm differential competitive advantage in its own markets. If the company is a reseller, the salesperson may show how his offering enhances or rounds out the product-service mix of the reseller. Often the service offered the reseller is assistance in the promotion of the line to ultimate purchasers. As another example, cosmetics sales representatives can make slight product mix changes so that their line can fit into parts of the store other than the cosmetics department, such as in sports equipment, sportswear, and high school and college fashions.

Level of Competition

The salesperson must also learn who the direct and indirect competitors are. He must find answers to such questions as, "How much business of the kind I am seeking does each competitor enjoy?" How long has each competitor been doing business with the account? "What is each competitor doing to develop and sustain his place in the account?" The salesperson must make a detailed study of each competitor to determine strategic areas in which he can achieve the greatest advantage. This information also enables the salesperson to answer questions and objections that the customer may raise as a result of experience with competing products and services.

Most of this information about accounts and competitors must be generated by the salesperson through observation and inquiry, although his firm may acquire some knowledge through executive-level contacts, marketing research, and trade and industry sources. He may gain some of it, too, by interrogating noncompeting sales representatives and reading trade publications.

In addition, the salesperson can make reasonably accurate estimates of required quantities of a product by calculating the quantity of goods manufactured or sold by the customer or prospect. Most employees of a customer or prospect account will react favorably to a request for a tour of their premises. This affords the salesperson an opportunity to observe what goods are in inventory, what production lines are running, and the volume of outgoing orders. He may also engage in casual conversation with plant supervisory employees—a source of information not otherwise available. Even though such personnel do not contribute directly to purchasing decisions, their unfavorable comments can block purchases.

STRATEGY IN CUSTOMER ACCOUNTS

It is good business for the salesperson to devote his primary efforts to existing customers. Firms do not want new accounts generated at the expense of those already established. In customer accounts the strategic objective is to *render the account as invulnerable as possible to the inroads of competitors*. The stance is protective. This does not mean that the salesperson may not seek to cultivate and increase the amount of business, but his prime concern is to prevent any loss of business.

All too often a salesperson feels there is more potential business in his competitor's accounts than in his own accounts. As a result, he expands his business by opening up new accounts. Unfortunately, the salesperson frequently fails to realize three key points. First, he has a limited amount of time. He can not possibly be all things to all people; he can not properly serve all the accounts in his territory. Second, while the salesperson is out generating new business, one of his competitors may be lining up one of his present accounts. If the salesperson fails to realize this, he will not give enough attention to his present accounts, and as a result, they will become vulnerable to competition. Third, it will take him a great deal of time and effort to establish a positive relationship with the prospect's key decision makers and to understand the prospect's buying process. This process has already been accomplished with his present accounts, and the salesperson should make every effort to capitalize on it.

Interaction Among Key Decision Makers

The interaction among decision makers is illustrated as "who's who" in Figure 9-1. In a particular account the salesperson is likely to have one member of the "who's who" he views as his key entry point (in Figure 9-1, the purchasing executive). The salesperson usually begins his round of calls with this person. However, he also makes an effort on each visit to see the plant manager, the director of research, and the store manager. He has determined that these persons influence which products are purchased. He also assumes that each of his competitors has identified this "who's who" and is seeking an entry point into it.

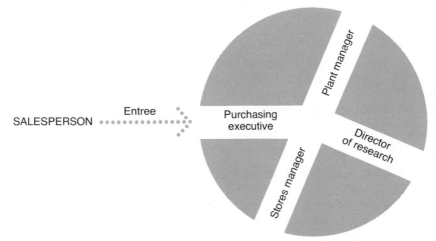

Figure 9-1 "Who's Who"

The salesperson reasons that, all other things being equal, each competing salesperson is seeking to identify the person *who is least pleased with things as they are*. He is the one most vulnerable to the overtures of the competitor. Accordingly, the salesperson makes every effort to leave no weak link in this people cycle. The salesperson also is on the lookout for "comers" in the organization—persons who will be part of the "who's who" in the future. He knows that if he can cultivate these persons now he has an advantage when they move up and can contribute to the buying decisions. The salesperson is also alert to any impending shifts or changes in the organization that may influence the composition of the "who's who." He needs to eliminate those who no longer have a role in decision making, as well as to spot successors in the group.

Movement of the Product or Service

The salesperson must be aware of the cycle of events that his products and services move through in each organization he sells to. This is the "what's what" (Figure 9-2). The steps are set forth for the same organization as in Figure

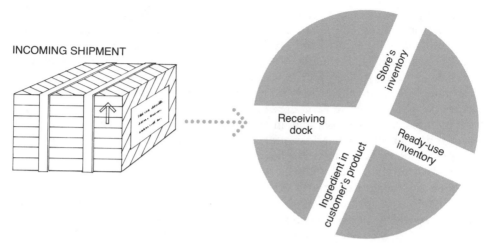

INCOMING SHIPMENT

Receiving dock

Store's inventory

Ready-use inventory

Ingredient in customer's product

Figure 9-2 "What's What"

9-1. The salesperson determined that purchased goods arrive by common carrier on the receiving dock of the company, and are then moved to stores inventory. As the merchandise is needed, it is moved to ready-use inventory on the production line. These goods then become an ingredient in the company's products. In a customer account the strategic stance is protective. The salesperson must insure that no troubles or difficulties arise as his goods pass through these steps. In fact, he may be able to show that his products, in contrast to those of his competitors, are easier to unload and require far less handling in getting them into inventory. He may be able to demonstrate that they are easier to stack. He also may have learned that on the production line greater uniformity of quality from batch to batch in his own firm's goods results in fewer stoppages of production. Whatever the situation may be, he knows that each competing salesperson is seeking any weak spot in the "what's what" cycle of events. In customer accounts, then, the objective is to prevent trouble. This means that the salesperson must thoroughly follow through on all transactions.

STRATEGY IN PROSPECT ACCOUNTS

Even though maintaining present customers is critically important to the salesperson, there are times when he will want to prospect for new accounts. This may occur because he might occasionally lose an account to a competitor, or after examining his total situation, he feels he can afford the time to open new accounts while keeping his present customers satisfied. With prospect accounts, the salesperson is the outsider trying to get in. The strategic objective is to find some way to change the present situation. His first task is to identify the decision makers, those who comprise the "who's who." As he calls on each of them, he seeks ways and means of showing them that they are not as well off by purchasing from his competition as they believe they are. In customer accounts, the major emphasis is on *posttransactional satisfaction*. In prospective accounts, the emphasis is necessarily *pretransactional*. No orders have been placed yet. The salesperson is looking for a key entry point into the decision-making team. If he is unable to locate such a person, he may have to take a longer-term view and place his emphasis on the "comers" in the account. If, however, he is successful in locating one or more persons in the current decision-making team who are favorably disposed to what he is offering, he then attempts to make each of these persons an internal salesperson who, it is hoped, can influence the other decision makers who are satisfied with the firm's present suppliers.

The salesperson must also concern himself with the "what's what." His objective is to find difficulty or trouble in the present situation. For example, he may gain entry by suggesting an improved work method on the production line, even though he has been unable to demonstrate product superiority as such.

Specific Strategies

The salesperson has several specific strategies open to him in his efforts to convert the prospect into a customer. These can be used singly or in combination, as the salesperson deems appropriate on the basis of the information he has gathered.

Differential Competitive Advantage.   In his initial efforts, the salesperson may push an item in his product line which has the greatest differential competitive advantage compared to the goods now being purchased. It may not be the product with the greatest volume or profit potential but one most amenable to dramatic presentation. Once the prospective customer sees the advantages of the first product, it is hoped that he will be favorably disposed to buying the rest of the salesperson's product line. The important point is that the salesperson uses the product that "looks" best compared to competition to sell the rest of his product line.

Trial Order.   Under certain circumstances, the salesperson may settle for a trial order. This means that the customer is willing to purchase enough of the product to test under actual conditions in his organization, but he is not ready to commit his firm to the purchase of large quantities of the product. If this procedure is followed, the salesperson must make sure his goods are given a thorough objective test on a comparative basis with the products now in use. Ideally, the salesperson should be on hand for such testing. This provides him with an excellent opportunity not only for observing and inquiring about procedures in the prospect account, but also for establishing face-to-face contact and interchange of ideas with people in the firm other than his entry person.

Free Sample.   Another possibility, but not quite as desirable as the trial order, is to furnish the prospect with a sample for testing purposes. It is axiomatic that what individuals or firms get for nothing they are likely to treat as having no value. Thus, if samples are furnished it is even more imperative that the salesperson be sure they are tested and that he is furnished with the results. The salesperson must also be wary that he does not supply free goods beyond those needed for trial and evaluation.

Plant Visit.   In some situations it is sound strategy to invite one or more decision makers in the prospective account to make a plant visit. This affords an opportunity to give them VIP treatment and to show off the spectrum of people and physical resources backing up the salesperson in the field. Guests on such occasions are likely to feel an obligation to at least give a fair trial to the offerings of the host company. Another advantage of this is the opportunity that can be provided for technical personnel from the prospective account to meet and exchange ideas with the specialists in the salesperson's firm.

Technical Assistance.   If the potential in the prospective account warrants it, the salesperson may, on a speculative basis, commit technical assistance to the prospect on problems that are of concern to him. If this is done, the salesperson must plan the arrangement with care. He must brief his technical people on the "people" as well as the "thing" aspects of the account. It is important for them to realize that their knowledge and efforts are being committed with the hope of generating a lasting selling-buying relationship. It is important that they build favorable personal relationships with their colleagues in the account.

Testimonials.   Recognizing the impact of testimonials from satisfied users, the salesperson may arrange a visit to a customer's installation. This has the advantage of letting the prospective customer see the product under "real world" conditions. He will have a chance to talk not only with plant executives, but with the people who are responsible for the day-to-day handling of the product. Such a visit obviously requires advance clearance and careful planning with the customer. The salesperson must also make sure that the customer he chooses will have prestige in the eyes of the prospect and that the visit will not prove disruptive to the customer.

There are other forms of testimonials that the salesperson might find useful. For example, he might ask a satisfied customer to write a letter of introduction or recommendation for him to a prospective customer. Or he might ask the satisfied customer if prospective customers could telephone him for a recommendation.

However, there are three important problems with any testimonial. First, the customer may feel it is improper to make recommendations about a salesperson to someone outside of his company. Second, the satisfied customer, to be effective for the salesperson, must be well known and respected in his area of business. If he is not, the recommendation will not carry much weight with people outside his company. Finally, the salesperson may misread the signals from his supposedly satisfied customer. If the customer is not really satisfied, it could be disastrous for the salesperson to use him for a recommendation.

The salesperson must, of course, use good commercial judgment in the efforts he expends to open a new account. The important thing he must remember is that "you can't win them all." He must know when to quit as well as when to persist. Sometimes a salesperson becomes so ego-involved in the challenge provided by a prospect that he devotes undue effort to his attempt to gain an order. If he were more rational, he would realize that the same energies expended in other directions might provide far more business than he could possibly achieve in that single account.

Timing Strategy in the Account

It is naive for the salesperson to assume that each decision maker has equal influence on what is purchased. It is equally naive to assume that the influence of each decision maker remains constant with them. For example, if an account is experiencing difficulty in meeting production schedules, it is likely that the plant manager will have a major voice in purchasing, and the source that offers time- and labor-saving ideas is likely to command major consideration. As another example, if a firm is encountering difficulty in meeting its marketing objectives of volume and profit, it is likely that the marketing vice-president will have much to say about the products and services being purchased. In this situation a supplier who can offer advice and assistance with the pressing marketing problems facing the company is likely to get the order. As still another example, if a company is finding it increasingly difficult to obtain the necessary skilled labor for its operation, the industrial relations director may have a strong voice in purchases. Here, the vendor firm that offers products and services that are "idiot proof" and labor saving may have the competitive advantage. For a final example, recurrent in the case of resellers, if the customer or prospect account is having financial problems brought about by a lag in its own receivables, a financial vice-president may become an important decision maker and support the supplier who offers the most favorable terms. The salesperson is thus challenged to maintain a current picture of conditions in each account and to formulate a strategy based on them.

Outside Influences on Strategy

If we ended our discussion of account strategy at this point, we would be oversimplifying the selling-buying relationship. Regardless of what is being considered for purchase, it is unlikely that final buying decisions are arrived at independently of outside influences. Factors such as the degree and types of competition, trade relations, multiple sourcing, and publicity all play important roles in the purchasing decision process. The salesperson must understand these factors if he is to be successful.

Competition.   The ingredients in each competitor's promotional mix—*personal selling, advertising, sales promotion,* and *merchandising*—exert varying degrees of influence on each member of the decision-making "who's who." This means that the salesperson must not only be alert to his own firm's promotional forces, but also to those being used by each competitor. The successful salesperson will continually ask himself what *differential advantages* he has compared with each competing salesperson and what *differential advantages* his firm has over its competitors. In this way the salesperson not only will learn what he should stress in his presentations, but he will also be keenly aware of the specific points his different competitors are likely to use to sell their products. As an example, if company A's advantage is its delivery time, then Company B's salesperson will not want to talk about delivery; rather, he will want to stress other important areas, such as after-the-sale-service. However, if Company B's salesperson were competing with Company D, who had extremely slow delivery, then he might wish to stress the importance of his firm's three-week delivery schedule.

Trade Relations.   Reciprocity, or trade relations, is another external influence in many industrial sales situations. This refers to the fact that a company may buy from a given supplier because that firm is a customer for the company's goods and services. The salesperson may then face one of two strategic situations. The first is where he can take advantage of the fact that his company buys from the customer or prospect; the other is where he has learned that a competitor is gaining advantage through reciprocity. If the first situation prevails, the salesperson has another potential source of information about the company he is calling on—namely, his own purchasing department and others who have become involved with procurement. He can also find out what volume of business the account enjoys with his firm. He is then in a position to use this information as reinforcement in the case of the customer account and as a basis for entry in the case of a prospect account.

   If he learns that reciprocity exists with one or more of his competitors, his strategy is to show the customer that he may not be buying the best products for his firm and to imply that captive purchasing is not profitable purchasing. He may challenge the purchasing department to carefully examine his product against the competition's products. (This procedure is called value analysis and is discussed in detail in chapter 18.)

Multiple Sourcing.   Another external factor is multiple sourcing. This occurs when the customer or prospect allocates shares of its business among a number of vendors. This, too, poses two distinct sales situations: (1) where the salesperson now has an assigned share of total business, and (2) where he is the outsider trying to get in. In the first instance, the salesperson's objectives are likely to include obtaining an increased share of the total business. To accomplish this he must show that buying a fixed share from him has limited benefit for the account. The first step in formulating the appropriate strategy in the second instance may be to find out on what basis the allocations have been made.

Generally speaking, this purchasing policy is justified by a firm not wishing to become too dependent on its suppliers. Proponents also cite the disadvantages that would occur if a natural catastrophe (such as a flood or fire) or a man-made one (such as a strike) were to curtail or even eliminate supplies from a sole source. It is also argued that by having several suppliers there will be competition among them to provide maximum value.

The salesperson desiring a larger share of the business may build his strategy around the economic stability and favorable labor conditions of his firm as well as the savings that would result if larger orders were placed with him. In the second situation, the salesperson's strategy may center on the prospect's unwarranted assumption that he is now doing business with the best combination of sources. In this instance, the salesperson may seek a trial order or even ask that a free sample be evaluated in comparison with the products now in use.

Important Companies and Individuals.   In every market there are likely to be "spheres of influence" who set the purchasing patterns. These persons and accounts warrant an effort to cultivate them beyond their direct payoff. If a salesperson can establish a selling-buying relationship with several of these in each part of his territory, he has a real promotional asset. A sales manager once referred to these prestige accounts quite appropriately as his "unpaid sales force."

Publicity.   Another important outside influence is the unsolicited favorable publicity that may, from time to time, be accorded in the public media. The salesperson must be alert to this when it occurs so that he can exploit it with both customers and prospects. He also must be able to offset the impact of a competitor's good press. A number of years ago a major oil company received widespread national publicity for its "drive safely" efforts. In one state the governor declared a day in honor of the firm. This resulted in an immediate boost in the firm's market share!

It is also important in today's world for the salesperson to be able to handle unfavorable, and at times unfair, criticisms of his firm. When publicity is unfavorable but true, the salesperson should admit that, like most human beings, people in his company make some mistakes. Hopefully, he will be in a position to assure the customer that his firm is doing all it can to correct past errors and to see that they do not occur again. However, if the criticisms are truly unfair and unfounded, the salesperson should respond to questions about the problem area by stating clearly and unemotionally, within the bounds of good taste, why the publicity is in error.

Account strategy gets even more complex when the nature of the marketplace is such that two or more independent individuals or firms become directly or indirectly involved in purchasing decisions. The following examples illustrate some of the complexities that exist in the areas of consumer and industrial goods.

CONSUMER-GOODS EXAMPLE

A pharmaceutical salesperson seeks to influence each of three physicians who practice noncompetitive medical specialities and who share a common suite in the Medical Arts Building. The salesperson has several products that fit the practice of each of these men, as well as some general-purpose pharmaceuticals that each of them might have occasion to prescribe. In formulating his strategy, the salesperson assumes that these three physicians discuss common professional problems and that each one exerts influence on the prescribing habits of the other two to some degree. However, this is not the total situation facing the salesperson. It also involves two local hospitals with which these physicians are affiliated.

The salesperson has the task of influencing each of these institutions to place his products on the formulary (approved list) of the hospital pharmacy. In each institution he has a "who's who" to influence. This may include the chairman of the formulary committee, the hospital administrator, the chief pharmacist, and the purchasing agent. Assuming he is successful in each hospital, the salesperson still has not concluded his task with these physicians.

He must also make sure that the local retail drugstores patronized by the physicians' patients stock his products. If a physician prescribes one of his products and it is not in stock, the pharmacist may call the physician for permission to substitute with a competitive drug. Thus, in turn the salesperson must influence the "who's who" in each retail drugstore so that his products are in inventory. If the salesperson allows a weak spot to develop in this external "who's who" and "what's what," he can be reasonably sure that the competitor will discover and exploit it.

INDUSTRIAL-GOODS EXAMPLE

The same kinds of complications caused by independent individuals or accounts interacting in consumer-goods buying decisions also occur in the industrial sector of the economy. For instance, a salesperson representing an air-conditioning equipment manufacturer seeks to have his equipment purchased for a new office building. He learns about the impending construction from a newspaper article describing the land purchase and noting the names of several realty developers and an insurance company who are jointly engaged in the undertaking. His task is to identify and penetrate the "who's who" in each of these participating firms. It is his job to show each of them the benefit of designating his firm as the preferred supplier. However, the likelihood is that the persons called on will indicate that they are going to be guided by the recommendations of their architects when that firm is appointed. The salesperson then has the objective of learning who this is, hopefully before his competitors do.

The sales representative's next step is with the firm of architects. Obviously, the needs and wants of the architecture firm are quite different from those of the promoters. It may be that the salesperson will seek to give technical assistance to the architecture firm in designing the air-conditioning system of the projected building. Certainly, the salesperson would want the resulting design to incorporate his own firm's products. At a minimum, he would hope that the design would be such that his products and services would have a competitive advantage.

The next step would be to learn which contractors are likely to get the contract for the building. Several will probably put in bids. At this stage, the salesperson has the task of cultivating each of these general contracting firms. Again, he is likely to encounter a unique pattern of needs, different from those of the architectural and financial interests. Each general contractor may then have his own views about the subcontractor he will want to work with in the event he gets the building contract.

When the bid is finally let, the salesperson must call on each firm involved to insure, if he can, that he gets the business. Notice in this example that it is not enough for the salesperson to achieve favorable results internally in each of these varied firms; he must see each of them as a part of an interlocking, decision-making whole. It would not be unusual in a case such as this for the sales effort to extend over a period of one or two years. It also might happen that thousands of dollars of technical assistance would be committed on a speculative basis. The external "who's who" and "what's what" in a situation such as this could undergo many changes from the time the salesperson made his first call on the financial interests to the day when an order was finally obtained.

SUMMARY

Just as it is with individuals to be influenced, so it is with accounts: the salesperson's stragetic objective is *to accord uniqueness*. To accomplish this, the salesperson must identify the decision-making group—the "who's who." He must also know the steps his products (and those of competitors) go through following purchase—the "what's what." Finally, he needs to find out as much as possible about direct and indirect competition in each account.

In customer accounts the strategy is protective, that is, to make the situation impenetrable by competitors. The salesperson emphasizes the *post-transactional* phase, a personal follow-up designed to maximize satisfaction. In contrast, in the case of prospects, sales strategy is aimed at disturbing the *status quo* and thus gaining entry. Six specific methods were suggested for opening new accounts.

Circumstances and priorities within each account change with time, and modifications in strategy must be made accordingly. In addition to internal influences, there are numerous external factors that affect strategy—the competitors' promotional efforts, trade relations or reciprocity, multiple sourcing, spheres of influence in the market, and publicity.

In many markets each transaction involves influencing two or more individuals or firms that operate independently of one another. Trade relations or reciprocity may be a factor. Also, large users may allocate shares of existing business among several suppliers. Strategies for handling such conditions were described, using as examples consumer goods and industrial goods.

PROBLEMS

1. Differentiate between the strategy used in customer accounts and that used in prospect accounts.
2. What are some of the pitfalls in relying on other persons (e.g., noncompeting sales representatives), for information about an account?
3. How important are the external influences on account strategy? List the most important external influences.
4. About which of the internal influences on strategy would it be easiest to obtain information? Most difficult to obtain information? Explain.
5. Which external influence on strategy would be most difficult to counteract? Why?
6. Referring to the industrial-goods example in the text, what are some of the changes that might occur during the time the salesperson is engaged in the project?
7. What are the most important differences, from the salesperson's perspective, between a trial order and a free sample?

Exercise 9

INFLUENCING ACCOUNT BEHAVIOR

Objectives: To obtain a salesperson's views about account strategy.
To compare this with what was learned from the text.

You are to interview a salesperson* and learn how he penetrates each account in sufficient depth to achieve effectiveness. Cover all questions set forth below, supplementing each where necessary to obtain full response.

Name of salesperson _____

Company _____

Product line _____

1. Who are your key customers and prospects?
2. In the largest accounts, how many people must be seen?
   What positions do they hold?

   a.

   b.

   c.

   d.

*May be arranged in class

3. In a new account, how do you determine which persons to see?

4. What kinds of things do you try to find out about each person?

5. How do you learn about the competition in these accounts?

6. What steps do products such as yours pass through once they are purchased?

7. What kinds of problems or difficulties might occur at each step?

8. How many calls are typically required before you obtain the first order?

9. Please describe the sales strategies you used to obtain a specific new major account.

Case 9-1 United States Post Office*

Mr. Gilbert Welks, a United States Post Office Customer Service Representative, is planning his sales approach to Crampton and Denton, a large stock brokerage firm. Crampton and Denton (C&D) has a number of branches located across the United States, and Mr. Welks feels it has a definite use for the Postal Service's express mail service.

One of the more popular of the Postal Service's new "products" is express mail. This service can be described loosely as a combination of registered mail, air mail, and special delivery based on a set pick-up time at the client's location and a guaranteed time at the delivery point. The service is rather expensive. As an example, the door-to-door service from Chicago to New York is $25.00 The guarantee furnished a mailer by the Postal Service consists of refunding the charge in the event the shipment is delayed.

Competition for express mail consists of a number of carrier services specializing in the careful handling of vital, timely material. Flying Cargo is a typical carrier organization which is occasionally used by Crampton and Denton. C&D simply calls Flying Cargo by phone and a courier comes to the office, picks up the pouch, and makes all of the necessary arrangements for handling, including delivery. Flying Cargo bills C&D at the end of each month and is on time about 85% of the time. Its charge from Chicago to New York is $11.25. The companies in this field are usually rather marginal as the competition is severe and many companies fail within a year.

Crampton and Denton is one of the many brokerage firms situated in a large Eastern city. C&D has recently opened up a number of branch offices in principal cities in the United States. As its geographic territory has grown, the problem of transporting documents on a timely and reliable basis has also grown. Time is extremely important in light of the volatility of the stock market. C&D is also concerned with the competitive pressures from other brokers who are expanding their efforts to attract smaller investors. C&D currently operates twenty-six branches and customarily has important daily messenger transactions in both directions.

Mailing and other messenger transactions of C&D are coordinated by the mailroom supervisor, Harry Esser. He reports to Patrick Lindsey, Director of Administrative

*This case was taken in part from a case developed by Donald D. Curtis, "Gilbert Weeks (A)" University of Virginia UVa:M-113R

Services of C&D. Mr. Lindsey's supervisor is Dale Holden, Vice President of Finance. Usually, the daily operating decisions are made by Esser, although he is restricted from making contract commitments for the company. Under C&D's policy such commitments are to be recommended by Mr. Lindsey for the approval of Mr. Holden.

Prior to making his first call on C&D, Mr. Welks did as much research as possible on the company by looking through their mailing records, and asking the postmaster to suggest people who know something about C&D. He gathered bits and pieces of information about people within the company. For example, he learned that Harry Esser is interested in health foods. He learned who would ultimately make the decision on whether or not to change its mailing policy.

On his first call to Esser, Welks specifically brought up the subject of health foods, and instead of suggesting a coffee break, they both went to a local health food restaurant and had carrot juice. In these relaxed surroundings some of the problems in the mailing of timely information to the branch offices of C&D were discussed. The highest priority for C&D was to have its mail in the hands of its account executives (stock brokers) before the opening of the stock market.

From his first call, Welks was able to determine the company's mail needs, and he obtained an estimate of the mail volume which might be converted to express mail. As he left this first meeting, Esser arranged for an appointment for Welks to see Lindsey and Holden.

1. What strategy should Welks use to gain the C&D account?
2. Should he handle the three C&D people differently during the meeting?

Case 9-2 The Madison Glove Company (B)*

Mr. Baker is attempting to design a strategy that will increase the sale of Madison Glove's products to the Claymore Steel Company. There are four individuals who play a role in purchasing at Claymore. These are Waxley, the company's purchasing agent; Fitzgerald, the plant foreman; Cardoza, a senior blue-collar worker; and Claymore, the owner of the steel service center.

Baker has already identified Waxley's traits (See Case 8-1). In addition to these, Baker feels that Waxley is generally interested in buying a quality product. Waxley is proud of stating, "I always feel that a few extra dollars buy a great deal of value." From his own experience, Baker knows that Waxley has been willing to trade-up in the products he buys from Madison when Baker was able to make a reasonable case for a better product. Finally, Baker feels that although Waxley has full authority to make purchasing commitments for Madison, he is reluctant to buy merchandise that has not been requested and "tested" by that part of the service center which will use the merchandise.

Mr. Fitzgerald wants a high-quality product, but he is also very concerned with price. He wants his employees well protected, yet his unit is charged with the product.

*The reader should examine the Madison Glove Company (A), Case 8-1, before analyzing this case.

Therefore, if Waxley buys more costly products than the men really need it comes out of Fitzgerald's budget not Waxley's.

Fitzgerald is also critically interested in delivery and inventory maintenance and control. Twice last year his men lost half a day's work because they ran out of heavy-duty steel reinforced workgloves. This occurred because the supplier does not have a warehouse located in the same town as Claymore. In addition, if Claymore had kept better records and control over its own inventory of workgloves this situation would not have developed. Finally, Baker knows that Fitzgerald is a real detail man. Whenever Baker has needed to talk with Fitzgerald, he sets up a lunch date because there are so many interruptions in Fitzgerald's office. These lunch dates present at least a minor problem because it is well known that Waxley does not approve of operations people being entertained by salespersons.

Mr. Cardoza is a well-respected long-term employee of Claymore. He is also the son-in-law of Fitzgerald. Although he does not have any direct management responsibility, it is generally felt that when Fitzgerald retires in 3 years, Cardoza stands better than an even chance of becoming foreman. Cardoza is frequently consulted informally by Fitzgerald about operations problems, and he would be the one who would oversee any tests on Madison's gloves.

Mr. Claymore is the owner and manager of the service center. He is not involved in these types of purchasing decisions as long as the merchandise is multiple sourced. Claymore feels that multiple sourcing is bound to keep the situation more competitive and assures the firm the most for its money. If a product is to be single sourced he wants to know precisely what his firm will gain from such a deviation from company policy.

The company is currently purchasing its gloves from four different glove firms. The standard gloves that Madison sells to Claymore cover direct expenses but do not contribute to profits or overhead. The competitors are good companies who manufacture quality products. The Burke glove company is the one which had the two delivery problems with Claymore. Baker thinks that this was really Claymore's fault, but it might give the other competitors a better chance to get Burke's portion of the business. Neither of the other two competitors has had any problem with Claymore that Baker knows about.

Claymore buys four basic types of gloves—one from each of its suppliers. The standard workglove is purchased from Madison, Burke supplies the thermal insulated glove. The two other gloves are heavy-duty gloves with steel fiber running through them to help protect the employee from sharp objects. All the gloves that Claymore buys could be purchased from any of its suppliers at approximately the same price. Madison's thermal glove is slightly better than Burke's.

Baker has considered several alternative strategies for getting a larger share of Claymore's business. Two years ago he gave Claymore's two free samples of Madison's $65.00 per pair thermal gloves. He knows that they were never tested; in fact he is aware that Fitzgerald and Cardoza each took a pair to use at home for working on their cars.

1. How much added business should Baker try to get from Claymore?

2. Why did Baker's attempt to get Claymore to test Madison's gloves fail?

3. What strategy should Baker employ to increase his sales from Claymore?

SUGGESTIONS FOR FURTHER READING

Blickstein, Steven, "How to Find the Key Buying Influence," *Sales Management,* Vol. 107 (Sept. 20, 1971), pp. 51 54.

Cribbin, James, Jack Hanan, and Herman Heiser, "Welcome, Please, the Consultative Salesmen," *Sales Management,* Vol. 104 (June 1, 1970), pp. 59–61.

Harding, Murratt, "Who Really Makes the Purchasing Decision," *Industrial Marketing,* Vol. 51 (September 1966), 76–81.

10. Prospecting — Generating New Business

Sales representatives must have a large pool of prospective customers in order to sell enough to generate income for themselves and profits for their companies. In this day and age, most sales representatives operate in very dynamic environments. New products, new customers, and new competition make it critically important for the salesperson to monitor his assigned market closely so that he can act quickly to meet new challenges. Yesterday's customer may become a prospect again as he or she searches for solutions to new and old problems. In addition, aggressive sales representatives continually scan the market for opportunities to sell their merchandise to new prospects.

In this chapter we examine how the salesperson prospects for new accounts. Specific topics include the importance of keeping established accounts satisfied, ways of generating leads for new accounts, uses and types of information that the salesperson will want to gather on prospective accounts, and the effective routing of sales representatives.

NEW BUSINESS FROM OLD ACCOUNTS

It is vitally important for the salesperson to have a thorough understanding of his present accounts. Without this understanding, it is impossible for him to effectively plan future efforts. The questions set forth in Table 10-1 provide a quick test for the salesperson to use in assessing his current business. Unfortunately, all too often sales representatives can not answer a majority of these questions. When a salesperson is unable to do this, he is probably taking his established accounts for granted, although they represent the foundation for the present and future business of the firm. The salesperson must realize that when he is out wining and dining prospective accounts, someone else may be doing the same thing with his established accounts. The successful salesperson should be aware of the concept of established key accounts and their strategic implications.

Key Accounts

The typical salesperson has a large number of accounts. Yet a very small percentage of them usually represents most of his volume of sales and profits. A typical example might be a cosmetics salesperson who has 150 accounts distributed as shown in Table 10-2. This particular salesperson has 15 "A" accounts, which make up 50 percent of his volume, whereas he has 69 "D" accounts, which provide only 10 percent of his volume. This same example can be applied to profits.

TABLE 10-1 A SALESPERSON'S TEST FOR ASSESSING CURRENT CUSTOMERS

How many customers do you have?

Which are your key accounts?

Which are unprofitable to you?

What's the typical sales coverage pattern for each of your major classes of customers?

How many hours does each class require?

How many selling hours are needed to service your present business without wasting precious time in overlong calls?

Source: Adopted from *Sales Management: The Marketing Magazine,* April 1, 1971, p. 17.

TABLE 10-2 COSMETICS SALESPERSON'S CATEGORIZATION OF CUSTOMERS

Account Classification	Number of Customers Ranked by Volume (or Profit)	Percent of Volume (or Profit) for Total Territory
A	15	50
B	20	25
C	46	15
D	69	10

The salesperson must spend proportionately more time on those accounts that represent a large portion of his business. He can not try to get a small account to buy more of his merchandise if this means he must neglect one of his larger accounts. Many sales representatives plan their communications with customers based on the amount of business the customer does with them. Table 10-3 continues the example of the cosmetics salesperson. This salesperson visits his "A" accounts three times per month and telephones them three times per month, or as often as necessary. At the other extreme, he visits the "D" accounts only once each year and telephones only twice a year. Of course, if a "D" customer telephoned the salesperson he would return his call or possibly even visit with him. The salesperson has a limited amount of time, and he must try to spend a proportionately larger amount of it with his key accounts.

TABLE 10-3 COSMETICS SALESPERSON'S COMMUNICATION WITH ACCOUNTS

Account Classification	Personal Visits	Telephone Calls
A	3 per month	3 per month or as often as necessary
B	1 per month	3 per month
C	4 per year	1 per month
D	1 per year	2 per year

Strategic Implications of Key Accounts

Often the salesperson wants to go after new business from accounts that he has not sold to before. Although these accounts represent substantial new opportunities for the salesperson, they probably have been doing business with another firm for a number of years. Even if the salesperson penetrates a new account, the chances that it would develop into one of his key accounts are quite remote. As a result, it is frequently good strategy for the salesperson to try to get more penetration with his present accounts than to spend too much time visiting new accounts. A good account can become better either by buying larger quantities of the same merchandise or by purchasing new products from the salesperson. If the salesperson has provided good posttransactional service to the customer, he will be given a fair hearing when he suggests that the customer buy more of his products.

GENERATING LEADS FOR NEW ACCOUNTS

There are many situations where it is important for the salesperson to look for new business. For example, no matter how well the salesperson monitors his existing accounts, he will occasionally lose some of them to competition. In addition, a firm will periodically ask its sales representatives to attract new business as plant capacity increases or as new opportunities become available. In some markets, such as door-to-door encyclopedia sales, there is very little repeat business, and the salesperson is always looking for new accounts.

There are several avenues available to the salesperson in generating new accounts. The effective salesperson will examine each carefully and then select that method or combination of methods that best fits his needs. Nine basic ways to generate new accounts are presented below.

Endless Chain

This technique has proven successful for many sales representatives. Here the salesperson asks each prospect to provide him with three or four names of individuals that might be interested in purchasing his product or service. A good salesperson handles his interviews so that the prospect feels the visit was worthwhile even if no purchase is made. The salesperson asks for leads even if he did not successfully complete the sale.

A good example of this approach is a local lawn fertilizer service that asks each of its customers for the names of their immediate neighbors. The lawn service then mails each of these neighbors a notice about their service and offers them a free estimate.

Referrals

Referrals involve asking the customer to go one step further than he was asked to do with the endless chain. That is, the salesperson asks the customer not only to provide names of individuals who might be interested in his product, but also to contact these individuals for him. Often the customer can say things about his experience with the salesperson and with the salesperson's products and services that would not be believable if they came directly from the salesperson. Obviously, this approach works only if the salesperson and the customer have a positive, long-standing relationship. (This technique is discussed in more detail in Chapter 12.)

Important People

In most sales territories there are individuals or firms whose buying behavior is directly influenced by others. If the salesperson is to maximize his success within his territory, he will want to identify and cultivate such influential accounts even if it means spending more money and time on them than they justify on their own merits. An excellent example of this process comes from a study done several years ago by *Fortune* magazine of the home air-conditioning market. Investigators observed that air conditioners occurred in clusters rather than being randomly distributed through the market. The research found that in each instance some one individual began the buying process in each cluster. Once this key person had purchased an air conditioner, his neighbors, who viewed him as a pace-setter, purchased theirs. Research in the pharmaceutical field corroborates these findings. Certain physicians tend to be looked upon by their colleagues as leaders in the use of new successful medical practices. As a result, their behavior is often followed. In the industrial marketplace, small firms frequently look to the larger ones to determine what to buy and whom to buy it from.

Noncompeting Sales Representatives

Noncompeting sales representatives provide another important source of prospect leads. This is particularly useful if there is a reciprocal relationship—that is, the two salespersons provide leads for each other and thus both feel a need to continue the relationship. This source may not be able to provide enough information for the salesperson to classify the leads as likely prospects. In this situation, the salesperson should tap other sources to complement the initial information.

Occasionally, the noncompeting salesperson may be able to furnish a direct entree, either through a joint call or through permission to cite him as a source. Before this entree is used, however, the salesperson should make sure that his colleague has a favorable buying-selling relationship with this account. If this is not the case, the reference may have a very negative effect. Usually, leads from noncompeting sales representatives are suspect and should be examined very closely to determine how much potential business is available and how the account should be approached.

Junior Sales Representatives

Younger sales representatives are frequently used as "bird dogs" to determine how much business might be available from a number of accounts.[1] This is done because it gives the young salesperson good experience in the field and because the experienced salesperson's time is too valuable to have him looking down a large number of blind alleys. Normally when this procedure is followed the

[1]Charles A. Kirpatrick and Fredrick A. Russ, *Salesmanship,* 5th ed. (Cincinnati: Southwestern Publishing, 1976), p. 235.

junior salesperson turns any good leads he has established over to an experienced salesperson, who then attempts to close the sale.

Acquaintances and Friends

Acquaintances and friends in the business community are also potential sources of leads. Bankers and other people in the financial community are extremely valuable to the salesperson whose products represent substantial capital outlays. Executives of trade associations, industrial groups, and chambers of commerce can also be useful in providing sales representatives with information concerning new businesses and shifts in the objectives of existing firms in a specific territory. Frequently, these people do not want to have their names cited as having furnished information to the salesperson. If this is the case, the salesperson must respect this confidence if he wants to maintain this source of information.

Telephone and Mail

Telephone and mail inquiries and responses to advertising comprise another important source of leads for the salesperson. These require that the salesperson do a careful job of screening the good leads from those that do not have much potential with a minimum investment of his time and effort. It is prudent for the salesperson to phone or write such prospects before making personal calls. For example, in one case a sales manager gave one of his electronics equipment salespersons an advertisement coupon that had been mailed in by an individual. The salesperson drove more than 30 miles only to find that the coupon had been sent by a junior high school student writing a science paper.

Directories

In some areas of selling, special directories, reports, and open-to-bid announcements comprise an important source of leads. These categories vary greatly from industry to industry. Each salesperson should acquaint himself with such information if it exists in his field, and by his own experience and the experience of his fellow sales representatives he should determine whether or not they are valuable sources of leads.

Cold Canvassing

Sales representatives in some fields discover new business by cold canvassing. This consists of calling on a number of people who may or may not be potential users of the salesperson's product or service. If this method is to be used effectively, the salesperson should have at least some criteria to apply before investing his time in an actual interview. This may involve such observations as the size of the establishment, traffic flow in the case of a wholesaler or retailer, the amount and type of inventory in sight, and the general appearance and upkeep of the premises. If the salesperson feels that an account is worth calling on, he must have a quick method of determining if it has any real potential that could lead to profitable sales. A good way to do this is to develop a series of questions designed to identify how much potential business the account has, who its present supplier is, and how happy the prospect is with the present supplier.

USES AND TYPES OF PROSPECT INFORMATION

Once he has generated some leads, the salesperson needs to collect information on each prospect. This information will permit him to qualify the prospect, to determine what the prospect's real needs are, and to decide the best way to approach the account. The salesperson finds out as much of this information as possible before he makes the actual call. We will examine the types of information the salesperson must collect to make these determinations.

Qualifying the Prospect

Evaluating or qualifying leads is one of the most important aspects of a salesperson's job. At this stage, the salesperson is trying to learn which accounts are really worth pursuing. If this is done well, the sales representatives will not waste time working on prospects that simply do not have the potential to be profitable, nor will he overlook prospects that might become profitable accounts. Areas the salesperson will want to investigate for evaluating prospects include financial ability, potential business, special requirements sought by the prospect, the likelihood of a long-term relationship, and the prospect's location.

Financial Ability.   Information on the financial ability of the prospect can be obtained through observation, questioning, references, and credit-reporting agencies. Whichever sources of information the salesperson uses, there is a premium on his sound commercial judgment. The salesperson has a natural tendency to discount or override adverse credit information. He frequently feels that he is in the business of selling, not financing. This attitude is reinforced by the fact that the salesperson is paid a commission that is based on sales. The professional salesperson is aware that, in the long run, he can not make too many sales that cause his firm collection problems.

Volume of Business.   With regard to the volume of business, it is important for the salesperson to keep in mind his company's best interests. There are fixed costs, such as billing expenses, that exist regardless of the volume. Some accounts are so small that their business would not cover these fixed costs; therefore, they do not warrant any attention on the part of the salesperson. The effective salesperson, however, may see future potential in some small accounts even though their present volume is small. This insight often allows the sales-person to gain an important account that his less competent competitors have overlooked. Therefore, he should carefully weigh a prospect's current potential against the fixed costs for his company, but he should also keep in mind the prospect's future potential when he makes the decision whether or not to pursue an ostensibly small account.

Special Requirements.   The salesperson must convince himself that it is his objective to sell his firm's products in the form in which they are manufactured. If the firm has done its homework, its products are designed to meet the needs of market members. Although this implies that the product in question will prob-ably not fit the exact needs of every customer, each time the salesperson is talked into a modification of the product, he not only causes substantial production costs for his company but his action may be interpreted as indicating a short-coming in the product. In the final analysis, the salesperson must weigh the costs of special services or production modifications against the benefits that the firm will obtain from this step in the long run.

Continuity.   For many firms, maintenance of long-term contracts with custom-ers is a vital consideration. There is little chance to make a profit on an account until several orders have been written. (One specialty chemical house estimates that it must receive three orders before a profit is generated.) Thus, it is up to the salesperson to estimate whether the new account has a substantial probability of becoming a long-term customer.

Location.   This is an important factor when buying is done in one office and shipments are made to other sites of the new customer. If a large amount of follow-up service and contact is involved, the salesperson will want to balance the extra cost of traveling to a customer against the expected profit that should develop from his efforts.

The Prospect's Needs

Once the salesperson identifies a lead as a prospective customer, he determines the exact needs of the account. In Chapter 2, we saw that the marketing concept is based on determining the needs of the customer so that the firm is in the best possible position to satisfy them at a profit. Although sophisticated survey research can reveal many things about customer attitudes, sales representatives are still the best sources of information about a customer's behavior. As a result, the salesperson will do his best to determine what the prospect's problems are by talking with the purchasing agent, engineers, production personnel, and plant management. In this way, the salesperson can provide the prospect with those items in his firm's product line that best meet his requirements. By relaying customer needs to his firm, the salesperson keeps his organization on top of changes that are taking place in the market.

Improving Sales Effectiveness

The salesperson's effectiveness in approaching a prospective account depends in large measure on his knowledge of the problems facing that account. This may take a great deal of effort on his part. It involves talking with people within and outside each customer and prospective account. However, this one activity does more to enhance the salesperson's effectiveness than anything else.

In addition, it is helpful to the sales representative to identify all those who are in formal and informal decision-making positions in the prospect account. Some individuals, such as a purchasing agent, may appear on the prospect's organizational chart to have a great deal of authority over purchasing decisions. Yet, in many firms the purchasing agent handles only the day-to-day decisions, whereas the decisions leading up to actual purchase are handled by other members of the firm's management. Often the purchasing agent will consult with appropriate "knowers" (e.g., director of research or the chief engineer), when technical products are under consideration. The key idea for the salesperson to remember is that it may be as important to reach these people as it is to talk to the person who actually makes the purchase decision.

Still another consideration is that the salesperson neither oversell nor undersell. This involves judicious use of the proper types and amounts of promotional material. The salesperson's strategy is to stay in the conscious awareness of all those who can influence buying decisions. Some buyers feel that if they do not hear regularly from sales representatives, they are being neglected. In contrast, some buyers like to have regular, well-organized visits but do not want to be harassed with promotional material between visits.

ROUTING

Routing is the formal procedure used to determine which customers and prospects the salesperson should call on during a particular time period. A salesperson's route may be established for as short a period as an afternoon or for as long a time as several weeks. We will examine who creates the salesperson's route and then discuss six specific routing techniques.

Responsibility for Routing

There are at least two perspectives on who is responsible for routing the salesperson. Some think it is strictly a management responsibility, whereas others feel the salesperson should play an important role in determining his route. We will examine each of these perspectives, along with some special circumstances that may influence policy on routing.

Management's Responsibility.   Proponents of management's handling of routing feel that a full, systematic coverage of the territory will not occur if the salespersons are left on their own. They also contend that a proper mix of customer and prospect calls will not be maintained. They assume that most sales representatives prefer to call where they are already established and that personal convenience will influence the salesperson's decisions. As an example, advocates of this perspective suspect that the salesperson who is left to handle his own routing will backtrack and criss cross his territory in an attempt to be home every night. Some companies have pointed up this problem by analyzing the percentage of potential business realized from each account. They find that a circle can be drawn around the salesperson's home that represents the maximum distance the salesperson can travel and still be home at night. Accounts within the circle yield a disproportionate amount of business compared with those outside the circle.[2]

Salesperson's Responsibility. A case can also be made for the salesperson to determine his own route. He is, after all, the territory manager. One way to handle this is to have the salesperson plan his routing subject to approval by management. This system not only gives the salesperson a great deal of responsibility in planning his activities in his territory, but it also helps management know where its sales representatives are in case they need to be contacted.

Proponents who recommend giving the salesperson the routing responsibility argue that salespersons are professionals who know their territories better than any management personnel possibly could. The salesperson knows how much time should be devoted to each account, optimum times to call, which accounts expect entertainment, and what the current sales potential of each account is. As one account heats up, the salesperson who monitors his market closely will be in the best position to adjust his call pattern to this new development.

It is also argued that sales representatives are more independent than other employees. Salespersons consider themselves to be virtually independent businessmen, in full charge within their territories. They do not speak of the area in which they sell as the company territory but as *their* territory. This is why management provides a freer rein to sales representatives than to other non-supervisory employees.

Other Special Considerations. There is no one best answer for determining who should route the salesperson. The overriding factor may turn out to be how good a sales force the firm has and what its members want to do. A truly top flight sales organization that wants to do its own routing should be given a chance to do so. There are, however, two other factors to be considered—the nature of the product and the extent of market development.

In dealing with frequently purchased products, such as foods, drugs, tobacco, fuel, and hardware, it is best to have a detailed routing plan worked out by

[2]William J. Stanton and Richard H. Buskirk, *Management of the Sales Force* (Homewood, Ill.: Irwin, 1974), p. 608

management. If the salesperson misses a call with these types of products, a competing salesperson is likely to take over the account very quickly. In this case, one of the most important benefits a firm can offer is the regularity of its visits. Management can not afford any mistakes in this area. In contrast, if a firm sells products that are not purchased regularly, such as heavy equipment, it is less appropriate for the sales manager to do the routing. With such products, a good salesperson does much better by relying on his own judgment rather than on some predetermined route set up by management.

Similarly the extent of market development and the identification of potential buyers are related factors that influence who is responsible for the routing. In the early stages of developing a market, when the salesperson is busy locating new customers, he must be prepared to spend as much time with each account as the situation requires. This is not the type of selling that permits extremely close supervision by management. The salesperson will have to make changes in his schedule as new circumstances develop. In contrast, if the market is highly developed and prospects and customers have already been identified, it may be possible for management to determine who the salesperson should call on and at what time intervals.[3]

Special Routing Techniques

Virtually any systematic routing plan is superior to a haphazard coverage of the territory. The size of the territory, concentration of business, number of accounts, call frequency, likely length of each call, and mode of transportation are factors that must be considered in deciding on the best method to use. We will examine six routing plans—circular, cloverleaf, leap frog, straight line, skip stop, and computerized models.

Circular. The circular approach to routing is appropriate when the salesperson's accounts are distributed uniformly, when few limitations exist on accessibility, and when the call frequency is about the same for each account. With this approach, the salesperson draws concentric circles, or a spiral, around his accounts. He then begins calling on the accounts closest to his office and works out around each circle until he has called on each account. Or he could begin at the edge of the outer circle and spiral his way back to his office. Figure 10-1 illustrates the circular approach.

Cloverleaf. This approach is useful when there are concentrations of accounts in specific parts of the territory. A hub point is used in each area and calls are made in loops. Alternate sales calls and those made less frequently can be placed on the schedule for each loop. This technique is illustrated in Figure 10-2.

[3]D. Maynard Phelps and J. Howard Westing, *Marketing Management* (Homewood, Ill.: Irwin, 1960), pp. 628–629.

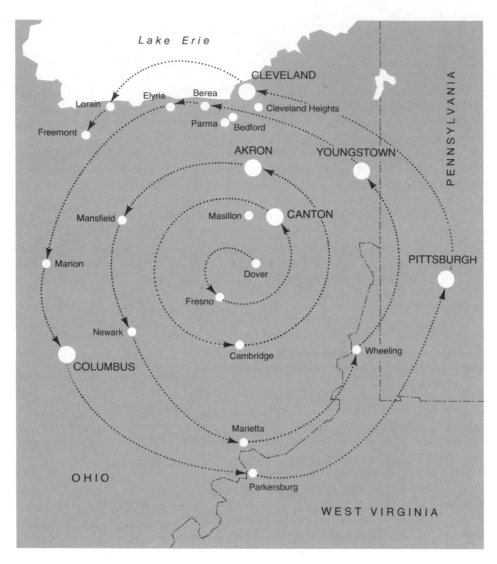

Figure 10-1 Circular Approach to Routing

Leap Frog.   When it is important that the salesperson maintain a frequent call pattern on each account, the leap frog routing is feasible. With this approach, the salesperson starts at a distant point in his territory and works back to his office, making sales calls as he goes. He would appear to be jumping to each account in a random manner; yet this is not the case. Rather, the salesperson has figured out the best route to return home that will at the same time take him through each of his accounts. Figure 10-3 demonstrates this approach.

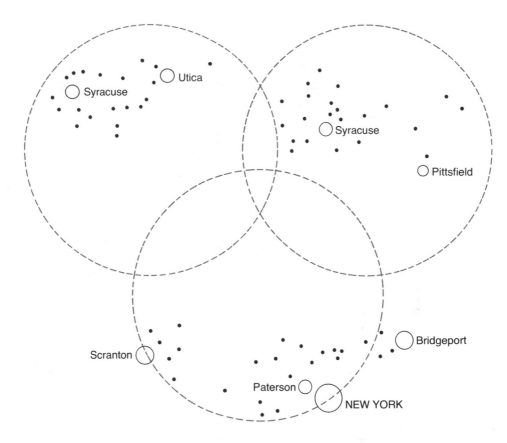

Figure 10-2 Cloverleaf Approach to Routing

Straight Line.   The straight line approach works best when business is concentrated in several clusters that are scattered from each other. The salesperson makes a straight line to each cluster. He calls on each account within that cluster and then makes a straight line to the next cluster. This approach is illustrated in Figure 10-4.

Skip Stop.   With this approach, the salesperson routes himself through all of his accounts during one sales trip. However, the next time through the territory, he will skip those accounts that are not among his more profitable accounts or that do not have the potential to become more profitable. During this follow-up trip through the territory, the salesperson may visit only 10 to 20 percent of his accounts.[4] Figure 10-5 illustrates this approach.

---

[4]William J. E. Crissy and Harold C. Cash, *The Psychology of Selling,* Vol. 11, "Selling in Depth" (Flushing, NY: Personnel Development Associates, 1965), pp. 52–54.

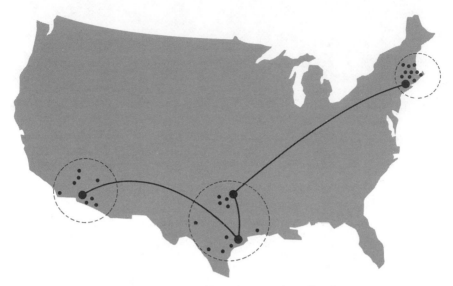

Figure 10-3 Leap Frog Approach to Routing

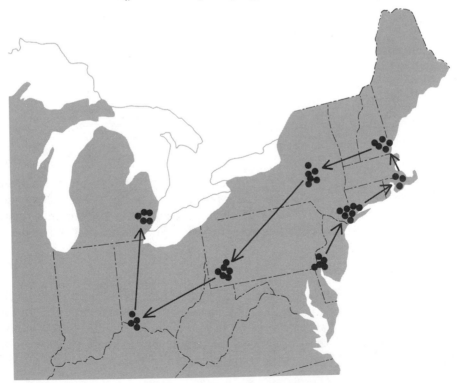

Figure 10-4 The Straight Line Approach to Routing

Figure 10-5 Skip Stop Approach to Routing

Computerized Models.   Mathematical models, such as linear programming, also help the salesperson develop a routing plan. Normally, these models are programmed for use on a computer because they require a great many calculations. The inputs to such a model would include length of call, number of accounts, location of accounts, and when specific accounts wish to be visited. A number of models have been developed that will help minimize total travel time or cost.[5]

[5] Stanton and Buskirk, *op. cit.*, p. 609.

SUMMARY

In this chapter we focused on prospecting for new business. We saw that one of the best sources of new business is current satisfied accounts. Business with these accounts can be improved by getting the customers to buy more of what they currently purchase from the salesperson or by purchasing other products from his firm. When searching out new accounts, the salesperson must not neglect his key accounts because competing sales representatives will be trying to win them over.

We looked at nine methods for generating new accounts: the endless chain, referrals, important people, noncompeting salespersons, junior salespersons, acquaintances and friends, telephone and mail, directories, and cold canvassing. Each salesperson must evaluate these methods to determine which combination works best for him.

We also discussed the use and types of information the salesperson must collect on each of his prospects. Before he qualifies the prospect as a potential customer for his firm, the salesperson investigates the prospect's *financial ability,* the *current* and *future* potential volume of business, any *special requirements* the prospect may demand, chances for a *long-term relationship* between the two firms, and the prospect's *location.* The more information the salesperson is able to generate about the prospect, the better his chances are of providing a product that would solve the prospect's needs and the more effective is his sales presentation.

We concluded with a discussion of routing. A good case can be made for either management or the salesperson having primary responsibility for routing. We examined several special considerations that would influence this decision. We then looked at six techniques for routing—circular, cloverleaf, leap frog, straight line, skip stop, and computerized models.

PROBLEMS

1. Why is it so important for many salespersons to spend a large proportion of their time on a few "key accounts". Under what circumstances would a salesperson have few if any key accounts?
2. Compare and contrast the endless chain method vs. the referral method for generating new leads.
3. Under what type of selling situations is cold canvassing the normal method for generating new leads?
4. What are the most important factors in qualifying a prospect? Is determining who the key decision makers are in the prospect's firm a part of the process? Explain.
5. Explain the advantages and disadvantages of having the salesperson do his own routing. Under what conditions should management perform this function?

Exercise 10

PROSPECTING— GENERATING NEW BUSINESS

Objective: To appreciate the importance of routing as a means of covering existing accounts and prospective accounts.

Assume that you are a salesperson and that the map on page 210 is your territory. Key customers are depicted by ●; other customers by ○. Key prospects by ■; other prospects by □. You see key customers and prospects at least twice a month. You call on other customers and prospects at least monthly. Your home is your office and is in suburban Detroit.

1. What methods are available for planning your route through the territory?
2. What method or methods of routing would you use?
3. Would you use the same route each time? If not, why not?
4. Plot your progress through the territory, bearing in mind prescribed call frequency.

Case 10-1 Beatty Chevrolet

David Johnson is in charge of the new car fleet-leasing program for George Beatty Chevrolet of Houston, Texas. At one point in time, Beatty Chevrolet did a substantial business in fleet leasing. In 1973, the firm had 32 customers who leased an average of 23.5 vehicles for one year or longer.

However, business slipped substantially since 1975 when their fleet leasing manager retired. At that time, Beatty felt that he would try to cut costs and take over the leasing

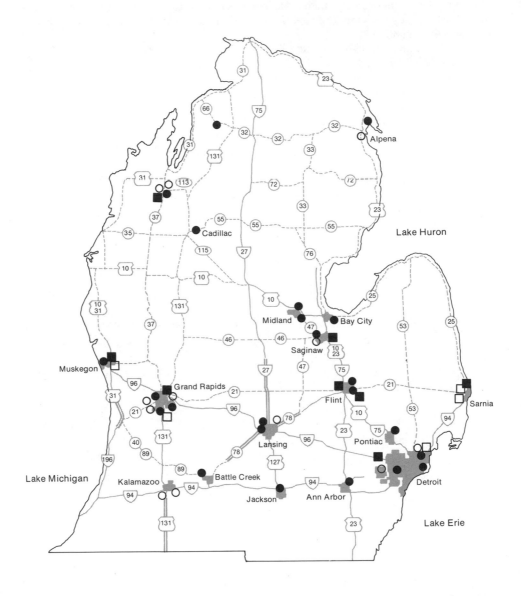

business himself. Unfortunately, he did not have the time or the flair for running this side of his dealership, and as a result the new car leasing business fell off substantially. In the six months prior to hiring David Johnson, Beatty Chevrolet received only one contract for fleet vehicles. This order was for twenty Caprices, which were leased to a cousin of George Beatty.

David has been with Beatty for two months. In that time he has established a fleet-leasing service program and received two contracts for a total of fifty units. The fleet-leasing service program consists of little more than a half-time service representative who deals with all the service problems of the fleet customers. David feels that Beatty lost so many contracts so fast because there was no one person in service who worked solely on fleet leaser's problems.

The two new contracts that David landed are Dix's Delivery Service for thirty delivery vans and Houston Oaks Bank for ten Caprices. David became aware of the Dix's contract through a public announcement that they would be accepting bids on the vans. David knew Dix's reputation for leasing strictly on price; and because he needed to land a good contract to build momentum in the leasing program and to show Mr. Beatty he was making progress, he bid very low on the contract and was the winner.

David became aware of the Houston Oaks Bank's need for ten vehicles from Mr. Beatty who is a friend of the bank's senior vice-president. Only one other firm bid on the vehicles and Beatty Chevrolet received the order. David's bid was not quite so low as it had been with Dix's, and as a result the firm made a good profit.

Mr. Beatty thinks David is doing a good job with the leasing business. However, he feels that David's performance must continue to improve if Beatty is to stay in the new car and truck fleet-leasing business. Beatty feels that the firm's break-even point for this segment of the business is approximately 400 new vehicles leased each year for a period of one year. Beatty told David that he will have at least one year to build up to this point, but at the end of that period, he will have to review the fleet-leasing business to determine if it can be profitable again.

1. What can David do to attract new customers?

2. Is there any possibility that some of Beatty's old customers can be lured back to the firm?

3. What techniques would be useful for David in generating new leads for Beatty Chevrolet?

Case 10-2 The Magic Screen Corporation

Magic Screen Corporation is a small consulting firm located in Austin, Texas. It was founded in 1973 by two professors of the University of Texas, Dr. William Witt and Dr. Edward Alpert. Both men had been involved with researching and developing teaching systems which would be effective for large classes (from 200 up to 1,000 students).

Witt and Alpert have written several articles on the subject and investigated proven teaching methods for large classes.

The present policy of state and other public universities forced colleges to increase class sizes in order to serve an ever larger number of students with limited budgets. However, very few teaching innovations had been introduced, and the professors had to lecture to 400 or 500 students, with very poor results. Witt and Alpert experimented with several types of audiovisual aids, such as overhead transparencies, slides, television cassettes, and movies. After a full year of research they developed a package which combined all these techniques in what they thought was an optimum and most effective manner.

They were professors of marketing at the University of Texas, and as such they saw the opportunity for developing their idea into a small consulting business. This is how Magic Screen Corporation originated. After one year, the firm was ready to proceed and market its services which were divided into four different package offerings.

The major problem facing Magic Screen Corporation was to identify and contact their prospective customers. The academic community was close knit and not very sensitive to commercial appeals. The two associates were convinced that personal calls were the best way to get the job done.

1. What should Witt and Alpert do in order to contact the major public universities which appear to be their target market?

2. Whom should they contact within those universities?

3. Design a presentation for the Magic Screen Corporation services.

SUGGESTIONS FOR FURTHER READING

Carney, Gerard, "Finding New Sales and Profits with Your Present Customers," *Sales Management,* Vol. 106 (April 1, 1971), pp. 17–20.

Everett, Martin, "Why the Future of Your Company May Ride with Its Key Accounts," *Sales Management,* Vol. 114 (May 19, 1975), pp. 28–31.

Gadel, M. S., "Concentration by Salesmen on Congenial Prospects," *Journal of Marketing,* Vol. 28 (April 1964), pp. 64–66.

Russell, Frederic A., Frank H. Beach, and Richard H. Buskirk, *Textbook of Salesmanship,* 9th ed. (New York, N.Y.: McGraw-Hill, 1974).

Sales Management, "Cold-Calls—The Heat's On," Vol. 104 (February 1, 1970), pp. 21–25.

Stuteville, John R., "The Buyer as a Salesman," *Journal of Marketing,* Vol. 32 (July 1968), pp. 14–18.

Taylor, Thayer C., "Pinpointed: The Most Promising Prospects in the Middle-Wealthies," *Sales Management,* Vol. 92 (April 3, 1964), p. 30–34.

Taylor, Thayer C., "Turning Prospects into Accounts," *Sales Management,* Vol. 109 (Oct. 30, 1972), pp. 12,16,62,64,66,68.

Woodward, Harry, "Sarah Uses the Direct Approach," *Sales Management,* Vol. 94 (Feb. 5, 1965), pp. 33–36.

FOUR

Selling Tactics

This section contains six chapters, all dealing with selling tactics. Given competitive conditions, the universal sales tactical objective is to influence subtly– to be in control without seeming to be. All of these chapters are aimed toward showing how this can be accomplished.

In Chapter 11, "The Sales Call as a Tactical Situation," we develop the proposition that the other person's reactions during face-to-face meetings are the key inputs for the salesperson's tactics. Thus, a sales tactic may be defined as any adjustive reaction on the salesperson's part to a reaction observed in the customer or prospect. Reactions are categorized as positive-voluntary, positive-involuntary, negative-voluntary, and negative-involuntary. We describe tactics for handling each of these categories of reactions.

In Chapter 12, "The Approach–Gaining Entree to Sell," we deal with ways and means of getting face to face with a prospect or a customer. We emphasize the tactical considerations involved in each method presented.

"The Presentation–Satisfying Wants Persuasively," is the topic of Chapter 13. The presentation is viewed as effective when four criteria are met– understandability, interest, believability, and persuasion. We describe ways of accomplishing these, with emphasis on the basic human processes–perceiving, and thinking–as described in Chapter 4.

In Chapter 14, "Demonstration–Reinforcing the Presentation," we see the demonstration as encompassing any and all means employed to reinforce the oral presentation. Much of this chapter deals with principles to follow in preparing and using visual aids.

Sales resistance is virtually omnipresent and is of two kinds–logical and psychological. In Chapter 15, "Objections–Managing Sales Resistance," we define both kinds as well as the tactics for handling each. Traditional methods of handling objections are analyzed from a tactical viewpoint.

In Chapter 16, "The Close–Facilitating Decision Making," we present the close of the sale. This is seen as any effort by the salesperson to influence acceptance of his presentation. But no salesperson can sell and forget about it if he seeks an ongoing selling-buying relationship. Therefore, this chapter also describes posttransactional follow-up as an essential part of sales tactics.

11. The Sales Call as a Tactical Situation

The salesperson is uniquely the firm's marketing tactician. He is where the action is—face-to-face with customers and prospects, competing for their business. The salesperson, like the military person, can only be a good tactician if he is, first and foremost, a sound strategist. This means that he has objectives in mind and a plan for achieving them. It is important to remember that strategy is based on the known and the predictable, whereas tactics are triggered by the unknown and unpredictable. Prior to each call the salesperson reviews what he knows about each individual in the account, how his products and services meet needs, who the competitors are, and what has occurred on previous visits. Even with such a careful analysis, seldom, if ever, does a call go exactly as planned.

Almost always there is an unanticipated problem, a change in the competitive situation, or a shift in the thinking of those who must be influenced. In this chapter we examine unexpected situations that the sales representative may encounter on a call and ways in which he can best respond to them. In this regard he must be particularly aware of those factors that will require on-the-spot tactical maneuvering—positive and negative, voluntary and involuntary reactions of the customer or prospect, as well as the mood he or she is in and unexpected time limitations.

TACTICS ARE ADJUSTIVE REACTIONS

Strategy is always future oriented—an integral part of planning. Tactics, in contrast, are in the "now," a part of executing a plan. In fact, tactics are needed because things do not always work out as intended. From this viewpoint, tactics are seen as modifications of strategy. They comprise the adjustments the salesperson makes to the situation as he finds it once he is face to face with it. The sales call is depicted as having three parts or phases: *before, during,* and *after.* (Chapter 7). The *before* phase consists of planning and strategy. The *after* phase is devoted to evaluation. The *during* phase is the tactical phase, and this is our concern in this chapter.

Background factors, traits, and motives are the key inputs for effective strategy in influencing individuals. They are the basis of individual differences among people. They are what give each of us our uniqueness. In combination they may be viewed as the consistencies in the behavior of the other person—that which can be counted on and predicted. In contrast, individual reactions are the inputs for tactics during the sales call. Reactions include what the other person does and what he says, how he does it and how he says it—a hearty handshake, a pleasant greeting, a scowl, a hesitant rejoinder to a question.

Sales tactics may be defined as *adjustive reactions* on the part of the salesperson to the reactions he observes in the customer or prospect. The salesperson, to be an effective tactician, must be both *perceptive* and *flexible.* If he lacks perceptiveness he will miss cues in the other person's behavior—that is, in his reactions. However, observing them is not enough. He must be flexible in order to react appropriately to what he observes. It is the salesperson's task to adjust to the person called on rather than to expect the customer or prospect to adjust to the salesperson. Obviously, though, each is influencing the reactions of the other.

THE KEY TACTICAL OBJECTIVE IN SELLING IS SUBTLE CONTROL

The tactical objective in selling is to *be in control without seeming to be.* Subtle influence is crucial. Customers and prospects react adversely to coercion. How, then, can a salesperson be in control without seeming to be? Answers to this question derive from a consideration of reactions as they occur during the sales interview. In the following section we set forth a plan for classifying reactions and relating tactics to each category.

Positive Versus Negative Reactions

An observed reaction is *positive* from a tactical standpoint if, as the salesperson sees it, there is an increased likelihood of achieving his call objective. Positive reactions might include questions such as, "When can we expect delivery?" and "Does the product come in other sizes?" or such statements as, "I like the texture," or "This seems to be a convenient package." Positive reactions would also include movements and gestures, for example, picking up the sample, moving forward in the chair, smiling, using the intercom to exclude incoming calls.

In contrast, *negative* reactions, from the salesperson's viewpoint, indicate a decreased likelihood of achieving call objectives. Illustrations would be such statements as, "Your price is too high," or "I am satisfied with my present sources of supply," or "Don't take up my time with that." Other examples would be gestures and movements such as head moving from side to side, squirming in the chair, looking out the window, or engaging in other matters such as signing mail.

By definition, the salesperson is seeking to elicit positive reactions—those that indicate he is making progress. He knows that each time a positive reaction follows another positive reaction there is less likelihood of a negative reaction occurring. He is establishing a favorable view of his proposal. The tactical principle, then, is that the salesperson, in the face of a positive reaction, ought to continue doing what he is doing. On the other hand, if the salesperson causes a negative reaction, he must shift and do something else. Furthermore, it is evident that each time a negative reaction follows a negative reaction, it is going to be more difficult to bring about a positive reaction. Figure 11-1 illustrates this point.

Voluntary Versus Involuntary Reactions

Voluntary reactions are those that are made with conscious awareness. They include thoughtful statements and questions and deliberate movements and actions, whereas involuntary reactions occur without conscious awareness, such as a smile, a head nod, a spontaneous exclamation, or a symbolic rejection of the proposal by pushing the sample away from where the salesperson placed it. The customer or prospect is aware of his voluntary reactions, and consequently the salesperson must use more careful and deliberate tactics with these reactions than he would for involuntary ones. For example, if a customer or prospect asks a thoughtful question, it is a sound tactic for the salesperson to stop his presentation to answer it. If the salesperson ignores the question and continues with his own remarks, he is likely to lose the attention of the other

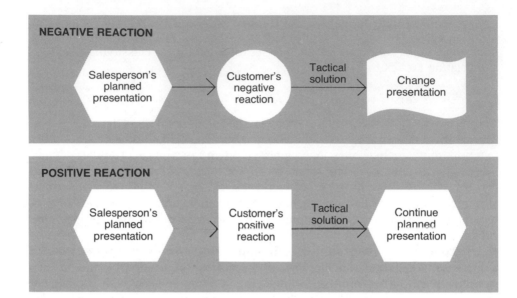

Figure 11-1 Tactical Solutions to Perceived Customer-Positive and Customer-Negative Reactions

person. The prospect or customer is likely to be directing his thoughts to the point he raised rather than to what the salesperson is saying. As another example, if a prospect says, "I would like to buy some," it is both a sound tactic and common sense for the salesperson to cease his presentation and thank the person for the order. He should not talk his way out of the sale by continuing his presentation in the face of an offer to buy.

Involuntary reactions are subtle, and the tactics used with them should be equally subtle. For example, if a salesperson sees that he is losing the attention of the other person (the prospect looks away and starts to wind his watch), he may rearrest his attention by finding some way to pass him a sample to examine or by injecting the buyer's name into the presentation. While he holds a sample and hears remarks about it, it is virtually impossible for the prospect not to pay attention. The objective is to convert the involuntary positive reaction into a positive voluntary one.

Tactics as Adjustive Reactions

If you combine the two dimensions of reactions into a four-way classification scheme, *any* reaction during any call will fit into one of four categories: negative-voluntary, negative-involuntary, positive-involuntary, and positive-voluntary. Figure 11-2 depicts this classification scheme and the tactics the salesperson should employ with each of these reactions.

	Positive	Negative
Involuntary	Tactic— No shift	Tactic— Subtle shift
Voluntary	Tactic— Close	Tactic— Radical shift

Figure 11-2 Reactions as a Basis for Sales Tactics

Negative-Voluntary Reactions. These reactions are consciously made and are indicative of a decreased likelihood of achieving the call objectives. Examples include such statements as; "Your price is too high," and "I'm not in the market right now." Additional illustrations would be to stand up and show the salesperson the door, or to interrupt the salesperson and use the intercom to summon the secretary. Here, the customer is clearly disagreeing with the salesperson and letting him know it, and thus a radical shift in tactics is called for to hopefully elicit a positive reaction.

The single most powerful tactic for such a situation is a question so phrased that it forces the other person to respond positively. For example, if the negative-voluntary reaction observed was a statement, "I am satisfied with my present suppliers," the salesperson might respond by asking, "What criteria do you expect your suppliers to meet?" While the other person is indicating the various things he expects of his suppliers, the salesperson can mentally weigh the extent to which his company meets the stated criteria. It may be that the salesperson just did not realize what specific criteria the customer was interested in. As an example, if the customer feels that delivery is critical and the present supplier is offering ten-day service, the salesperson's firm may be able to offer five-day service. The danger in this approach is that the customer, by verbalizing his feelings, may become even more convinced that his present supplier is satisfactory and that there is no reason to consider a change.

Negative-Involuntary Reactions. These reactions are not in conscious awareness and indicate a decreased likelihood of achieving the call objectives. There are two subcategories of these reactions—beginning disagreement or disbelief and waning attention. Examples of beginning disagreement or disbelief are a frown, head wagging instead of nodding, leaning back in the chair, or pushing away the sample. In each instance a *subtle shift* is called for. Obviously, the salesperson does not wish the other person to repeat such reactions. However, if he acts too deliberately himself he may cause a shift to a negative voluntary reaction on the part of the prospect. His objective is to do or say something in subtle fashion that will elicit a positive reaction from the other person. With waning attention, a pause by the salesperson may be all that is needed. Few people can stand silence. Another tactic useful in these circumstances is to have the customer or prospect examine the sample or hold the visual aid.

In the case of beginning disbelief or disagreement, the rhetorical question is a powerful tactic. A road-building equipment salesperson calling on a contractor observed a slight wagging of the head to a remark he made. He countered by saying, "Mr. Contractor, I know you are wondering whether your people are going to be able to operate this new equipment effectively. I wouldn't even sell it to you unless you would permit me to explain the operation thoroughly to all of your personnel." A key consideration here is to direct the other person's attention to a positive point before what is bothering him reaches conscious awareness.

Positive-Involuntary Reactions.   Such reactions are not in conscious awareness but indicate an increased likelihood of achieving the call objectives. Examples include smiling and nodding, moving closer, examining a sample furnished by the salesperson, spontaneous "uh-huh's" and other affirmative verbal signals. From a tactical standpoint, *no shift* is called for. Rather, the salesperson should do everything possible to reinforce the point that elicited this kind of reaction. This is a prime application of the summation aspect of perception (Chapter 4). The salesperson is at a tactical advantage if he has several different ways of making the same point or expanding on the point. Thus equipped, he can reinforce the favorable reaction and hopefully convert it to positive-voluntary. Some caution is needed here, however, because sometimes the salesperson mistakes a positive-involuntary reaction for agreement and moves off the point before it has reached the conscious awareness of the other person.

Positive-Voluntary Reactions.   These reactions are consciously made and indicate an increased likelihood of achieving the call objectives. Examples include such remarks as: "When can I get delivery?" "I'll ask our engineering department to test this sample." "You can write up this order." In response to such a reaction, the salesperson must either *close* the sale or move to the next point, as appropriate. It is tactically unsound for the salesperson to continue stressing a point once conscious agreement has been achieved. Further elaboration may raise questions and doubts in the other person's mind. Unfortunately, some salespersons become so enamored with what they are saying that they talk their way out of many sales.

In summary, negative reactions call for a tactical shift, radical when the reaction is voluntary, subtle when it is involuntary. Positive-involuntary reactions call for staying on the point and reinforcing it; positive-voluntary reactions are signals to close or to proceed to the next point.

To reiterate, the salesperson's tactical objective is always to be in control without seeming to be. The key to achieving this lies in responding appropriately to all reactions, especially the involuntary ones. This can only be achieved if the salesperson is well prepared for each call so that he can focus full attention on the other person and not miss any cues. Missed cues lead to lost control, lost control to lost sales.

OTHER TACTICAL CONSIDERATIONS

The salesperson's sales tactics not only include all of his adjustive reactions, but also large-scale changes and modifications that he makes in the call plan as he goes from the *before* to the *during* phase of the call. It would be difficult to compile an inclusive list of the innumerable factors or conditions that can cause such tactical adjustments. We will examine some of the more frequently encountered ones, which every salesperson is likely to face at some time in the course of his work. Each in turn calls for tactical adjustments on his part.

Mood

A person's mood may be defined as his particular state of mind which colors his perceptions and thoughts. In the first few seconds of the sales call, it is important for the salesperson to gauge the mood of the customer or prospect. If he finds the other person's feelings disturbed, this may call for a radical departure from his initial call plan. The best single tactic to use with a person whose feelings are upset is *to provide warm and attentive listening.* To the extent that the salesperson shows concern for the other person and lets him ventilate his upset feelings, he is likely to sustain a favorable relationship. On the other hand, if the salesperson is insensitive to the feelings of the customer or prospect and attempts to carry on a sales presentation with an unhappy person, he is not likely to permeate the emotional fog shrouding his perceptual and thought processes.

Often, of course, the sales representative finds the other person in a good mood, referred to technically as *euphoria* or state of well-being. This represents a tactical opportunity for accomplishing more than the salesperson initially planned. The person feeling "up" may take a favorable view of the salesperson and his proposal and agree to purchase without much resistance.

Goal Gradient

This is a psychological term that refers to the fact that when an individual is engaged in purposeful, goal-seeking activity, the closer he gets to the goal, the less interruptible he is. Often the person called on is too polite not to see the salesperson, particularly if he has arranged an appointment in advance. Yet when the salesperson comes face-to-face, he recognizes that although the prospect is physically present, psychologically his mind is elsewhere on a task that has been interrupted. When the salesperson senses this, the best tactic may be to offer to wait or return at some other time, if this is feasible. Alternatively, he may take advantage of the situation to get permission to see other people in the account from whom he might be blocked under normal circumstances. The insensitive salesperson in this situation may carry on a presentation, only to find to his dismay that the other person has paid little or no attention to him.

Limited Time

The salesperson may have counted on far more time than he finds available once he opens the interview. Several tactical alternatives are available to him. First, he may attempt to streamline the presentation and get the essential ideas across in the limited time. This has several disadvantages, one being that he may unwittingly set too fast a pace for comprehension on the part of the customer or prospect. Also, in his anxiety to cover everything, he may not give the other person a chance to actively participate in the interview. Buying is as active and participative a process as selling. Another danger is that he may, without intending to, discredit the importance of what he has available by the very cursory way in which he treats the presentation under the duress of the deadline.

Alternatively, he may simply stress the importance of what he has to offer and seek another occasion when time is available to do justice to what he has to say. This tactic has the advantage of underscoring the importance of what is to be presented, but it has the disadvantage of delaying the buying decision. During the interval between the present visit and the next call, a competitor may move in and get the order. Fortunately, it often happens when this tactic is employed that the other person's curiosity causes him to adjust time for the presentation. A third alternative is to take advantage of the situation as a way of reaching someone else in the account.

Unexpected Problems and Difficulties

In the first few minutes of a call, the salesperson may discover one or more prospect problems that he had not planned on. These may range from delay in delivery to defective merchandise, or they may be totally unrelated to the salesperson's products and services. It is up to the salesperson to adjust to the situation as he finds it and, consequently, he must depart from his planned presentation to assist in any way possible with the problems encountered. If he is helpful in solving them, he is likely to strengthen the selling-buying relationship more effectively than if he had been able to follow his original plan for the visit. If he is unable to help directly, he may enhance his position by just being a good listener.

Another Person Present

On some occasions, the salesperson faces the situation where the individual he calls on has another person with him and makes no effort to dismiss that person. The soundest tactic may be for the salesperson to remain silent and wait for the customer or prospect to fill him in on who the other person is and what his potential interest may be in the presentation. If this is not done, the salesperson may have to question either the person he is calling on or the guest in order to have a basis for relating the presentation to both parties. The key difficulty is likely to be the relative naivete of the third party with respect to what has occurred on previous calls. Because of this, it may be best for the salesperson to encourage a recapitulation from the customer or prospect of what has happened thus far. This affords the salesperson an opportunity to reinforce what has been accomplished to date, as well as to amend any misinformation.

Unanticipated Competitive Activity

Some sales tactics are countermeasures to tactics employed by competitors. For example, a salesperson might encounter an unanticipated price concession by a competitor. This may require him to amend the presentation he had contemplated making. As another example, he might discover that a competitor had offered an unreasonably large amount of technical assistance on a speculative basis, with a view to making an inroad in one of his accounts. The salesperson cannot match the offer because of his firm's policy on such matters. Even where it is feasible to meet the offer, such a maneuver is tactically dangerous, because it gives an impression of being a ''me-too'' organization and of having held back legitimate assistance. A better course of action is to come up with a countermeasure.

In the case of an unanticipated price concession, the sales representative may engage the other person in a discussion on what values he is actually looking for in the offering. In fact, he may be able to turn this price concession of the competitor into an indication that the competitor is not able to sell on a quality basis. In the situation where the competitor has overcommitted technical resources on a speculative basis, the salesperson may raise the question of whether you ever get something for nothing. Even when the competitor makes a questionable move to obtain the business, however, it is unwise to criticize him. This is too likely to arouse an unfavorable reaction in the other person.

''Brain Picking''

In selling-buying situations where technical advice and service comprise a considerable part of what is purchased, sales representatives must be wary of the professional ''brain picker.'' Some buyers, fortunately few in number, attempt to generate needed technical information, advice, and service from sources that are competent to provide it. Once these have been obtained, they turn to less competent firms for the actual products needed. When this situation is encountered, the salesperson is challenged to try to sustain a relationship without overcommitting the requested advice and service. Sometimes this can be offset by arriving at a dollar value for such help by astute questioning of the person who is seeking to get it free. To control this situation, one firm limited such commitments by charging its sales representatives' expense accounts for services of headquarters' technical personnel—thus the salespersons were more careful about such costly commitments when they were personally charged for them.

SUMMARY

Throughout this chapter we stressed the need to adjust to the unknown during a sales call—the importance of tactical considerations. To assist in developing a sensitivity to situations that require tactical adjustments, we classified the reactions of the prospect or customer into four categories: negative-voluntary, negative-involuntary, positive-involuntary, and positive-voluntary. For each of these reactions, an appropriate tactic is required to help move the sales call closer to a completed sale. There are many factors that may cause the need for tactical maneuvering by the salesperson. Among these are mood, goal gradient, limited time, unexpected problems and difficulties, another person present, competitive activity, and brain picking. In each case, on-the-spot adjustments must be made to the unanticipated situation.

PROBLEMS

1. The text suggests that "an effective tactician must be both perceptive and flexible." Explain.
2. What additional traits would be helpful for a sales tactician?
3. Explain and illustrate the four kinds of reactions cited in the text.
4. What are some examples of goal gradient that you have observed in your own behavior or in that of others?
5. What are some circumstances that might limit the time a customer or prospect makes available to a salesperson?

Exercise 11

THE SALES CALL AS A TACTICAL SITUATION

Objectives: To illustrate reactions and tactics as they occur in selling.
To apply basic tactical concepts to personal experience.

A. Reactions and Tactics

In the designated spaces, classify each reaction positive-voluntary, negative-voluntary, positive-involuntary, or negative-involuntary); and indicate an appropriate tactic.

Reaction	Classification	Tactic
1. Smiles		
2. "When can I get delivery?"		
3. Shuffles papers on desk		
4. "Your price is too high."		
5. Looks out window		
5. "I have too large an inventory now."		
7. Winds watch		
8. "That sounds good."		
9. Frowns		
10. "What company did you say you represent?"		

B. Reactions and Tactics

We suggested that any reaction observed during face-to-face communications may be classified as either positive-voluntary, negative-voluntary, positive-involuntary, or negative-involuntary. Provide three examples of each. For each example, provide an appropriate tactic.

	Positive Reaction	Tactic	Negative Reaction	Tactic
	1.		1.	
Voluntary	2.		2.	
	3.		3.	
	1.		1.	
Involuntary	2.		2.	
	3.		3.	

C. Applications of Other Concepts

All of us have encountered examples of mood, goal gradient, limited time, an unexpected problem, and another person present in our interpersonal relations. Set forth your own experiences, indicating how you handled each situation. Be specific.

1. Mood:
2. Goal gradient:
3. Limited time:
4. Unexpected problem:
5. Another person present:

Case 11-1 The Inconsistent Prospect

Dale Werner prided himself on being a pretty good salesperson. Yet Jim McManus baffled him. Dale has been trying to get business from Jim for over two years. He has learned two things for sure about Jim. He is a man of many moods and he seems impossible to pin down to a buying decision. As today's call opens here is the conversation:

Jim: Hi, Dale. You don't give up easily do you?

Dale: Good morning, Jim. I sure don't. Not when I know how useful and profitable you'd find our product line.

Jim: Yea. That's what every salesperson tells me. What did you think of the ball game last Saturday?

Dale: It sure was a cliff hanger. The folks that started leaving in the last few minutes missed the best part.

Jim: Well, Dale, go into your spiel. I always like to listen.

Dale: Well, Jim, I think you know our products as well as I do. You've heard me talk about them and you've seen our literature. I'm sure, if you try them, they'll sell themselves.

Jim: Dale, every salesperson thinks that way about his products. If he didn't he would be in the wrong field.

Dale: Well, the real proof of such claims is profitable use. However, today my purpose is to ask your advice.

Jim: That's a switch. What about?

Dale: In analyzing my twelve calls on you I've been trying to find out where I've gone wrong. You see a lot of sales representatives. What mistakes have I made in calling on you? Why haven't I obtained an order?

1. Was it sound tactics for Dale to avoid another presentation of his product line?

2. What do you think of the tactic of asking for advice?

Case 11-2 Morrison's Jewelry Store

Morrison's is an independent firm serving a middle-class clientele. It enjoys a good reputation in the community. Engagement and wedding rings comprise a significant share of total business. Vera King is a salesperson at Morrison's. She is straightening up the stock when a young man enters the store. He is hesitant in manner and looks around at the dazzling display cases. Then he slowly approaches the display of engagement and wedding rings. Vera moves behind the counter and greets him as he moves toward her.

Vera: Good evening. I'm Vera King. May I assist you?

Young man: Errr. Well, I want to look at engagement rings.

Vera judges his age at about 25. She notices that he is neatly dressed and his clothes are of good quality.

Vera: A lucky girl. Let me show you some of our popular styles. By the way may I ask your name?

Young man: I'm Tom Gorman.

Vera: Mr. Gorman, all the rings on this display tray are KeepSake. Your fiancée will know that name. It's famous for quality.

Tom: They are beautiful. Can you give me an idea of the prices?

Vera: Well, they range considerably. Also, you'll notice that in the lower two rows we have ensembles of engagement and wedding rings. And, if you have a double ring ceremony, there is a complementary band for the groom for each of these sets.

Tom: Yes, I see. Of course our wedding is still a long way off.

Vera: The advantage of the ensemble is that the rings are designed to go with one another.

Tom: I hadn't thought of that. If I were to select an ensemble could the wedding rings be put on layaway?

Vera: Yes. The advantage of KeepSake is that models are numbered and kept in stock.

Tom: What is the price of that ensemble?

Vera: You certainly have excellent taste. The engagement ring is a full carat and the wedding band has individually cut diamonds in it. The price for the set is $990. The groom's band is $110.

Tom: Whew. That's a lot of money.

Vera: Of course you're really making a life-time investment. When you look at it that way price is unimportant. Besides many of our customers finance their purchases.

1. Criticize Vera's tactics.
2. As the call proceeds should Vera suggest that Tom bring his fiancée to the store before making a final decision?

SUGGESTIONS FOR FURTHER READING

Matthews, H. Lee, David T. Watson, and John F. Monoky, Jr., "Bargaining Behavior in a Buyer-Seller Dyad," *Journal of Marketing Research,* Vol. 9 (February 1972), pp. 103–105.

Doody, Alton F., and William G. Nickels, "Structuring Organizations for Strategic Selling," *Business Topics,* Vol. 20 (Autumn, 1972), pp. 27–34.

Sales Management, "How Well do you Read Body Language," Vol. 105 (Dec. 15, 1970), pp. 27–29.

12. The Approach – Gaining Entree to Sell

In Chapter 7, we mentioned the *preapproach*, in which all the factors that need to be considered in planning a call on a particular customer or prospect are determined. Once the preapproach is accomplished, the salesperson must consider his *approach*—the strategy and tactics he will employ in gaining entree and in establishing rapport. Obviously, there is no sharp line that divides the pre-approach from the approach. No matter how careful the salesperson has been about his call plan, he may have to modify it once he is face-to-face with the prospect. Further, as the call progresses, his task is to adjust tactically to the reactions he observes in the other person. We will discuss the different situations that exist for the salesperson when calling on customer and prospect accounts, the direct and indirect methods he may use to gain entree, and the beginning of the face-to-face interview.

ESTABLISHED VERSUS PROSPECTIVE CUSTOMERS

With established customers, there is usually no difficulty in arranging a call. The salesperson's main concern is what remarks to make in order to start the interview on a favorable basis. The salesperson almost always has one or more matters to discuss from the previous call. For example, he may have committed himself to obtaining some technical information for the customer which he can furnish at the outset of the visit. In the same way, delivery on an order placed previously may give the salesperson a good topic on which to open the conversation. These "bridges" or "links" which join calls are invaluable in making the ongoing relationship smooth and continuous.

If the salesperson has done business with the other person for a number of years, he has accumulated trustworthy, comprehensive inputs for his strategy and can size up the situation very quickly. At the other extreme, the first call on a prospect is strictly a tactical situation; little if any strategically useful information is available. Under these circumstances, the salesperson is likely to have, at best, only scant pieces of secondary information about the person and the firm that he can use for openers, assuming that he is granted the interview. Every sales representative faces situations in which he can not even gain entree to talk to someone in prospective accounts.

The most difficult approach situation is when the call represents the first face-to-face contact and there has been no prior communication by telephone or correspondence. This is what sales representatives refer to as a "cold call."

DIRECT METHODS OF GAINING ENTREE

In trying to gain access to a new prospect, the salesperson must first decide whether to attempt entree directly, through his own efforts, or indirectly, through the efforts of others. Although the indirect method has several advantages, more often than not the salesperson must gain entree on his own. There are three direct methods available to the salesperson: a personal visit, a telephone call, or a letter. Each has unique advantages and disadvantages.

Personal Visit

A personal visit has some decided advantages over the other two methods. First, the salesperson is on the scene and ready to conduct the call if he is able to get in.

Second, he has a chance to observe at first hand the physical facilities of the prospective account. Third, he may be able to generate information by observation and inquiry while waiting in the reception room. Fourth, the salesperson's investment of time and effort to call in person gives the prospect an indication of the importance the salesperson attaches to the visit. Fifth, it is usually more difficult for the prospect to refuse to talk face-to-face than it is to refuse on the telephone or to answer a letter.

Role of the Subordinate.   If a personal visit is made, the salesperson almost invariably talks first to a subordinate, usually the receptionist. He must induce that person to arrange the actual interview. Tactically, the salesperson's objective with such a person is to convince her that she is fulfilling her responsibility by *getting him in* rather than *by keeping him out*. Even though the receptionist may contribute little or nothing to the actual buying decisions of her firm, she is an important person to the salesperson. The way in which she indicates his presence, the impression she conveys of him to her superior, may determine whether he gets the interview or not.

In general, it is not good tactics to deceive the subordinate. This can be disastrous if discovered. If the subordinate asks directly, "Are you a salesperson?" the individual calling should be proud to indicate that he is. He might want to add that his mission is to help the company make a profitable purchase. The salesperson's manner in this situation may have greater impact than what he actually says. If he can manifest confidence, sincerity, and conviction he increases the likelihood of getting in. It may be a good tactic, before asking for the actual interview, to seek some advice about the company from the receptionist. For instance, a salesperson might say: "Miss Jones, we have a proposal that means real money to your firm. I am confident Mr. Blank will want to discuss it with me. What would his reaction be to my requesting an interview right now?"

Precautions to the Personal Visit.   If a personal visit is used, some precautions should be taken lest the salesperson invest his travel and waiting time unproductively. The salesperson should occupy waiting time purposefully by reviewing printed information on the prospective account, tactfully questioning the receptionist, conversing with noncompetitive sales representatives, making sure that he is well organized, or doing something else associated with this work. In some fields of selling, the actual "wait time" exceeds the total amount of time the salesperson spends in face-to-face interviews. This large portion of the salesperson's working time must be *invested* rather than *spent*.

To gain a payoff from necessary travel time in the event that an actual interview does not occur, the salesperson should plan in advance for alternate calls as close by as possible. A salesperson must recognize that even if a prospect wishes to see him, it often happens that he cannot do this on the spur of the moment.

The Telephone Call

The second direct method of gaining entree is to phone in advance for an appointment. This has the key advantage of a greater likelihood that the sales representative will be able to see the prospect than if he walks in off the street to seek an interview. Furthermore, if the prospect adheres at all rigorously to his appointment calendar, this method will result in far less waiting time. Thus, the salesperson may be able to schedule more calls closer together than he would otherwise be able to do. In addition, there is some evidence that long-distance calls requesting appointments are honored more frequently than local calls. (Chapter 20 deals in depth with effective use of the telephone in selling.)

Other Advantages to Calling Ahead.   Another advantage is that the salesperson, in most instances, can get through to the person with whom he desires the interview. He does not need to depend on the receptionist to get him in. Even when he fails to talk to the decision maker directly, he can usually get to his private secretary and arrange with her for the visit. Still another advantage is that at the time of the actual interview, both parties are aware of the purpose of the visit. This allows the salesperson to get down to business more quickly than he would otherwise be able to do.

Disadvantages to Telephone Calls.   There are, however, some problems in using the telephone call method. For example, the salesperson may not know in advance who would be the most appropriate person to see. A personal visit will often permit him to obtain this information from the receptionist. Although this problem sometimes can be solved by seeking information from the switchboard operator, there is always a danger that the call will be directed to the wrong person. Another problem is that the prospect may be attending a meeting outside of his office or he simply may not be available to receive telephone calls from sales representatives at that time.

In addition, the salesperson may be inclined to ask for more information over the phone than is prudent to furnish. It is usually sound telephone strategy not to go beyond *need and want development and identification and assessment of want satisfiers* (phases 1 and 2 of the selling-buying process, discussed in Chapter 6). Finally, it is easier for many customers to turn down a request for an interview when made by phone than when the salesperson has made the trip to the prospect's premises. This may explain in part the greater effectiveness of the long-distance call. A person receiving such a call recognizes that an investment has been made by the salesperson and that the salesperson places considerable importance on getting an appointment.

Personal Letter

The salesperson covering a large territory often finds it effective to write to prospects in a particular city or area well in advance of his planned calls in that area. This is a particularly appropriate method if products and services offered are technical in nature and represent large dollar outlays. The salesperson may enclose appropriate company literature with his letter requesting the interview. This method may also be used in combination with the long-distance telephone request as a confirmation and reinforcement of the arrangements.

This method can result in time economy, and the likelihood of gaining entree is even greater with arrangements made by mail than with those made by telephone. It is reasonable to suppose that the person to be seen will be briefed for the interview and that he has read the literature furnished him. It is unwise, however, for the salesperson to assume that this has been done. With this method, it is imperative that the salesperson construct the letter with considerable care. It is sound practice for him to have one or more persons in his firm read it and make suggestions before it is sent. The letter, like the telephone request, should not go beyond determining how the prospect's needs are being satisfied. The letter should be designed to meet the following objectives:

1. To let the recipient know the salesperson's awareness of his need.
2. To raise doubts and questions in the recipient's mind about how to best fulfill his needs and wants.
3. To request the interview.

In connection with the third objective, it is a good practice for the salesperson to offer *two* alternative dates. He is more likely to get the interview with this approach than if he asks, "When can I see you?"

INDIRECT METHODS OF GAINING ENTREE

The indirect methods of gaining entree may take one of several forms. A third person may serve as an intermediary and pave the way for an appointment request or, less frequently, he may actually set one up. This is done by face-to-face contact, correspondence, a phone call, or simply by the intermediary giving the salesperson permission to use his name in making the request.

The salesperson ought to weigh two considerations before deciding to take an indirect course of action: (1) the impact on his relationship with the intermediary if he asks for such a favor, and (2) the effectiveness of the intermediary in dealing with the prospect versus the results the salesperson might obtain on his own. The first of these considerations is, of course, irrelevant if the intermediary is the one who has taken the initiative and has suggested the particular prospect. The second is greatly affected by the reputation of the intermediary in the business community.

The Customer as an Intermediary

The indirect method can have a decided advantage over the direct method in that it has all the impact of a testimonial. For this reason, the best possible intermediary is a satisfied customer who is willing to share with the prospect the benefits that he has derived from the selling-buying relationship. An additional advantage of having the customer pave the way is that he is equipped to handle technical questions with confidence, and he can do this from the buyer's standpoint.

Other Persons as Intermediaries

An intermediary, such as a mutual friend, lodge brother, or a key person in the community presents the salesperson with a different kind of situation. If the help of such persons is enlisted, the salesperson should make sure that the other person can give sufficient briefing so that he does not misinform the prospect or make commitments that the salesperson is unable to fulfill.

Other Important Considerations

If an intermediary agrees to write to a prospect, the salesperson should request a copy of the letter to facilitate his personal follow-up in the matter. Routing a copy of the letter to the salesperson lets the prospect know that the salesperson is aware of the request that has been made on his behalf. If the intermediary handles the matter by telephone or personal contact, the salesperson should be sure that he has some way of knowing when the contact has been made, so that he may follow up at an appropriate time.

Sometimes the intermediary is unwilling to become directly involved in setting up the appointment. He may, however, give the salesperson his business card with a personally written note on the back to his contact in the prospective account. This then becomes a means of entree that the salesperson can use directly. Alternatively, the intermediary may merely tell the salesperson that he is free to use his name and the name of his company as a means of getting the appointment.

In some sales situations there is another indirect method open to the salesperson: He may have an appropriate executive of his company's management write a letter of introduction for him to the executive in the prospective account. The advantages here are the impact of the executive suite and the opportunity it affords management to build up the sales representative in the eyes of the person to be seen. Another advantage of this method is that the executive can indicate the spectrum of resources the company has available to support the efforts of the salesperson. This back-up commitment coming from an executive has more believability than if it were stated by the salesperson.

COMMENCING THE FACE-TO-FACE INTERVIEW

Before the salesperson begins the interview, he should remind himself of several critical factors such as the basic assumptions underlying each sales call, and the importance of first impressions.

Five Basic Assumptions

There are five basic assumptions to remember at the outset of an interview: (1) the salesperson is interrupting the prospect, (2) the salesperson must invest his and the prospect's time, (3) the prospect is the eyes and ears of his company, (4) the prospect is presently satisfied, and (5) the prospect wants to buy profitably.

The Salesperson Interrupts the Prospect.   Generally, when the salesperson calls on the account, he will be interrupting purposeful activity on the part of the other individual. One sales manager was fond of reminding his sales representatives that the best prospect was the one too busy to see you. For a person engaged in his work, the salesperson is a barrier standing between the prospect and the goal he was pursuing. The salesperson, therefore, has an immediate objective of redirecting the person's attention to the matters he wishes to discuss. This has to be done tactfully and uncoercively.

The Salesperson Must Invest His Time.   The salesperson also needs to remind himself that the person called upon is as busy as he is. The salesperson has an obligation to *invest* the face-to-face time, not spend or waste it. Thus, he has an objective of making every minute count, both for the prospect and for himself. This places a premium on being carefully prepared and well organized.

The Prospect Is the Eyes and Ears of His Company.   The third assumption the salesperson must keep in mind is that the individual being called on is as much the "eyes and ears" for his company as the salesperson is for his own firm. Accordingly, one basis he will have for deciding on the worth of the salesperson's visit is the *amount, relevance,* and *value* of the information he gains from it. The knowledge and expertise of the salesperson may provide a prime basis for differential competitive advantage.

The Prospect Is Satisfied.   The salesperson must assume that the prospect is satisfied with things as they are (need homeostasis). *Prime prospects are satisfied customers of the competitor.* Thus, the immediate tactical objective is to disturb need homeostasis as quickly as possible. Provocative questions are a key method of doing this.

The Prospect Wants to Buy Profitably.   The prospect is as desirous of buying profitably as the salesperson is of selling profitably. If the call is to be effective, it must be mutually beneficial. This is why it is often said that the effective salesperson is a good buyer for the prospect.

First Impressions

The salesperson has two considerations with regard to first impressions: (1) he must try to have the best possible impact on the other person; and (2) he must guard against jumping to conclusions concerning the prospect.

Personal appearance is superficial, but it has considerable initial influence. Grooming and attire should be congruent with the expectations of the salesperson's clientele. One successful construction equipment salesperson had occasion to call on the heads of road building firms and members of city, county, and state road commissions, as well as job bosses out on construction sites. He carried a hard hat, overalls, and work shoes in his car and changed into them whenever he made field calls.

The salesperson's behavior should be adjustive to the other person. For example, he should wait for his prospect to ask him to be seated. Also, in more and more offices, smoking is taboo, and thus it is presumptuous for a salesperson to light up unless the host takes the initiative. Good manners add to the favorable impact made by the salesperson.

It is critically important, however, that the sales representative does not jump to first impressions when dealing with the customer. If he does make this mistake, all too often he will later make errors based on an initially incorrect perception of the customer. The following are five pitfalls of first impressions.

Manifestation of Traits.   People do not manifest all their traits at one time or under one circumstance. The traits displayed on a first call may not be in evidence several calls later. Conversely traits observed on later call often are not in evidence initially. Furthermore, the traits a person shows in a buyer-seller relationship may be different from those observed under social conditions. In Chapter 8 we stressed the importance of observing a prospect under varying conditions over time before judging his traits. As a result, the salesperson must be quite cautious before he comes to any conclusions about the real personality traits of a prospect.

The Nervous Prospect.   Some people may be nervous in their first meeting and not appear at their best. However, once the salesperson gets to know them, they seem to be completely different persons. When a salesperson feels that this may be true of a particular prospect, he should go slowly and try to win the confidence of the prospect. The salesperson may have to make several calls on this type of an individual before he can begin to try to close a sale.

Voluntary Control of Expressive Movements.   Many expressive movements are subject to voluntary control, hence do not reflect true feelings. Many times an angry person will conceal his anger and force a smile. In the same way, many purchasing agents will try to keep from giving the salesperson their immediate reaction, particularly if it is positive, so that they are in a good position to drive a "hard" bargain. Therefore, until the salesperson gets to know the prospect quite well, he can not be sure that the prospect's true feelings are reflected in his overt behavior.

Present Behavior is Influenced by Past Behavior.   A person's present behavior is markedly influenced by his immediate past behavior. If the salesperson can determine what a prospect or customer has done just before the call, he will have a clue to the person's behavior. Often, pent-up feelings are spilled on the salesperson because he is the first target for displaced aggression. Unfortunately, when the prospect is making a cold call, he normally does not have an opportunity to control his prospect's immediate past behavior. However, one of the reasons why many salespersons feel they should take customers out to lunch is not because they will discuss a great deal of business over a meal, rather because after a pleasant relaxed lunch, the customer will be in a good mood to talk business with the salesperson.

Expectations.   First impressions are influenced by a person's expectations. As a result, if a salesperson is predisposed to thinking either positively or negatively about a prospect he will let his first impression be colored by his expectation. Unfortunately, the predisposition may be based on incorrect hearsay which could lead the salesperson into making a mistake.

THE CRITICAL BEGINNING OF THE INTERVIEW

It is obvious that the salesperson has many things to accomplish in the first few seconds of the interview. He must decide if the prospect is interruptible. If he is, the salesperson must determine the best way to redirect his attention quickly to the matters he wishes to discuss. If the prospect is really too busy to see him, the salesperson must decide whether to call back, wait, or attempt to see someone else. The salesperson must also gauge the mood of the prospect. Is the emotional climate favorable for a presentation? Finally, the salesperson must determine how satisfied the prospect is with his present supplier. How, then, can the salesperson best open the interview?

The Introduction

The salesperson should begin by introducing himself. If the secretary has taken his business card in and arranged for the appointment, the salesperson may take advantage of the summation aspect of perception and reinforce his name and his company's name with the other person. As part of the introduction, he can also thank the other person for seeing him and assure him that he is going to make the interview worthwhile. For example, the salesperson might begin by saying: "Mr. Jones, I am Frank Smith of the XYZ Company. My firm and I both appreciate your willingness to see me. I will do my best to make this visit profitable and worthwhile for you and your company." In these few words he sets a climate with the other person, sets a purpose for the call, and accords the other person higher status than himself. Such rapport is crucial for it influences how the call will proceed.

Questions as a Useful Tactic

The salesperson wants to show the prospect that he may not be as pleased with his present supplier as he thinks he is. A good tactic for achieving this is to question the prospect. If he has little or no information on hand about products now in use and the competing companies being patronized, the questions asked must be universal enough in application to be pertinent. On a cold call, the salesperson must guard against asking questions that might seem to the other person to be presumptuous on short acquaintance. In the early stages of the call, the questions should be ones the prospect can answer without difficulty or hesitation. They should deal with matters of fact rather than opinion. The questions should be phrased so that the answers are positive rather than negative. The salesperson must be sure in framing his questions that he does not reflect his own opinion. Questions should not be leading.

The Proper Use of Displays

As an alternative to opening with questions, the salesperson may open with a display or sample designed to attract the attention and whet the curiosity of the prospect. For example, when calling on jewelry retailers, for a firm manufacturing wristwatch bands, the salesperson starts each call by handing the prospect a sample with the request "Tie a tight knot in it." He has found that this arrests the prospect's attention, and after a moment's hesitation, the other person complies. The salesperson then asks the jeweler to untie it. The band snaps back immediately to its original form. In a few seconds he is able to show the ruggedness and resilience of his product.

As another example, a tool steel salesperson had a potentially profitable account in his territory but he could never get beyond the purchasing agent to the operating personnel. To add to his difficulty, the purchasing executive had comparatively little technical knowledge pertinent to the salesperson's products and services. So on one occasion, the salesperson commenced his visit by placing two patches of velvet on the purchasing agent's desk. On each one he placed a nugget of steel. Each had a brightly burnished surface. He began the conversation by asking, "Mr. Purchasing Agent, can you tell me which of these steels is a miracle metal?" The purchasing agent replied gruffly that he was not a metallurgist, but he did examine each one. The salesperson then said, "Would you like to find out?" As the salesperson said this, he handed the purchasing executive a three-cornered file. Then he said, "See whether you can scratch them." One of the nuggets was far more scratch resistant than the other one. The salesperson then proceeded to play down the importance of this characteristic and went on to tell the purchasing agent that there were other more conclusive tests the purchasing agent could make to prove the uniqueness of the metal. He pointed out that these additional tests would require the use of certain tools and the spectographic equipment in the laboratory of the plant. The purchasing agent's curiosity was sufficiently aroused and the salesperson briefed him in the testing procedure. He agreed to take the salesperson into the plant to do the other tests. This provided an additional benefit to the salesperson. It brought his product to the attention of the tool room supervisor and the plant metallurgist.

The use of displays in the initial stage of the interview has both advantages and limitations. If the display is successful, it will arrest and redirect the attention of the prospect more quickly than questions are likely to. Also, it provides immediate participation for the other person. Often it provokes additional questions from the prospect concerning the product being shown and thus provides an easy transition to the salesperson's presentation on the product. On the other hand, it may be construed as a stunt or gimmick and arouse unfavorable feelings on the part of the prospect. By the affective expansion principle, the adverse feelings aroused are then applied to the salesperson and his company. Likewise, if it is overdone, it may so arrest the attention of the other person that it is difficult for the salesperson to discuss the business at hand.

"LIGHT TALK"

Inasmuch as the selling-buying relationship involves social interaction, the question of light talk is a pertinent issue in connection with the sales approach. From a practical standpoint, the salesperson is safer to be guided in light-talk conversation by the prospect. Obviously, if the prospect takes the initiative, the salesperson should join in. If the salesperson takes the initiative, he should be alert to the other person's reaction to the topic. In addition, it is good practice to avoid topics that are controversial—sex, religion, and politics can only cause difficulty. Finally, just as the sales representative views the occasion as a business appointment, it is reasonable to assume that the prospect has the same perspective. If too much time is devoted to chit-chat, the prospect may resent it in retrospect even though he accepted it at the time. Furthermore, if the salesperson carries light talk to extreme, he may find himself investing more time on a call than the potential sale warrants.

The Importance of Being Receiver-Oriented

To be a good conversationalist, the salesperson must be *receiver-oriented*. This implies first, that he will accord the other person uniqueness and talk about topics of interest to that person. Second, he must have something to say. This puts a premium on the salesperson being as broadly based as possible in his knowledge about contemporary happenings and business news. Third, it is up to the salesperson to avoid argument. If controversy develops, he should be mature enough to shift to another topic, which requires a fourth condition: tolerance for the other person's viewpoint. To the extent that the other person is encouraged to express his viewpoint, there is a better chance that he will change it. Obviously, if there is no participation on the prospect's part, he is likely to have little conviction about what is being discussed.

There is one other aspect of light talk that deserves consideration from a tactical standpoint. If the salesperson is both attentive and retentive with regard to what the other person likes to talk about, he has a basis for accomplishing a smooth transition from one visit to the next. For example, if a prospect has discussed his children and some of their school activities, this may pave the way for the salesperson on his next visit to bring something to the prospect of likely interest to his children.

The Role of the Salesperson

The sales representative should have on tap ways and means to turn light talk back to the business at hand. On any conversational topic the salesperson initiates there ought to be some direct or indirect relationship to the call agenda. In our business culture, light talk is so likely to occur that it underscores the need for the salesperson to be an adept coversationalist.

Perhaps the biggest barrier to approaching the prospect is the salesperson himself. It is natural to fear the new. This is why most sales representatives, given a choice, prefer to call on customers rather than prospects. Why not? With customers, he is on familiar ground, has strategic inputs for his visit, knows the people to be seen, and is likely to be received cordially. However, every salesperson needs to generate new accounts if he is to be effective. If he has a genuine conviction about the worth of his offering for the prospect, he should go in with confidence. After all, he is there to help the other person to buy profitably.

SUMMARY

In this chapter we examined the most important time in any sales call—the first few moments. The initial impression is generally a lasting one, or one that is very difficult to change. The two methods of gaining entree are via direct approach (personal call, telephone call, or letter) or indirect approach (use of a mutually respected intermediary). We discussed the advantages and pitfalls of each approach.

Once the salesperson has "his feet in the door," he must make the most of the opportunity or he may not have a second chance. A forthright introduction and statement of the purpose of the call are most appropriate. Then, the salesperson can go into the specifics and the tactical considerations required to make a successful visit. We noted a number of successful methods for opening a sales call, but these are by no means the only ones available—nor should they be used by every one in sales. The need to develop personal "door openers" is very important for each salesperson for two main reasons. First, his own personality and other characteristics may make it difficult for him to adopt the methods of other people. And second, because of the individual differences that are sure to exist among prospects, a salesperson must use different approaches on different persons. What might be appropriate for one individual may be very inappropriate for others.

The use of light talk during a sales call was also discussed. This can be a very effective device with certain prospects and customers—but not with all. When light talk is used, the salesperson must introduce it at the right time and allow it to continue for only an appropriate amount of time. In other words, the salesperson should be in control of the use of this tool. We also saw how the salesperson himself is seen as the greatest barrier to smooth approaches with new accounts.

PROBLEMS

1. Attack or defend the statement, "The salesperson is at a tactical advantage with a prospect if he has gained entree by indirect means."
2. Assume that you are a salesperson waiting in the reception lobby of a new prospect. You have an opportunity to talk to a noncompeting salesperson. What are some of the questions you would ask?
3. What are the advantages, limitations, and cautions in using each of the direct methods of gaining entree?
4. What are some questions a salesperson might use to disturb homeostasis in a cosmetics buyer?
5. How can you judge the mood of another person?

Exercise 12

THE APPROACH-GAINING ENTREE TO SELL

Objectives: To illustrate a way of obtaining an appointment.
To illustrate "opening remarks."

A. Entree by Letter
You are a salesperson handling a well-known line of young ladies' fashions. You have learned that a large-volume suburban ladies specialty store has changed ownership, and you hope to convince the new owner-manager to stock and sell your line. Your efforts with the previous management were unsuccessful. The store is an hour's drive from your headquarters. Write a letter requesting an appointment.

B. Opening Remarks
Assume you have been granted an appointment. Set forth your opening remarks.

Case 12-1 Acme Machinery Company (A)

Jim Johnson sells construction equipment for Acme Machinery Company, a distributor for Allis-Chalmers. He works out of Grand Rapids, Michigan. While skimming the week's accumulation of newspapers and magazines one weekend, a note in the *Regional Contractor* catches his eye:

> Mr. Atchison, President of Atchison Construction Company, has announced an expansion program for his firm which will include opening two new branches. One of the branches will be located in Grand Rapids.

Jim is excited by this news. He knows of Atchison's reputation. It is based in Columbus, Ohio, and has been a major contractor in road building throughout Ohio, West Virginia, and the western part of Pennsylvania. Jim thinks of what steps to take in order to see Mr. Atchison and other members of his management, especially, whoever is to head the Grand Rapids operation.

Jim jots down some things he will do Monday morning:

1. Check with boss and others to see if anyone has any personal contacts within Atchison.

2. Look up Atchison in the national and Ohio directories of contractors to find out:
   (a) "Who's who" in the firm,
   (b) size and structure of the firm,
   (c) information on brands of equipment being used by the firm, if given.

3. Request a Dunn & Bradstreet report and see what information is given; check for additional information either at the office or at the local library.

4. Phone Allis Chalmers sales representative to see if he can find out anything, in the meanwhile, through his home office.

5. Depending on what is discovered, use either a direct or indirect approach for obtaining the appointment.

Monday morning Jim is able to pull together a considerable amount of information. However, no one has a direct entrée with Mr. Atchison, so Jim decides to write him a letter with the hope of seeing him in Columbus. Here are the bits and pieces he has for possible inclusion:

Full name and address: James R. Atchison, President
Atchison Construction Company
2100 Leland Ave
Columbus, Ohio 43214

Vice-president, operations: Michael L. Murphy

Company founded: 1958

Dunn & Bradstreet Rating: Excellent

Number of branches (excluding the two new ones): four

Fleet: mixed; no known Allis-Chalmers equipment

He also sees his own company, Acme, as having these points of competitive advantage:

—in business for over 50 years

—recognized as having a strong repair shop and reliable field service capable of handling all labels of equipment

—small enough to give personal attention

—strongest Allis-Chalmers distributor in out-state Michigan

1. What tactics should Jim use to get to see Mr. Atchison?
2. Compose a letter from your company to Mr. Atchison.

Case 12-2 Acme Machinery Company (B)*

Jim arrives in Cleveland elated. He has an appointment with Mr. Atchison. During the short plane trip Jim read and reread Mr. Atchison's letter:

> Dear Mr. Johnson:
>
> This is an answer to your letter of June 17. All of us in Atchison are eager to obtain any ideas which will help our business. I am circulating your letter and enclosures to appropriate members of my team.
>
> I must advise you, however, that we are not now in the market for equipment. Initially, we expect to move existing units to any new jobs in Michigan.
>
> If you still wish to visit us, we will be pleased to see you on June 26 at 9 A.M.
>
> Sincerely,
>
> *James R. Atchison*
>
> James R. Atchison
> President

Jim asks himself: What kind of fellow is he? How shall I start off my meeting with him? He arrives at the Atchison offices at 8:50 and presents his card to the receptionist and tells her of his 9 A.M. appointment. Promptly at 9 o'clock Mr. Atchison's secretary ushers Jim to a conference room and introduces him to Mr. Atchison. In turn, Mr. Atchison introduces him to: "Mike Murphy, our number 2; Jim Ellis, our controller; Sam Cohen, our chief engineer and the guy who helps us bid our jobs; and young Jim, my son, who's learning the ropes."

Inwardly, Jim is flabbergasted. He never expected this kind of reception. He tried not to show his surprise and uneasiness.

Mr. Atchison continues, "Jim, we don't stand on ceremony. Frankly, we've never really had a serious approach from an A-C distributor sales representative. We're impressed by your initiative and willingness to come to see us. Tell us about yourself."

What should Jim say?

*The reader should examine Acme Machinery A (case 12-1) before analyzing this case.

SUGGESTIONS FOR FURTHER READING

Bethards, H. Gordon, "Keeping Those Calls Ringing," *Sales Management,* Vol. 106 (May 1, 1971), pp. 46–47.

Furst, Bruno, "How to Remember Names and Faces," *Sales Management,* Vol. 77 (Dec. 7, 1956), pp. 38–40 and 42.

Henry, Porter, "Use of 2-D Principle for Making the Most of Sales Time," *Sales Management,* Vol. 114 (May 19, 1975), pp. 24–26.

*The reader should examine Acme Machinery A (case 12-1) before analyzing this case.

Kahn, Robert, and Charles F. Cannell, *The Dynamics of Interviewing* (New York, N.Y.: Wiley 1957).

Kurtz, David L., H. Robert Dodge, and Jay E. Klopmaker, *Professional Selling* (Dallas, Tx.: Business Publications, 1976), Chapter 7.

Russell, Frederic A., Frank H. Beach, and Richard H. Buskirk, *Textbook of Salesmanship,* 9th ed. (New York, N.Y.: McGraw-Hill, 1974), Chapters 7 and 8.

Sales Management, "How Buyers Rate Salesmen," Vol. 106 (Jan. 15, 1971), pp. 21–23.

13. The Presentation — Satisfying Wants Persuasively

If the approach has been handled effectively, the prospect is now in a favorable perceiving, thinking, and feeling state to hear what the salesperson has to offer. The salesperson has an assessment of the prospect's needs and wants and can relate his remarks to them. Thus, both parties are ready for the next step, the *presentation*. (Review Chapter 6, if necessary.) This is Phase 3 of the selling-buying process and involves placing the firm's want-satisfier system in the best possible light from the standpoint of the customer or prospect. In this chapter we analyze preparation for the sales presentation, criteria for an effective presentation, and the proper use of suggestion.

PREPARATION FOR THE SALES PRESENTATION

Sales representatives face a key communication task in preparing effective presentations; that is, they must translate the company's resources, its products and services, and its people into benefits, uses, and want satisfiers for those comprising the markets. The more technical the product line, the more difficult this translation task becomes. Let us consider feature-benefit matrices, competition, and the specific presentation.

Feature-Benefit Matrices: Development and Communication

In preparing for a sales presentation the salesperson should develop a set of feature-benefit matrices which deal with (1) special features of his company, (2) the product group he hopes to sell, (3) any associated services that accompany the product group, and (4) the special personnel talents that exist within his firm. A feature-benefit matrix is a table which forces the salesperson to think through the prominent features of his firm, how they relate to his customers, and how they can be effectively communicated to his customers.

Table 13-1 illustrates a feature-benefit matrix for the salesperson's company. The prominent features listed are size of the firm, number of years it has been in business, and geographic location. For each feature, several critical customer benefits are listed along with alternate ways of expressing these benefits to the salesperson's customers. Tables 13-2 through 13-4 provide examples of the three other types of feature-benefit matrices just mentioned. According to each situation, more feature-benefit entries could be worked out for each matrix. We shall examine the three sequential steps for developing and implementing these matrices: (1) determining the prominent features, (2) converting the features into benefits, and (3) expressing and demonstrating each benefit to the customer.

Determining the Prominent Features.   The salesperson must list the prominent features for each feature-benefit matrix. For instance, a feature for the firm would be number of years in business. A product feature might be the fact that it is offered in different forms. As to associated services, an example might be the availability of a corporate field-service organization staffed by engineers. Talent might be exemplified by the size of the firm's research staff and the caliber of all company personnel.

Converting Features into Benefits.   Once each list of features has been drawn up, the next step is to convert the features into benefits, uses, and want satisfiers. This involves showing the significance of the features to the customers and prospects. As an example, if one company feature is that the firm is large in size, the benefits that would accrue to the customer might include the availability of a

TABLE 13-1 COMPANY FEATURE-BENEFIT MATRIX

Features	Customer Benefits	Alternate Ways of Expressing
Large size	Spectrum of resources available	Have a wide variety of talents and equipment available to service customers' needs
	Economies of scale in production	Low-cost producer because of large-scale operation
Number of years in business	If old:	
	Stable source of supply	Have been providing the products for years
	Reputation built over a number of years	
		Not a fly-by-night operation
	If new:	
	Young, aggressive company	Willing to try the new
	Very desireous of making new customers	Hungry for business
Geographic location	Can give good service and quick delivery	Always nearby to give good service
	Near the customer's location so have reduced shipping costs	Transportation time and costs less than competitors

TABLE 13-2 PRODUCT GROUP FEATURE-BENEFIT MATRIX

Features	Customer Benefits	Alternate Ways of Expressing
Assortment available	Wide variety from which to select	Can meet most customer needs because of selection available
	As fashion or style changes, will still be able to have the right type to sell	As colors, styles, etc., change (fads) the right types of goods will still be available because of wide assortment
Inventory supply	Can meet emergency needs of customers because of backup inventory available	When customers need quick delivery, can ship almost immediately from inventory
	Reduced production expenses because make in large quantities	Competitive prices because of economical production runs
Available in alternate forms	Better able to meet specific customer needs	Can tailor to customer desires because of varieties of configurations available
	Not in direct competition with other sellers because of product variations available	Product differentiation created by selling different varieties

TABLE 13-3 ASSOCIATED SERVICES FEATURE-BENEFIT MATRIX

Features	Benefits	Alternate Ways of Expressing
Field service organization	Technical advice available to customers	Producer's people available to work on customer's problems
	Qualified assistance for special problems	When particular problems are encountered, will send people out to work on them
Cooperative advertising	Will help promote the reselling of the product by paying a portion of the reseller's advertising expenses	Provide ad layouts or drawings to use in advertisements
	Helps develop an awareness of the reseller's existence	Creates more business for resellers for specific product as well as for other products handled
Company school	Insures top-flight training for customer's key personnel	Customers gain competitive advantage through expertise of their people
	Keeps employees from getting in a rut—they exchange ideas with others in the industry	Employees improve their attitude; they learn from others at the company school

TABLE 13-4 TALENT RESOURCES FEATURE-BENEFIT MATRIX

Features	Benefits	Alternate Ways of Expressing
High caliber of management	Willing and able to work with customers on business problems	Help customers to make more profit by knowing about and working with them
	By associating with a progressive supplier can be sure of being on top of significant changes or trends	Can be kept informed of industry changes
Qualified technical personnel	Guarantee of best brains in industry on customer's problems	In effect, each customer has the company's technical staff as his own
	Insurance of continuing development and refinement of product line	Way of keeping out front technologically
Customer-oriented salesperson	Each salesperson is an unpaid consultant for the customer	Salesperson's availability is an important value added in each purchase
	Provides direct personal linkage with supplier	Makes supplier and customer "partners in profit"

wide range of resources and cost savings as a result of significant economies of scale in production. An example in the services matrix might be the company school, which would provide benefits for the customer in terms of good training programs for his personnel plus an exposure to other people in their industry.

Expressing and Demonstrating Each Benefit.   The salesperson must develop as many ways as possible of expressing and demonstrating each benefit. There are several reasons why it is important to have alternate ways of expressing the want-satisfier aspects of each element in the offering. Because of the summation aspect of perception, which is discussed later in this chapter, there is no assurance on a particular call that expressing something once will reach the conscious awareness of the customer. More likely, a given point that arouses interest will need to be made in many different ways before full comprehension occurs. A second application has to do with successive calls on the same person. Often the salesperson must present essentially the same want satisfiers during each of a number of visits. It is important that he have a fresh approach in such presentations, lest he bore the other person by repeating almost verbatim what he said during the last call. Third, relating this to the discussion of tactics, the salesperson needs to have different ways of handling a particular point if he is to cope effectively with positive-involuntary reactions as he encounters them (these reactions were discussed in Chapter 11).

   Time and effort invested in these three steps can be amortized over all the presentations the salesperson makes. Essentially, these three steps are done just once although a review and refinement of them is essential from time to time based on the salesperson's accumulated experience, change in customer or prospect behavior, shifts in competitive strategy, and, of course, any innovations his firm makes in the want-satisfier offering.

Competition

It is helpful for the salesperson to analyze each of his competitors in the same manner as he does his own firm with feature-benefit matrices. If this is feasible, it gives the salesperson an opportunity to anticipate the essentials of each competing salesperson's presentation. This in turn allows him to work out ways of differentiating his claims from those his competitors are making. As a result, the salesperson has a substantial advantage because he can emphasize his firm's relative advantages without attacking each competitor directly.

The Specific Presentation

The salesperson is now equipped to prepare a specific presentation for a particular account. In view of his call objectives, he selects elements out of each relevant matrix for the presentation. For instance, with a current customer, the objective might be to acquaint the account with a new product the firm is introducing. The salesperson might first consider which products the customer is now buying and from which of these he is deriving greatest satisfaction. In this case one element might be to remind the person of these benefits as an indication or likelihood of deriving similar benefits from the new product. The second and main element in the presentation might be the variety of benefits provided by the new product. Inasmuch as the customer is not familiar with this product, the salesperson might enumerate its many benefits. Then, he could elaborate any points arousing interest and favorable reaction.

In contrast, if the contemplated call is on a prospect and the key objective is to establish the salesperson's firm as "a good place to do business," the salesperson's preparation would be mainly a study and refinement of the matrix reflecting the benefits of the firm. In general, it is easier to prepare a more individualized presentation for a customer account than for a prospect account. In fact, in the extreme case, with a new account the general-purpose matrices are about all the salesperson can use as a basis for his presentation.

CRITERIA FOR AN EFFECTIVE PRESENTATION

Whether the individual called on is a prospect or a customer, and whether the points to be covered are simple or complex, the presentation itself must meet four basic criteria: it must be *understandable, interesting, believable,* and *persuasive*. These criteria are interactive in that each one is dependent on the others. It is difficult to conceive of an interesting presentation if it is not understood by the other person. If the presentation is to be believable, then what is said must be understood and interesting. However, the acid test is that it must be persuasive. Let us examine how a presentation can be prepared so that it meets these four criteria.

Understandable

There are four concepts that combine to make a presentation understandable: (1) the way in which an event is perceived, (2) the customer's attention span, (3) the mind's attempt to make concepts concrete rather than abstract, and (4) the customer's state of mind.

Perception.   How a person perceives incoming stimuli is greatly dependent on his past experience. Thus, to the extent that a salesperson knows the background of the prospect or customer and presents his ideas in terms of that background, he is likely to be understood. This involves using examples, illustrations, analogies, and comparisons in order to relate what is being presented in the perceptual present to the individual's prior experience. It is easy for a salesperson to violate this principle by using technical terms, concepts, and examples beyond the understanding of the other person. In addition, the salesperson must avoid discussing points that are not of interest to the customer's needs and wants.

The salesperson must also be aware of the fact that he may have to present his point several times and in several ways before the customer really understands what he is trying to get across. As an example, let us consider a young salesperson who is very successful at selling stereo equipment in a retail store. After he has determined the customer's real needs, he presents the technical aspects of the equipment. When this is completed he plays the stereo softly and reiterates the benefits of the equipment that is being listened to. Finally he asks the prospect what types of music he would like to hear, and asks him to adjust the volume to the level that he desires. At this point the salesperson tries to answer any questions the prospect has.

This salesperson recognizes two very important aspects of perception. First, he realizes that he needs to reiterate his message several times if it is to be understood. Second, he recognizes the importance of the use of visual stimuli to help the prospect understand his message. That is by showing the prospect the equipment and by asking him to set the volume at the level he wishes the prospect has a better chance of understanding the salesperson.

Attention Span.   The prospect's attention span must be considered if understanding is to occur. An abundance of research evidence indicates how limited human beings are in the number of stimuli they can attend to at once. The less familiar they are with the stimuli, the smaller is the number of stimuli that can be held within their attention. If the presentation is to be understood, the number of points or concepts incorporated should be few enough for the listener to grasp. In addition, the very *pace* of the presentation will influence how well it is understood. The better informed the salesperson is, the more likely he is to set too fast a pace in his presentation for comprehension on the part of the listener.

Concrete Rather than Abstract Terms.   The salesperson who avoids abstract terms and uses image-provoking language will be more understandable. If technical terms need to be used, they should be defined adequately to avoid misunderstanding and confusion. This is particularly important for technically trained salespersons who call on purchasing agents who are not technically trained. Often this type of salesperson might find himself talking in a language that the purchasing agent does not understand, resulting in very little successful communication. Since most individuals do not like to admit their own ignorance of a subject, the salesperson must use clear language and be attentive to the other person so as to catch cues that let him know how he is coming across. As we discussed in Chapter 4, the extent to which the salesperson elicits feedback, he is likely to minimize noise in the receiver and thus increase the receiver's understanding of the presentation.

The Customer's or Prospect's State of Mind.   An individual's feelings or state of mind also influence understanding. To the extent that the salesperson establishes a favorable feeling state in the other person during the approach, he is enhancing the likelihood of his presentation being understood. Understanding may be blocked by the unwitting use of words and phrases that have emotional overtones for the other person. "Homemade" might cause a favorable feeling response in one person because the expression elicits in him an image of apple pie baked by mother for Sunday dinner. For another person it might be a reminder of impoverished youth, when the family could not afford "store-bought" clothing. Another person might give the term a meaning of less than adequate, or imperfect. Generally, understanding is enhanced when some feelings or emotion is aroused. It is difficult to communicate effectively to a person who has no feeling whatsoever for what you are saying. At the other extreme, if too much emotions are aroused, this may block that person's perception and thought process and thus impede his understanding of the presentation.

Interest

The second criterion to insure a successful presentation is obtaining the interest of the other person. The salesperson has several sources of information from which to infer the likely interests of the prospect or customer. These include both personal background and professional role. We will examine these, along with tactical considerations of how the salesperson can sense the degree of interest the prospect has in his presentation.

Personal Background.   The kind and amount of formal education the customer or prospect has may provide some clues. With an individual who has substantial professional experience, inferences about his interests might be drawn from a knowledge of his work background. A prime aspect of this kind of information is the person's life values. These values give rise to his attitudes and interests, and are critical in that they let the salesperson know the kinds of values the prospect looks for in the presentation. In addition, the more the salesperson knows about the other person's traits and motives, the better equipped he is to interest him. All those personal characteristics that give the other person his uniqueness are important considerations.

Professional Role.   Another set of clues to a person's likely interests stems from the position he holds in the firm and particularly the role he plays in the decision-making "who's who." For instance, the marketing manager and the controller are likely to have quite different interests.

Fundamentally, of course, the salesperson recognizes that to obtain the interest of the prospect he must make him realize that he is not as satisfied with his present supplier as he thought he was. In doing this, the salesperson faces a dual task. He must meet the individual's needs and wants as well as the needs and wants of the firm as that individual interprets them. The salesperson's best assumption is that the person called on is satisfied with things as they now are, and therefore he must disturb this complacency; until this is done there will be little or no interest in the presentation. The exception, of course, is the sales representative's own satisfied customer. The salesperson may reinforce this person's interests by encouraging him to describe the many benefits and advantages he sees in the present selling-buying relationship.

Tactical Considerations.   The salesperson must be able to sense the waxing and waning of interest as he continues with the presentation. The best single indicator he has of this is the degree of attention accorded the presentation by the prospect or customer. Attention is a dimension of perception, and until incoming stimuli receive a substantial amount of attention they do not reach the level of conscious awareness. Until they reach conscious awareness there can be no interest.

Because the salesperson must satisfy the personal needs and wants of the individual as well as those of the individual's firm (as he interprets them) suggests the importance of "you" appeal. Sales representatives should avoid as much as possible referring to "I" or to "my" company. One of the weakest sales appeals is for a salesperson to seek the order on the basis of "I need the business." On the contrary, one of the strongest appeals is to the ego of the other person.

Believability

The third criterion for a successful presentation is believability. This is a function of several key variables, which include the (1) image of the salesperson, (2) the personal conviction of the salesperson, (3) overlearning the presentation, (4) the ability to reassure the customer, and (5) third-party selling.

Image of the Salesperson.   To a great extent, believability is not a function of the content of the presentation as much as it is a function of the personal image the salesperson conveys. If the customer or prospect approves of the salesperson's conduct, he is likely to believe what the salesperson says. Conversely, if he disapproves or feels threatened by the salesperson's values, he is not likely to put much credence in the presentation.

In addition, the salesperson's image is a function of the firm he represents. Take, for example, an IBM computer salesperson contrasted with a "Hot Shot Electric" salesperson. The IBM salesperson has an image of being honest, forthright, and an expert in his field. The salesperson who represents "Hot Shot" begins with the handicap that the buyer has never heard of "Hot Shot" before. As a result the IBM man has a positive image because he represents IBM, whereas the other salesperson has either no image or a negative image in the mind of the buyer.

Personal Convictions.   This is the feeling on the part of the salesperson that his offering represents a good value for the prospect or customer. The salesperson has to be sold on the proposition if he is to sell it to another person. Belief or conviction on the salesperson's part, by suggestion, encourages a similar reaction in the other person. The salesperson must be sincere for his presentation to ring true. The manner of presentation is more important in accomplishing this than what is said.

Overlearning the Presentation.   A third factor influencing believability is the extent to which the salesperson has overlearned what he is presenting. Overlearning is a technical term from psychology which refers to the situation where a person has learned something to the point that it is second nature to him, a part of himself. The importance of this can be illustrated by what happens when the salesperson has *not* overlearned his material. If the salesperson has only learned his presentation, but not made it part of himself, and some unanticipated reaction occurs in the other person, the salesperson may stumble or direct his attention inwardly to think through what to say or do next. This stumbling and hesitation may be interpreted by the prospect or customer as a lack of expertise and conviction on the salesperson's part.

Reassurance.   The salesperson can increase believability if he is able to reassure the other person. With a customer, this can be done by citing many favorable experiences and benefits that have been derived in the past from the selling-buying relationship. With a prospect, this may be accomplished by reminding the other person of the reputation of the firm, of the salesperson's willingness to personally back up any purchase, and, if appropriate, by reference to any guarantees and warranties associated with the product.

Third-Party Selling.   The last method of instilling believability is through third-party selling. This involves the judicious use of testimonials of people who presumably have no vested interest in influencing the other person to buy. Such statements are given more credence than claims by the salesperson. Testimonials may range from formal statements on the part of customers to evaluative data prepared by a testing laboratory, or to such endoresements as a *Good Housekeeping* Seal of Approval.

The issue of credibility cannot be overemphasized. In most instances, prospective purchasers are likely to be skeptical about claims made in ads, direct-mail pieces, and sales presentations. Unless the salesperson is believable, a sale will not result.

PERSUASION

As important as understandability, interest, and believability are, still the acid test of a presentation is persuasibility. Unless the presentation meets this critical criterion, it will be ineffective. The salesperson accomplishes this by some combination of suggestion and reasoning. Generally, customers who are already deriving satisfaction from the selling-buying relationship are more amenable to suggestion than are prospects. Customers know the salesperson, his company, his products, and his services. They are convinced of their worth. Prospects, in contrast, are usually deriving satisfaction from competing offerings and consequently have to be reasoned with if they are to shift to other want satisfiers. We shall examine the strategic and tactical considerations of persuasion.

Strategic Considerations

The salesperson must weigh three strategic considerations in deciding whether the emphasis in the presentation should be through suggestion or through reasoning. These include his trait and motivational analysis of the customer or prospect, the salesperson's analysis of the situation within the account, and the relative emphasis on suggestion versus reasoning.

Trait and Motivational Analysis.   The salesperson should begin by considering his trait and motivational analysis of the prospect or customer (review Chapter 8 for details of this method). As an example, an insecure person is more open to suggestions, while a self-confident person must often be provided with many logical reasons for taking a particular action. The extremely impulsive person may act immediately on suggestion, whereas an extremely deliberate person is apt to weigh any proposition with care. An individual with a relatively low level of intelligence and with little technical knowledge is likely to be more open to suggestion than a bright, technically able person.

Analysis of the Situation within the Account.   A second strategic consideration in deciding whether suggestion or reasoning should be used is the salesperson's analysis of the situation within the account. If there is a deadline by which the buying decision must be made, suggestion may be adequate. On the other hand, if there is no compelling reason to purchase immediately, the decision makers may want to weigh each detail of the presentation very carefully. The closer the proposal relates to the prior experience of the firm, the more the salesperson can rely on suggestion. In contrast, the more unprecedented the proposal, the more likely it is that the salesperson will have to supply excellent reasons why his offering should be accepted. If the salesperson is dealing with only one decision maker, depending on the trait and motivation analysis, that person may be amenable to suggestion. In contrast, if the individual called on must become an internal salesperson within the decision-making "who's who," it is important for the salesperson to provide him with a comprehensive rationale for such a presentation.

Products and Services Being Offered.   A third strategic consideration that will influence the salesperson's relative emphasis on suggestion or reasoning involves the products and services being sold. If the products are relatively simple and nontechnical, suggestion may be sufficient. If they are complex and highly technical, the emphasis should be on reasoning. In addition, if the unit order represents a *small outlay* from the standpoint of the customer or prospect, he may be open to suggestion, but if it represents a substantial investment, reasoning will be needed. Finally, the better known the products, services, and expertise of the company are, the more likely it is that suggestion will be effective, whereas if neither the product nor the company is known, reasoning will be necessary.

Tactical Considerations

Going beyond these strategic considerations, the salesperson must recognize that certain tactical factors also influence the use of suggestion versus reasoning. We will examine mood and rapport along with the salesperson's assessment of the attention level and goal gradient.

Mood and Rapport.   If the salesperson finds the customer or prospect in a pleasant mood, he can rely more heavily on suggestion and accomplish more than he had expected. Also, the more the salesperson establishes rapport and makes a favorable impression, the more likely his suggestions will be acceptable.

Assessment of the Attention Level.   As the call continues, the salesperson's assessment of the attention level of the other person provides an additional tactical consideration. Usually if he has the full attention of the prospect or customer, the accompanying thought processes are logical, analytical, and evaluative. With this mental set, reasoning is called for. The salesperson can gauge the level of attention by the cogency and number of questions asked. In contrast, if part of the person's attention is diverted to other matters, he is likely to be open to suggestion.

Goal Gradient.   Still another tactical consideration in using suggestion versus reasoning is the *goal gradient* principle, discussed in Chapter 11. This principle implies that the closer an individual gets to an important goal he has been seeking the less interruptible he is. Thus if the salesperson interrupts someone in this situation and he cannot command the attention of the preoccupied individual, he may request permission to see someone else in the company. And because much of the other person's attention is on his uncompleted task, he is more open to suggestion and may accede to the request.

   Strategic and tactical conditions often interact in influencing the desirability of suggestion and reasoning, so the salesperson must be skilled in responding to both kinds if his presentations are to be persuasive. Because suggestions are so critical to the presentation let us consider them in more detail.

SUGGESTIONS TO THE CUSTOMER OR PROSPECT

Suggestions can be direct or indirect and positive or negative. We will analyze these aspects, together with several other principles of suggestion.

Direct Versus Indirect Suggestion

When a direct suggestion is used, it is usually evident to the customer or prospect what the salesperson wants him to do. For example, a salesperson might bring a sample to a prospect and say, "Try this and you will see what I am talking about." In contrast, an indirect suggestion does not reveal the desire of the person making it, nor does it spell out the desired action. For example, a salesperson might say, "Dealing with the firm that has the lowest price may be very costly in the long run."

Indirect suggestion has two tactical advantages over direct suggestion. First, it puts the burden on the other person to make a decision. Therefore, if the customer decides to perform the desired act, he feels that it is his own idea. This decreases the likelihood that antagonistic ideas, which may serve as a source of sales resistance, will develop. Second, if it does not work then a more direct suggestion can be used. However, if the salesperson uses a direct suggestion and it doesn't work, he has provided the opportunity for a negative-voluntary reaction, and it will be difficult for him to regain a favorable position.

Positive Versus Negative Suggestions

A positive suggestion indicates an action to be taken or a decision to be made. In contrast, a negative suggestion indicates an action or decision to avoid. "Order now while we can still guarantee delivery," is positive. The same suggestion in negative form would be, "Don't postpone the decision or we may not be able to make delivery." The tactical weakness of the negative suggestion arises from the fact that there are two elements present: what is to be avoided as well as what is to be acted upon. The difficulty is that the other person may react only to the negative element.

Principles of Suggestion

In addition to the principles of direct versus indirect suggestions and positive versus negative suggestions, let us analyze ten other principles of suggestion that are applicable to the selling-buying process.

The Prestige of the Suggestor.   The greater the prestige of the person making the suggestion, the greater the likelihood that his suggestion will be followed. There are many factors that contribute to prestige. One of these is the reputation of the company. Others, such as social standing, financial resources, physical size, age, and educational attainment may reside in the salesperson. The suggestion that a certain stock is a good investment is less likely to be questioned when coming from a person known to be a successful investor than from a person with no comparable record of success. A salesperson may be able to use this type of suggestion by quoting persons of prestige. These can be executives in his company, persons well known in the trade, or persons from the community.

The Impact of Numbers.   In a difficult sales situation, it may be profitable to back the salesperson with other company personnel. A joint call with a sales executive, a company engineer, or another person of authority will increase the likelihood of success from the standpoint of suggestion.

Attention Level.   There is a widespread idea that if a high level of attention is devoted to the subject at hand, there is a greater likelihood that the suggestion will be acted upon. A person becomes so concerned over a problem that his ability to weigh the pros and cons objectively diminishes. (This supports the idea that stepping back—relaxing attention—to get a fresh view is an aid to clearer understanding.) While there is no experimental evidence for this, it may be that, at the other end of the scale—inattention—there is also an increased likelihood of suggestions being acted upon. This is based on the idea of dissociation. Suppose a salesperson calls on a prospect who is completely immersed in thinking about a problem. The salesperson may present his proposition, but the prospect never really shifts his attention to the salesperson. If the salesperson makes the sale, he has done so without the prospect attending to or critically evaluating the proposition.

   If this reasoning is correct, then suggestion is most likely to be effective when the customer is either barely attending or completely engrossed in the problem. At the middle level of attention, the prospect is most likely to think critically about the proposition.

Absence of an Opposing Idea.   In psychology, one often sees the statement that every idea that enters the mind will be acted upon unless there is an antagonistic item present. One way, then, to minimize opposing ideas is to keep the desired idea in mind. The more time a prospect devotes to the desired idea, the less time he can devote to inhibiting ideas; hence, if an idea is kept before a person long enough, it will be acted upon.

Repetition of the Suggestion.   When an idea is repeated often enough over a period of time, the subject tends to forget the origin of the idea, and may eventually accept it as his own. This is an aid to the salesperson, because it is easier for the buyer to act on his own ideas than on the ideas of the salesperson. Many times such an idea can be planted through company advertising, which is a good reason for coordination of advertising and selling. The advertising copy and the sales representative's presentation should be couched in the same style as much as possible. This allows the salesperson to make maximum use of the advertising as a preselling device.

Ignorance of the Topic Under Discussion.   This occurs when the person lacks information with which to disagree. For example, if a person were having a house built, how would he know what material to use on the exterior? He has a choice of wood, concrete, brick, and a variety of metals such as stainless steel and aluminum. If the contractor "suggests" a material and the person lacks any knowledge of the materials, he usually will adopt the ideas of the contractor. If a contractor built a house for himself, he might very well use the same material. The difference would be that the contractor would select the material after a process of reasoning rather than as the result of suggestion.

A Disturbed State.   Any disturbance of a physical (fever, fatigue, drunkness) or psychological (depression, excitement) nature will reduce a person's ability to think clearly and hence leave him more open to suggestion. There are many examples of people making purchases under the influence of alcohol that they would not have made otherwise. While perhaps less dramatic, purchases made under other forms of disturbances are equally likely to be unsatisfactory.

Previous Performance of the Act.   Any novel act is likely to require a conscious effort and be accompanied by critical thought processes. As far as selling is concerned, this would indicate that a salesperson should not expect his first sale to a prospect to be achieved by suggestion. Initial contacts require undivided attention and a full presentation. Subsequent sales may be accomplished by suggestion and without the customer's full attention.

Of course, it takes more than suggestion to account for the ease of the second sale to a customer over the first one, such as satisfactory service from the first purchase and the salesperson's increased knowledge of the customer's needs.

Wording of the Suggestion.   There is experimental evidence to show that leading questions, definite rather than indefinite articles, and positive rather than negative phrasing influence the individual's reply.

For example, "Did you see the horse?" is more likely to produce an affirmative answer than "Did you see a horse?" In order to suggest that a dog was dark colored, this would be accomplished more readily by asking, "Was the dog dark colored?" than by asking, "What color was the dog?"

Another way language can increase suggestibility is through the use of technical terms. A liberal sprinkling of such terms, especially if they are spoken easily and habitually, may influence the listener. Dramatic effect through the use of colorful words, intonations, and gestures also increase suggestion.

Seeing the Act Performed.   There is a tendency to imitate the actions of other persons unless some inhibiting factor is present. Any audience can be used to illustrate this. If one person coughs, it triggers off a whole series of coughs. A salesperson who realizes this will be alert to perform any motor act, the imitation of which will bring the prospect nearer to an affirmative buying decision. For example, an order form calling for the signature of the customer might contain a space where the salesperson could sign also. The salesperson should sign the form first as a way of reducing the resistance of the customer to placing his signature where needed.

SUMMARY

Each part of a sales call is very important and is developed on the basis established in preceding sales call activity. If the initial impression conveyed in the approach is not favorable, then the presentation will not be well received. Conversely, if a favorable *set* is established at the start, the presentation is likely to go well. The presentation, although not any more important than any other part, is perhaps the "core" of a sales call.

The first step for a good presentation is preparation. One way of being sure all the salient points are covered and related to the prospect's or customer's needs is to develop four feature-benefit matrices, one about the salesperson's company, one about the product group, one about the available associated services, and one about the company's people. Elements from these matrices can then be used as the basis for an individualized presentation.

The four criteria used to evaluate a presentation are: understandability, interest, believability, and persuasion. For a presentation to be effective, all four of these criteria must be met. The key factors in understandability include individual differences in perception, attention span, salesperson's ability to think concretely, and the customer's state of mind.

The next criterion is interest. Relevant considerations here are the educational level of the recipient, life values, need homeostasis, attention, and "you" appeal.

The third criterion is believability. Factors considered important in establishing believability are: image, personal conviction, sincerity, manner of presentation, overlearning, reassurance, and testimonials.

The final criterion, persuasion, is accomplished by suggestion and by reasoning. The decision as to which to use in any specific sales call depends upon strategic as well as tactical considerations. Strategic considerations include: customer's or prospect's trait pattern and motivation, urgency of the buying decision, prior selling-buying relationships, products and services being offered, relative size of the proposed purchase, and prior knowledge of goods being sold. Tactical considerations are the mood of the person, the rapport, and the attention level.

PROBLEMS

1. You have been asked to address a group of high school seniors to influence them to enroll at your college or university. Prepare a feature-benefit matrix as a basis for your presentation.
2. Prepare a checklist of principles, methods, and techniques peculiar to each of the four criteria of an effective presentation.
3. Give at least one example of each of the following kinds of suggestion: direct, indirect, positive, negative.
4. What traits on the part of the customer would be influential in the salesperson's decision to use reasoning versus suggestion?

Exercise 13

THE PRESENTATION-SATISFYING WANTS PERSUASIVELY

Objective: To apply the *matrix* method to a company offering.

Continue your role as a salesperson of ladies fashions. (See Exercise 12) Work out entries for each feature-benefit matrix. (You may wish to peruse recent issues of such magazines as *Mademoiselle* and *Seventeen* for ideas.)

A. Your Firm as a Source

Feature	Benefits	Alternate Ways of Expressing
1.	1a.	
	1b.	
2.	2a.	
	2b.	
3.	3a.	
	3b.	

B. Your Product Line

Feature	Benefits	Alternate Ways of Expressing
1.	1.	
	1b.	

2.	2a.
	2b.
3.	3a.
	3b.

C. Your Associated Services

Feature	Benefits	Alternate Ways of Expressing
1.	1a.	
	1b.	
2.	2a.	
	2b.	
3.	3a.	
	3b.	

D. Your Talent Resources

Feature	Benefits	Alternate Ways of Expressing
1.	1a.	
	1b.	
2.	2a.	
	2b.	
3.	3a.	
	3b.	

Case 13-1 Robinson's Carriage House

Marjorie Smith is a young housewife on the sales staff of Robinson's Carriage House, one of the finest furniture stores in the greater Providence area. She has worked there for almost two years and has built up a following. In fact her principal source of leads is referral by satisfied customers.

A well-dressed, middle-age woman enters the store and asks for Marge by name. Marge comes to the front of the store and greets the caller and introduces herself.

Mrs. Jackson: Mrs. Smith, I'm Mrs. Jackson and I've been recommended to you by my good friend and neighbor, Mrs. Jarrett. She sure thinks a lot of you.

Marge: Mrs. Jackson, I'm delighted to meet you. Mrs. Jarrett is very kind. Doesn't she have a lovely home?

Mrs. Jackson: She certainly does. She told me that you recommended several excellent pieces to her for her living room.

Marge: Yes. One of the reasons her living room is so attractive is the mix of woods and fabrics.

Mrs. Jackson: I certainly agree with you, Mrs. Smith. I'm really here to see you and your store. Right now I'm not planning to buy. However, my husband and I are thinking of replacing our dining room set. It's been in use a long time. The years fly by. We have our twenty-fifth wedding anniversary coming up a few months from now.

Marge: Congratulations. You certainly must have married very young. If you can spend a few minutes, I would like to show you through the store. We're very proud of Robinson's and the high-quality furniture we carry. You probably know that Mr. James Robinson is the third generation of his family to run the business. Every piece in the store has been approved by our interior decorator and Mr. Robinson, himself.

We find the two women strolling through room settings of dining room furniture.

Mrs. Jackson: Marge, that certainly is an attractice dining room set.

Marge: Yes, Mrs. Jackson, we just got that in. Mr. Robinson saw it at the last market and felt it was one of the best designed sets he had seen in years.

Mrs. Jackson: What's the price on it?

Marge: Well, Mrs. Jackson, you have fine taste. It's the top set now in stock and a great value. It sells for $1400.

Mrs. Jackson: My, that is a lot of money.

Marge: Well, often the best is the least costly in the long run. It will give you the many years of service your present set has provided you. You'll be proud too, knowing you have the very best.

Mrs. Jackson: I certainly do like it, Marge.

Marge: Mrs. Jackson, may I be presumptuous. I'd very much like to see your home before you buy anything so that I may serve you better.

Mrs. Jackson: Why, Marge, that surely is nice of you. Let's finish our tour and we'll go now if that's all right. It will only take us a few minutes to drive out and I'll be glad to bring you back.

Marge: Oh, that's wonderful. Let me tell Mr. Robinson I'll be out of the store.

1. What has Marge accomplished so far?
2. What might have improved her efforts?

Case 13-2 WMSU (FM)

Bill Carr is a one-man sales force for WMSU. The station features classical and semi-classical music and provides a national and local news summary four times a day. It is on the air from 7 A.M. to 11 P.M. The city and suburban population is about 300,000. The urban area is heavy industrial; the suburbs mainly "bedroom" communities. It is one of three FM stations in the local market. The others feature country and rock, respectively. The reach of the signal is about 20 to 25 miles.

Bill keeps an active prospect file and about two-thirds of his time is devoted to calling on them. He has obtained an appointment to see the head of a general insurance agency.

Set forth below are the notes he made for preparing his presentation.

What I know about the prospect?

Company:	Hughes Insurance
Head:	Mr. J. W. Hughes
Time in business:	18 years
Size:	about 15 employees
Reputation:	excellent; Mr. Hughes well known and active in community
Other:	WMSU carries casualty policy with Hughes

Why should Hughes advertise on WMSU?

—caters to people of substance and culture
—has an excellent reputation
—is independent, locally owned business
—programs convey image of good taste
—at present no other insurance advertising
—rates are competitive
—will provide free assistance in preparing commercials
—one exclusive news sponsorship now available

Prepare a presentation that will be effective for Bill.

SUGGESTIONS FOR FURTHER READING

Bauer, Raymond A., "Self-Confidence and Persuasibility: One More Time," *Journal of Marketing Research,* Vol. 7 (May 1970), pp. 256–258.

Garardi, N.,"Salesman: Face to Face with Today's Buyer," *House and Home* (July 1975), pp. 45–61.

Henry, J. P., Jr., "Make Your Suppliers' Presentations Count," *Industrial Distribution,* Vol. 63 (October 1973), pp. 69–70.

Hovland, Carl I., Irving L. Janis, and Harold H. Kelly, *Communication and Persuasion,* (New Haven, Conn.: Yale University Press, 1953).

Jolson, Marvin A., "Should the Sales Presentation be 'Fresh' or 'Canned'?" *Business Horizons,* Vol. 16 (October 1973), pp. 81–88.

Jolson, Marvin A., "The Underestimated Potential of the Canned Sales Presentation," *Journal of Marketing,* Vol. 40 (January 1976), pp. 68–70.

Kuesel, Harry N., "Brush Up Your Sales Talk," *Sales Management,* Vol. 101 (Sept. 1, 1968), pp. 38–39.

Raudsepp, Eugene, "How to Sell Ideas Persuasively," *Sales Management,* Vol. 105 (Nov. 15, 1970), pp. 34–35.

Roth, Charles B., *Successful Sales Presentations,* (Englewood Cliffs, N.J.: Prentice-Hall, 1955).

Sales Management, "What Makes a Good Presentation? It Depends on Where you Sit," Vol. 111 (Nov. 12, 1973), pp. 44.

Schuchman, Abe, and Michael Perry, "Self-Confidence and Persuasibility in Marketing: A Reappraisal," *Journal of Marketing Research,* Vol. 6 (May 1969), pp. 146–154.

Vohs, John L., and Roger L. Garrett, "Resistance to Persuasion: An Integrative Framework," *Public Opinion Quarterly,* Vol. 32 (Fall 1968), pp. 445–452.

14. Demonstration – Reinforcing the Presentation

IN THIS CHAPTER

Considerations for the Use of the Demonstration
Materials and Tools Used in Demonstrations
Timing in Relation to the Selling-Buying Process
Requirements for a Good Demonstration
Advantages of Visual Aids in Oral Presentation
Cautions in Using the Demonstration

However skillful in oral communications the salesperson is, he can no doubt increase his effectiveness by employing additional perceptual channels for reinforcing his message. This involvement of additional channels is what we call *demonstration*. There are a number of considerations that go beyond the characteristics of the perceptual channels themselves (as described in Chapters 4 and 13), which influence the use of demonstration to reinforce the sales message.

In this chapter we examine these considerations along with the materials and tools of the demonstration. We then focus on important concerns with regard to the actual demonstration, including the timing, the requirements, the advantages of visual aids in oral presentations, and cautions to observe in using the demonstration. The demonstration can be a key factor in the sales presentation, but if it is to be effective the salesperson must be aware of its relationship to the rest of the presentation and know when and how it can best be used.

CONSIDERATIONS FOR THE USE OF THE DEMONSTRATION

The primary considerations, here, are the individual differences that exist between auditory and visual learning. Other considerations include selectivity, principles of learning, and forgetting. These considerations are important in determining the usefulness of demonstrations in the particular sales presentation.

Auditory Versus Visual Learning

As the salesperson plans his presentation and reflects on how to meet the basic criteria, *understandability, interest, believability,* and *persuasion,* he may ask himself, "Is there anything I can show the other person that will increase the likelihood of meeting each of these criteria?" For instance, an equipment salesperson might decide that a schematic diagram of the machine will help the prospect understand how the equipment is designed and why it is virtually maintenance free. The same salesperson might use a miniaturized model of the equipment to arouse or maintain interest in his presentation. He might attempt to achieve believability by showing pictures of the equipment in operation in a situation similar to the prospect's. He might also plan to take the prospect on a visit to one of his customers to see the equipment in actual use if his presentation as contemplated does not persuade the prospect to place an order. The demonstration not only supplements the oral presentation with additional information but also provides contrast that is useful in maintaining the prospect's attention and increasing his persuasibility.

Selectivity

The demonstration also capitalizes on an additional aspect of perception: *selectivity.* When the prospect's eyes as well as his ears are enlisted, there is increased likelihood of getting the message across. The visual device used may be deliberately designed to direct the prospect's attention selectively to specified characteristics of what is being sold. For example, the equipment salesperson might have a schematic diagram of each component of the equipment; each schema would enable him to direct attention to one or two ideas at a time.

Principles of Learning and Demonstrations

When visual and other stimuli are included in the presentation, they add realism and facilitate learning on the part of the prospect or customer. Specifically, the demonstration facilitates the use of four principles of learning: participation, association, transfer, and insight.

Participation.   Learning is an active process and the more the other person is actively engaged in the situation the more he will learn from it. In a demonstration in which the product in question is tested, the prospect has an opportunity to see with his own eyes how the product performs. To illustrate this, a retail furniture salesperson might stand on top of a certain coffee table to demonstrate how strong and scratch resistant it is. The important point is that the more the salesperson can get the customer involved with the product, the more likely he is to sell it.

Association.   The more sensory channels are involved in a presentation, the more likely learning will take place by association. The two inputs for thought process are the past (memory) and the present (perception). By using a greater number of stimuli in the perceptual present, the salesperson ensures more ties or associations with the individual's past experience.

For this reason, it is critical for the salesperson to be aware of the customer's background. Then, he is in a position to use the right types of demonstrations to draw on the customer's past to help with the current sale. A good example of this might be an insurance salesperson who is selling property insurance. If the salesperson knows that a close friend or relative of the prospective customer had his home damaged by fire, the salesperson might want to demonstrate, through the use of figures, his company's coverage of this type of claim.

Transfer.   To the extent that the demonstration materials show the product in use, the other person will find it easier to visualize and understand the use of the product in his own firm.

Thus, it is critically important for the salesperson to try to demonstrate his product under actual conditions in the customer's plant. If this is not possible, other alternatives involve taking the prospect to view the product in question in another customer's facility, demonstrating the product's use in the firm's test facility, or simply outlining on paper the test results of the product. The first of these alternatives can be particularly effective if the customers are not competing with each other and if the salesperson has a very strong and positive relationship with the firm they visit. This transferability of learning from the sales call to on-the-job use is particularly pertinent to technical products and services.

Insight.   The demonstration also capitalizes on another learning principle— insight. The presentation alone may give the customer or prospect relevant details about the offering, but it may be necessary to use a demonstration to show the big picture—the total impact and use of the products and services. In this sense the demonstration acts as the "clincher" for the sale. It helps the sales-person pull into focus all the important points about the product.

Forgetting

Forgetting is as much an active process as learning. In many fields of selling an appreciable time lag occurs between when the salesperson conveys information and when the other person has an opportunity to use it. This challenges the salesperson to reinforce his ideas in a way that will minimize forgetting. The demonstration is a critically important means for accomplishing this. In fact, this is why many sales representatives are furnished with items they can leave with the customer or prospect. For example, one steel company provides its custom-ers and prospects with one-foot rulers made of stainless steel. Imprinted on each is the company's name, address, and phone number as well as similar informa-tion about the salesperson managing the account. Pharmaceutical salespersons often leave samples of their products with the physician, with the thought that he will have them readily available for trial prescription if a patient requires such medication.

MATERIALS AND TOOLS USED IN DEMONSTRATIONS

The materials and tools used in the demonstration may take an unlimited number of forms, ranging from a simple price list to a full-scale demonstration or model of the product. Let us look at some of the more frequently used materials.

Pictures

Color pictures are preferable to black and white. If color is used, it should be realistic and do the product justice. It is better to show the product in its normal use or setting rather than in isolation. Blow-ups or enlargements of parts may be used to show details.

Schematic Diagrams

These are extremely useful for conveying ideas about highly technical products. The use of color to differentiate each component or system is helpful for clarity. These may be printed on transparent sheets and mounted in sequence. In this way, the salesperson is able to begin with the basic chassis of the equipment and build on it the various systems and components until he finally shows the complete unit.

Mock-ups

These have an advantage over pictures and diagrams in that they are three-dimensional portrayals of the product. Individuals with limited space perception have difficulty visualizing in three dimensions from the two dimensions provided by pictures and diagrams. Although mock-ups should be realistic to be effective, they are normally oversimplified as compared to the product itself in that they are designed to reflect only the product's salient features.

Miniaturized Models

These differ from mock-ups in that they are exact replicas of the product scaled down for use in the demonstration. They have the obvious advantage of greater realism, but they may convey too much information all at once. Also, the cost of such items may preclude their use in many situations.

Samples

For the salesperson of small consumer and industrial goods, the best demonstration tool is the product itself. Nothing is more realistic. The salesperson must, however, have ways and means to insure that he does not distribute the samples beyond what commercial judgment would dictate. If the salesperson is too generous with samples, small users may accept them in lieu of purchase.

Tests

In many fields of selling, especially in the industrial sector, the presentation can be reinforced by reports of product testing done by independent laboratories. The chemicals salesperson may show that his product exceeds government specifications of purity. The pharmaceuticals salesperson may furnish a report from a medical journal indicating the efficacy of his firm's drug.

Another use of tests is when the salesperson can induce the prospect to use his own facilities to test a sample of the product. If this is done, the salesperson should be present for the test, to insure that it is performed properly and fairly. Too, he can influence the decision makers who are present. Based on the favorable results, he can immediately press for an order. If the results are unfavorable, however, he can take immediate steps to recoup his position. If the prospect is reluctant to have him present, the salesperson should be sure to follow up and seek a report on the tests. It is easy for a firm to promise to test a product and then neglect to do so.

Full-scale Demonstrations

A key consideration for a full-scale demonstration is where it is to be conducted, all things considered. The least costly arrangement is to take the prospect to a customer's place of business to see the equipment in use. A key advantage of this, in addition to economy, is the testimony of the satisfied customer. There are, however, certain strategic and tactical advantages in conducting the demonstration on the premises of the salesperson's firm. This affords the opportunity to provide VIP treatment and to control the situation fully. Also, it is likely to cost relatively less than if it is scheduled at the prospect's place of business. However, this last location also has strategic and tactical advantages, because the prospect and his personnel can see the product in use in their own work setting.

If the demonstration is brought to the prospect, the salesperson should, of course, check out the equipment to be used to be sure that it is in perfect running condition. If other people from the firm are going to accompany him on the call, the salesperson should brief each of them about all phases of the prospective account—for example, what has occurred up until now, what applications he sees as the crucial ones for this account, and who the decision makers are. The demonstration will have greater impact if the salesperson can produce something of value to the account in the course of the demonstration. For instance, an office equipment salesperson might do a specified job for the prospect, such as duplicating a memorandum. The salesperson should also make sure that the decision-making group in the prospective account is present to observe the demonstration. In addition, if anyone in the account is to participate actively, the salesperson should instruct him in advance and give him an opportunity to practice what he is to do before the decision makers assemble.

TIMING IN RELATION TO THE SELLING-BUYING PROCESS

Although the demonstration may be used at any stage in the selling-buying process, the most logical times are during the initial stage of the sale, at the time of the presentation, or when an attempt is made to induce buying action.

The Initial Stage of the Sale

The demonstration may be used to begin the call as a dramatic way of gaining attention. If this strategy is used, the salesperson must be sure that what is shown is easy to understand and appreciate. If the salesperson knows from previous calls what competing products are now being used, he may place the demonstration at the beginning of the call to show how favorably his products will contrast with presently used products. An additional consideration for using a demonstration initially may be the restricted amount of time the salesperson has available for the call. It enables him to get down to business quickly. However, the great danger of placing the demonstration in the first phase of the selling-buying process is that if the other person rejects it, it is difficult to regain a position from which to continue the presentation. The salesperson's big gun has been fired.

At the Time of the Presentation

By definition, of course, the usual place for the demonstration is the presentation itself. Well-conceived visual reinforcements are particularly important if the salesperson is to sustain the attention of the prospect for long periods of time.

They are also invaluable in providing a change of pace. The salesperson must ensure that he synchronizes his demonstration with his presentation. It is very easy, for example, for a visual aid to distract from, rather than reinforce, what is being said.

To Stimulate Buying Action

Occasionally, the demonstration may be used for inducing buying action. For example, in some fields of selling the product may be left for trial use with a commitment to buy if it measures up to the claims made for it. If this is done, it is imperative for the salesperson to make sure the "who's who" in the prospect company fully understand the product and that any personnel using it are familiar with its operation. The salesperson must avoid being exploited by unscrupulous prospects who may use this means to obtain free service. Let us examine some of the potential problems that can exist with demonstrations and how to avoid them.

REQUIREMENTS FOR A GOOD DEMONSTRATION

Unfortunately, the demonstration as a means of effective communication still leaves much to be desired. All too often, the salesperson making the presentation appears more intent on justifying his effort than on helping his audience understand the material. To avoid this and other pitfalls and—even more important—to capitalize on the unique strengths of this type of communication, the salesperson must have a working knowledge of the four basic requirements for an effective demonstration. These requirements are (1) clear understanding of the audience, (2) precise definition of the purpose, (3) sound organization of the material, and (4) effective delivery and proper length.

Clear Understanding of the Audience

The salesperson must ensure that he has a firm understanding of his audience, so that he can tailor his presentation to fit that group. Thus, he must know who the people he will be speaking to are, what level they occupy in the customer's organizational hierarchy, and what specific responsibilities they have. Is his audience made up of decision makers, of technical specialists, or of conduits to the decision makers? What are the interests of this particular group? If most of them are engineers, the salesperson may wish to couch his presentation and demonstration in technical terms. If the audience consisted primarily of non-technical people, however, a technical demonstration would be a disaster. In the same manner, if there is one particularly high-ranking person attending the demonstration, the salesperson may wish to aim his presentation at that individual.

Other important factors the salesperson should consider are: how long the prospect has been doing business with the competition, who the competition is, what the prospect sees as the central problem the salesperson's firm might be able to solve. If the salesperson has been doing business with this particular account, he will know the answers to many of these questions; if he has not, he will have to do his best to obtain the information from other sources.

Precise Definition of the Purpose

The salesperson must have a clear purpose, not only for the presentation but also for the demonstration. The demonstration itself is always in the position of supporting the presentation. It may be that the demonstration is the highlight of the entire interview, but even then it must be designed to help get a particular point across—which is the objective of the presentation.

Sound Organization of the Material

The way in which a salesperson organizes his material and times his delivery hinges directly on his selection of visual aids (such as text visuals, charts, graphs, flow diagrams, and maps). This selection offers the greatest potential for improvement of demonstrations because the salesperson is actually putting together a show, each part of which is designed to bring the audience closer to the climax. If the show is orchestrated properly, with the appropriate visuals at the appropriate time, it will have a much better chance of success.

Effective Delivery and Proper Presentation

Although each individual has his own style for making a presentation to a group, the salesperson who has a hard-hitting dramatic style will tend to keep his audience's attention longer than will the salesperson who simply speaks on and on in a monotone. A salesperson can not sell if he can not keep his audience's attention.

It is also important for the salesperson to practice his presentation and demonstration before he talks to the audience. The successful salesperson is confident of himself, his product, and the role of the demonstration in his presentation. Most good speechmakers practice their presentations until their talk and its interwoven demonstrations become second nature to them. Finally, the entire presentation, including the demonstrations, should be kept to a relatively short period of time. An audience's mind can wander even when a good talk goes on too long. It should be short and exciting.

ADVANTAGES OF VISUAL AIDS IN ORAL PRESENTATION

Isolated statistics are useless data. They take on significance only when a relationship can be established among them, when something is rising or declining, overtaking or falling behind, remaining constant or changing. A football center, for example, may weigh 200 pounds. That figure, by itself, is of little value to a football coach trying to determine team strategy or to estimate his team's chances for victory. But the figure does assume a meaningful dimension when compared with the weight of the center of the opposing team, say 275 pounds.

In similar fashion, a sales figure of $6.3 million for the current year is of little use to a company president until he contrasts it with a sales figure for the previous year, say $3.1 million or $9.2 million. Only then will he have a meaningful basis for judging company performance. Let us examine several topics designed to help the salesperson with his visual aids.

The Use of Graphs

Statistical relationships can be expressed verbally, in tabular form, or pictorially —that is, in text, in tables, or by means of visual aids. The graphic form of presentation, however, offers the following distinct advantages over textual counterparts:

Direct: The mind is presented with a ready-made image.
Revealing: When well designed, the main features of the data are shown at a glance.
Quick: When the key points are highlighted, the audience can focus immediately on what is truly significant.
Convincing: Instead of being merely stated or described, the relationships among statistics are demonstrated.
Appealing: It attracts the attention of the viewer better than text or tables.

Graphic Aids Can Confuse the Audience

It is important to note, however, that if a message can be stated just as clearly and convincingly using text or tables, the salesperson should not turn to charts merely because "they look good" or "will help break the monotony." Graphic aids that are ingenious in themselves but are not really needed to clarify or to point up relationships, serve only to distract from the continuity of a presentation. Also, precisely because of their strong dramatic impact, these graphic devices, if overused, may wind up stressing everything, but emphasizing nothing.

In deciding whether and where charts should be used, the salesperson should carefully weigh advantages against possible disadvantages. Thus, a good starting point is to ask, "Will this chart contribute appropriately to the effectiveness of my presentation?" "Will it communicate my message more quickly and more clearly than other means available?"

Key Elements of Effective Chart Design

Obviously, a salesperson making a presentation to an English-speaking prospect is not going to use visuals written in Chinese. Such visuals would be self-defeating. For the customer or prospect to gain any benefit from them, the salesperson would have to take time out to translate each visual, simply to establish a common ground for understanding.

Yet, the charts used in many presentations might just as well be written in a foreign language for all their value as aids. Because they are poorly designed, such charts force the salesperson to waste valuable time translating and interpreting them. In such instances, audience impact—and often the message itself —is weakened.

Thus, proper design of charts is not a luxury, it is a necessity. In the following we discuss and illustrate in detail each of the four basic elements of chart design: simple visualization of relationships; clear, easy to understand titles; minimum detail; and eye appeal. When combined, these elements contribute substantially to making an effective chart.

Simple Visualization of Relationships.   Merely plotting lines on a piece of graph paper does not necessarily make a useful chart. The design of the image must go beyond a mere visual statement of facts and figues. The impact of the design must target on the critical relationship borne out by the facts and figures so that the image projected emphasizes the specific point the chart is intended to present. In Figure 14-1 the design does not concentrate on any specific idea. Rather the audience must of necessity wait for the speaker to translate the maze of lines into the intended message.

In contrast, Figure 14-2 clearly expresses the relationship between the data and its significance. The visualization focuses attention on the specific point the chart is intended to convey. The dark "mountain caps" emphasize the critical elements, and the arrows add to the clarity of the message. Also, the production unit scales have been omitted in this second exhibit. Quite simply, they were not needed since they did not contribute to the essential point being made with this chart. In short, a good presentation chart should make only one major point at a time. Subordinate ideas should not detract from the key thesis.

Clear, Easy-to-Understand Titles.   The surest way to make a chart understandable is to say in the title what the chart is trying to illustrate. That way, the message is conveyed quickly, leaving the salesperson free to develop details and to point out its significance. (One familiar example of the value of clear titles is the newspaper headline, which enables the reader to quickly grasp the gist of a story before actually reading the article.)

The title of Figure 14-3 states exactly what the chart is intended to show. It serves to reinforce the impact of the oral message, since the listener reads it himself and simultaneously hears it from the speaker. The salesperson can then

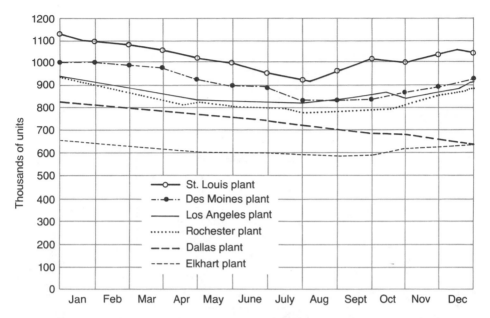

Figure 14-1 Unit Production in Six Class "A" Plants (January 1, 1975 through December 31, 1975)

proceed to concentrate his time constructively on relating the significance of this particular chart to the rest of his presentation.

Unless a great deal of thought is given to shaping the title, the chart itself can become misleading. Clearly, a title should not introduce any subjective interpretation or editorializing. But since the title should state what the chart has been designed to show, a degree of interpretation—if based on objective facts—is permissible, and even desirable.

Minimum Detail.   Unlike a reference chart, which is used time and again for analytical purposes, a presentation chart must get its message across quickly. Its function is to communicate in the brief time it is on display. For this reason, the salesperson should siphon off any material that does not constructively contribute to the message of the chart. Detailed statistics, excessive grid rulings, lengthy legends, complex qualifying footnotes, and extensive sources should be minimized. Since any material included in a chart is open to discussion, the salesperson might find himself needlessly involved in a detailed explanation of a point that is of no significance to the presentation.

In the process of simplifying a chart design, the rough sketch is an important first step toward deciding how much should be omitted in the finished product. Figure 14-4 is an example of a rough sketch, which includes all analytical details. The figures are computed to decimals, a footnote is included, the source is mentioned. There is no grouping of the elements. The title merely lists the elements. In no way is the intended message clear.

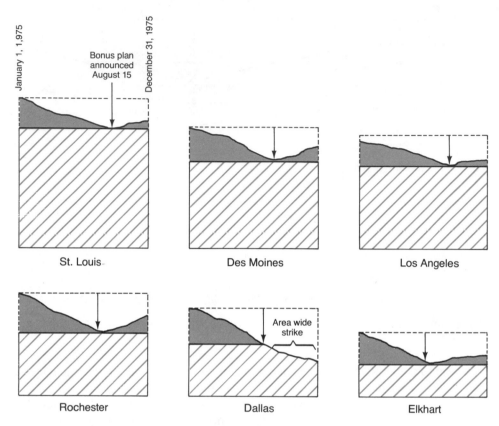

Figure 14-2 In All But One of the Six Class "A" Plants the New Bonus Plan Reversed the Dropoff in Production

In contrast, Figure 14-5, is the finished product ready for presentation. The title spells out the critical relationship to be emphasized. All unnecessary elements have been removed. The groupings have been clearly indicated and shading reinforces the critical segments.

Eye Appeal.   For a chart to serve its purpose, it must attract the attention of the viewer and then hold it. Therefore, a certain amount of eye appeal is mandatory. However, the chart is first and foremost a medium of communication and not a work of art for art's sake. Its purpose is to convey a message clearly, quickly, and convincingly.

CAUTIONS IN USING THE DEMONSTRATION

Properly employed, the demonstration can significantly increase the presentation's effectiveness. Improperly used, it can seriously impair the selling-buying

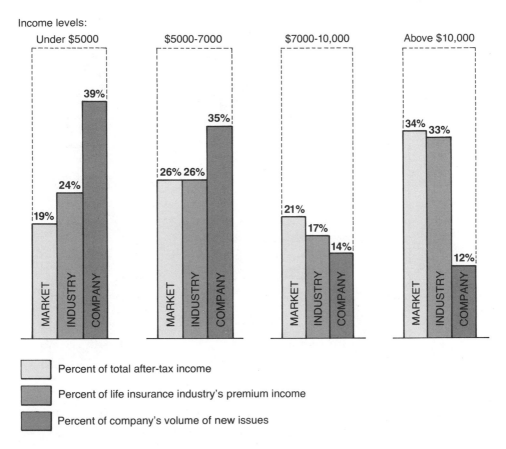

Figure 14-3 Industry Sales Match Market, While Company Sales Concentrate on Low-Income Groups

process. If the following cautions are observed, the demonstration can contribute much to the salesman's success.

Necessity of the Demonstration

If the presentation alone is enough to bring about a buying decision, a demonstration may only raise doubts and questions. An example of this situation would be the attempted sale of a new home. Although the prospect was ready to buy, the salesperson volunteered to bring the plans over for his inspection. Unfortunately, the plans revealed several aspects about the house that were not appealing to the individual. Thus, as a result of this demonstration, the sale was lost.

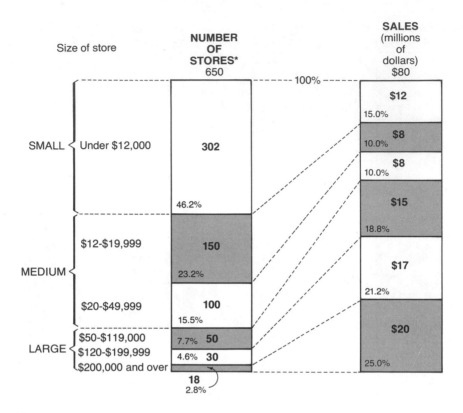

*The number of stores is for the United States only. (Source: U. S. Department of Labor, 1973).

Figure 14-4 Number of Stores and Dollar Sales*

Check Out and "Debug" Materials

The salesperson is responsible for checking out and debugging any materials that will be used in the demonstration. It is better not to use a demonstration than to use one that employs poor or defective equipment.

Mechanical aspects employed in a demonstration can fail to function at no fault of the salesperson. If this occurs, it may spoil an otherwise successful sales presentation. A dramatic example of this occurred several years ago at the Paris air show, when the Russian Super Sonic Transport crashed while on a demonstration flight. This certainly did not help the Russian's efforts to sell their plane.

Organization of Materials

The salesperson must organize the items in his demonstration so that they can be used effortlessly. If the salesperson has to fumble in his bag for his visual aids he may lose the attention and interest of the prospect. The smoothness of the presentation, including the demonstration, contributes to its credibility. If it

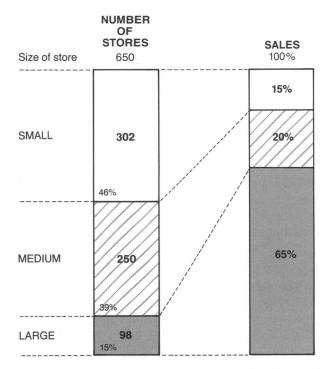

Figure 14-5 15% of the Stores Account for 65% of the Sales

does not go well, it will make the salesperson and the customer very nervous. This will give an atmosphere of tension to the selling-buying process, which will hurt the salesperson's chances of success.

Role of Additional People

If other personnel from the salesperson's firm are involved, the salesperson must see that they are briefed on the account and their roles in executing the demonstration. It is better for the salesperson not to have helpers if they are inept in their roles. In the same way, if the prospect's or customer's personnel are to take part in the demonstration, they must be properly instructed and briefed. Since the objective is to show that the product can be used effectively by the account, advance instruction is imperative.

Demonstration Synchronized with Presentation

If the demonstration is not synchronized with the presentation it becomes a distraction rather than a reinforcement. Materials for the demonstration should not be in view until they are ready for use and they should be put out of sight once they have served their purpose. A classic situation in which disaster can occur because of poor synchronization is a sales presentation that uses slides. If this is done well, it can be extremely effective. However, if the slides are out of order and do not relate to what the salesperson is talking about, they will distract from his presentation and reduce his chances for a successful sale.

Selection of Demonstration Site

The setting for the demonstration site should be as lifelike as possible. This is why it is eminently desirable (if feasible) to arrange for the demonstration on the prospect's premises; otherwise, there may always be a nagging feeling on the part of the prospect that the demonstration went well but it was under "laboratory" conditions. This can be eliminated if the presentation is done at the prospect's place of business under his actual working conditions.

Dramatize without Distracting

The salesperson should see to it that the demonstration is as dramatic and vivid as possible without being distracting. Sometimes the demonstration becomes so attention compelling that it distracts from the primary message of the presentation. An example of this is the clever advertising used by a firm for its well-known stomach-headache remedy. Unfortunately, their research showed that the prospect all too often became so interested in what was going on in the advertisement that he missed its point. As a result, the company's commercials won several advertising awards, but its sales did not increase.

Time Interval

If a time interval occurs between the presentation and the demonstration, the salesperson should try to keep the presentation in the conscious awareness of the prospect to minimize forgetting. The usual way of accomplishing this is to give a prospect some "assignment" associated with the forthcoming demonstration. For example, the prospect may be asked to give each of the people who will be present at the demonstration a descriptive brochure on the equipment with instructions for each of them to come prepared with questions.

SUMMARY

The importance of using visual aids and demonstrations to help reinforce an oral presentation is an accepted principle in selling, but far too often these auxiliary tools are not used or are used improperly. Care must be taken in planning, organizing, and using such techniques to help establish a sale. There are a number of psychological phenomena that should be understood regarding the use of demonstrations. They include participation, association, transfer, insight, and forgetting.

A number of different demonstration tools were delineated in this chapter, including pictures, schematic diagrams, mock-ups, miniaturized models, samples, tests, and full-scale demonstrations. There are cautions and requirements that should be employed with the use of visuals as well as several key elements to effective chart design.

The test for a good visual demonstration is whether it serves the needs of its intended user and audience. Using techniques suggested in this chapter will help a salesperson achieve that result. Such use of demonstrations and visuals will not only sharpen the focus and increase the impact of the message, but will also facilitate the task of organizing the material and strengthening the delivery. Further, it will enable the salesperson to make full and proper use of his prospect's time—and both parties will be much richer for the experience.

PROBLEMS

1. In which of your college courses have you observed the most effective use of visuals for reinforcement? Describe them and be specific.
2. To appreciate the need for other than auditory stimuli in communication, sit on your hands and describe a circular staircase. What are your reactions?
3. Scan a current magazine and mark up or clip out ads that illustrate the principles of perception and learning described in this chapter.
4. Formulate a checklist of precautions for a full-scale demonstration. Justify each entry.
5. Outline a speech on the topic, "The Sales Demonstration."
6. What type of visual or audiovisual aids would be most appropriate for meeting each of the four criteria of an effective presentation (understandability, interest, believability, and persuasion)? Justify your choices.

Exercise 14

DEMONSTRATIONS-REINFORCING THE PRESENTATION

Objective: To provide examples of how visuals can be used during a sales call.

Continue your role of selling young ladies fashions (see Exercises 12, 13). You have convinced the new owner-manager of the ladies specialty store that your line has real potential. However, understandably he does not want to make the decision unless his buyer is as convinced as he is. You are now scheduled to make a presentation to both of them. You have a big stake in this! The following are available as potential ways of reinforcing your sales message. Indicate which ones you will use and how, why, and when you will use each.

1. Samples of next season's fashions.
2. Color photograph of the firm's display at a recent market.
3. Preprints of ads to be used in national media.
4. Statistical data in table form on company sales versus leading competitors.
5. Specimen point-of-sale display unit.

Case 14-1 Carter Chrysler-Plymouth

Carter is located in a southwestern community of about 200,000. It competes with three other dealers representing other major auto companies. Mr. Tom Carter is the owner-manager, Jim Harrison is sales manager, Ed Luckman is service and parts manager, and Viola Albertson handles financial and office matters.

Jim Harrison is conducting a sales meeting with Ed Luckman and the sales staff: Bill Baker, George Downing, Ben Lyons, and Pete Smith. "Fellows," says Jim Harrison, "we have a problem. New cars are moving pretty well considering business conditions. However, our used cars are almost standing still. In the past three months we've had to wholesale too many units. I think you know that when we do that we lose money."

Jim continues, "I want to try something different. Effective today, I'm naming you, George, used car sales manager. You will have complete responsibility for this end of the sales effort. You can feel free to dress up the lot, change anything you like. Just keep 'em moving out."

After the sales meeting, George met briefly with Carter and Harrison. These are his thoughts about the new assignment.

✔ The attractiveness of our showroom, the company-furnished, multi-colored displays, the brochures all help to sell our new cars. What steps can I take to make our used car lot more attractive? How can I dress up the cars . . . perhaps, feature a daily special?

✔ In selling a new car, the salesperson can negotiate from a known base, the window "sticker." Can I develop something comparable . . . perhaps a posted "retail book value?"

✔ The big problem is to generate traffic to the lot. What new steps can I take to do this?

✔ What about having each prospect fill out a simple rating sheet each time he takes a trial drive?

✔ What special tools can I provide the salespeople (and myself) for reinforcing our presentations?

    1. How should George approach this problem?

    2. What are some examples of effective ways he could use demonstrations?

Case 14-2 Selling Vacuum Cleaners Door-to-Door

Bill Zimmerman felt pretty good. He was ready to start selling in his own territory. He had completed his training with flying colors and was ready to make it big.

His company, *Zenith*, generated sales leads from inquiries in response to their national advertising. However, each sales representative is expected to prospect on his own.

With some apprehension Bill rings his first doorbell. A middle-age, pleasant lady greets him.

Bill: Good morning, Ma'am, my name is Bill Zimmerman. May I show you our Zenith cleaner. It's the best in the world.

Lady: Mr. Zimmerman, I'm terribly busy and besides, I don't need a new vacuum.

Bill: May I help you by cleaning one of your rugs?

Lady: None of my rugs is really dirty.

Bill: Well, ma'am, our vacuum gets down deep and reaches dust and grit other cleaners miss.

Lady: If it will only take a few minutes you can demonstrate on the hall carpet. (*She shows Bill in.*)

Bill: Incidentally, Ma'am, what is your name?

Lady: I am Mrs. Underwood.

Bill shows Mrs. Underwood how a clean, disposable bag is inserted in the vacuum. He then plugs in the machine. He goes over the carpet very carefully and then stops the machine. He spreads a sheet of white paper on the floor and removes the bag and empties it. Very little dirt has accumulated.

1. What should Bill do next?

2. How might he have provided a more convincing demonstration?

SUGGESTIONS FOR FURTHER READING

Burnett, R. W., "Weber Stretches its Promotion Dollars with Sales Shows on the Road," *Industrial Marketing,* Vol. 56 (September 1971), pp. 46, 48, and 50.

Carter, D. C., "Showmanship and the Salesman," *The American Salesman,* Vol. 15 (February 1970), pp. 21–24.

Industrial Marketing, "Mobile Demonstrator Sells Doubtful Buyers," Vol. 50 (January, 1965), pp. 106–107.

Leterman, Elmer G., *How Showmanship Sells* (New York, N.Y.: Harper & Row, 1965).

Sales Management, "Selling by Seminar (Herman Miller)," Vol. 106 (Jan. 1, 1971), p. 24.

Tarrant, J. J., *Tomorrow's Techniques for Today's Salesman* (New York, N.Y.: Hawthorne, 1969).

Wood, Dean M., " 'Back to Basics' Has Garlock O. E. M. Salesmen Flipping Over Flip Chart," *Industrial Marketing,* Vol. 59 (January, 1974), pp. 42–45.

Wright, G. B., *The Art and Skill of Ingenious Selling* (West Nyack, N.Y.: Parker Publications, 1967).

15. Objections — Managing Sales Resistance

Sales resistance may be defined as anything the other person says or does to prevent the salesperson from achieving his call objectives. Whenever such resistance occurs it is evident that a conflict exists between acceptance and rejection of the salesperson's offering. Thus, sales resistance can provide a tactically desirable situation, and if the salesperson handles it effectively a sale may result. The resistance encountered lets him know that some interest is present.

In this chapter we focus on psychological and logical sales resistance. Psychological sales resistance occurs in the form of an emotional reaction that is a function of the customer's attitude toward such factors as being disturbed by a salesperson, having to give up money to receive a product, or the dislike for making decisions. In contrast, logical sales resistance is easier for the salesperson to handle because it stems from aspects of the proposition itself, such as the product or its price, over which the salesperson has some control. We also deal with devious reasoning on the part of the prospect which occurs when he does such things as uses emotionally toned words, takes extreme positions or uses ambiguous terms. We conclude with a discussion of eight specific methods for handling sales objections.

PSYCHOLOGICAL SALES RESISTANCE

Even if there were a perfect match between the want satisfiers offered by the salesperson and the needs and wants of the account, there might still be substantial sales resistance. Although there would be no logical basis for failure to purchase, psychologically founded resistance might still exist. Indeed, far more sales resistance encountered by salespersons is psychological than logical. In this section, we examine several of the more important reasons for psychological sales resistance, timing of psychological resistance, and nine specific types of psychological sales resistance.

Reasons for Psychological Sales Resistance

One of the most important causes of psychological sales resistance is the availability of competitive offerings which makes decision making difficult. There may be apprehension on the part of the buyer that all alternatives have not been explored. The more options available, the more difficult it is to decide. A second reason is the interactive nature of the three basic processes of perceiving, thinking, and feeling. Rarely is a buying decision, even in the industrial marketplace, exclusively the result of logical thought process. The prospect's perceptions and feelings are found to be influential. He may experience a vague feeling of uneasiness and uncertainty which prevents him from buying. A third reason is that human beings tend to engage in rationalization—that is, after-the-fact justification of decisions and actions. He may think the proposal is satisfactory but yet hesitate to buy because he has not mustered a sufficient number of reasons why it is a good idea. Finally, many types of psychological resistance derive from attitudes and feelings as they occur in interpersonal relationships. In these instances, resistance might stem from such causes as lack of attention on the part of the customer during the presentation or unwillingness on the part of the customer to admit his ignorance of a specific area.

Timing of Psychological Sales Resistance

Psychologically founded sales resistance may occur at any time, but it is generally experienced during the first and fourth phases of the selling-buying process.

The most recurrent causes of such resistance during phase 1, are homeostasis and goal gradient. We noted in the discussion of homeostasis in Chapter 6 that it is more comfortable not to need anything than to have one's needs disturbed. The more pleasant a person finds the status quo, the more likely he is to resist any disturbance of it. After all, there is always some risk in making a change.

As to goal gradient (Chapter 11), the best assumption for the salesperson to make as he comes face-to-face with a customer or prospect is that he is interrupting purposeful activity on the part of the other person. The nearer that person is to completing the task at hand, the more difficult he is to interrupt. Hence, he views any attempt to talk to him as unwelcome interference. If the salesperson were to terminate his visit each time he heard a prospect say "I don't need any" or "I am too busy" the salesperson would make very few sales.

Psychological resistance may build up as the presentation draws to a close, and the salesperson attempts to induce the action of purchase. Many people find the decision to buy painful—either because they are parting with money, or because they are uncertain of the purchase. This, by the way, is why the salesperson should use the word *value* rather than *price*, in talking with customers and prospects. Most people associate price with laying out money; they view value as what they are receiving.

Specific Types of Psychological Sales Resistance

Psychological sales resistance presents a more complex tactical problem than logical resistance. To handle it, the salesperson must first determine the psychological or social needs the other person is satisfying by engaging in it. Once this is done, the salesperson must find some way to meet these needs of the prospect and still achieve his call objective. Let us consider nine specific types of psychological sales resistance and techniques for handling each type when it is encountered.[1]

Resistance to Interference.   Except when a customer seeks out a salesperson, a visit from a salesperson constitutes interference. The prospect has to stop what he is doing and attend to the salesperson. In cases where no interview is granted, there is probably an even stronger feeling of interference. If the prospect is not interested in the line the salesperson represents, he may be annoyed to think he was approached at all. And, even if he is interested in hearing the salesperson's proposition, he may be engaged in another task so he still might consider the visit an interruption.

There are several suggestions for reducing resistance of this kind. First, the salesperson should be attentive to his physical appearance and personal manner so that he is likable on sight. This will tend to overcome the initial impulse to deny an interview. Second, he should try to set up interviews in advance. This

---

[1]Harold C. Cash and William J. E. Crissy, *The Psychology of Selling,* Vol. 9, "Managing Sales Resistance" (Flushing, NY: Personnel Development Associates, 1965), pp. 11–21.

can be done through correspondence or over the telephone. In some instances regular calls, such as those by route men, can be made without a prior appointment. It is improbable that this type of psychological resistance can be eliminated, but it can be held to a minimum by a little forethought and planning.

Preference for Established Habits.   Habits are a stablizing influence on society and on the individual. If it were not for habits, behavior would be less predictable than it is now. Habits are a paradox to the salesperson. When he can get information about a prospect's habits, the salesperson feels he has a better chance of selling to him; yet the very nature of selling is such that a sale almost invariably calls for a change of habits. More specifically, it is necessary to get the buyer to agree in advance to a change of habits before the sale can be made. It becomes obvious, then, that anticipated change is a potent source of sales resistance.

To the salesperson who is aware of this resistance to change, there is no substitute for the knowledge of how his prospect will use the goods. It is part of a salesperson's job to demonstrate how products fit into the buyer's life pattern. When a change of habits is shown to result in increased satisfaction, it is more attractive than when the increased satisfaction is not apparent. For example, a housewife with a nonautomatic washing machine has a habit of staying near the washer for as long as two hours at a time. With an automatic washer, she starts the operation and goes away for half an hour. She must prepare herself for this change in her housework habits before she is ready to switch to an automatic washer. Hence, the salesperson should present the advantages to be enjoyed through greater freedom.

Another way of reducing the resistance to changing habits is to reduce the gap or apparent difference between the old habit and the new one. This can be done by talking in language and terms familiar to the customer, by making reference to people known to the customer, and by minimizing the novel aspects of using the new product.

Resistance is as likely to be focused on the dislike of giving up old ideas as it is on the dislike of adopting new ones. The salesperson should not make the mistake of repeatedly stressing the product benefits when they have already been accepted by the customer. Rather, he should concentrate on minimizing the change in habits resulting from using the new product.

Apathy or Lack of Desire for New Product.   It is natural for a customer to resist a proposition for which he feels no need. After all, accumulating money is an important objective and making a purchase is often perceived as going counter to that objective. Human beings are usually happier receiving money than they are spending it. Hence, it is necessary to develop a need for the product that is greater than the desire to save money.

To supply product information and customer benefits convincingly is the best method for overcoming this type of sales resistance. The salesperson who takes the time to develop a presentation which stresses the quality of his merchandise in relation to its price and how it can help solve the customer's specific problems will have a good chance of overcoming the resistance.

Resistance to Giving Up Something.   One of the painful realizations of adulthood is that "you can't get something for nothing." Normally, acquiring one item requires giving up something else. A purchase involves giving up money in exchange for the commodity. This triggers an unpleasant awareness of the realities of life and constitutes a source of sales resistance. When this type of resistance appears, there is no point in rushing the sales process. The salesperson should visualize a balance scale with money on one tray and desire for the product on the other. At the beginning of the sales process, the customer perceives the tray containing the money as the heavier. Selling consists of adding to the desire for the product until it balances, and finally outweighs, the desire to retain the money.

If the buyer continues his resistance on this basis, the salesperson may not be able to make a sale in a short enough period of time for it to be profitable. In the same amount of time, the salesperson might get several orders from other prospects. We will consider this situation more fully later.

Traditional Unpleasant Associations Triggered by Sales Representatives.   The original names given to salespersons, such as peddler, drummer, and the like, indicate the contempt and suspicion with which salespersons were and are sometimes viewed. Enlightened persons, however, accept the fact that our high standard of living and state of prosperity depend on sales representatives to a large degree. Nevertheless, many persons experience a feeling of resentment when approached by a salesperson.

This basic problem must be approached through public relations. It is up to the companies and trade associations to attack this type of resistance. Still, if the salesperson encounters this form of resistance he cannot ignore it. He should try to allay such suspicions by referring the prospect to customers who will speak well of him. If appropriate, he can appeal to the fairness of the prospect by asking if it is proper to condemn all salespersons on the basis of experience with one who was unscrupulous. This resistance can be eliminated gradually if all sales representatives conduct themselves in a businesslike and dignified manner.

Tendency to Resist Domination by Others.   The nature of the sales process is such that it must be largely controlled or dominated by the salesperson. Most people have a tendency to resist domination of any sort, especially from those considered to have an inferior status. Domination from some sources, such as parents, teachers, police, and clergy, is accepted. But sales representatives do not fall in this category. As soon as the customer feels pressure, he tends to resist. In fact, he may anticipate domination and show resistance from the beginning of the sales contact. Even though he wants the product, he may be inhibited from purchasing it until he has found a face-saving mechanism that makes it appear to others that he bought the product, rather than that it was sold to him.

The salesperson should recognize this need of the customer to feel that he, rather than the salesperson, controlled the interview. The salesperson's satisfaction should be derived from getting an order, not from dominating the interview. If the salesperson looks for opportunities to make the customer feel important and superior, he will eliminate this source of resistance. The technique by which this is accomplished is *low-pressure selling*.

Predetermined Ideas About Products or Services.   Many times a customer has a preconceived idea regarding a product. Such ideas and feelings, even though they are not warranted, may close his mind to the purchase. If the salesperson ridicules the prospect's belief or tries to change his mind with logic, he will probably intensify the prejudice.

The first step in dealing with a prejudice is to accept the fact that it is held as firmly by the prospect as if it were based on actuality. The salesperson should show that he can appreciate the point of view expressed. The prejudice, however, is undoubtedly inconsistent with something else the prospect believes. If such an inconsistent belief can be discovered, it can be used by relating the purchase to this alternate idea rather than by meeting the prejudice head-on. This is risky, though, because one does not like to be made aware that he is holding inconsistent ideas. In any event, the salesperson should not try to dispose of the prejudice on the basis of logic or his own belief.

When an inconsistency is exposed, very often the only result is that the prospect offers another equally inconsistent reason for not buying. It should be recognized that the problem is deep-seated and represents emotional resistance. Such problems may be beyond the responsibility of sales representatives. It may be necessary to ignore the prejudice and try to make the sale on some other basis.

Dislike of Making Decisions.   Making a decision is a painful process for some people. They fear the consequences of their actions and dread disturbing the status quo. Yet, before an order is obtained, a decision must be made—namely, a decision to buy. Many sales are carried to the point where the order is ready for signature, but the salesperson cannot overcome the resistance of the customer to that final act.

Thinking about this situation will reveal that things are not as bad as they seem. Obviously a strong tendency to buy exists or this point of conflict would never have been reached. The barrier may be a lack of self-confidence on the part of the customer. One technique for dealing with this situation is to refer the prospect to customers who have bought and are satisfied. The greater the prestige of such references, the more effective they will be for this purpose. The important thing to remember is that there is a strong motive to buy, and the problem is not so much one of talking about the product but of thinking about the customer and searching for ways to reduce his apprehension about making a decision.

Neurotic Attitude Toward Money.   Extreme attitudes toward money result in refusal to spend it and often lead to the accumulation of money as an end in itself. This results, in some instances, in deriving pleasure from talking about purchasing articles. There is little likelihood that a purchase will take place, however, because the individual feels that by denying himself the purchase he is actually rewarding himself by saving the money. Such a person is completely capable of inviting a salesperson to initiate a conversation about a product. He soon loses sight of the fact that he initiated the interview and feels that the salesperson is forcing him into an uncomfortable position. He then pities himself as the victim of the salesperson's aggression and refuses to buy. If such an individual is asked to make a purchase he may assume that the questioner considers him a wishy-washy person. He won't say "no," but he tends to become aggressive.

If a prospect's excitement over spending money is out of proportion to the amount of money involved, the salesperson may suspect that the customer has a neurotic attitude toward money. When this occurs the salesperson may be wise to back off and spend his time on other more promising accounts. This does not mean to imply that this individual cannot be sold. However, one of the salesperson's most valuable assets is his time and he cannot afford to waste it on an individual who finds it difficult to spend money.

LOGICAL SALES RESISTANCE

When logical sales resistance is encountered, the prospect sees a discrepancy between his needs and wants and the want-satisfier system offered by the salesperson. In this section, we will examine reasons for logical sales resistance, types of this resistance, and tactics that may be used to overcome it.

Reasons for Logical Sales Resistance

A main cause of logical resistance is noise in the communication on the part of either the sender or the receiver. The salesperson may not have obtained a comprehensive picture of the needs and wants of the account, or he may have misunderstood or misinterpreted the information obtained. The resulting presentation in either instance is likely to be less than ideal. Sender-induced noise might also occur as a result of the salesperson's use of words and phrases that might have one meaning for him and a different meaning for the receiver. Abstract words and phrases and technical jargon cause misunderstanding and, therefore, sales resistance. Although *logical* sales resistance can occur throughout the selling-buying process, it is most likely to occur during the presentation.

It is at this point the other person is considering the salesperson's proposition on its merits.

Specific Types of Logical Sales Resistance

Let us now consider seven types of logical sales resistance and techniques for effectively dealing with each of them.

Price.   In many fields of selling, the most recurrent form of logical sales resistance centers around price. Price is the value, in monetary terms, placed on the offering by the seller. Unless the prospect sees value in the proposal that is equal to or greater than the quoted price, no transaction will occur. That is why it is important for the salesperson to avoid mentioning price until he has thoroughly explored the needs and wants of the other person and determined as much as possible where he places his values. Almost without exception, when it comes to value the prospect centers his thinking on the product itself. He does not take into account associated services, the reputation of the source, or the problem-solving and creative-thinking ability of the salesperson. It is up to the salesperson to include these in his presentation and to induce the prospect to place a value on them. Otherwise, he may not be able to offset the price being quoted by a competitor on the basis of product alone.

A Direct Factory Price.   When the same product is available either directly from the manufacturer or through an intermediary, the intermediary's salesperson often encounters a special type of price resistance. The prospect points out that he is getting a direct deal at a price lower than the wholesaler can quote. Questioning may reveal that the larger quantity that must be purchased to gain a direct price is more than offset by the materials-handling costs, inventory costs, and the cost of the capital tied up in the purchase. The Steel Service Center. Institute, an association of steel resellers, conducted a highly successful marketing campaign on the theme, "Cost of Possession," to offset this kind of resistance. This same tactic can be used by any salesperson when he faces this situation.

Product Characteristics.   Almost as frequently as a salesperson encounters the price objection, he faces objections to one or more characteristics or properties of the product he offers. Often what is objected to is new to the other person and hence not completely understood. This kind of objection can be minimized if the salesperson becomes thoroughly familiar with the products now in use and in his presentation explains what his product has in common with them as well as the unique features of his offering. These can be presented in "benefit" terms. One of the key uses of the feature-benefit matrices (Chapter 13) is to prevent this kind of resistance or to deal with it when it arises.

No Demand for the Product.   Sales representatives calling on resellers often encounter the objection, "We have had no call for that product." In most instances this is the problem of the chicken and the egg. Until the product is stocked, it will not be promoted and hence customers will not seek it. When the salesperson notes the competing products in stock, he may offset this resistance by inquiring about the volume of turnover in the other items. He may then be able to show, using marketing research information, that in this kind of establishment his product line does better than those now being used. In some retail situations, it can be shown that offering alternative brands of a product increases the total volume being sold.

Delivery Schedules.   In many fields of selling, delivery schedule provides a basis for objection. If the salesperson has been able to penetrate the prospect account in depth, he should have a fairly accurate idea of delivery needs. With manufacturing firms, these needs often relate directly to the production schedule. With resellers, the needs are a function of volume turnover of the item being sold. Sometimes the purchasing executive does not have the full picture of his firm's delivery needs and hence insists on immediate delivery as a precautionary measure. To the extent that the salesperson is able to understand the true needs of the customer in terms of delivery requirements he will be in a good position to see that his company is able to meet them.

Salesperson's Company.   Sales resistance with regard to the company as a source often takes this form: "You are a giant firm, we are just a small business. We prefer to do business with companies our own size." In face of this objection, the salesperson can show the many advantages that can be gained from a big supplier—for example, certainty of source of supply, a spectrum of technical resources to assist with problems, and the fact that bigness in itself reflects success. Alternatively, the salesperson may be able to demonstrate that, by virtue of the divisionalized structure of his firm and its decentralized sales organization, in reality his firm is functionally no bigger than the prospect's.

   In contrast, the large prospect may indicate that the salesperson's firm is too small to meet its needs. The salesperson may rejoin by indicating that the prospect will be considered a key account and that it will be accorded all the care and individual treatment that such a situation implies. He may also show that a small firm provides considerably more flexibility in meeting the needs and wants of the prospect than a large organization would.

Age of the Firm.   Sometimes the age of the firm constitutes the basis for sales resistance. There may be a reluctance to deal with a new firm that is in the course of getting underway and establishing a reputation. The salesperson representing such a firm may indicate the years of experience represented in the human resources of the firm. He may also show that, because it is new, the firm is far more innovative than many of its older competitors. In addition, he may imply that, being new, the firm is going to have to try much harder to please each account than would a firm that is older and that has grown complacent. Rarely is there likely to be an objection to a firm on the basis of its being too old. Most people equate time in business with stability and reliability. If, however, the salesperson does encounter this objection he may show how innovative and progressive his firm really is and its track record in good and bad times.

Tactical Adjustments

Tactics for combating logical resistance are quite different from those used to reduce psychologically founded resistance. They are based on the premise that people place more credence in what they say themselves than in what others tell them. Thus, the salesperson's task is to get the prospect to answer his own objections. Logically founded objections are negative-voluntary reactions. In this case, a radical shift is called for, and the salesperson must do or say something that will elicit a positive reaction. Let us consider four steps which are designed to help the salesperson deal with logical sales resistance.

Positive Set.   The first step is to establish a positive set in the other person. For example, if the prospect says, "Your price is too high," the salesperson may respond, "With profit margins so narrow, money is pretty important today, isn't it?" He may continue, "As a professional purchasing agent, I know you are going to submit my proposal or that of anyone else to rigorous value analysis. Your job is to purchase at a profit to your firm, isn't it?" To establish the proper set or readiness, the salesperson must accomplish two things: (1) he must show an appreciation of the prospect's viewpoint, and (2) he must accord him the status he deserves as the prospective purchaser.

Clarify and Define Objections.   The second step is to clarify and define the actual objection. Through questioning, the salesperson must get the prospect to be as specific as possible about what it is he is objecting to, or after such questioning, the salesperson may state the objection as he understands it and see if this is in agreement with the thinking of the prospect. For example, with price objection the salesperson would want to clarify such points as:

1. Is this a general objection not only to my offering but the offerings of competitors as well?
2. If this objection is to my offering, is it based on a comparison with competitive offerings? If so, which ones?
3. If the basis of the objection is judgment on the part of the prospect, what basis is he using to arrive at the judgment?
4. How much would he consider a fair price; in other words, how much money is standing between us?

5. If price varies with quantity purchased, on what quantity is he basing his objection?

The Best Answer. The salesperson's third step is to formulate in his own mind the best possible answer to the objection as it has been clarified. He should not, however, furnish the prospect with the answer directly. Rather, it is important that the customer be given the opportunity to take an active role in the selling-buying process and thereby help sell himself the product.

Questioning the Prospect. The fourth and last step is to question the prospect in such a way that he answers his own objections. The dialogue as set forth in Figure 15-1 illustrates this four-step method of handling logically based resistance.

Step 1–Establishing Readiness

PROSPECT:	That price is far too high.
SALESPERSON:	Everything seems to cost more today, doesn't it?
PROSPECT:	You're sure right about that.
SALESPERSON:	Your firm expects you to make profitable purchases?
PROSPECT:	Yes, I do my best.
SALESPERSON:	This means you have to analyze carefully the full value in any proposition, doesn't it?
PROSPECT:	Yes, but I still say that your price is out of line.

Step 2–Clarifying the Objection

SALESPERSON:	Might I ask what you consider a fair price based on your value analysis?
PROSPECT:	Well, I don't have exact figures, but I'd say about 30¢ a unit less than you quote.
SALESPERSON:	What unit value would you place on our guarantee of uniform quality from batch to batch?
PROSPECT:	I don't know, but that doesn't amount to much. We test a sample out of each delivery ourselves.
SALESPERSON:	That sounds like a good precaution if you are not certain of quality. What does that cost?
PROSPECT:	I'd say about 5¢ prorated over the normal order.
SALESPERSON:	From a cost standpoint what is your optimum order quantity?
PROSPECT:	About 1000 units.
SALESPERSON:	Would it increase your unit cost very much to order 4000 at a time?
PROSPECT:	There would be some dollars tied up on inventory, but I can't think of much beyond that. However, with our plant expansion, storage space is at a premium.

Step 3–Mentally Formulating the Answer

SALESPERSON: (Our price breaks 30¢ a unit at 4000 quantity. His own estimate of testing cost is 5¢. I can meet his price if I can get an order for 4000 with delivery in modules of 1000 as he needs them.)

Step 4–Questioning to Have the Prospect Answer His Own Objection

SALESPERSON: If you could eliminate testing incoming purchases it would save at least 5¢ a unit wouldn't it?
PROSPECT: This is right, but we'd need to be certain of quality if we did.
SALESPERSON: Would a guarantee covering replacement of goods plus any and all costs or damages incurred through faulty quality be attractive?
PROSPECT: Yes.
SALESPERSON: Would you place an order if you could save 5¢ under your own unit value estimate?
PROSPECT: I sure would.
SALESPERSON: By ordering 4000 units, you gain the advantage of our volume price, which is 30¢ less per unit than when purchases are in smaller quantities. We will deliver your order in modules of 1000 on dates you specify. We will guarantee quality as I've outlined above so you can save the 5¢ unit cost of testing.

Figure 15-1 An Example of the Four-Step Method of Handling Sales Resistance

DEVIOUS REASONING AS A FORM OF SALES RESISTANCE

It would be naive for the salesperson to assume that each prospect will entertain his propostion on an open-minded, logical basis. It is a fact of life that some people are not straight thinkers. Sales representatives should be aware of this and be ready to cope with it when it occurs. We will consider several different kinds of devious reasoning a customer may follow.[2] Each is illustrated in terms of how it might occur in the selling-buying relationship.

Emotionally Toned Words

This type of reasoning is illustrated by the use of "cur" or "mongrel" when referring to a dog. In the field of selling, "dog" might be used to refer to a slow-moving product. Another example is "peddler" to describe a salesperson.

The defense against the technique is simple. All that is required is to restate the sentence with the proper rather than the emotionally toned word and ask whether that is the intended meaning. For example, a customer might say, "You

[2]*Ibid.*, pp. 49–57.

peddlers are all alike." A reply might be, "I consider myself a salesperson. Is that the same as peddler?"

Imply "All" When "Some" Is True

An illustration of this would be, "Redheaded people have bad tempers." This implies that all redheaded persons have bad tempers. Likewise, salespersons may be told, "Your products are terrible." This again implies that all of the products are terrible.

The defense is to put the idea "all" into the statement to show that it is then false. For example, "Do you mean that every one of our products is terrible?" The next step would be to say, "Let's take them one at a time and analyze them." As soon as one satisfactory product is discovered, the fallacy in the statement is obvious.

Divert the Discussion to Side Issues

When a customer denies the ability of a product to meet the specifications and switches to a complaint he had with the previous salesperson, he has diverted the discussion to a side issue. He may be right about the previous salesperson and hopes that through this device he will appear right about the specifications.

The antidote in this instance is to point out that there are now two issues under discussion. The salesperson should be willing to take up either issue, but he should also make it clear that a resolution of one issue will have no bearing on the soundness of the other issue.

A Compromise Solution

Politicians are noted for taking a middle road to avoid conflicts rather than arriving at sound decisions and standing by them. Customers may do the same thing. When a salesperson recommends 100 units and the customer has in mind 50 units, he may suggest a compromise and place an order for 75.

To demonstrate that this kind of reasoning is not sound, it is necessary to show that compromise is not a useful method for discovering the truth. Any position can be made to fall between two extremes. If, in the above instance, the customer feels 50 units are proper, the salesperson need only select 150 as his objective to make the middle ground 100. If the salesperson's recommendation is based on past experience and correct arithmetic, there is no reason to compromise. It may be that there are other reasons for not placing an order of the proper size, but it is better to isolate the true reasons than to arrive at an unsound conclusion that may hurt future calls.

When a salesperson knows that a customer is prone to use compromise to reach a decision, he has the alternatives of trying to show the fallacy in this approach or going along with it. If he decides to go along, he must inflate his objective so that a compromise will result in a reasonable order.

An Extreme Position

A customer can stall a presentation by making a demand that the salesperson cannot possibly approve and that would not be approved by the home office or met by a competitor. An example might be to request a discount or a delivery schedule that is unrealistic.

The remedial step would be to explore and, if possible, point out that the demand is not necessary from the buyer's standpoint, nor is it in keeping with industry practices. A further step is to demonstrate an awareness and understanding of the technique and request that it be dropped so that the presentation can continue.

An Unqualified Authority

Becuase a person has reached a position of prominence as an expert in one field, it does not follow that he is an expert in every field. A chemist may be renowned as a discoverer of scientific compounds, but it does not follow that his opinion on financial affairs or sales techniques is equally valuable.

When a customer refutes a sales point by reference to an "authority" not known to the salesperson, it is well to ask for a statement of the person's qualifications before accepting the rebuttal.

Provoking Anger

By directing criticism to the salesperson rather than to the issue under discussion, it is sometimes possible to cause the salesperson to lose self-control and attempt to defend himself. In the process of defending himself, he inevitably loses the argument.

The salesperson's response to this method is to point out that he has no personal interest other than to carry out his company's policy. He can restate the basic issue and try to continue his presentation.

An Overstated Position

When a salesperson shows enthusiasm for some aspect of his product or service, a customer may appear interested and bait the salesperson to overstate the performance that can be expected. He then forces the salesperson to back down on that point and implies that the entire proposition is unsound.

The salesperson must be cautious and objective in the claims he makes for his proposition. He must resist the temptation to exaggerate or even to agree with the prospect's exaggeration. If he has fallen into this kind of a trap, he should concede his overstatement on the particular point and proceed to show that the rest of his presentation is sound and warrants consideration.

Inability to Understand the Proposition

On the basis that a salesperson cannot expect a person to buy something he cannot understand, some customers act as though they do not see its application to their problem.

In such an instance, the salesperson must repeat his presentation in simpler terms and use questions to cause the prospect to state the relationship between his needs and the product features and benefits. If he fails in this approach, the salesperson must decide whether to challenge the prospect by alluding to his feeling that he does not wish to understand, or merely to abandon the attempt.

An Inappropriate Analogy

Suppose a salesperson were selling a machine tool as capital equipment on the basis that it would pay for itself by lowering production costs. The customer rejects the proposition by relating an incident where he listened to a salesperson who "sold" him on a new accounting system and, while he did save some labor costs, the extra forms required wiped out most of the profit.

This can be refuted by distinguishing between capital expenditures and expenditures for expendable supplies and showing that examples of one are not a valid basis for evaluating the other.

The Use of Ambiguity

An example of ambiguity would be a discussion as to whether a third person has an "inferiority complex." This is almost certain to result in confusion because the term is ambiguous. Each person gives it a different meaning. Unless time is taken to agree on the exact meaning for the purposes of the discussion, nothing can be accomplished. In a similar manner, a customer or prospect may use a term that is ambiguous, so that it appears there is a difference of opinion as to the merits of the proposition when, in truth, the point of discussion has not been established.

Salespersons should ask for clarification of ambiguous words or phrases and be willing to use the customer's meaning during the actual sales presentation. This requires that the salesperson be flexible in his terminology and, if necessary, use a different definition with each customer.

Trade Jargon

Asking for acetylsalicylic acid when an aspirin is wanted illustrates this method. Every business and industry develops words and phrases that have special meaning to their particular group. An example is the word "spiff," which refers to a special commission given to sales representatives in the jewelry and related fields. When a buyer uses these terms on a salesperson who has not yet mastered them, he is trying to evade a direct discussion.

A Slight Change

Air conditioning is designed to control heat and humidity so that employees devote their energies to their work rather than have it drained off by uncomfortable weather. Assume that the average temperature of a locality is 73 degrees and the air conditioning salesman gives 72 degrees as the proper temperature. The prospect may say, "Is it worth all that money to change the temperature one degree?" Put that way, it does not seem warranted.

In this instance the salesperson should point out that any issue can be made to seem important by comparison. While there is a definite difference between water at 60 degrees and at 160 degrees, the temperature can be raised one degree at a time so that there is no significant point at which it is hot rather than cool between each degree. Yet it is still a fact that between 60 degrees and 160 degrees there is a real difference. Air conditioning is not installed to combat the average temperature. It is installed for the high temperatures of summer months.

SPECIFIC TECHNIQUES FOR HANDLING OBJECTIONS

Thus far we have differentiated between psychologically based and logically based sales resistance, and the appropriate tactical handling of each. However, there are several specific techniques for handling objections that may be appropriate for either psychological or logical resistance.

Boomerang

Turning an objection into a reason for buying is a standard practice with many salespersons. A typical example is to answer such a statement as, "While the proposition seems very desirable, I have no money," with, "The reason I brought this to your attention is that it will save you money." Another objection is, "Your organization is too small to provide the service we need." This can be boomeranged by replying, "Our small size is one of our assets: it permits us to give personal service."

Coming To That. . . .

Often the salesperson will avoid answering an objection because he plans to present the information at a later point. This is particularly true in a fully structured or "canned" sales talk. The salesperson, instead of answering the objections, says, "I plan to cover that later," and continues his presentation. This technique can also be used when the salesperson lacks a good answer to objections. By giving himself time, he may come up with a good answer. It is also possible that the prospect will drop the objection so that it may never need to be answered.

Yes, But. . . .

This is an attempt to show the prospect that he can have his cake and eat it too. It appears that the salesperson is conceding the objection, but in reality he supplies more information to support his point of view. For example, if a salesperson is told that his firm's price is too high, he might counter by stating, "Yes, our prices do seem higher than competition, *but* when you consider the free service that we provide at the time of installation and our two-year guarantee, I feel you will conclude that our prices are very competitive."

Comparison or Contrast

This is a special case of offsetting or minimizing an objection. Rather than offer a counterargument or play down the importance of the objection, the salesperson contrasts or compares it with something that is quite acceptable. A sophisticated machine that is designed for many years of service might appear expensive in terms of its list price. By pointing out that it is about the cost of a quart of milk or a pack of cigarettes a day, however, the cost can be made to seem inconsequential. Such a comparison may have the effect of neutralizing the objection.

Humor

A good laugh may cleanse the atmosphere when a critical point is reached in a sales presentation. If the salesperson can introduce a funny story or anecdote, it may relieve the tension and allow the presentation to continue even though the objection has not been fully met.

Ask Questions

Questions can be helpful in handling objections by turning some of the responsibility for the answer back to the customer. Suppose the objection is, "Your product is not as good as your competitor's." A simple question, "Why?" may bring out the fact that the objection is not well founded. If there is a basis for the objection, the salesperson can either provide a satisfactory answer or request information from his superiors. The question also helps clarify the objection in both the minds of customer and salesperson.

Direct Denial

Sometimes the customer offers an objection that is not valid. This could be due to misinformation on his part, or it might be an attempt to harass the salesperson. In either case, a direct denial of his objection together with a statement of the facts may be in order. Caution must be used, however, as such an outright contradiction may cause the customer to take offense.

SUMMARY

Sales resistance includes anything the prospect or customer says or does that prevents the salesperson from achieving his call objectives. It is of two kinds: *psychological* and *logical*. Psychological resistance is more recurrent and difficult to counteract. Nine types of such resistance were described. Handling this kind of resistance involves identifying the psychological and social needs underlying them and finding ways to help the other person fulfill them.

Logical resistance occurs mainly during the sales presentation and is directly related to elements in the presentation. Four frequently encountered, logically founded objections were examined. Handling such resistance effectively hinges on the premise that people place more credence in what they say themselves than in what others tell them. Four specific steps must be taken to overcome logical resistance: (1) establish a positive set: (2) clarify and define the actual objection; (3) formulate, but do not reveal, a "best" answer, and (4) through questioning, obtain the answer from the other person.

We also dealt with devious reasoning on the part of the prospect or customer. Unfortunately, since many people are not straight thinkers, the salesperson must be ready to deal with them. Thirteen examples of devious reasoning were discussed along with techniques the salesperson can use to handle them.

We conclude with a discussion of several specific techniques for handling either psychological or logical resistance.

PROBLEMS

1 Differentiate, in your own words, between logically founded and psychologically founded resistance.
2. Which of the nine forms of psychological resistance would you consider easiest to overcome? Which ones would be most difficult?
3. Select one form of psychological resistance and list as many tactics as possible for coping with it.
4. Differentiate between price and value.
5. What examples of devious reasoning have you encountered?
6. You often hear the expression, "They say. . . ." Who are "They"?

Exercise 15

OBJECTIONS—MANAGING SALES RESISTANCE

Objectives: To illustrate various kinds of psychological resistance.
              To illustrate logical resistance.

A. Psychological Resistance

Many of the nine types of psychological resistance occur in every-day interpersonal relationships, especially in situations where one person is seeking to influence another to do something. For each enumerated type, indicate from your personal experience its frequency of occurrence; and, for each one you have encountered, indicate how it was handled.

1. Resistance to interference.

2. Preference for established habits.

3. Apathy or lack of desire.

4. Reluctance to giving up something.

5. Unpleasant associations with other person.

6. Tendency to resist domination by others.

7. Predetermined ideas.

8. Dislike of making decisions.

9. Neurotic attitude toward money.

B. Logical Resistance

Assume your role as fashion salesperson. Prepare a hypothetical dialogue that might occur between the buyer and yourself.

Buyer: We are successful with our present brand-name line.
You:
Buyer:
You:
Etc.

Case 15-1 Bonne Bell Cosmetics (A)

Maria Alameda is an account manager for Bonne Bell and has a territory covering the Phoenix, Tempe, Scottsdale area. The Bonne Bell product line includes skin-care lotions and creams, lipsticks, eye make-up, etc. The company has received many awards for its products and has served as cosmetician to the United States ski team. Bonne Bell is retailed through cosmetics departments in leading department stores, specialty stores, and better drug stores. In large outlets, Bonne Bell contributes to the salary of a salesperson. Such firms are designated "demonstration accounts." In lower volume accounts, Bonne Bell pays a commission to a sales representative. These are called "PM accounts" (Preferred Merchandise).

Maria is calling on Mrs. Jackson, cosmetics buyer for a new, luxury department store, which has recently placed a large branch in Scottsdale.

Maria:	Mrs. Jackson, I can understand why you haven't had calls for Bonne Bell. Many of your shoppers rely on what they see displayed and they are greatly influenced by the recommendations of your salesladies.
Mrs. Jackson:	That's true, I guess, but as you know we carry only the best labels and these are well known.
Maria:	Yes. The brands you display are well known and of high quality. However, our Bonne Bell products are specialty items which will not compete directly with your other labels. For example, our *TEN O'SIX* is a skin cleanser and stimulator for women of all ages. It has been approved for skin care by the American Medical Association. Our lipsticks keep the lips moist and prevent chapping.
Mrs. Jackson:	Well, I don't question the quality of your products. However, our department can carry just so many labels.
Maria:	I can certainly appreciate that. You have to be highly selective considering the number of brands available.
Mrs. Jackson:	You're certainly right about that.
Maria:	Here are our mark-up and turnover figures for stores comparable to yours. (*She shows Mrs. Jackson a table of such information.*) May I ask what profit performance you set for any brand you carry?
Mrs. Jackson:	Well, I don't have an exact norm but those Bonne Bell figures are impressive.

1. If you were Maria, what would you have done differently?
2. Is there a basic objection that Mrs. Jackson seems to have to Bonne Bell cosmetics?

Case 15-2 Providence Realty (A)

Donna Stark is one of six sales people comprising the sales force of Providence Realty. The company has a policy of sharing advertising expenses with any of its personnel who choose to generate leads by this means. Donna decides to run the following ad in the *Sunday Examiner:*

> *NEW LISTING–7 rooms, 3 bedrooms, located at 429 Hillcrest Ave. Large lot, fireplace in living room, close to schools. Immediate possession. Call Donna Stark, Providence Realty, 332-3534, evenings 332-3253.*

She receives a call at her home from a Mrs. Leonard.

Mrs. Leonard: Miss Stark or is it Mrs. . . . .

Donna: Mrs. But please call me Donna.

Mrs. Leonard: We are interested in that home you have listed provided it isn't too expensive; what's the price?

Donna: It's a real bargain, Mrs. Leonard. You'll have to see it to appreciate it. I'll be glad to show it to you any time tomorrow. Can we make a definite appointment?

Mrs. Leonard: Well, my husband and I don't want to waste time looking at homes we can't afford.

Donna: I can certainly understand that. However, I think you're going to like it. If by chance you don't, I can show you other listings. By the way, how big is your family?

Mrs. Leonard: We have two children, a boy and a girl. Our son is almost six and our daughter is almost four. That's why we'd like to find a home with three bedrooms. We only have two now, and besides we are not very close to a school.

Donna: How lucky you are to have two youngsters. They're going to like the big backyard. Mrs. Leonard, may I jot down your full name, address, and phone number? (She does.) It may be easier for you to have me drop by for you and your husband. Is 6:30 tomorrow evening convenient for him?

Mrs. Leonard: Let me check. Yes, we'll be ready at 6:30. I have a nice neighbor who will mind the youngsters.

Has Donna done a good job of handling the call? Explain.

SUGGESTIONS FOR FURTHER READING

Bohon, David T., *How to Overcome The 101 Most Frequent Objections in Selling Real Estate* (Englewood Cliffs, N.J.: Prentice-Hall, 1965).

Dreyfack, Raymond, "How to be One Up on Customer Objections," *The American Salesman,* Vol. 9 (January 1964), pp. 45–49.

Finsley, Dillard B., and Vinay Kothari, "Unfreezing Your Prospects," *Sales Management,* Vol. 114 (June 2, 1975), pp. 51–52.

Goldstein, A., *Secrets of Overcoming Sales Resistance* (West Nyack, N.Y.: Parker Publications, 1969).

Kirpatrick, Charles A., and Frederick A. Russ, *Salesmanship* (Cincinnati: South-Western Publishing, 1976), Chapter 17.

Leterman, Elmer G., *The Sale Begins When the Customer Says "No,"* (New York, N.Y.: Hillman Books, Bartholomew House, 1961).

Mauser, Ferdinand F., *Salesmanship: A Contemporary Approach* (New York, N.Y.: Harcourt, Brace, Jovanovich, 1973), Chapter 8.

Reinfeld, G., "Selling and Salesmanship: Objections: What Are They? Their Causes, and Cure," *Inland Printer/American Lithography,* (January 1975), p. 70.

Rosene, Lee, "The 'Why' Factor Brought an Order," *Printer's Ink,* Vol. 267 (April 17, 1959), p. 96.

16. The Close — Facilitating Decision Making

In a general way, all strategy and tactics employed by the salesperson are directed toward the close. Looking at this another way, the salesperson could do everything that has been described thus far in superlative fashion and yet fail miserably if he did not succeed in inducing purchase. Specifically, then, the close may be defined as the tactics used by the salesperson to induce purchase or acceptance of the proposition.

In this chapter we examine (1) reasons why some individuals have a difficult time closing the sale, (2) closing signals the salesperson should watch for, (3) the trial close, (4) the "psychological moment," and (5) the situation in which a sale is not the call objective. We then describe the specific techniques and the follow-up activities necessary to successfully complete the sale.

WHY SOME INDIVIDUALS FAIL TO CLOSE

There seem to be three basic reasons why individuals fail to close sales: (1) they do not have the required confidence in themselves, their company, or their product; (2) they feel guilty about asking people for an order; and (3) they are poor sales representatives. We will explore each of these problems.

Lack of Confidence

Many people find it difficult to attempt any form of a close. They do not have the confidence to look the customer in the eye and ask him if he wants to purchase the product. The salesperson must remember that if he represents a company that sells a product of good value, then most of his prospects need to see him. When the sale has been completed, not only have the salesperson and his company profited, but the customer is also better off than before he purchased the product.

If the salesperson lacks confidence in one of the products he is promoting, he should communicate this feeling to his superiors and stop emphasizing the product in question. If his company can explain that his misgivings are not justified, the salesperson will then be in a stronger position than before to sell the product because he has a better understanding of it. If, however, the company cannot alleviate the salesperson's doubts, he may have to quit selling the product indefinitely.

If the salesperson's lack of confidence stems from the realization that he does not have trust in either his products or the company he is working for, then he should probably leave the organization and find a new job. One salesperson used to say that he sold "an inferior product at a high price." Although he made a good living for his family in that job, he is now making more money and is much happier with a firm he can be proud of.

Guilt Feelings

Some individuals fail to close sales because they feel guilty about their career. They feel that selling is not a profession they can be proud of no matter how much money they make. A study done by the Life Insurance Institute determined that the greatest single cause of failure among new life insurance agents was that they felt guilty about their work.[1] They felt they were intruders who were begging for a living rather than helping people solve legitimate problems.

The feeling of guilt relates closely to the first reason why people fail to close —lack of confidence. Apparently these life insurance salespeople did not understand their very important role in delivering a vital service to society. Life insurance companies might overcome this attitude by asking new salespersons to go on a call with an agent when he is notified that one of his clients has passed

[1]Federick A. Russell, Frank H. Beach, and Richard H. Buskirk, *Textbook of Salesmanship,* 9th ed. (New York, N.Y.: McGraw-Hill, 1974), p. 384.

away. Although the benefits provided by the salesperson's firm cannot bring back the deceased individual, the fact that financial support will be provided to his or her family to help ease their burden will show how important the job really is.

If, however, an individual cannot be convinced of the importance of his position, he should consider changing careers for his own good. Not all people are cut out to be sales representatives, and the sooner the individual who feels guilty about selling realizes this and begins to look for a new job, the better his or her chances will be of achieving a successful career in another field.

Poor Selling

This is probably the predominant reason that salespersons fail to close a sale. If the salesperson does not correctly read the cues he is receiving from the prospect, he will not know when the appropriate time to close the sale is. This often occurs because the salesperson is so wrapped up in himself or his product that he is not looking for feedback during his presentation.

Other examples of poor selling center around the fact that the salesperson did not do his homework prior to the call. He did not spend sufficient time and effort to learn about the prospect's problems, who the key decision makers are in the organization, who his major competitors are, or how his product might fit into the prospect's future.

Finally, the salesperson may fail because he does not adjust tactically to the prospect's situation. If the prospect is nearing a decision on an important matter (goal gradient), it may be wise for the salesperson to return at another time. Similar adjustments must be made when the salesperson encounters unexpected competitive activity. The more the salesperson is able to think on his feet and adjust his sales presentation to fit the new situation, the better his chances of closing the sale.

CLOSING SIGNALS

The salesperson must continually monitor the prospect to determine if he is emitting any signal that could be interpreted to mean that he is ready to have the sale closed. Let us now review the prospect's reactions and examine three types of specific closing signals.

Prospect's Reactions

We pointed out earlier that the prospect has two types of reactions: positive and negative, and voluntary and involuntary (See Chapter 11). If the salesperson sees that the customer is acting in a *positive-involuntary* manner, such as nodding or picking up the product and examining it as the salesperson talks, he may wish to try to close the sale at this time or to continue with the points he is emphasizing. Positive-involuntary reactions indicate a weak closing signal.

However, only experience will enable the salesperson to separate those posi-tive-involuntary reactions which are closing signals from those that are only indications of interest.

In contrast, *positive-voluntary* reactions such as, "When can I get de-livery," or, "I'll ask our engineering department to test this product," require the salesperson to close the sale or to move to the next item on his agenda. Positive-voluntary reactions are stronger closing signals than positive-in-voluntary reactions.

Specific Closing Signals

There are three specific types of closing signals the salesperson should watch for: physical actions, statements or comments, and questions. Although there is no way the salesperson can be absolutely sure he is correctly interpreting a situation, he should be alert to these signals. If the salesperson focuses on the prospect rather than the product, he will not miss many of them. Examples of these three categories are illustrated in Figure 16-1.

Figure 16-1 Closing Signals

Physical actions indicating readiness to purchase are:

1. The prospect reexamines the product carefully.
2. He takes possession of the item—as, for example, strapping on a wristwatch.
3. He begins to read the order form.
4. He nods in agreement as the salesperson summarizes.
5. He points at the samples on display.

Statements or comments indicating a readiness to buy are:

1. "I always wanted a hi-fi set."
2. "These new machines should reduce the number of breakdowns we've been having."
3. "The letters typed on your electric machine are attractive."
4. "I've always liked dealing with your company."

Questions signaling a closing are:

1. "Can we open a joint account?"
2. "When must you have the full down payment?"
3. "When can you make delivery?"
4. "In what colors is it available?"

Source: Albert W. Frey, *Marketing Handbook* (New York, N.Y.: Ronald Press, 1965), pp. 9–26.

TRIAL CLOSE

Once specific closing signals have been identified, the next step, according to many sales representatives, is the *trial close*. This is an attempt to determine whether the other person is ready for a full-scale close. This term has little or no tactical significance or utility. If trial close has meaning at all it refers to *any close that is not successful.* Whenever the salesperson attempts to close it should be for real! Almost inevitably, some psychologically based resistance occurs when a close is attempted. Not every close works, but when failure occurs it is up to the salesperson to try again.

The following describes a typical sales situation in a retail appliance store.[2]

Prospect: Do you carry the "X" washing machine that sells for $229.00?

Salesperson: We certainly do. It is an excellent machine, and I can have one installed for you by tomorrow afternoon.

Comment– *If the prospect agrees with the salesperson, a close has been made. If not, then the sales process continues.*

Prospect: Oh, can you show me how it works?

Salesperson: Of course, just step this way.

Comment– *After a good demonstration, the salesperson again tries to close.*

Salesperson: It does seem to accomplish your objective. May I write up the order?

Comment– *If the prospect says yes, then the sale has been closed. If not, the sale continues.*

Prospect: I like this machine, but do you have any others?

Salesperson: Yes, we do, but none of them is on sale. In addition, I feel that even if this machine were not on sale, it would still represent the best buy for the money.

Prospect: I see. It is important to me that the machine be delivered by noon tomorrow.

Salesperson: This will present no problem. I will get my order blank.

The important point is to realize that the salesperson made two attempts to close the sale before he was successful. These attempts, however, were not "trial" closes; each was a sincere effort to close the sale. When the prospect made it clear that she was not yet ready for the close, the salesperson continued the presentation until another attempt could be made to close the sale.

PSYCHOLOGICAL MOMENT

Another term that is widely used in selling is the *psychological moment*. This implies that there is one optimum time during the call to ask for the order. This

[2]Adopted from Albert Frey, *Marketing Handbook* (New York, N.Y.: Ronald Press, 1965), sec. 9, p. 26.

term has no more tactical utility than does *trial close*. During any call there may be a number of times when the other person emits signals that indicate a close is possible. It is important that the salesperson minimize or eliminate sales resistance by giving the prospect adequate information to understand the proposition and to anticipate satisfaction with the purchase before he attempts to close. Each time these conditions are met, a closing attempt is appropriate. As we already noted, however, any attempt may cause resistance on the part of the other person.

One executive in the sales field prefers the term *getting favorable action* to *close*. He explains:

> We recognize that in most of our operations the sale is the result of a number of calls, but each call must achieve definite objectives and build to the final contract. As a result, every call must produce some form of favorable action.
>
> If follow-up calls are necessary, and they generally are, dates, times, places, and people must be firmly committed. It is important to stress that there are many cases where a sale can be closed in four calls instead of five, or five instead of six, by bringing the appropriate decision makers together. In most cases, decisions involving large sums of money are made on a multiple basis, so that if all the people affecting the decision can be brought together at one time, the ultimate action that we seek may come about sooner.
>
> One problem we face with sales engineers is overcoming an attitude that they are "prostituting themselves on the altar of commerce." They feel that if they provide the technical advice that the customer needs, he will let us know when he is ready to buy. There is, on occasion, great reluctance to supply the catalytic agent that is necessary to bring about favorable action.

Even when a perfect match occurs between the want-satisfier system as presented by the salesperson and the needs and wants to be satisfied, there still may be psychologically based sales resistance. Even when the presentation meets the four basic criteria of understandability, interest, believability, and persuasion, there is no assurance that the customer or prospect will automatically choose to buy what is offered. It is still up to the salesperson to ask for the order. His request must be accomplished in a manner that is not perceived, thought, or felt to be coercive.

WHAT IF A SALE IS NOT THE CALL OBJECTIVE?

Many situations exist where purchase, as such, is not the call objective. In such situations, the close is tactically more complex and the salesperson has less conclusive evidence of having achieved it. There are two main categories of selling-buying situations where this is the case: (1) when more than one call will be required to complete the sale, and (2) when the salesperson is not dealing with the ultimate user.

When More Than One Call Is Required

The most common situation of this type occurs when the salesperson knows in advance that he will need to make several calls before he can expect a purchasing decision. Under these circumstances, the salesperson must have specific objectives to achieve on each individual call. The close in each case consists of obtaining agreement up to that point. In the time between calls, however, the salesperson can expect changes in the situation, forgetting on the part of the decision makers, shifts in competitive effort, and, perhaps, new personnel to be influenced. Therefore, on each succeeding call he must determine the extent to which agreement still does exist, and where it does not, he must rebuild the relationship.

The Salesperson Is Not Dealing with the Ultimate User

The less common situation, though, is where the person called upon cannot take the action of purchase; he can only prescribe the product or recommend the purchase to others. An example of this is the pharmaceutical salesperson calling on the physician. The salesperson's key call objective is to convince the doctor to prescribe his firm's products for his patients. The textbook salesperson provides another example. He hopes to convince instructors to require the use of his firm's textbooks in the courses being taught. In industrial selling, where there are two or more persons comprising the "who's who" in a given account, it is usual for one of them to be designated as the person who finally places the order. Thus, the industrial salesperson cannot expect an action of purchase from each person he sees. For example, it would be rare for the director of research to place an order. The objective with such a person is to convince him that he should recommend the products being proposed for use by the firm.

Whether or not a sale is the objective of the particular call, there are several methods the salesperson can use in making the close.

SPECIFIC CLOSING TECHNIQUES

Whenever a salesperson closes he is likely to use a combination of closing methods, rather than a single one. The considerations that will dictate the actual choice of methods are (1) the salesperson's strategic analysis of the other person's background, personality, and motivation, and (2) the amount and kind of resistance the salesperson has encountered. Let us examine eight methods of closing the sale. We will define each one and indicate the strategic and tactical considerations for their use.

Direct Method

With the direct approach, the salesperson asks the prospect to buy, prescribe, recommend, or use his product. This can be an effective method when a logical, straightforward presentation has been made and the salesperson has encountered little or no psychological resistance. The prospect has been businesslike, and his objections have had logical foundations and have been handled to his satisfaction. The self-confident buyer is likely to appreciate this kind of forthrightness on the part of the salesperson. In contrast, directness may scare the insecure person and actually cause psychological resistance.

Summative Method

With the summative method, the salesperson recapitulates the points of agreement and thereby induces the buying decision. It is a particularly appropriate method if negotiations have occurred over several calls and if many sales points were covered. It has the additional advantage of offsetting the inevitable forgetting that may occur, particularly on points that were made early in the selling-buying relationship. It also has the advantage of reinforcing those points where resistance may have been present.

With this method, the salesperson has a choice to make with regard to the sequence of the recapitulation. He may reaffirm points in the order in which they have occurred. This has the advantage of logic, and it is likely to be the best way of reminding the person of what has taken place. Alternatively, he may choose to recapitulate in inverse order, picking up the last point agreed upon first, and working backwards. This sequence has the advantage of starting with points still in the conscious awareness of the other person. From a tactical standpoint, a superior sequence to either of these is for the salesperson to take up points in order of *minimum likelihood of encountering sales resistance*. Thus, he commences with the point of most likely continued agreement and follows this with the one of next most likely acceptance until he has covered sufficient points to obtain the order. This sequence elicits a series of positive responses and establishes a favorable set or predisposition to buy. Each time the prospect agrees with a point, he is less likely to disagree with the next point made.

This method has other advantages. If the close is made with several of the "who's who" present, either of the other sequences will cause trouble because individual differences exist on what will be remembered and on the importance accorded various points. The effectiveness of this method is enhanced to the extent that the salesperson can use questioning to get the prospect to recap the points. As we indicated previously, people put more credence in what they say than in what others tell them. If the salesperson finds that he must make one or more of the points himself, he should ask for a direct affirmation on each point before proceeding to the next one.

Demonstration Method

With this method the salesperson closes by showing the product or equipment in use. It is strictly low pressure because it places the prospect or customer in seeming control and in a position to make the buying decision. It has a unique advantage of providing the prospect or customer with a sample of the post-transactional satisfaction that will attend the purchase. In all other forms of close, such satisfaction is anticipatory. This is a particularly appropriate close for use with the cautious, skeptical prospect. It is frequently used in the sale of equipment and machinery. It affords an opportunity for the decision makers and other personnel who will be concerned with the equipment to see it first hand.

If the salesperson uses the demonstration, he should identify one or more persons in the "who's who" who are fully convinced about the merits of the proposal, so that they can act as "internal sales representatives" to convince other members of the "who's who." If the demonstration is shown to a group, the salesperson can ask the satisfied persons for agreement first, with the hope that others will be reluctant to say no.

A variant of this closing method is to add a provision allowing the customer to return the product if he is not satisfied with it. Also, in some fields of industrial selling, equipment and machines are rented or leased with a purchase option.

Assumptive Method

With this method, the salesperson assumes an agreement has been reached. For instance, he might say to a purchasing agent, "I will help your secretary write up the order." This is an appropriate method to use when the salesperson notes that commitment and decision making are painful experiences for the other person. If suggestion has been used effectively during the presentation, it is reasonable to expect that an assumptive close will be appropriate.

Another factor that influences the effectiveness of this kind of close is the confidence the other person has in the salesperson. For example, if there has been an ongoing selling-buying relationship over a period of years, the customer is likely to accept the salesperson's offering in relatively uncritical fashion.

As to personality and motivational factors, the submissive person who depends on his environment for security is more likely to accept this form of close than the strongly independent individual. A unique tactical advantage of this method is that it is certain to bring any latent sales resistance out in the open. If the salesperson assumes the order and the prospect or customer is not ready to buy, the salesperson will certainly learn this very quickly.

Positive-Choice Method

This method falls, from a tactical standpoint, between the direct and assumptive methods. The salesperson presents the prospect or customer with two or three positive alternatives and says, in effect, "Do you want A or B?" This makes it difficult for the prospect to respond negatively. You may have observed this selling-buying situation in retail stores where you have been the prospect. For example, you may have gone in to purchase a camera. The effective salesperson brings out several cameras for your perusal. He quickly removes any that you seem to reject. At no time does he allow you more than two or three cameras from which to make a selection. An important principle relevant to this method is that as the *number of alternatives or options increases, the decision making becomes more difficult and consequently less likely to occur.* This method is particularly appropriate if the salesperson senses psychologically founded sales resistance. This closing method minimizes the likelihood of such resistance by making the decision easy and simple. It is especially effective with an indecisive person.

Minor-Decision Method

With this method, the salesperson seeks affirmation on the smallest possible decision that encompasses the full order. This is often used in selling big-ticket consumer items. For example, an automobile salesperson who has a husband and wife as prospects might get a decision from the wife on the color of the paint or upholstery for the new car. Any decision involving a large dollar outlay can be painful. The effectiveness of this method is based on the principle that small decisions are made more easily than big ones. This method is particularly appropriate where suggestion has been effective. During the presentation and demonstration, the salesperson may have noted favorable reactions to one or more aspects of the product. Obviously, these are the characteristics he should use to present the minor decision to the other person. In the example above, the salesperson may have noted the husband's interest in engine options. He might ask the husband to indicate which engine he prefers. If psychological resistance has been encountered during negotiations, this is an additional reason for attempting to close on a minor point.

Challenge Method

With the dominant, self-confident, innovative person the salesperson may choose to close by offering him the opportunity to score a first. Sometimes it is appropriate to use this close on the entry person in the decision-making "who's who"—for example, if the purchasing agent won't allow the salesperson to go beyond the purchasing department to discuss matters with other personnel. In this application, the tactic may be for the salesperson to say to the individual, "Mr. Purchasing Agent, once you are convinced of the soundness of my proposition, I know you can arrange for me to make a presentation to some of the line management of your company." Even if he normally does not have such authority, the purchasing agent may rise to this kind of challenge.

Scare Method

Sometimes this is referred to as the negative close. "This is what you are missing if you don't buy now." With this closing method, the salesperson shows the disadvantages and discomforts of failing to act. Examples include implying that a general industry price rise is imminent, that inventories are low, or that delivery may be questionable later on. One paper products salesperson wished to sell his line to a large chain of supermarkets. He closed by computing the opportunity losses that would be incurred by not stocking his company's products during their special promotion. This method is particularly appropriate with the suggestible, complacent, emotional prospect. However, this method has the limitations of negative suggestion, and it should not be used except when more conventional closing methods fail.

Reflection on these eight closing methods reveals that the first three— *direct, summative,* and *demonstration*—are appropriate when few, if any, psychological "hang-ups" were encountered during the presentation. In contrast, the latter five methods—*assumptive, positive choice, minor decision, challenge,* and *scare*—are more appropriate if psychological resistance has been encountered. A very important additional consideration for choosing how to close is the strategic analysis of the prospect—his *background, personality,* and *motivation.*

POSTSALE ACTIVITY

Once the sale has been closed, the salesperson's job is only partially completed. This follow-up activity is critical to the salesperson's long-term success. If he handles the postsale activity well, the next sale will be much easier; if he does not, he will face considerable resistance the next time he approaches that customer. Two areas of the postsale activity are analyzed here: the time immediately following the close, and the longer, posttransactional phase (this is phase 5 of the selling-buying process; see Chapter 6 for review).

Immediate Postclosing Activity

Salespeople are frequently told that once they close a sale, they should leave as quickly as possible. This has merit in that it will prevent further conversation that might raise doubts or questions. In many instances, however, details must be worked out on such things as best time for delivery and purchase terms; it is important that these steps be easy to complete. If the decision maker might be called upon to defend the purchase with other members of the "who's who," the salesperson will want to provide ideas to serve as rationalization for the purchase. For example, research suggests that when a wife buys a particular furniture item, say a chest or a chair, she needs to be able to justify the purchase in her own mind and (more importantly) to her husband. Thus, if a furniture salesperson senses that the points covered for the close are not sufficient for the wife to use in justifying her decision, additional points should be provided. Related to this is the desirability of giving reassurance to the buyer by painting a vivid picture of the satisfactions that will result from owning the product.

Posttransactional Behavior

Posttransactional satisfaction, must be linked with the closing effort. The salesperson must never sell and forget. If appropriate, he may arrange for a follow-up call in order to provide necessary services, such as start-up of equipment, instruction on using the product, or assistance in merchandising if the customer is a reseller. Even when such services are not needed, the salesperson is likely to increase posttransactional satisfaction by making a commitment to return at the time of delivery to make sure everything is as promised. This has the advantage of being a logical bridge to the next call and ultimately to the next sale. Here are two salespersons' views of posttransactional behavior:

> Scheduling a follow-up call when the initial order is received is a policy point with our firm. It reassures the buyer at the time of purchase and also affords me carte blanche in choosing an ideal shelf and counter location at the time of the follow-up call. We refer to these as "set up" calls. . . .

> The point that you make on posttransactional responsibility is most important. We say that the sale is not completed until the customer is receiving the value we promised. As a result, there is an entire area of responsibility that must be considered as part of the sales follow-through. To mention a few:

> 1. Expediting shipments and deliveries.
> 2. Training personnel.
> 3. Adjusting equipment.
> 4. Installation and applications advice.
> 5. Proper billing and procedures and the interpretation of policy and practices.
> 6. People to contact in cases of difficulty in any of these areas.

A key psychological reason for follow-up is that it relieves the buyer's *cognitive dissonance*. In varying degree, each time a substantial purchase is made the person making it experiences qualms, wondering whether he or she has done the right thing. The salesperson tries to make sure the buyer has a rationalization for his purchase as a final step following the close. The follow-up visit contributes further to the buyer's conviction that he has made the right decision.

SUMMARY

In a general way, everything the salesperson does is directed toward Phase 4 of the selling-buying process: the action of purchase. The salesperson could perform superlatively in all aspects of his work but fail miserably if he were unable to close.

We discussed three reasons why salespeople fail to close sales. Although some people lack confidence in themselves, their product, or their company, and some people have guilt feelings about selling, a major reason why salespeople fail to sell is that they are poor or lazy sales representatives. They are unwilling to devote the time and effort to determine the best strategy and tactics to effectively sell to their clients.

We also examined the various closing signals the salesperson should watch for. Although there is no guarantee that a specific gesture, comment, or question means that the prospect is ready for the close, the salesperson who pays close attention to the prospect will have a better feel for when to close the sale. Thirteen specific closing signals were illustrated.

The concepts of *trial close* and *psychological moment* were also considered. However, there really is no such thing as a trial close—each time the salesperson tries to close it is for real. If he does not succeed, he simply continues his presentation and tries again at a later time. Psychological moment implies that there is only one time during the sales call when the salesperson can close the sale. We feel, however, that each time the salesperson eliminates sales resistance a closing attempt is appropriate.

The close becomes tactically more complex when the call objectives are not to induce purchase. Two such situations exist: when it is anticipated that several calls will be needed before purchase occurs, and when the person called on can only prescribe or recommend the product.

Eight commonly used closing methods were examined from a strategic and tactical standpoint.

Whatever methods are used, the salesperson must not "sell and forget." Instead, follow-up must occur to insure that phase 5 of the selling-buying process —posttransactional satisfaction—is accomplished.

PROBLEMS

1. Describe, in your own words: *close* and *psychological moment*.
2. Which are likely to be the call objectives of the following sales representatives?
   (a) Furniture manufacturer's salesperson
   (b) Machine tools wholesaler's salesperson
   (c) Cosmetics retailer's salesperson
   Justify your answers.
3. Which of the closing methods described would be most effective for use with you as the customer? Why?
4. If you were a salesperson, which closing method would appeal most to you? Why?
5. What traits in a salesperson would predispose him to misinterpreting closing signals?
6. Scan a current magazine and mark up or clip out ads that illustrate any of the closing methods described in this chapter.

Exercise 16

THE CLOSE—FACILITATING DECISION MAKING

Objectives: To reinforce knowledge of closing methods by case analysis.
    To illustrate ways of insuring posttransactional satisfaction.

A. Closing Methods

An industrial salesperson used the following closes during the course of his work. Identify the method(s) and indicate what factors may have influenced the choice he made—for example, antecedent events, characteristics of the other person(s), and kind of sales resistance encountered. Remember that often combinations of methods are used. Don't miss any.

1. *Presentation to a purchasing agent in a prospect account:*

Salesperson: ". . . I sure appreciate your willingness to have your technical people test our product. It's bound to look good against anything in the field. May we set a time for my next visit? You indicated the lab might need a week for the test. What day next week would be better for you? Wednesday or Thursday?"

2. *Presentation at a conference where three people in a customer account are present: Ed White, the chief design engineer; Bill Black, the director of purchasing; and Don Brown, the production manager.*

Salesperson: ". . . Gentlemen, may I summarize where we are in this new project. Incidentally, I'm sure our firm will be able to do as fine a job for you this time as was done on the last one.

First of all, I believe the specifications as revised are now firm. Is that correct, Mr. White?''

Mr. White: "Yes. They are cleared with production."

Salesperson: "Second, our #201 switches and #342 transducers meet your specifications without modification. Believe me, this was good news to our plant people.

Third, purchasing is about ready to receive final bids on specified quantities. Mr. Black, when do you anticipate having the quantity schedule drawn up?''

3. *Presentation to a vice-president of manufacturing in a customer account.*

Salesperson: "... I can understand your hesitation to make this change. As you indicate, there have been no major headaches using the XYZ component, and your personnel are used to handling it. On the other hand, have you considered how much you would save in labor alone if you switched to our unit? You've said yourself our other products you use have been excellent in every respect. May I ask you just one question—can you afford the loss you are incurring by not at least trying our component?''

B. Posttransactional Satisfaction

1. List as many ways as you can think of that this industrial salesperson might use to provide posttransactional satisfaction to each of his accounts.

2. Again assuming the role of the fashion salesperson, list as many ways as you can to provide posttransactional satisfaction to your customers.

Case 16-1 Bonne Bell Cosmetics (B)*

Maria Alameda's call on Mrs. Jackson continues.

Maria: All our products are profit-makers. I'd like to demonstrate how they can make money for you.

Mrs. Jackson: Well, as I indicated, we've had no calls for Bonne Bell and we may have too many brands in stock now.

Maria: Mrs. Jackson, if you are willing, I'd be glad to work with your assistant in compiling your turn-over and profit figures for the items you now carry. This will enable you to evaluate how Bonne Bell can fit in.

Mrs. Jackson: I don't think I should open up our records to an outsider. I'm sure the other salespeople who call on us would be upset if they found out.

Maria: I'm sorry. I was only trying to be of service. By the way, you're free to share these Bonne Bell figures with anybody. We're proud of our acceptance and record.

*Examine Case 15-1, Bonne Bell Cosmetics (A), before analyzing this case.

Mrs. Jackson:	Well, thanks for stopping by.
Maria:	Mrs. Jackson, will you do me a favor? Accept these Bonne Bell samples and try them yourself. I think you'll be convinced that you should stock them.
	A week later Maria phones Mrs. Jackson.
Maria:	Mrs. Jackson, this is Maria Alameda, the Bonne Bell representative. What did you think of our *TEN O'SIX?*
Mrs. Jackson:	It certainly is a fine product. I enjoyed the tingly feeling it gave me.
Maria:	Might I see you either this afternoon or tomorrow morning? I have a proposal I'm sure you'll like.
Mrs. Jackson:	Well, I'm very busy, but I can give you fifteen minutes at about 4 o'clock today.
Maria:	Thanks very much. I'll see you then.
	Maria plans to get an order with the stipulation that she will work behind the counter training the sales ladies in handling Bonne Bell.

1. How should Maria try to accomplish her objective?
2. What closing method should she use?

Case 16-2 Providence Realty (B)*

Donna Stark drives up to a modest, well-kept home and rings the bell. Mrs. Leonard greets her and introduces her husband. Donna noticed an older model station wagon in the carport as the three of them set out to see the listing. After exchanging initial pleasantries, Donna and Mr. and Mrs. Leonard leave to see the house in Donna's car. The following conversation takes place.

Mr. Leonard:	Mrs. Stark, I must tell you we don't want to bite off more than we can chew. We pride ourselves on paying as we go. Our only debt is the mortgage on our present home.
Donna:	That's certainly the way to live. I guess if more people lived that way we'd all benefit.
Mr. Leonard:	I told my wife specifically to ask the price and I find she doesn't know it yet.
Donna:	Mr. Leonard, I must apologize for that. This house you are going to see is such a buy I didn't want either of you to miss seeing it. Here we are. (*Donna pulls into the drive.*)
Mrs. Leonard:	Isn't this a nice neighborhood. The lawn and shrubbery are well cared for.
Donna:	Wait till you see the inside and the backyard. You'll love it. (*Donna unlocks the door and ushers them in. She turns on lights as they proceed through the house.*)

*Examine Case 15-2, Providence Reality (A), before analyzing this case.

Donna: (*as they look at the basement*) Mrs. Leonard, think of the space the children have down here to play on rainy days.

Mrs. Leonard: Will the washer and dryer be included? They are a lot newer than mine.

Donna: Not as a rule. However, I can find out. Perhaps we can strike a bargain.

Mr. Leonard: Before we go any farther just what is the asking price?

Donna: It's listed at $39,900.

Mr. Leonard: Wow. That's over my head.

Donna: Well, it is a lot of money. However, I think you'll both agree that this is a lot of house.

Mrs. Leonard: It certainly is. And it's such a nice neighborhood.

Mr. Leonard: What's wrong with our neighborhood?

Mrs. Leonard: Nothing at all, dear, but you'll agree this is more residential and nearer to the school.

Donna: You know, it occurs to me that you may wish to trade in your present home. My firm can handle such an arrangement.

Mr. Leonard: Well that sounds OK but I've got to know what it's going to cost if we go ahead.

Donna: I'm sure we can work things out to your satisfaction. Our assessor can give me a price on your home tomorrow. He'll need to know such details as status of the mortgage, your tax rate, things like that. This home has a transferable mortgage with a face value of $29,000, Mr. Leonard. That tells you something about the value of this property.

Mr. Leonard: $39,900 still sounds too big to me. However, since my wife likes the home, I'm willing to look at some figures.

Donna: Our Mr. Ed Jones will come by tomorrow, and tomorrow evening I'll come to the house with a definite proposal. It's been a pleasure to meet you.

Here are the figures Donna has prepared for her meeting the next evening:

Leonard's Present Home

Allowance: $27,000
Mortgage: 7%, 20 year, $20,000 face, $9,200 still owed, mo. payment $155.04
Taxes: $755/annum; 64.58 mo.
Total monthly: $219.62

429 Hillcrest

Asking: $39,900
Mortgage: 7½%, 20 year, $29,000 face, $25,500 still owed, mo. payment $233.63.
Taxes: $1,125/annum, 93.75 mo.
Total Monthly: $327.38

She muses. Any way you figure it, the Leonard's will be paying an additional $108 per month. Our office has found that Leonards are an A-1 credit risk and Mr. Leonard's salary is in the $20,000 to $25,000 range, so the payments are not out of reach.

How should Donna proceed?

SUGGESTIONS FOR FURTHER READING

Connolly, Robert, "Courage and Audacity: Keys to Closing Sales," *Marketing Times* (March–April, 1973), pp. 24–26.

Crissy, William J. E., and Robert M. Kaplan, "Tactics and Strategies of the Close," *Sales Management,* Vol. 106 (June 1, 1971), pp. 58–63.

Gross, Walter, "Rational and Nonrational Appeals in Selling to Businessmen," *Georgia Business,* Vol. 29 (February 1970), pp. 2–3.

MacDonald, John A., *Strategies that Close Sales* (Englewood Cliffs, N.J.: Prentice-Hall, 1959).

Roth, Charles B., *Secret of Closing Sales* (Englewood Cliffs, N.J.: Prentice-Hall, 1970).

Stuteville, John R., "The Buyer as a Salesman," *Journal of Marketing,* Vol. 32 (July 1968), pp. 14–18.

Tralins, Robert S., *How to Be a Power Closer in Selling* (Englewood Cliffs, N.J.: Prentice-Hall, 1960).

Yoho, David, "13 Steps in Closing Sales," *Marketing Times* (September–October, 1973), pp. 21–23.

FIVE

Types of Selling

Up to this point we have noted the variety of selling jobs that exist in our economy, as well as the many viewpoints of the selling-buying process. In addition we have provided insights into sales strategy and tactics. Now, we are ready to take these principles, methods, and techniques and apply them to different selling situations.

In Chapter 17, "Selling to the Final Consumer," our attention is focused on individuals or family buying units in the community and the home. The spectrum of kinds of selling extends from over-the-counter retail selling to selling capital-level goods and services through house calls. Special mention is made of tie-in sales, trading up, and generating business through word of mouth.

Chapters 18 and 19 are devoted to selling to organizations. In Chapter 18, "Selling to Organizations–Manufacturers," considerable detail is provided on the buying process such as the role and functions of the purchasing agent, value analysis, systems thinking, and speculative advice and service expected of the salesperson. Buygrid is presented as a way of analyzing the selling-buying process.

In Chapter 19, "Selling to Organizations–Government, Nonprofit, and Resellers," we gain insight regarding the peculiarities involved in selling to organizations in the public and voluntary (not-for-profit) sectors. These include: rigidity of specifications, bidding, and the provision in some instances of goods and services not applicable to any other markets. Also included is a discussion of selling to various categories of resellers. Such firms must buy profitably in order to sell profitably. Hence, selling to them invariably requires helping them sell the goods purchased.

Because of its pervasiveness and utility in all kinds of selling, the telephone as a selling tool is the subject of Chapter 20, "Selling to Individuals and Organizations by Telephone." Among its many applications, the telephone is used for lead generation, follow-up, and setting appointments. Special techniques are presented for effective use of the telephone.

17. Selling to the Final Consumer

Despite the energy crisis and the depletion of some of our natural resources, Americans still enjoy the highest standard of living in the world. What are viewed as unattainable luxuries in most other countries are considered necessities by many Americans—for example, note the labor-saving appliances in almost every home, the number of families with more than one television, and the sheer amount of wearing apparel each person has.

Over 200 million Americans are prospective customers for a limitless variety of goods and services. Their needs, wants, and desires are catered to by about 6 to 8 percent of the work force who are engaged directly in selling to individuals. The institutions and establishments patronized by consumers range from small, independent grocery stores to national chains of supermarkets; from automobile dealerships and used-car lots to real estate firms and banks; from beauty parlors to health clinics. In this chapter we examine the scope of retail selling activities along with retail sales procedure, selling in the home, four special selling strategies, and a brief discussion of some of the more important managerial issues in selling to the final consumer.

SCOPE OF RETAIL SELLING ACTIVITIES

The scope of the retail selling process is as vast and complex as the consumer market it serves. The amount and kind of selling done depends on who does the buying, what is bought, where it is bought, the value of the purchase and the expertise needed to help the customer make the buying decision. Many consumer goods and services are obtained with no direct selling effort. Consider the air traveler who obtains his flight insurance out of a machine; the housewife who selects food and a variety of other goods in the supermarket; the youngster who buys a candy bar from an automatic dispenser. Virtual self-service extends even to hard goods in a discount store, although a small staff is usually scattered about to offer help as needed.

At the other extreme, retail salespeople play an important role in influencing purchase decisions. As examples, think about the selling-buying process involved in the purchase of an automobile, or life insurance, or an engagement ring. The stakes are too high and the required expertise too great for the typical customer to risk buying any of these without guidance. Also, many shoppers, even for small items, prefer to patronize a store where they are waited on—for example, a department store, a fabric shop, or a local meat market. Frequently, salespeople in such establishments build a personal following of customers who like to do business with them. Part of the *value added* is this personal attention.

There are many facets of the retail selling process. These facets include selling in the community, specific tasks of retail salespeople, and knowledge needed by retail salespeople.

Selling in the Community

The great diversity of retail businesses—the bank, the car dealership, the supermarket, the department store, the drugstore, the beauty parlor, the specialty shop—share a common characteristic from the standpoint of selling. Customers and prospective customers seek them out, drawn by a variety of promotional forces, advertising, direct mail, word of mouth, recommendations of friends, and, most important, prior satisfaction with purchases made. Thus, many shoppers enter the retail establishment with clearly defined needs and wants. Below we examine the role of the retail salesperson, counter selling, and open-stock selling.

Role of the Retail Salesperson. Given the special nature of the retail situation, sales positions in the consumer sector may vary from mere ordertaking to highly creative problem solving and information sharing. This spectrum of responsibilities is often demonstrated in the same retail outlet. Some salespeople are satisfied to merely furnish what the customer seeks with no attempt to sell a greater quantity, a better quality, or additional items. On the other hand, there is scarcely a retail business where the salesperson, with imagination and initiative, cannot influence additional purchases and insure repeat business.

For example, the teller at the bank may remind a customer it is time to start a Christmas Club. The car salesperson may "trade up" the prospect from a used car to a new one. The checker at the supermarket may direct attention to some of the impulse items at her station. The saleslady at the hosiery counter in the local department store may remind a customer of a special on scarves. The clerk in the drugstore may influence the purchase of a larger package of what is requested. The beautician may tie in a manicure while she performs her services. The haberdasher may sell slacks to go with the jacket.

Large establishments with a great variety of merchandise departmentalize their offerings and locate their groupings to insure optimum traffic flow. In some departments the goods are sold over the counter. In others they are arranged so that shoppers can circulate among the wares on display. Some departments combine the two. In either arrangement, it is critical that the salespeople keep stock neat, well organized, and in tasteful display. This can be done during the times when customers are not being waited on. The effective salesperson is a department merchandiser.

Counter Selling. Typically, counter departments handle small goods and goods that are relatively *homogeneous* in intended use. The effective salesperson knows the stock and has in-depth information about related items and where they can be obtained.

When shoppers crowd the counter, it is important to assure each one that he or she will be waited on in turn. It may be appropriate to see that each person has something to examine so as to hold them in readiness rather then letting them wander off. In order to let them know that they have been noticed, the salesperson may want to reassure them and say: "I'll be with you in a moment." Courtesy is a prime requisite, as is competence and efficiency, in handling the actual transactions. All of us have heard a salesperson say, "Will this be cash or charge?" It brings the sale to a close and, after the paperwork is accomplished, paves the way to handling the next customer.

Open-Stock Selling.   Open-stock departments handle goods that are physically large, such as furniture and major appliances, as well as those that come in a variety of combinations, sizes, and styles, such as ladies' and men's ready-to-wear. Most open-stock goods represent relatively large outlays in contrast to those sold over the counter. And, although some goods sold over the counter require special expertise, open-stock wares almost always involve special knowledge. Customers seek answers to a variety of questions before making purchases. Consequently, salespeople in such departments must find ways of keeping informed on styles, trends, competing labels, and the like. These salespersons may require more formal education and greater experience, as they must command respect and confidence on the part of the customer.

Specific Tasks of Retail Salespeople

Retail salespeople have specific duties and responsibilities to perform in the store. In addition, they must develop a positive relationship with the customers.

Duties and Responsibilities of the Salesperson.   Although their main objective is to satisfy customers' needs by selling them products at a profit, five specific tasks should be added to this general goal: (1) ascertain customer needs and give information about different products, (2) provide adequate service to customers before and after purchase; (3) handle customers' complaints; (4) provide assistance when products are returned or exchanged; and (5) generally help customers through the store.

In addition, retail salespeople may have to perform other tasks that are not directly related to selling, but that are vitally important for the overall sales performance of the retail organization. These functions often include: checking and marking incoming merchandise, maintaining adequate shelf inventory, building displays, taking inventory, and informing management of perceived trends in customer needs.

The Retail Salesperson-Customer Relationship.   The relationship that a retail salesperson has with his customers is extremely important. Buyers are seldom absolutely certain of the product they want to purchase, and they often value the salesperson's information. Thus, it is essential that a retail salesperson be able to closely relate to his customer.

It is, obviously good practice and good manners for the salesperson to be courteous in his treatment of customers. The consumer should feel that the salesperson and the store take true interest in his or her problems and that they are sincere and willing to help. Rudeness discourages customers from returning to the store, and lack of patronage will cause a considerable deficit.

Likewise, it is important for the salesperson to establish a long-run relationship with a customer. He should not consider each prospect as a potential one-time sale; rather, he should try to make sure the customer will return to the store as often as possible. He should not pressure the customer into making unsuitable purchases, but rather he should advise him as to the advantages and disadvantages of each particular decision. If the customer has confidence in the honesty and competence of the salesperson, he will no doubt continue to patronize the store.

Knowledge Needed by Retail Salespeople

To give adequate counseling to his customers, a retail salesperson must have knowledge about several important variables: he must be able to convey information about the store he represents, the merchandise he sells, and the customers he serves.

The Store. Retail organizations frequently differentiate themselves from competitors by selling particular lines of merchandise and offering special services. The salesperson should be aware of these policies so that he can pass the information on to the customer. Price, quality, or specific guarantees on products may be crucial factors in the purchasing decision. Also, store services, special promotions, delivery, and availability of credit are appealing to customers and should be pointed out whenever they may favorably influence the purchase.

To illustrate the importance of the salesperson's knowledge let's take an example. Imagine that a consumer enters a store to purchase a particular portable radio. She has a specific model in mind and asks the salesperson: "Do you have model X of Brand Y transistorized portable AM-FM radio?" One possible answer, assuming the store does not carry that particular model, is the following: "No, Ma'am, we do not carry it." It is likely that the customer will then leave the store and continue her search somewhere else.

If, however, the salesperson knows the product lines his company carries, he could try the following approach: "We have a wide assortment of AM-FM portable transistorized radios, Ma'am. The model you have in mind is a good product, but unfortunately we do not have it in stock at the moment. However, we do have two other models that are very comparable to the one you had in mind; may I show them to you?"

The customer might be very interested in seeing possible alternatives to her initial choice. A careful and honest description by the salesperson of the *advantages* and *disadvantages* of each model and how each compares to Model X of Brand Y will help the customer make a purchase decision. She may eventually choose one of the models the store has in stock rather than continue her search.

The Merchandise. The salesperson's thorough knowledge of the merchandise handled by the store is another important type of information. Most buyers are willing to learn more about the products they are considering for purchase. The salesperson is often considered an expert on the merchandise he sells and should be able to answer at least the most common questions about his products.

Consider the following situation: a customer enters a store to purchase a color television set. After looking at several sets on the floor, he is approached by a salesperson who offers to help him with his questions. The customer is undecided between two brands. He cannot really tell the differences in the sets' image, color, or hue, but the two televisions are priced differently: one is $50.00 more expensive than the other. The customer's question to the salesperson is: "What is the difference between these two brands? Why is this one more expensive?" It is very important, at this point, that the salesperson be able to give the customer a thorough explanation of the technical differences between the two products so that the price differential can be justified.

The Customer.   Finally, a good retail salesperson knows his customers. It is very important to many people to know that a salesperson remembers their name, the type of products they like to purchase, particular merchandise they have been looking for, and so on. Although a salesperson may not be able to keep all of this information in his head, he should keep records to which he can refer when it is needed. When new merchandise reaches the store, a salesperson may want to call some of his regular customers and let them know about particular products.

Knowledge about the store's general type of consumer is useful to the salesperson when approaching new customers. This information will aid him in asking pertinent questions and suggesting possible choices.

RETAIL SALES PROCEDURE

There are six steps involved in retail sales. These comprise a logical sequence of events when a consumer enters a store: (1) the salesperson greets the customer; (2) he asks questions to determine the customer's needs; (3) he selects the products that he feels would satisfy these needs; (4) he shows the merchandise to the customer and describes the important features; (5) if the customer has any objections, the salesperson tries to answer them; and (6) he attempts to close the sale. Let us examine each of these steps.

Greeting the Customer

It is essential that a customer feel welcome when entering a store. The salesperson who ignores the customer's presence and continues intent in his busywork or talking to other salespeople will cause a negative impression and may eventually lose the customer altogether.

The initial greeting should encourage the customer to stay in the store, look around, and ask questions about the merchandise. Some traditional greetings are often considered acceptable, such as "Good Morning! May I help you?" It is important, however, to encourage the customer to share ideas about the product he has in mind, and questions such as "May I help you?" often elicit an automatic response: "No, thank you, I'm just browsing." More pointed approaches that might encourage a dialogue are preferred: "We are featuring Brand C this week at a special price," or "This is a product that has pleased many of our customers."

Embarrassing questions (e.g., "Can you tell me exactly how you would use this product?") should be avoided. The customer must feel free to browse and ask for information without being pressured into buying.

Determining the Customer's Needs

A good salesperson observes and listens to the customer so that he can properly assess his needs. By encouraging the customer to share ideas and feelings about a product, the salesperson can determine his preferences and tastes, and thereby can suggest specific alternatives to him.

Screening questions are especially useful in this regard. For example, a person selling furniture might ask:

Is your home modern or traditional?
What rooms are you furnishing?
What pieces are you particularly anxious to buy?
What price range are you considering?

In the case of a men's clothing department, the salesperson would note what the shopper is examining as well as how he is attired. If he is looking at slacks, he might ask such questions as:

Do you prefer straight or flair?
Are they for business or leisure?
What colors do you prefer?
What is your waist size?

Often it is possible to suggest additional items once the shopper has made his or her basic selections. With furniture, attention can be directed to small pieces such as end tables, wall decorations, and ornaments. With men's clothing, the salesperson may suggest sport shirts, ties, or a jacket. The ability to induce tie-in purchases is an important attribute of effective open-stock selling.

Selecting Merchandise

The salesperson at this point has already identified some of the product attributes the customer is interested in. He will, therefore, make his initial selection of merchandise based on these attributes.

Variables such as the model, size, price range, or color of the product may be the initial selection criteria, but it is rare to find a customer who has already made all of the product decisions before entering the store. A common mistake, however, is for the salesperson to show product after product to the consumer without attempting to match his needs. This method is confusing and tiring and certainly does not offer the customer a solution to his immediate problem.

Describing and Demonstrating the Product

Even though most American consumers are sophisticated and knowledgeable about the products and services available in the market, it is still important for the purchasing alternatives to be clearly presented to them by the salesperson. Actual demonstration of product uses may be crucial to the buying decision, as well as oral description of important product characteristics.

The customer's reactions give the salesperson helpful hints about what points should be reiterated or strengthened. These hints encourage the salesperson to show additional products to the customer.

Handling Objections

Very frequently the customer voices some kind of objection to the products presented by the salesperson, which relate objectively to features of the product —for example, "This color is too dark," or "I really would like a smaller size." When this happens, the salesperson can respond easily by choosing more desirable alternatives.

A more serious type of objection may reflect deep-seated feelings about the product that the customer is not willing to state clearly. For instance, the customer may decide that he is not financially able to buy the product he likes, but he does not want to tell this to the salesperson. In this case, vague objections such as "Well, I am not really sure. . .," or "I will talk to my husband about this," might be voiced by the customer. Here, the salesperson would encourage the customer to be more specific by adding comments related to special purchase plans, or by asking the customer general questions that may bring out his or her real feelings.

There are times when the salesperson can not satisfy the customer's objections. But a salesperson knows that coping with frustration is part of his task.

Closing the Sale

The retail salesperson should know when the customer is approaching his buying decision. A good salesperson is able to promptly recognize closing clues and should offer his customer the opportunity to terminate the purchase.

At this point, the salesperson should stop showing merchandise to the customer so as not to confuse him. Instead, he should ask for the customer's agreement in order to eliminate any possible indecision on his part. He should not, however, rush the customer into buying. Some frequently used closes are:

"Should I charge this to your account?" or "Would you like us to deliver this to your home?"

Purchases of big-ticket goods, such as furniture and appliances, often require approval of a spouse. Returns are extremely costly for the store to handle, and therefore it may be a sound sales practice to do the "paperwork" but not to process the sale until both parties approve the sale. Some home-furnishings retailers go even further—they suggest a house call to make sure that what is selected will fit in compatibly. Other stores may have the consultative expertise of a certified interior decorator available to advise on such purchases.

SELLING IN THE HOME

Opportunities exist for selling a wide range of goods and services in the home—ranging from cosmetics to insurance, from magazine subscriptions to vacuum cleaners, from small sundries to central air conditioning. In addition, some retail establishments augment their sales effort on their premises with in-the-home calls made by field salespeople.

While many of the recommendations given for retail selling also apply to in-home selling, there are some key differences. One of the most important is that the retail customer enters the store voluntarily, whereas the in-the-home salesperson is usually interrupting the privacy of the prospect. Therefore, *prospecting* plays an important role in this type of selling. In addition, there are special types of in-home-selling schemes that have been devised to adapt to this special selling situation. Of course, this special type of selling also has its problems.

Prospecting

In this kind of selling, prospecting is of prime importance. It ranges from cold-canvass door-to-door; to following up on leads generated from mail, coupon returns, and telephone inquiries; and to a preliminary canvassing by telephone. The effective door-to-door salesperson generates leads as he makes his cold calls by asking each person he calls on for names of others who may be interested in the product.

Those individuals who sell items involving large expenditures try to govern their call schedule to reach both husband and wife so that cancellations are minimized. This means that much of the actual selling is done during the evenings. Calls during the day are used to screen and qualify prospects for later follow-up.

When the nature of the product line is such that there is repeat business (e.g., cleaning materials and cosmetics), it is important to develop a personal following. There are two payoffs—continuing purchases and references to other prospects.

Special Types of In-Home Selling

"Party selling" and "pyramiding" are two special types of in-home selling. We will examine each type.

Party Selling.   A variety of consumer goods are sold by having a prospective customer invite guests to a party where the salesperson can present the product line. The hostess usually receives a gift for the commitment plus additional commission awards depending on attendance and how much is purchased. She handles the orders, takes care of delivery, and makes the collections. At each party the salesperson is on the lookout for additional hostesses. From the firm's standpoint, as well as the salesperson's, this arrangement is ideal. The unit sale is large, responsibility for payment is fixed in one person, and bulk delivery can be made. In addition, it provides a pleasant get-together for the customers.

Pyramiding.   Some home selling organizations increase market coverage by pyramiding—that is, by enlisting each customer to recruit his own sales force and set up his own business. He is offered an override on each sale his people make. Each of them, in turn, is given the same opportunity of pyramiding. This method quickly reaches a limit; it has the same potential evils as the chain letter.

Unscrupulous promoters of such schemes have swindled hapless participants by selling each one a manual, selling aids, and other equipment, together with a sizable inventory. The third or fourth "generation" in a given trading area finds no prospects left and is left with a sizable investment, whereas those at the top of such pyramids make a financial killing. As a result, pyramiding is now considered to be a violation of the Federal Trade Commission Act which is discussed in some detail in Chapter 23.

Problems with In-Home Selling

Unethical behavior on the part of a few firms and individuals has given in-home selling a bad image. As a result, many people are fearful of letting salespeople into their homes. Some communities ban this mode of selling altogether. Others require such salespeople to be licensed and bonded. Some door-to-door salespeople tend to force purchases, which has led to legislation in several states stipulating a two-or three-day "cooling-off" period in which the purchaser can cancel the order.

To overcome this widely held preconception of the public, in-home salespeople must be certain to establish their honesty and integrity. They should carry official identification and employ polite, courteous, and sincere behavior at all times.

SPECIAL SELLING STRATEGIES FOR SELLING TO THE FINAL CONSUMER

Selling to individuals, whether in the community or in the home, provides an opportuntiy for numerous strategic adjustments, as we have observed in our discussion thus far. We will analyze the use of specials and sales along with narrowing the choice of alternatives, trial use, and credit.

Specials and Sales

One widely applicable strategy is associated with specials and sales. Alert salespeople can bring such events to the attention of their regular customers by phoning them to give them the opportunity to take advantage of the bargains. Such attention enhances the relationship with each customer even if he or she is not interested in what is offered. In dealing with shoppers who are attracted to the store, the special pricing facilitates closing. An example of this would be a person who has a weakness for imported ties. The salesperson with whom he does business at the local haberdashery always calls him when a new shipment of French ties arrives. His approach on the phone is: "I have some beautiful new European ties in stock, which will complement your wardrobe. Can you come by sometime to look at them? I am afraid that they will be in great demand, and I would like you to have first choice. . . ."

Narrowing Choice Alternatives

Still another strategy, applicable where wide choices are possible, is to avoid showing the shopper too many items at a time. Continuing the tie example, if a tie is rejected, the salesperson immediately puts it aside. If the choice narrows to one of the three ties but uncertainty exists, the salesperson brings out an additional tie which he thinks will appeal to the customer. The stretegic principles involved in this example are simple. First, avoid providing too many choices; a buying decision becomes more difficult to achieve as the number of options increases. Second, offer a limited number of positive alternatives; it minimizes a "no purchase" response as one of the options.

Trial Use

With some items, demonstration or trial use is an effective strategy. Consider the following examples.

A wife shopping in a supermarket is offered a cut of a new sandwich meat.
A shopper at the cosmetics counter watches a beautician apply makeup.
A local automobile dealer encourages a prospect to take a test drive.
A vacuum cleaner salesperson cleans a rug for the housewife.
A professional model shows off a new dress style.

In effect, this strategy challenges the prospect to see for himself. It also manifests the firm's confidence in its product.

Credit

Credit can also be used as a sales strategy. If the salesperson senses that a customer is hesitant to make a purchase because he or she cannot make the necessary cash outlay, he may encourage the opening of a charge account, or, if appropriate, suggest extended terms of financing. It is important to note that the firm makes about as much money from the credit extended as it does from the goods sold.

MANAGERIAL ISSUES

The selling-buying process is uniquely personal. Hence, it is important to attract salespeople who have the appropriate talents, personality, and motivation. Retailing firms have been notoriously low-paying, which makes it difficult to compete for quality personnel. Also, the mode of reimbursement does not always include incentive pay; thus salespeople are not motivated to exert initiative in closing sales.

Many studies of consumers' reactions to retail salespeople reveal such varied complaints as: too much pushiness, lack of enthusiasm and interest, limited product knowledge, bad manners, and ignorance of other offerings in the store. Obviously, many of these can be offset through proper training and supervision of salespeople.

Typically, in a retail situation, the *buyer* purchases the merchandise offered and is expected to sell it. Sometimes the latter responsibility is neglected due to administrative demands on the buyer's time. It is extremely important for the buyer to be on the floor as much as possible. There are a number of reasons for this. First, personal insight is gained of shoppers' reactions to what is offered. Second, personal selling skill is kept sharp. Third, guidance can be given to sales personnel on a one-to-one basis.

More and more establishments are being located in shopping centers and malls, and it is important for management and salespeople to be familiar enough with these other businesses to answer general questions about them. Salespeople should be cautioned against knocking the competition.

Retailers are often asked to cooperate with the local schools in distributive education and cooperative programs. If such a request is made, management has an obligation to provide a learning experience for the young people. Some retailers tend to view the students only as cheap help and fail to fulfill their educational role.

SUMMARY

In America, selling opportunities exist wherever there are people. Most of the buying is done in a great diversity of establishments in the community, though some is done in the home.

A wide spectrum of selling activities exists, and a considerable range of talent is used. We noted distinctions between the selling activities and talents needed in counter selling, open-stock selling, and in-home selling. We analyzed the basic tasks of retail salespeople and the knowledge they need to provide useful information to their customers.

There are six different steps involved in retail sales: greeting the customer; determining the customer's needs; selecting merchandise; describing and demonstrating the product; handling objections; and closing the sale.

We also examined selling in the home. Two types of special in-home selling activities were discussed: "party selling" and "pyramiding." We concluded with a discussion of four selling strategies for the final consumer and a discussion of some important managerial issues in selling to the final consumer.

PROBLEMS

1. Describe, *in your own words*, the scope of retail selling.
2. What useful distinctions can be drawn between counter selling, open-stock selling, and selling in the home?
3. What are some examples of creative selling you have experienced while shopping?
4. Define *in your own words*, "party selling" and "pyramiding." Give an example of each. Are both these ethical sales practices?
5. Which of the strategies listed in this chapter would be most challenging to the salesperson? Why?

Exercise 17

SELLING TO THE FINAL CONSUMER

Objective: To appreciate the problems and challenges faced by an open-stock salesperson.

Interview a salesperson in an open-stock department in a local store. Obtain answers to these questions:

1. What do you like best about your job?
2. What do you like least?
3. How do you handle the situation when a number of customers are seeking your attention?
4. What talents are needed to succeed in your kind of selling?
5. How would you describe a typical day's work?

Case 17-1 Integrity Life Insurance

Integrity is a medium size company now in its fourteenth year. It is cleared to do business in four midwestern states. It sells mainly through independent agents* although it is building its own sales force in southern Illinois where it has its headquarters. It relies heavily on advertising with coupon returns to generate leads. These in turn are furnished to the appropriate company salesperson or agent depending on the address of the prospect. The company processes each lead by a letter which tells the individual to expect a personal call. This costs Integrity roughly $8.00 per coupon, so salespeople and agents are reminded to handle the leads with care.

Bob Williams, a salesperson for a general agent in Indiana, receives a coupon-lead filled out as follows:

---

*Independent agents sell insurance for a number of companies. They are paid on a commission basis.

NAME ___M·C· MARSTON_____

ADDRESS __31 OAKLAND RD._____

____GREENVILLE, IN   47124_____

____SINGLE   ✓ MARRIED

OCCUPATION: ___CARPENTER_____

✓ YES. I want to hear more about the double benefit life policy.

Bob notes that Mr. Marston lives about 30 miles away. He has only one customer near Marston's address so he decides to phone Mr. Marston and screen him as a prospect before he makes a trip to see him. After the telephone conversation, Bob decides it is worth a trip and makes a date to see Mr. Marston at 7:30 P.M. on Thursday. He is greeted pleasantly.

Mr. Marston:	You must be Mr. Williams. Come right in. This is Mrs. Marston.
Bob:	Good evening folks. Thank you both for seeing me.
Mr. Marston:	Pull up a chair. We generally do our business right here at the table. (*After a brief discussion about the weather and what a pleasant community Greenville is, the following conversation takes place.*)
Bob:	Before I talk about insurance, I'd like to know about you. Your answers to my questions will help me help you. First of all, Mr. Marston, as a carpenter, do you work for yourself, or are you on a company payroll?
Mr. Marston:	On my own all my life and proud of it.
Bob:	I would be too. Might I ask you what your approximate income is?
Mr. Marston:	Well, work is seasonal but I'd say overall, about $15,000 a year.
Bob:	How much life insurance do you now have in force on yourself and on Mrs. Marston?
Mr. Marston:	We have an old policy for $1000 on Mrs. Marston. Dates back before we got married. Her parents took it out and transferred it to us. I have my veteran's policy for $10,000.
Bob:	The way things are today a $10,000 coverage isn't very much.
Mr. Marston:	That's why we sent in the coupon. Your company has insurance that provides protection for a husband and wife and builds a retirement income, too, isn't that right? See, I've saved the ad.
Mrs. Marston:	Actually, Mr. Williams, I think we've talked about having more insurance for years. Now that our boy is on his own, maybe we can afford it.
Bob:	Oh. How old is your son?
Mrs. Marston:	Nineteen. He joined the navy a year ago and he's doing just fine. My husband was a navy man during Korea.
Mr. Marston:	I'm still navy in spirit. Great outfit.
Bob:	You both look young but if your son is 19 you both must be in your late thirties.

Mr. Marston: Nope. I'm 44 and my wife is just past 40.

Bob: Our double benefit policy is just what you need. As you mentioned a few minutes ago it protects both husband and wife and builds up a retirement income. Here's how it works. (*He spreads a folder on the table.*) Let's use 42 as an entry, the average of your ages. Now, notice at the top of each column is the amount of protection needed. Let's say $20,000 in the event of the husband's death. Notice, under that number is $2000 which covers the wife's death. Notice there are two numbers where the age and coverage come together. The upper one, $161.50, is the monthly retirement payment which commences when the wage-earner reaches age 65. The lower one, $46.20, is the monthly cost if payments are made annually.

Mr. Marston: Just a minute. I have some questions. If I should die at any time, Mrs. Marston would get a lump sum of $20,000. Is that right?

Bob: Yes, unless we arranged the policy for monthly payments to her over a time period, say, 20 years.

Mr. Marston: Here's my next question, if Mrs. Marston were to die, I'd receive $2000 but then what happens to the policy?

Bob: It remains in force and you are still covered. We have found that the most sought-after coverage on the wife is 10% of the face.

Mr. Marston: Well, we already have $1000 on my wife's life. If we wanted only $1000 additional coverage could that be arranged?

Bob: It would be difficult since we have developed our double benefit insurance based on the 10% formula.

1. Critique what has occurred thus far.

2. What should Bob do next?

Case 17-2 Campus Toggery

The Toggery, owned and operated by Mr. and Mrs. Owen, is one of several shops catering to the fashion needs of coeds at Central Michigan University. It has a choice location, opposite the Student Union. The store is a regular advertiser in the Central Daily. This ad appeared, late fall, in the Monday edition:

SPECIAL! SAVE 25%
on Polyester Knits

SHIRTS, Long-sleeve classics in soft, washable polyester. Choose from delicate pales, richer tones, pretty patterns. Available in sizes 10 to 18.

5^{25} and 6^{75}

regular $7 and $9

PANTS, Color compatible polyester double-knit
pants. With smooth-fitting elastic waistbands.
Proportioned for Tiny, Typical and Tall.

8^{99}

regular $12

About thirty girls were waiting for the store to open. There was a rush for the clothing on sale. More girls continued to arrive.

Mrs. Owen and one salesperson, Sue Hartley, were the only ones available to handle the mob. They dashed about trying to help and to answer questions. Everyone seemed to be talking at once. Confusion and delay occurred in making sales. The small dressing room area was soon crowded. Mrs. Owen noticed that some of the girls were leaving and their facial expressions showed their displeasure.

1. What should be done?

2. What steps might have been taken to avoid the mixup?

SUGGESTIONS FOR FURTHER READING

Ashell, Ben, "Let's Make Retailing More Profitable: A Salesperson's Guide to Better Selling," *Department Store Economist* (March 1966), pp. 26–29; (April 1966), pp. 26–28; and (May, 1966), pp. 32–33.

Bruce, Grady D., and Charles M. Bonjean, "Self-Actualization Among Retail Sales Personnel," *Journal of Retailing,* Vol. 45 (Summer 1969), pp. 73–83.

Cotham, James C., III, "The Case For Personal Selling," *Business Horizons,* Vol. 11 (April 1968), pp. 75–81.

Drucker, Peter, "Careers in Retailing, by Retailing and for People," *Stores,* Vol. 51 (February 1969), pp. 5–8.

Duncan, Delbert T., Charles F. Phillips, and Stanley C. Hollander, *Modern Retailing Management: Basic Concepts and Practices,* 8th ed. (Homewood, Ill.: Richard D. Irwin, 1972).

Gist, Ronald R., *Management Perspectives in Retailing,* (New York, N.Y.: John Wiley, 1967).

Jolson, Marvin A., "Direct Selling: Consumer vs. Salesman," *Business Horizons,* Vol. 15 (October 1972), pp. 87–95.

Merchandising Week, "The Sears Salesmen: Three Basic Points," Vol. 102 (July 13, 1970), p. 54.

Monaghan, Patrick C., *How to Sell at Retail: T.V., Appliances, and Home Improvements* (New York, N.Y.: Fairchild Publications, 1968).

Olshausky, Richard W., "Customer-Salesman Interaction in Appliance Retailing," *Journal of Marketing Research,* Vol. 10 (May 1973), pp. 208–212.

O'Shaughnessy, John, "Selling as an Interpersonal Influence Process," *Journal of Retailing,* Vol. 47 (Winter 1971–1972), pp. 32–46.

Lessig, V. Parker, "Consumer Store Images and Store Loyalties," *Journal of Marketing,* Vol. 37 (October 1973), pp. 72–74.

Pennington, Allen, "Customer-Salesman Bargaining Behavior in Retail Transactions," *Journal of Marketing Research,* Vol. 5 (August 1968), pp. 255–262.

Robinson, O. Preston, W. R. Blackler, and W. B. Logan, *Store Salesmanship,* 6th ed. (Englewood Cliffs, N.J.: Prentice-Hall, 1966).

Zimmer, A., *Strategy of Successful Retail Salesmanship,* (New York, N.Y.: McGraw-Hill, 1966).

18. Selling to Organizations – Manufacturers

IN THIS CHAPTER

A Definition of Industrial Goods and Services
General Characteristics of Industrial Markets
Who Does the Buying?
How Is Buying Done?
A Planned Approach to Industrial Selling

The market members in the manufacturing sector represent all sizes and varieties of organization. For example, Uniroyal sells tires to various divisions within the big four of the automobile industry but also to small custom builders of specialty cars. Typically, with accounts in these markets, many persons need to be influenced before a purchase will occur. In a single General Motors division, approval of tires must be made by six department heads in addition to the purchasing executive assigned to such products. Often there are professionally trained purchasing executives who screen prospective vendors and their market offerings.

A considerable amount of market segmentation exists today. A firm's mix of products and services may involve widely different technologies and uses in its varied markets. Because of this, the sales force may be specialized by products or industry or both. For example, IBM's sales representatives for its computer markets are specialized to a single industry—banking. In this case, the selling process is likely to extend over a long time period and several calls. Extensive negotiation is commonplace. Often the salesperson must use supportive personnel from his company in his promotional efforts—ranging from engineers and scientists to various marketing specialists.

In this chapter we examine the selling-buying process as it pertains to manufacturers, with special attention to the purchasing agent. We analyze industrial goods, the general characteristics of the industrial market, who does the buying, how the buying is done, and a planned approach to industrial selling.

A DEFINITION OF INDUSTRIAL GOODS AND SERVICES

Industrial goods and services include everything except what is intended for personal consumption by the ultimate consumer or for resale to him. At one extreme, an industrial good may be a paper mill purchased on a "turn-key" basis —that is, fully constructed, equipped, and ready for operation. But industrial goods and services more often include the raw materials needed to construct the mill, the paper-making equipment, the power plant and all auxiliary machinery, as well as the special services performed by the many subcontractors.

Continuing this example, in the course of operating the mill there would be purchases of such industrial goods and services as wood pulp, synthetic resin, bleach, and other ingredients for making the paper; fuel for the power plant; replacement parts and lubricants for the machinery; office supplies and equipment; telephone, telegraph, and mail-metering services; and a host of others. The major difficulty in defining industrial goods stems from the fact that many items similar to those needed for operating the mill are also bought by ultimate consumers (for personal consumption): for example, telephone service, paint, carpeting, and chairs. The main difference is the final use made of the product. Consequently, many products are sold in both the industrial and consumer markets.

GENERAL CHARACTERISTICS OF INDUSTRIAL MARKETS

Because of the very size and diversity of consumer markets, a huge industrial sector in the American economy is needed to supply and support them. Industrial goods and services amount to roughly 35 percent of the gross national product. These markets have four general characteristics, which are of particular interest to the salesperson: geographic concentration, derived demand, highly segmented markets, and short channels of distribution.

Geographic Concentration

While consumers are literally everywhere, industrial markets tend to be geographically concentrated, often with great distances between them. For example, firms in the electronics industry are heavily concentrated in lower New England, the Middle Atlantic states, the West Coast and, to some extent, the Southwest. Thirty percent of America's total manufacturing payroll is concentrated in five states: New York, Pennsylvania, California, Ohio, and Illinois. It is also accurate to describe the industrial sector as "big business." Less than 2 percent of our manufacturing establishments account for 50 percent of the total volume. Thus, although many salespersons travel a great deal, their travel is often restricted to small geographic areas where they deal with only a few customers.

Derived Demand

Demand throughout the industrial sector is derived rather than direct. This implies that the amount of goods demanded in the industrial sector is a function of how much demand there is for another product in the consumer sector. As an example, the amount of paint needed by a large construction firm is a function of how much demand there is for new buildings. Continuing this example, let's look at a salesperson who sells to two types of accounts for a paint producer—paint retailers and paint contractors. If the demand slacks off in the building industry he will spend most of his selling efforts on the retailers. Then when the demand picks back up in the construction business the salesperson can return to a more balanced selling effort.

In the same way, the industrial market demand shifts as the federal government's demand for goods changes. As a war shifts from hot to cold, huge reallocations of resources occur. Along the same line, current buying behavior in the industrial sector can be influenced by the forecast of future economic conditions. Buying decisions can be made or postponed depending on these predictions. This is particularly true of expenditures for capital-level items, such as replacement or expansion of plants and equipment. Because of the postponement option, fluctuations (both seasonal and cyclical) are much greater in the industrial sector than in the consumer sector.

Purchases of capital-level goods are also markedly affected by tax and regulatory bodies of government as well as the condition of the money markets. For example, a number of years ago when the federal government removed the tax advantages of accelerated depreciation, there was an immediate decline in capital equipment purchases. Once it became evident that the incentive was to be reinstituted, such purchases increased. When capital funds are in short supply and interest rates are high, firms in the industrial sector curtail their expansion and replacement plans.

Highly Segmented Markets

Markets in the industrial sector are far more segmented than consumer markets. The same industrial goods may move to several different markets. Each market segment has its own array of technologies associated with the use made of the same industrial product. This is why industrial sales organizations are often differentiated not only by products or product groups, but also (and more frequently) by markets served. The very diversity of uses and associated technical problems often prevents the single industrial salesperson from relating effectively to the diversity of his firm's customers and prospects. In the extreme case, four or five sales representatives from the same company may have the same firm as a customer! Related to this is the pervasive interdependence among industry groups and firms. Inputs for one industry are the outputs of another. Not infrequently, direct competitors in one market segment are key customers of one another for other products or in other markets. Dow Chemical has DuPont as a key customer, and vice versa.

Short Channels of Distribution

Channels of distribution in the industrial sector are shorter than in the consumer sector. As firms grow in size, they are likely to need multiple channels to reach all markets. As a recurrent example, an industrial firm might reach all companies that purchase large quanties of its merchandise directly, but it might employ two or three forms of indirect representation to cover those companies that purchase smaller quantities of its products. When the firm sells directly to the users of its products it will have a great deal of control over its sales efforts, because in this situation the salesperson's primary responsibility is to sell his firm's merchandise. However, when intermediares or wholesalers are used to reach the user of the merchandise, the salesperson not only has to sell goods but he may also try to convince the intermediary to sell the goods in the way his firm wants the products sold. These two selling positions may require two very different types of people.

WHO DOES THE BUYING?

Even in the smallest firm it is likely that more than one person influences the buying decision. In larger firms the number of people involved directly or indirectly can range up to seven or more. The people comprising this decision-making group, both individually and as a group, generally have greater sophistication and more rationality with respect to sales representatives offerings than, say, the family buying unit considering a large expenditure in the consumer sector.

In the small firm, a number of line management people might comprise the "who's who," and one of them may be designated to see industrial salespeople. In large firms, there is likely to be a department responsible for procurement, manned by professional purchasing executives. In the case of national and multinational firms with multiple locations, procurement policy may be established by corporate management, but purchases up to the level of capital-outlay items may be decided upon at the local level. It has been estimated that 75 percent of industrial purchases are made through professionally trained purchasing executives.

Organization of the Purchasing Department

Considerable variation exists in the level the purchasing department occupies in the management hierarchy, in the way it is organized, and in the authority it has for decision making. For example, where cost of goods purchased represents a large percentage of total costs for finished goods, purchasing is likely to be placed at the corporate level, headed by a vice-president. In contrast, if fixed costs and payroll are the main ingredients of the cost of finished goods, purchasing may be relegated to a lower spot in the total company structure. In some companies the purchasing department encompasses inventory planning, management and materials testing, and procurement.

Some purchasing departments have complete authority and responsibility for buying products and services. At the other extreme, some departments function strictly in a staff capacity and only fill requisitions and specifications set by others. If the firm is such that a great diversity of relatively technical products and services must be purchased, there is likely to be specialization within the purchasing department—specific buyers for each category of goods and services required.

Professionalism of the Purchasing Agent

No other business group, with the exception of accountants, has moved as far as purchasing agents in establishing a professional status. Typically, the purchasing agent takes his job very seriously and is motivated to improve his total effectiveness and his contribution to his employer. He views his assignment as being his firm's special "knower" on what to buy, where to buy, when to buy, and how to buy. Just as the salesperson is the firm's eyes and ears in the marketplace, so is the purchasing executive a seeker of significant information for his company. His prime sources of information are interviews with salespersons.

To function effectively, the purchasing executive must know his firm's internal organizational structure, the functions of various departments, and their special needs for goods and services. It is not unusual for the purchasing executive to face an "internal selling job" in the course of his work. For example, he may learn about a new product that, in his judgment, is far superior to the one now being used by one of the operating units of his own company. His task is then to convince the department concerned, and, of course, he is not always successful. The purchasing agent often faces frustrations and disappointments not too different from those of a field salesperson. As one salesperson pointed out:

There are frequent occasions when the salesperson cannot get to the spheres of influence within an account, or sit in on a committee meeting that will arrive at a decision. As a result, he must sell by "proxy." The importance of adequately preparing the individual that will represent you to other people within the account can make or break the sale.

HOW IS BUYING DONE?

There are several facets to the purchasing decision in the industrial sector. The most basic of these is the firm's decision whether to make or buy—that is, is it wiser for the company to produce the needed item itself or to purchase it from an outside supplier? Subsequent facets of the purchasing process are generally within the realm of the purchasing agent. Several of his most important functions are: optimizing inventory, annual buying, evaluation of sources, source development, negotiations, and value analyses. He must also follow up on purchases and deal with the special situations of reciprocity and gifts.

Make or Buy?

The selling-buying process begins with needs. For some needs in an industrial firm, an immediate decision must be made as to whether to make or buy an item. The answer to this question is not often simple. If the item is to be made, the company may thereby use available production capacity. On the other hand, the quantity needed may be such that economies of scale in production are not possible. Even if the firm has the necessary expertise and skills required, a "make decision" may divert personnel from other, more profitable activities. Often an argument in favor of making an item is that quality can be carefully controlled and availability can be assured. On the other hand, companies engaged primarily in the manufacturing and marketing of the desired items are likely to have accumulated expertise that enables them to turn out products of high and uniform quality and on a continuing basis. These factors must be weighed carefully before any decision to make or buy is made. Thus often the industrial salesperson's greatest challenge is to show that it is more profitable for the firm to buy from him than to use its own facilities to make an item.

The Role of the Purchasing Agent

If "buy" is the decision, a requisition is prepared by the department needing the item. If the product needed is such that it is manufactured to order for the customer, there may be a "bill of materials" specifying what is needed. During this early stage in the industrial buying process, the purchasing agent is viewed by line management as an "internal consultant." Depending on his expertise and the authority accorded him, he may significantly influence the final specifications.

Throughout the purchasing decision process and in the routine use of materials, the firm has a valuable source of knowledge available in the purchasing agent.

Optimizing Inventory.   Relatively standard items, used on a continuing basis, are generally kept in inventory. Each of these has a maximum inventory level and a specified reorder point. The purchasing department is responsible for seeing that adequate quantities of these items are kept in stock.

On many items, the optimization of inventory may contribute favorably or adversely to a firm's profit picture and may markedly affect the smoothness of the production process. For example, a recent research study found that metal service centers (resellers in the steel industry) had a running excess inventory amounting to some $150 million. A reduction of this by more effective inventory management changed the profit picture for that part of the steel industry. As an example of the impact of the size of inventory on work flow, the typical automobile plant has on hand sufficient tires for the output of one shift. It is up to the people responsible for procurement to see that deliveries of this product are on regular schedule. A pileup causes congestion at the unloading piers and extra material handling; delay in delivery can shut down a production line.

Annual Buying.   If an item is used in large quantity and on a continuing basis, the actual buying may consist of annual or semiannual contract negotiations. In such instances, specifications are usually given to several selected sources and bids are evaluated. In this form of procurement it is not unusual for the buyer to specify an annual efficiency improvement, say of 3 percent. The rationale, here, is that the manufacturer must improve efficiency in order to remain competitive. The firm then passes this requirement on to its key vendors as a condition of the selling-buying relationship. One of the problems associated with this criterion is that there may be different potentials for improvement in the various technologies involved in designing and manufacturing the many items purchased. Three percent may be too low for the supplier of one product and beyond all reason for the supplier of some other product.

Evaluation of Sources.   Another important function for the purchasing agent in the industrial selling-buying process is the continuing evaluation of sources.

Purchasing departments are responsible for knowing where the various goods and services may be procured. Appropriate criteria must then be applied in evaluating the merits of each source. Most firms are reluctant to depend on a sole source for any product or service essential to their continuing operation because it would place them in a vulnerable position. In addition, by having several sources of supply, there will be competition among the suppliers to improve quality, reduce price, and add services. Some large firms even set quotas on the percentage of business allocated to each supplier.

Source Development.   All too often there are goods and services needed for which a source is not readily available, and considerable effort must be made by the purchasing department to find suppliers. In the extreme case, a company may be forced to develop and maintain its own source. In the mid-1960s one of the automobile manufacturers financed the establishment of a tool and dye shop and provided managerial assistance to the enterprise in order to have a dependable source near one of its largest plants. In Latin America, Sears and Roebuck helped start many firms which would be able to supply merchandise to local Sears stores. In most cases, Sears did not own a portion of the business, rather they merely provided financial and managerial assistance to aid the firm's development.

Negotiations.   Once internal needs are determined and sources found, the actual negotiations are initiated. The purchasing agent's prime objective is to buy profitably just as the industrial salesperson's objective is to sell profitably. For many standard industrial goods, prices for a given quality and quantity are nearly identical. In these instances, the availability of technical and other services becomes a determining factor in the buying decision.

Value Analysis.   For many industrial purchases, there is a need for systematic evaluation of alternate offerings; the process used for this purpose is value analysis. Value analysis consists of answering questions, such as the following, with respect to products that the purchasing agent is considering:

What uses does the firm make of the item?

What values can be placed on each of the uses?

What is the cost of the item related to these values and associated with the uses?

Are any of its characteristics wasted?

If so, can these be eliminated and thus reduce the cost of the item?

Is there anything better for the intended use or uses than the item under consideration?

If the item is other than an in-stock item of the supplier, is there a standard product that can be used for the same purpose?

Considering the quantity of the product needed, does the price reflect economies of scale?

Answers to these questions facilitate a systematic comparison among alternate products available.

Value analysis of the product does not eliminate the need to evaluate the *total* offering of each vendor. Consideration must be given to a value analysis of the company as a source, for example, the depth of its technical expertise and resources, financial strength, flexibility in adjusting to the company's needs, and reliability of delivery. Similarly, value analysis must be applied to the service and assistance that are available from each source. Obviously, this process can and should be engaged in, whether purchasing is done by a professional procurement staff or the owner-operator of the business.

Follow-Up.   Just as the salesperson cannot afford to sell and forget, neither can the purchasing agent buy and forget. Follow-up by the purchasing agent is an important step in the industrial buying process. It is his responsibility to follow up on his purchases to see that deliveries are as promised, that quality of the product is as specified, and that any other commitments by the vendor are fulfilled. Just as the salesperson enhances his relationship with the purchasing agent by a follow-up once orders are placed, so the purchasing agent enhances his position with his own company's personnel by showing this interest. Furthermore, the purchasing agent learns by doing this. It provides him with information that will help him to refine his evaluation of sources and of products and services. It is good business to favor those sources that have been checked out as dependable and able to fulfill all commitments as promised at the time of the purchase.

Reciprocity.   Sometimes the purchasing department has imposed on it the restraint of reciprocity. Sources must be favored that are themselves customers of the purchasing agent's own firm. In general, this is an impediment to profitable purchasing because the department is precluded from investigating other sources of supply. In the extreme case, this type of buying might even raise the company's purchasing costs. It can also cause complacency in the vendors if they know they can count on the business.

The purchasing agent must carefully examine the reciprocity conditions and their effect on the firm's total efficiency. If such arrangements cause the firm to lose potential sales, the purchasing agent should prepare a detailed report for the top management asking them to consider the possibility of avoiding reciprocity agreements for specific items. On the other hand, if there is no significant problem in maintaining reciprocity, the purchasing agent may want to use informal contacts to obtain prompt delivery and good service. In addition, if reciprocity agreements substantially lessen competition, they could be in violation of the Clayton Act or the Federal Trade Commission Act. (These two laws are discussed in Chapter 23.)

Gifts.   Another troublesome aspect of industrial buying behavior involves the giving of gifts to those responsible for purchasing decisions. Some businesses, as a matter of policy, do not permit acceptance of gifts of more than nominal value. Each person who does so, even when not forbidden by policy, is vulnerable to the accusation that his business is being bought. Some firms feel so strongly about this that they prohibit their personnel from accepting any kind of gift, even a luncheon. Other firms encourage vendors to make a donation at Christmas to a charity in lieu of providing gifts.

Impact of Systems Thinking

One of the most recent influences on industrial marketing is the impact of *systems* thinking—that is, consideration of an operating unit as a complete entity. This affects the industrial buyers' perspective of the goods and services they need. With this viewpoint, few purchases of machinery and equipment can be made in isolation. Instead, such items are evaluated in terms of how they fit together in a man-machine system. This means that if the industrial salesperson is to influence customers and prospects favorably, he must be able to show the compatibility and contribution of his products and services to the total man-machine system of the firm.

One company, historically a major force in the manufacture and marketing of compressors, mud-pumps, and other equipment for oil fields, found that it had to diversify and broaden its offering to include whole systems of equipment for geophysical exploration and for the production of oil under various environmental conditions; market demands were no longer in terms of single units of equipment. Several of this firm's competitors lost market share by failing to consider the impact of systems thinking on buying behavior in that market.

A PLANNED APPROACH TO INDUSTRIAL SELLING[1]

Although many industrial sellers cling to the idea that their chief function is to mount an onslaught aimed at "making the sale," this type of thinking is rapidly going out of style. With the increasing complexity of industrial procurement it is no longer realistic to regard each purchase as an isolated event that "just happens." Both buyers and sellers are concerned with building long-term relationships that will allow them to exchange technical information and do business over a span of several years.

For the most part, though, the marketing literature depicts this romance as a one-way process that depends on the initiative of the seller. However, buyers should be equally concerned with staying on good terms with suppliers; this relationship is especially critical in times of shortage. Many purchasing manag-

[1]"Industrial Marketing, All Eyes are on the Buyer," *Sales Management, The Marketing Magazine,* Vol. 99 (October 15, 1967), pp. 71–78.

ers see their most important job as that of maintaining the company's reputation as a good customer. Why? Because this is the best way to make sure their company will receive prompt service and, perhaps more important, have continuous access to the design and inventive skills of its suppliers. For this reason, sellers should view their part in the purchasing process as much more than writing up orders. Companies don't make purchases—they establish relationships. And common considerations in the establishment of these relationships are team buying and selling and the question of tactics.

Also important to a successful buying-selling relationship in industrial marketing is an understanding of the complex processes involved. Particularly useful in this regard is a system for analyzing the various buying situations as they develop from the decision process within the purchasing areas of the industrial firm. One such system is the "Buygrid" framework, which we will discuss later in this section.

Buying-Selling Relationships

The relationships between the salesperson and the purchasing agent amount to more than a game of corporate gin rummy. Team selling and buying often characterize the industrial buying-selling process, and we will analyze the role of the marketer in this situation as well as the tactics that must be employed to establish effective relationships.

Team Buying and Selling.   Frequently, among large industrial concerns, buying and selling are performed by teams of specialists in every aspect of business —from production to cost accounting. Under this system, the role of the marketing department, especially of the industrial sales force, is primarily one of bringing about the best possible communication between the two teams. First, the marketer must respond to the concrete requirements of the buying organization and endeavor to persuade the potential customer that his company is best equipped to help the buying organization achieve its goals. For the successful marketer, however, this basic task is no more than a starting point. A salesperson using effective communication attempts to anticipate—and even to precipitate—forthcoming changes in customer requirements in order to direct them into channels advantageous to his firm.

This idea is so fundamental to success in modern industrial marketing that many people feel the entire marketing effort of a company should be based on a thorough analysis of buyer behavior. Not only does such an analysis entail the use of psychological and sociological principles (see Chapter 3), but it has direct implications for every-day marketing strategy. For instance, while the term *market segmentation* is conventionally applied to differentiating among buyers on the basis of, say, their needs for a certain product or their preference for high-priced or low-priced goods, it may also be applied to markets according to the circumstances in which buyers entered the market. Thus, a marketing organization may be expected to develop teams of specialists to deal with potential customers who are in the process of developing a new product and are seeking technical assistance. Or, the individual salesperson may make a career out of persuading noncustomers that they should forsake their current suppliers and switch to his company.

Tactics.   Not only is the particular buying situation of critical importance to salespeople, but they must also be aware of the tactics best suited to different stages in the buying process, and of the wide variation in information requirements among members of the buying team. The position of these decision makers gives each of the buying influences a formal stake in the outcome—each one views purchasing from his own peculiar vantage point. Design and development engineers try to minimize the risks of making an error, and yet their designs and specifications greatly influence the procurements that follow (their requirements often eliminate many suppliers who would otherwise be qualified).

Marketing people in the buying company tend to look at purchasing as a means of enhancing the salability of their own products. Manufacturing people favor simple items that make the production job as inexpensive and trouble-free as possible. Research and development people are important because they set the broad criteria within which the other technical decision makers operate, and they provide clues as to what the company's requirements will be in the future.

The "Buygrid" Framework

Understanding complex industrial processes requires a framework for analyzing the various buying situations and how they emerge from the continuous process of problem solving and decision making within the buying offices of a corporation. Usually, transactions are classified in one of three ways: (1) market segment or class of trade reached, (2) product or service marketed, or (3) end use of the product. But these classifications should be supplemented by a fourth system that takes into consideration the particular selling techniques required for each phase of the buying process. An illustration of such a system, the "Buygrid" framework, is shown in Figure 18-1.

"Buyclasses."   Using the Buygrid framework, all buying situations may be divided into buyclasses according to the newness of the problem. Thus, the "new task" situation is one that has never occurred before and consequently requires the buyer to learn much about an area in which he has had little experience. In contrast, the "straight rebuy" pertains to a recurring requirement that is filled by the same supplier as a matter of routine. The "modified rebuy" occurs when a company decides to consider other suppliers for a product that it has previously bought on a straight rebuy basis. The salesperson's tactics must be tailored to each situation, especially in the amount and type of information he provides to the purchasing decision makers, who are likely to pump him dry in a new task situation and turn him off when considering a straight rebuy.

Figure 18-1 Blueprint of a Buying Situation

	Buyclasses		
Buyphases	*New task*	*Modified rebuy*	*Straight rebuy*
1. Anticipation or recognition of a problem (need) and a general solution.			
2. Determination of characteristics and quantity of needed item.			
3. Description of characteristics and quantity of needed item.			
4. Search for and qualification of potential sources.			
5. Acquisition and analysis of proposals.			
6. Evaluation of proposals and selection of supplier(s).			
7. Selection of an order routine.			
8. Performance feedback and evaluation.			

"Buyphases."   The procurement process itself may be broken down into eight buyphases, as shown on the lefthand side of the Buygrid chart. Together these form a sort of chain reaction. Once the process gets under way, it will move from one phase to the next until the purchase is made or the deal is called off. Depicting the process as eight decision points underlines the importance of directing the sales effort toward the entire chain of events, instead of treating the sale as an isolated moment of truth that happens independently of the other events. As the process unfolds, there occurs a "creeping commitment" on the part of the buyer, which gradually narrows the field of potential suppliers. Thus, in most cases, it is difficult for a vendor to enter the selling-buying process during the late phases with any hope of success.

The Early Stage of the New Task.   In studying the Buygrid matrix, it becomes apparent that the most intricate selling-buying situations fall in the upper left-hand corner of the chart—that is, in the early stages of a new task assignment. It is here that management makes its most difficult decisions and, in many in-stances, it welcomes the advice of suppliers. But this is by no means the first stage at which an alert salesperson can influence the selling-buying process. Something must set off the chain reaction to begin with and, while that stimulus may come from within the buying organization, it frequently comes from a member of the selling team who anticipates or, better still, precipitates a need for a product or service within the purchasing company.

The Buygrid framework not only helps the seller visualize the decision-making process, it also helps him identify a number of decision points at which he can assist the buying company by providing technical data and advice. This assistance can favorably influence the trend of the process.

Most importantly, the Buygrid matrix illustrates the tremendous responsi-bility of the industrial salesperson as a communicator. Order taking is the least important part of his job. He is the communications arm of his company, constantly mediating between representatives of seller and buyer and ferreting out critical decision points. It is he who must provide meaningful data at just the right time to the decision makers on the buying team (whether they are engineers or purchasing agents). In short, his judgment or lack of it, can win or lose a contract for his company at any point in the procurement process.

SUMMARY

Selling to manufacturers is usually a complex, intricate team effort. Industrial markets are generally characterized by derived demand, highly segmented mar-kets, short channels of distribution, and special pricing policies. In the larger companies, the industrial salesperson must penetrate and influence a "who's who" with highly varied backgrounds.

A key figure in this "who's who" is the purchasing executive. He serves as the firm's agent in determining what, where, when, and how to buy. In this position, the contemporary purchasing agent is often influenced by *systems* thinking—that is, consideration of the operating unit as a complete entity.

Before the purchasing agent begins his search for a product, the firm must decide whether to make or buy the item. If the decision is to buy, the many functions of the purchasing agent are then put into operation. Of primary importance are: optimizing inventory, annual buying, evaluation of sources, source development, negotiations, and value analysis.

On the other side of the selling-buying relationship, the successful sales-person will take a planned approach to the industrial selling situation. He will seek, often using team selling and special tactics, to establish a working re-lationship between his company and the potential purchaser. One useful device for understanding the industrial selling-buying process and the salesperson's relationship to it is the Buygrid framework, which is illustrated in Figure 18-1.

PROBLEMS

1. What aspect of selling to manufacturers do you consider most challenging? Why?
2. Define *value analysis* for someone not familiar with business.
3. Who has the more difficult job—the industrial salesperson or the industrial purchasing executive? Defend your answer.
4. What is meant by: new task? modified rebuy? straight rebuy?
5. Summarize the differences in assignment among:
   (a) the door-to-door salesperson
   (b) the salesperson in an open-stock department of a retail store
   (c) the salesperson calling on manufacturers

Exercise 18

SELLING TO ORGANIZATIONS-MANUFACTURERS

Objective: To consider selling from the viewpoint of the industrial purchasing executive.

Complete this exercise either by interviewing a purchasing executive or by putting yourself in his place. (You may want to consult a text such as the *Handbook of Purchasing.*)

1. What are the key qualifications of a purchasing executive?
2. What are the key challenges and problems in the job?
3. How much working time is devoted to interviewing salespersons?
4. How much working time is devoted to interviews establishing needs within the company?
5. What criteria should be applied in establishing a source?
6. What are some common errors or "boners" on the part of the sales representative?
7. What qualities are most essential in an industrial salesperson?

Summarize what you have learned from the interview. What new insights did you get that were not covered in the textbook or in class?

Case 18-1 Satellite Stereo, Incorporated

Tom Swift represents RTA, a multinational manufacturer and marketer of electronic devices and components. Other divisions of his firm produce and sell end-products for use in navigation, control systems in plants, etc.

Tom is reviewing his accounts and making plans for the upcoming quarter. Of his key prospects, he decides that Satellite Stereo will be his prime target. He faces a difficult problem—RTA once was a major supplier of Satellite before he was assigned the territory. However, Satellite dropped RTA and vowed never to do business with them again.

RTA's version of what happened is as follows: Satellite was developing a miniaturized inexpensive tape recorder. It was to be supplied to a national discount chain and marketed under the chain's label. This represented a radical departure for Satellite. At that time they were producing only high-quality, costly products under their own label. RTA manufactured devices for the new product to Satellite's specifications. At the time they alerted Satellite to the hazards of printed circuits and inexpensive power units. The upshot was that many of the units were returned to the chain and caused considerable trouble and loss of good will.

Satellite's version of what happened: To be price-competitive, RTA cut corners in production and failed to maintain quality control. Furthermore, Satellite accused RTA of shipping devices without final inspection.

Tom has called on Satellite monthly for the eighteen months he has been in the territory. Bill Lynch, number two in purchasing at Satellite, has been willing to see Tom but has told him, "My hands are tied. Our production manager, George Young, can't bear to hear the name RTA." Tom pointed out to Bill that RTA furnished items to Satellite for use in other products and as far as can be determined only good results were obtained. Bill has indicated that Dick Zimmerman, Satellite's vice president of marketing, is also anti-RTA.

RTA's engineering department, at Bill's request, thoroughly analyzed specimens of Satellite's leading products and gave him a rundown on which RTA products might be used in various parts of the line. Where possible, they have also told Tom whose competitive products are now being used.

Tom recently learned that Satellite is phasing out of the private label recorder-player business. Thus, the disagreement which lost the account has little or no significance today.

Tom jots down the best description he can make of Bill Lynch:

Background: Engineering graduate; went to work at Satellite right out of college; married; about 35 years old; active in the local chapter of purchasing agents.

Personality: Mild, cheerful, conventional, serious, practical, dependent, courteous.

Motivation: Seeks status with own management and peers in purchasing. Aspires to be number 1. (His boss, Mr. Baker is 55.) Great personal integrity which influences how he does business.

As Tom sees it, unless he can find some way to reach and influence George Young and Dick Zimmerman, he cannot crack the account.

Outline a plan for Tom's next call.

Case 18-2 American Carbon—A Dream Come True

American Carbon manufactures and markets carbon in all forms. Customers range from municipal water purification plants to manufacturers of air filters. It divides its markets strictly along geographic lines. Thus a sales territory may include a great variety of potential business. Obviously, tremendous variations exist in the customer mix from one geographic sector to another.

Jim Coleman sells for American and his range of customers and prospects is quite varied. Ever since he was assigned his territory he has had a dream—to capture a share of the business from the two cigarette companies that have plants in his area. He estimates that there is about $500,000 worth of carbon being used in filter cigarettes being produced in those plants.

He calls regularly on both firms and has learned quite a bit about them. The objections he has encountered include: complete satisfaction with present suppliers; no need for a third source; carbon is carbon and both vendors deliver it to specification; no complaints about delivery.

Jim is challenged to come up with a new approach. He hopes that his persistence may some day pay off. He thinks: "Perhaps I will get some new ideas if I join a visitor group for a plant tour." Both companies provide such a public relations opportunity.

In the course of the tour, Jim chats briefly with a forelady on one of the lines. She makes a remark that startles him. "The girls like their work except when we have a run of filter cigarettes." Jim asks, "What's bad about the filters?" She replies: "The carbon dust gets in the air and smudges your face and hands." Jim can't wait to write up his discovery. Here is his letter to his manager:

Dear Ed:

I think I know how to crack the tough cigarette filter market! In the course of a plant tour I learned from a forelady that the girls on the line detest filter runs. The carbon escapes into the air smudging their hands and face. In fact, the forelady told me cleansing cream and disposable tissue have to be kept in the rest rooms for the girls to clean up. Also, she said when filter cigarettes are being run girls leave the lines far more often than when nonfilters are being run.

If we can get our technical people and our bag suppliers busy on this, we'll make a killing.

Sincerely,

In view of the tremendous potential in the total cigarette industry immediate action was taken. A valve was developed and patented for use on American bags which was leakproof. Jim's dream came true! He and American found a real winner.

You are Jim. Outline the presentation you will make to capitalize on this innovation.

SUGGESTIONS FOR FURTHER READING

Corey, Raymond E., *Industrial Marketing: Cases and Concepts,* 2nd ed. (Englewood Cliffs, N.J.: Prentice-Hall, 1976).

Hauck, Eugene C., "Industrial Selling: The Challenge of Sophistication," *Sales Management,* Vol. 103 (Aug. 15, 1969), pp. 63–64.

Martilla, John A., "Word-of-Mouth Communication in the Industrial Adoption Process," *Journal of Marketing Research,* Vol. 8 (May 1971), pp. 173–178.

Pruden, Henry O., and Richard B. Reese, "Interorganizational Role-Set Relations and the Performance and Satisfaction of Industrial Salesmen," *Administrative Science Quarterly,* Vol. 17 (December 1972), pp. 601–609.

Rowe, David K., and I. Alexander, *Selling Industrial Products* (New York, N.Y.: Hutchinson Press, 1968).

Steinkamp, Wilbert H., *How to Sell and Market Industrial Products* (Phildelphia: Chilton, 1970).

Thompson, Joseph W., and William W. Evans, "Behavioral Approach to Industrial Selling," *Harvard Business Review,* Vol. 47 (March-April 1969), pp. 137–151.

Walker, Orville C., J. Gilbert A. Churchill, Jr., and Neil M. Ford, "Organizational Determinants of the Industrial Salesman's Role Conflict and Ambiguity," *Journal of Marketing,* Vol. 39 (January 1975), pp. 32–39.

Webster, Frederick E., Jr., "Informal Communications in Industrial Marketing," *Journal of Marketing Research,* Vol. 7 (May 1970), pp. 186–189.

Wilson, David T., "Industrial Buyers' Decision-Making Styles," *Journal of Marketing Research,* Vol. 8 (November 1971), pp. 433–436.

19. Selling to Organizations — Government, Nonprofit, and Resellers

While markets in the government and nonprofit sectors have much in common with manufacturer markets, sufficient differences exist to warrant separate discussion of each. In this chapter we examine the individual complexities of the government and nonprofit markets, with particular attention given to the ways in which business can respond to these special situations.

Another broad and diverse sector that plays an important role in the selling-buying process is the reseller, who serves as an intermediary between the manufacturer and the use of the product. Many products are sold through a wholesaler, who in turn sells directly to a user (such as another manufacturer) or to a retailer, if the product is to be sold to the final consumer. Both the wholesaler and the retailer are resellers because they serve as a link between the manufacturer and the ultimate user of the product. The reseller must sell profitably as well as buy profitably, because his situation can provide benefits as well as limitations for the manufacturer. In the latter part of this chapter, we look at this special relationship between manufacturer and reseller and the problems and solutions that each provides for the other. In addition, we discuss those characteristics that most resellers hold in common, since they provide important clues for the salesperson.

GOVERNMENT MARKETS

The stock market crash of 1929 and the accompanying worldwide depression initiated the growth of "big government." Since that time, social legislation and hot and cold wars have resulted in further expansion of the public sector of the economy. We will examine the characteristics of the federal, state, and local government markets that tend to make them unique and then discuss the ways business has responded to these special markets.

Characteristics of Government Markets

The huge government sector of the economy is no more a homogeneous marketplace than is the industrial or consumer sector. It is more properly referred to as comprising many markets. The techniques used by local, state, and federal agencies to purchase products or services usually vary a great deal. However, some factors, common to each of these agencies, are significant in influencing the selling-buying process. Areas where common characteristics can be found include: annual budgets, decision makers, competitive bidding, fluctuations in demand, products' applications to the private sector, research and development, title to patents, and procurement policies.

Annual Budgets. Until recently, most government entities operated on annual budgets, and many still do. This means that an important first step in influencing the selling-buying process is to induce decision makers to make budget recommendations for future purchases if funds become available. Annual budgeting makes it particularly difficult for those selling capital-level equipment, because there is no way of arranging long-term financing, as might be arranged for the private sector.

This weakness in planning was, however, recognized by the Department of Defense, which instituted a five-year budgeting cycle (called the five-year force structure and financial plan—FYFSFP); this plan is now part of the total federal five-year plan. With this trend to five-year budget planning, the problem of long-range planning on the part of suppliers is somewhat lessened. Most defense-industry companies prepare their own five-year marketing and salesplans, using the Department of Defense's five-year planning cycle as a key input.

Decision Makers. With a government situation the salesperson is confronted almost invariably with a large number of decision makers. For instance, in marketing to the military, the sales representative must influence more than just the commissioned officers and civil-service employees in order to ensure a contract award. Given the tight controls on military and federal procurements, the salesperson of defense materials is confronted with a multitude of decision points during his "selling" process. For example, with a single Army program, it is usually necessary for the salesperson to be in contact with (1) the user command, that is, the branch or unit of the Army that will have the ultimate use of the equipment to be procured; (2) those within the Army who will be involved in the ultimate proposal evaluation and approval cycles; (3) those who will be involved in the procurement and procurement practice cycle; and (4) those in the Army Engineering Branches who are involved in the development and basic concepts of the equipment. In addition, there are units within the Department of Defense, such as DDRE (Department of Defense Research and Engineering), that play a major role in the approval of a particular procurement. In total, the sales representative who calls on the military is often confronted with as many as 200 different contact points in any one procurement. Perhaps only 20 percent of these are in the formal decision-making position, yet all are important to the total decision. Also, each command referred to in this example is located in a different part of the country, thus adding to the complexity of the challenge.

Competitive Bidding. Because of the huge quantities of items needed, purchases are often made on the basis of a competitive bid. This means that the salesperson's second task in cultivating such customers and prospects is to influence the way specifications are phrased, so that his firm's products and services will have a competitive advantage. We will discuss this process in more detail later in this chapter.

Fluctuations in Demand. As a result of political influence and world conditions, markets are necessarily tenuous and subject to wide fluctuations in demand. The most dramatic example of this is the purchasing behavior of the Department of Defense. When shifts occur in the temperament of the cold war, major changes in expenditures usually result.

The national, state, and local government agencies also go through cycles of expansion and austerity. As one political party replaces the other at the polls, there is usually a promise to reduce government expenditures, but as that party becomes entrenched, expenditures again increase. Oftentimes it happens that a vendor will cement close relationships with the incumbents only to find them defeated at the polls, just before a big order was to have been placed.

Products' Application to the Private Sector. Another aspect of these markets, particularly characteristic of defense purchases, is that many of the products and services as specified have little or no application within the private sector. The

firms involved in these situations must assemble the talent and material resources needed to produce the required products and services with the attendant
risk of sharp fluctuations in demand. Thus many firms doing business with the
government have set, as a matter of policy, maximum limits to the total business
done in these markets. Another related consideration is that public officials often
find it politically expedient to force these firms to limit their profits when demand
is high. Rarely, however, do they attempt to protect these same firms when
demand is suddenly curtailed.

Research and Development.   Large markets for research and development are
on the increase in the public sector—particularly in the Department of Defense,
the Energy Research and Development Administration (ERDA), and the Federal Energy Administration (FEA). For instance, when this country launched its
space effort, virtually all the products and services needed had to be developed
—there was no off-the-shelf supply of space capsules! Some of this research and
development is purchased on a "sole source" basis—that is, the government
chooses the firm that seems best suited for the project in terms of talent, material,
and fiscal resources. However, government officials are reluctant to make sole-
source decisions, because they become subject to the same vulnerability of an
industrial purchasing agent who depends on a single source for a product or
service vital to his firm.

      As a result, most contracts are now being let on a Request for Proposal
(RFP) basis. In this situation, the government asks qualified parties if they
would submit a proposal for a specific piece of research. When the filing date
expires, a government panel decides which company or nonprofit research
organization will receive the contract.

Title to Patents.   Another important aspect of the research and development
markets is the determination of who holds title to any patentable ideas—the
government, the firm, or the individuals on the project. Also, national security is
often involved in the project; thus, the contractor must make provisions for
maintaining necessary levels of security as the work progresses. This requirement can result in delays in obtaining key personnel or in clearing present
employees to work on the project. On the positive side, firms can seek such
research and development work in order to assemble scientific and technical
talents which can be applied to other products intended for the private sector.

Procurement Policies.   Still another aspect of the government market is the
relative rigidity of procurement policies and procedures. Even off-the-shelf
products and services often must be modified to meet detailed specifications.
Typically, special paperwork is required at the transaction stage, and it may take
weeks or months to clear bills and invoices for payment. In an ongoing selling-
buying relationship, such as would exist with a research and development
contract, special reports are likely to be required. Also, government auditors

and inspectors may visit the vendor and request information in addition to that routinely reported.

The Response of Business to the Government Market

Despite the difficulties and complexities of selling to government markets, increasing numbers of firms are viewing them as profit opportunities. Because of the peculiarities of these markets, many firms have established special divisions or other administrative units to maintain the necessary relationships—the salesperson must have special knowledge to be successful in government markets. In addition, a firm must be skilled in systems selling. A third consideration is the firm's relationship to elected officials. Let us consider these three topics in more detail.

Salesperson's Knowledge.   Sales representatives calling on such customers and prospects must have a thorough knowledge of their procurement policies and procedures, must be alert to any changes in their organization, must note competitive activity, and must be sensitive to the general climate as it affects shifts in demand. Companies selling to the defense establishment often will keep a sales representative in residence at large installations. Thus, such a salesperson has only one customer—for example, the United States Air Force at Wright-Patterson Field.

It is the salesperson's responsibility to keep his firm aware of all matters that might influence the selling-buying relationship. In addition, he brings in his firm's supportive personnel as necessary to maintain a favorable competitive position. In turn, his firm keeps him informed of developments in the higher echelons of government that may influence his local relationships. To continue this example, the firm may have to keep track of congressional committee agenda, of proposed legislation relative to national defense, and of changes in personnel at the top military level of the Air Force. At the same time, it must have local representatives at every major Air Force installation feeding back information. This information gathering is essential if the firm is to maintain an effective selling-buying relationship.

Systems Selling.   Virtually every unit of government thinks in terms of systems when purchasing capital-level equipment. It is not unusual for the government to purchase total systems, including provisions for training the human ingredient for such systems—this is the parallel to "turn-key" purchasing as it exists in the industrial sector. For the salesperson, this means that if he is not offering a total system himself, he must be able to relate his products and services as units that fit into existing systems. Alternatively, depending on the situation, he must be able to assist the prospect in structuring a new system in which his offering has a competitive advantage.

Relationships with Elected Officials.   The firm seeking a significant share of its total business in these markets faces the extremely delicate, but necessary, task of favorably influencing elected officials without being accused of unfair or unethical behavior vis-à-vis competitors and the public interest. A person who represents his firm in Washington or at the state capitol is a salesperson in a very real sense. Indeed, he has the most difficult of all selling jobs—to sustain favorable relationships with the government power structure. This can best be accomplished by providing officials with timely, reliable information. If an individual develops a reputation for giving elected officials data that are not accurate, he will soon be unwelcome in many government offices.

MARKETS IN THE NONPROFIT SECTOR

The nonprofit or voluntary sector has its own peculiarities which affect the selling-buying process. Although there are many similarities between the markets in the nonprofit sector and those in the government and private sectors, there are major differences the sales representative should be aware of. We will analyze the growth of the nonprofit sector and the key characteristics of its markets.

Growth in the Nonprofit Sector

The rapid growth of this sector in recent years is the result of three primary factors: increased interest in education, increased research and development activities, and new social programs. Let us consider each of these factors.

Increased Interest in Education.   The second half of the twentieth century has seen the evolution of a "knowledge industry." More Americans are attending schools and colleges than are engaged in all other activities combined. Thousands of employed persons are attending school at night or are continuing their education through short courses and seminars. The reason for this is the knowledge explosion which commenced with the global war in the 1940s and has since been accelerated through the race in space among the major powers. This increased emphasis on education is one of the most significant developments influencing growth in the nonprofit sector of the economy that lies between the private and public sectors.

Increased Interest in Research and Development.   Paralleling the emphasis on education at all levels has been the commitment of resources to research. New kinds of research institutes have sprung up around major universities, which tap faculty and student talent; sometimes they are referred to as "half-way houses" —not legally affiliated with universities but not wholly independent of them. Some foundations and associations have underwritten nonprofit institutes to bring research effort to bear on various problems and maladies facing mankind.

New Social Programs.   A third factor that has contributed to the expansion of the nonprofit sector has been the proliferation of social legislation at both the state and federal levels. This has, in turn, fostered all kinds of nonprofit organizations to meet the needs of individuals and groups unable to look after themselves. As increasing numbers of services become available through these quasi-public institutions, and as many of them are financed by the public sector, government bodies sometimes influence procurement policies and procedures in the nonprofit sector.

Characteristics of the Nonprofit Sector

As in the case of other sectors of the economy, this sector comprises several markets, not just a single market. This sector's needs for goods and services are similar to those of the consumer and industrial markets; few of its markets are specialized. Four general considerations influence the selling-buying process in the voluntary sector: the reputation of the seller, the key decision makers, tight budgets, and the prestige of the account.

The Reputation of the Seller.   Inasmuch as nonprofit organizations and institutions are dependent on government funds and private donations, they are likely to only consider vendors that have favorable, unimpeachable reputations in the community. Also, because of public pressures, it may be necessary for vendors to be headquartered in a particular geographic area.

Decision Makers.   The frequent presence of several echelons and categories of decision makers tends to complicate the selling-buying process. These "who's who" groups are often more complex than those found in the government sector. In the case of a hospital, for example, there may be an elected board of influential people from the community, several professional groups, and the administrative staff of the hospital. All of these must be influenced favorably if a purchase is to be obtained. If the products and services represent large expenditures, the sales representative may have to make formal presentations before all three groups as well as arrange calls on individual group members. He has to accomplish this without taking sides in any internal controversy that may develop.

   As another example, a company which markets fund-raising services often finds it necessary to make proposals both orally and in writing. A salesperson for such a firm, with a church as a prospect, may have to call upon the clergy individually and as a group, the board of elders, and, before the purchase is consummated, make a presentation before the entire congregation. Obviously, in these many interpersonal and intergroup relationships, the salesperson shapes the image of his firm. Because of the complex and diverse power structures of such organizations, it is important for the salesperson, once he has obtained the business, to follow through with each group to ensure continuing satisfaction.

Tight Budgets.   Characteristic of such organizations and institutions is the almost chronic condition of a tight budget, which causes special difficulties. In some cases, the vendor may have to arrange extended terms or find financing sources for the organization. Also, considering the nature of the customer, it is difficult to press for payment when delinquency occurs because of the adverse effect on the company's image in the community.

Prestige of the Account.   Because of the prestige value some vendors see in selling to such organizations, price concessions may be made to obtain the business on the grounds that an increased share of business in the private sector will result from this institutional patronage. Vendors should put together cost/revenue figures to substantiate their assumption; otherwise, it might turn out to be a rationalization for unprofitable business.

Some organizations in the nonprofit sector have their own markets to serve. For example, a hospital may purchase items for resale, such as toothbrushes, lotions, and the like that are put in "comfort kits" and sold to patients. As another example, a school or college may purchase books and student supplies that are sold at retail on campus. In these instances, the sales representative must be competent to advise prospects and customers on how to promote his products to the institution's own constituents.

Bidding

Many of the large-dollar contracts in the government sector of the market are put out for bid. This also occurs in the nonprofit sector. Sometimes the lowest bidder is awarded the job, sometimes not. But when the lowest bidder does not receive the contract, a very strong case must be made to justify the decision, such as the ability of one of the bidders to supply the goods more adequately, or to provide unique services, or even the fact that he possesses greater financial resources. Another complicating situation arises when identical bids are received. We will examine the implications of identical bids and some of the reasons why they occur.

Identical Bids.   One interesting phenomenon about the bidding system of selecting a supplier is the fact that two or more companies may submit an identical bid price—especially when supplying commodities or raw materials, or when the specifications for a contract are very tight and there is not much room for flexibility. When identical bids are received, an aura of suspicion immediately falls on the bidders regarding price fixing, conspiracy, and unlawful activity.

But the coincidence of identical bids does not necessarily mean that there had to be price fixing. This coincidence, as with any other bids, may or may not have been arrived at through conspiracy. In fact, many forms of nonidentical bids can be arrived at conspiratorially, for example, territory agreements or business sharing by firms which intentionally bid high.

Why Identical Bids Occur.   There are a number of common conditions which lead to identical bids without conspiracy. First, there are many industries which have only a small number of sellers in them (oligopolistic industries). In this situation, it is easy to keep track of what the competition is doing. Any price cuts one firm makes to secure a contract will surely bring about retaliatory action by the other firms when it comes time to budget the next contract. Second, the firms involved in these industries are constantly facing each other in competition and know the measures that would be taken in the case of price cutting. Generally, the demand curve for their kind of product is such that a drop in price will not sufficiently increase the quantity sold to make up for the loss of profits caused by a price cut. Third, in many business situations, the product is well specified as to such things as quality, standard, size, shape, and quantity. In such cases, not much room is left to calculate the costs for extras or minor differences. Fourth, the transportation cost of the goods is so small a part of the overall cost that it is often absorbed by the seller, or else the products are shipped via public transportation. The rate for this is established by the public transportation agency or is determined by trade sources. Thus, another potential area for price differentiation is often lost. Fifth, if the amount being sold via a bid system is small in relation to the firm's total output, the vendor will be less likely to upset the whole market by introducing an unusually low bid.

In fact, the methods by which job letting or contract awarding is done create a tendency for firms to make identical bids. For example, all bid prices are announced publicly. Thus any price cutting would be public knowledge and could lead competitors to take retaliatory action in their own pricing policies. It also exposes the pricing policies of all the firms so that over a period of time a generalization or pattern can be determined and used in predicting pricing behavior.

SELLING TO RESELLERS

As unique as selling to government and nonprofit organizations is the job of selling to resellers. There are two types of resellers: retailers and wholesalers. Retailers sell their merchandise to the ultimate consumer, whereas wholesalers sell their goods to manufacturers, to other wholesalers or to retailers but not to the final consumer. One important reason for the existence of these resellers is the economy of transaction that they provide. They accomplish this by assembling goods in large quantities and reselling them in smaller quantities and in various assortments and combinations.

Resellers do much to insure that the right goods, in the right form and quantity, are in the right place at the right time from the standpoint of ultimate users. Resellers also provide many services associated with the products they handle—ranging from maintenance of products to fulfillment of warranty and guarantee terms for consumer and industrial goods. It is appropriate to characterize the American economy as one of mass marketing and mass distribution, as well as mass production. These resellers are responsible in a major way for making mass marketing and mass distribution possible. We will examine five important considerations in selling to resellers.

Channels of Distribution

Products, once manufactured, must be sold to their ultimate users—be they consumers or business users. The different establishments through which the goods pass on their way to the end user comprise what is called the "channel of distribution" for that product. There is a great variety of these channels, and the choice of a specific one depends on many factors, including proximity of manufacturer to user, size and financial strength of manufacturer or middleman, availability of middlemen, speed required to get product to user (e.g., perishable foods or obsolescence of fashions), market coverage desired, degree of control over the marketing of the product, and the costs of using alternative channels.

The most common channels of distribution used for consumer and industrial goods are presented schematically in Figure 19-1. Part I represents the paths available for goods that are directed to the ultimate user—the consumer. Part II represents products that are sold to industrial, commercial, government, and institutional users. The major difference between these parts is the inclusion of *retailers* for consumer goods. The channels represented here show, in a very general way, the broad classifications of types of channels and some of the combinations of intermediaries. But in each channel, and in each company within each channel, the catalyst required to move the goods along to the next step is personal selling.

The Reseller's Contribution to the Manufacturer

From the viewpoint of the manufacturer, resellers make many contributions to a firm's total marketing mission. These include extending the firm's market coverage; modifying merchandise to fit local markets; reducing the amount of capital required by the manufacturer; and assisting in promotion and distribution, as well as in market development.

Market Coverage.   Resellers provide the manufacturer with far greater market coverage than would be possible if only direct representation and distribution were used. They do this by reaching users who may be geographically too far away from the place of production or whose order size and amount of consumption would not warrant direct selling-buying relationships. A good example of this can be seen in Figure 19-2. When there is not a wholesaler in the channel, each manufacturer must make three transactions to reach the retailers, and the entire manufacturer-retailer system must make nine transactions. However, when a wholesaler is introduced, each manufacturer makes only one trans-

I. FOR CONSUMER PRODUCTS

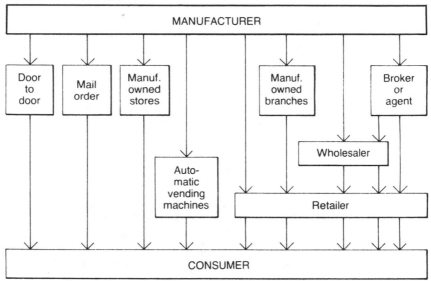

II. FOR INDUSTRIAL PRODUCTS

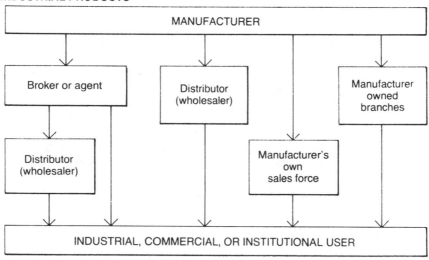

Figure 19-1 Major Types of Channels of Distribution

action, and the number of transactions in the entire system is reduced to six. The cost of these transactions is one of the manufacturer's key expenses; thus he can save substantial sums of money by using wholesalers. This same principle would be even more evident if the manufacturer calculated the number of transactions required to reach the final consumer directly rather than going through retailers.

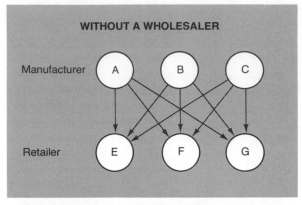

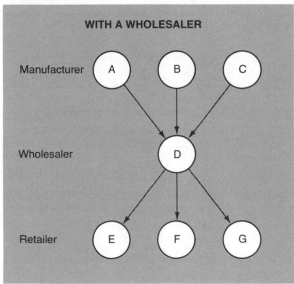

Figure 19-2 The Movement of Goods with and without a Wholesaler

Capital Commitments.   Resellers enable the manufacturer to substantially reduce capital commitments. Picture the millions of dollars of additional capital an
automobile manufacturer would need in order to own and operate all the retail
outlets for his product. In the same way, by using resellers, a manufacturer can
operate with a substantially smaller marketing organization than if all market
coverage were direct.

Promotional and Distribution Assistance.   In many instances, the manufacturer uses indirect representation to gain promotional and distributional effort
for which he does not have the internal talent or material resources. This is an

important consideration for a new firm whose expertise leans more toward research, development, and manufacturing than toward marketing. It is also important for the company that creates a product that differs significantly from its existing line, because special promotional expertise and distribution forces are needed to penetrate new markets.

Market Development.   Another consideration which favors the use of resellers is when the product or service is not protected by patent or other means and the manufacturer wants to cover all markets intensively before competitors can move in. In the consumer field, this is particularly applicable to items that are likely to have fad appeal. If this merchandise is not sold quickly to a large segment of the consuming population, its chances of success will be greatly reduced. Competitors will move in, and the price and margin will fall, or the public will lose interest in the product before the firm has made a profit from it.

Limitations on the Use of Resellers

Despite the advantages of using resellers, whenever a manufacturer employs indirect representation for part or all of his market coverage there are some tradeoffs. We will examine two of the more critical limitations on the use of resellers—loss of control and potential loss of profits along with a discussion of the fact that no one channel system is always the best to use.

Loss of Control.   When a firm uses resellers, it loses some control over how its products and services are sold. The exception to this is the company-owned wholesale or retail operation. However, such outlets account for less than 10 percent of all wholesale business in the industrial market, and an even smaller percentage in the retail market.

Inasmuch as resellers are independent businessmen, manufacturers must influence them by persuasion rather than by authority. Although each manufacturer feels that he knows best how his product should be priced and sold at the retail level, conditions vary a great deal from one territory to another. Thus, a strategy that may work well for many retailers will not work for all retailers. Therefore, major marketing plans, decisions, and actions have to be arrived at bilaterally rather than unilaterally. Unless the reseller flourishes, the manufacturer cannot.

Potential Loss of Profit.   Goods moving through indirect channels must be profitable for each firm to handle. Therefore, the manufacturer may anticipate less profit per unit for goods moving through indirect channels than for those moving through a direct channel. The longer the channel, the less unit profit for the manufacturer—inasmuch as each intermediary must cover his costs and make a profit. A wholesaler sells many products to his retailers, and each one must carry a portion of the firm's total overhead costs (i.e., administrative expenditures, salesperson's salary, depreciation on equipment, etc.). If the manufacturer sold directly to the retailer, his price would also have to cover all of the overhead associated with selling the product. Yet, the wholesaler usually deals in many products, so that his costs for selling are minimal for any one product. Firms that produce and sell only a few products could not absorb the expenses of selling directly to the retailer; and as a result, they realize greater profits by selling through wholesalers.

Individual Differences in Channel Selection. Many individual differences exist in the use of indirect channels, even among directly competing manufacturers. At one extreme, there are some manufacturers who rely solely on direct promotion and distribution. At the other extreme are manufacturers who depend solely on indirect representation. The great majority of firms fall in between and often use multiple channels for reaching their markets. For example, two directly competing manufacturers have a discernibly different channel structure. Firm A's sales force cover all accounts and shipments are made directly (direct channel). Company B, doing about the same volume, markets its goods exclusively through distributors (indirect channel).

If demand is on the increase and density of demand exists in prime markets, the manufacturer is likely to emphasize direct representation. In new, developing markets and in old, declining markets, the manufacturer often depends on indirect representation. Reliance on indirect channels is sometimes viewed as a short-term expediency to gain a foothold in the markets. This short-term strategy sometimes boomerangs, however, because less-than-top quality, indirect representation is often obtained by such firms. Furthermore, even in the short term the resellers may not provide the same kind of effort they would for permanent relationships.

Perspective of the Reseller

The reseller, like the manufacturer, has objectives of profit, growth, and perpetuity. The aim of every reseller is to buy profitably in order to sell profitably. To accomplish this, he places high priority on cultivating close selling-buying relationships with his own customers. His promotional strategy generally centers on his firm as "a good place to do business." Understandably, the manufacturers he represents focus their own promotional strategy on their products and brands; furthermore, they seek this same emphasis from the intermediary. This issue often becomes a major point of conflict in reseller-manufacturer relations. We shall examine this issue by focusing on the reseller's product-service mix, the reseller's competition, the manufacturer's promotional efforts, inventory allocation, and consumer services.

The Reseller's Product-Service Mix. The reseller must give priority to optimizing his product-service mix relative to his prime markets. To do this he must add and delete lines of particular manufacturers, as well as allocate promotional and distribution efforts for the lines being carried. The basic criterion for these decisions is profit maximization. To accomplish this, the reseller can rarely meet the desires of any single manufacturer. Each one, understandably, would like to have the reseller give primary attention to his products and services. This becomes a particularly sensitive issue in manufacturer-wholesaler relations when directly competing products are stocked by the reseller.

The Reseller's Competition.   Still another problem occurs when the same goods are sold through other channels in the reseller's markets. The reseller expects the manufacturers he represents to keep direct and indirect competition to a minimum. As an example, a jewelry store owner the authors are familiar with became very upset when he learned that the manufacturer of the inexpensive line of watches he carried had begun to sell watches not only to other jewelry stores in the neighborhood but also to local drug stores. The jeweler did not like seeing his watch line in other jewelry stores but having them also sold in drug stores was too much. As a result when the salesperson for the watch company made his next visit to the jeweler he found that he was phasing out the salesperson's line in favor of a new brand of inexpensive watches that he had decided to carry.

The Manufacturer's Promotional Efforts.   Another potential source of conflict from the viewpoint of the reseller is where the manufacturer places emphasis on his promotional efforts. The manufacturer's promotional efforts through indirect channels may be a "push strategy," in which advertising, personal salesmanship, sales promotion, and merchandising are focused on the intermediary, and the intermediary is then expected to push the line to the next step in the channel. At the other extreme, a manufacturer may employ a "pull strategy," in which most of his promotional efforts are directed at ultimate users. The reasoning here is that if a demand is created, the reseller will have to handle the product line to satisfy his customers. For example, a very successful soft drink firm deals entirely in "private label"—it promotes its products to regional and national chains. The consumer identifies his purchase by the store brand (push strategy). Contrast this with Coca Cola's strategy of stimulating world wide consumer demand (pull strategy).

Most manufacturers fall somewhere between these extremes in the way they cultivate and sustain demand—they employ a "push-pull" strategy. If the reseller perceives too little "pull" in his markets, he may drop a line or not promote it. At the other extreme, if he sees too much "pull" he may resent the manufacturer's preemption of his own customers and prospects.

Inventory Allocation.   Generally, a manufacturer seeks to move inventory as close to the ultimate users as possible. Each reseller, in turn, attempts to minimize his inventory. Thus, another problem in manufacturer relations involves the determination of minimum stock levels. The reseller is likely to view those stock levels specified by the manufacturers as too high, or he may seek terms on them so that the manufacturers share his costs of inventory maintenance.

Consumer Service.   Another problem area is the increasing kind and amount of service that ultimate users expect of the products they buy. By virtue of their position in the channel, resellers in many sectors of the economy bear the brunt of these increasing demands. Each additional service increases the costs, thus resulting in narrower profit margins. For example, not too many years ago the metal service centers, (the wholesale arm of the metal industries) were known as "warehouses." They provided little service other than breaking down bulk shipments and providing assortments of varying sizes and quantities. Most of the products handled went out the front door in the same form as they came in the back door. Today, prefabrication services such as edging, cutting, slitting, and burning are provided on 75 percent of these purchases. To provide these services, each metal service center has had to invest in capital equipment and in skilled personnel needed to handle such operations. One of the resulting promotional problems for these firms has been to persuade their customers and prospects that they are not just purchasing metal by the foot, pound, or ton but are also purchasing these added services. In fact, a key part of their offering is the provision of a readily available inventory that can be "customized" to the requirements of the individual account.

In general, the reseller expects to plan, decide, and act bilaterally with the companies he represents, in all aspects of the marketing effort. Furthermore, he expects the manufacturer to maintain quality of the product line, and he expects it to be priced so that he can make a profit on it.

Most resellers stress their companies as a source from which to buy certain types of products. Their selling, advertising, and promotion activities point up the advantages of dealing with a local firm and a member of the same business community in which the customers or prospects live or do business.

Characteristics of Small Resellers

In the American economy there is considerable diversity in types and sizes of resellers. In the industrial sector, they may include brokers (who simply bring buyer and seller together), manufacturer's agents (who cultivate and transact business but who do not take possession or title of the goods and services sold), limited function wholesalers (who provide little in the way of service), and merchant wholesalers and manufacturers' wholesale branches (both of which provide many services). In terms of size there are many more small resellers. However, a few large resellers often dominate a market.

Despite this diversity, resellers do have some common characteristics that must be understood in order to effectively influence their buying behavior. Let us now consider these characteristics.

Small Business.   Usually resellers are small businesses with very limited, specialized talent resources. Thus each product line offered to resellers must be accompanied by sound business advice and assistance—ranging from furnishing them with a standard cost accounting system to training their salespersons.

Owner-Managed Business.   Small resellers are typically owner-managed. Consequently, the maintenance of a favorable selling-buying relationship with such a firm, requires that the salesperson understand the owner's personal objectives. These objectives markedly affect the firm's objectives in terms of equity and profits. For instance, a research study of closely held retail establishments showed that growth was by no means a universally sought goal.

Undercapitalization.   Typically, small resellers are undercapitalized. Not infrequently, their receivables are discounted to provide operating funds. They view their suppliers as a source of operating funds, either through extended terms, provision of debt capital, or at least as aids in locating capital sources.

Local or Regional Markets.   Most frequently, small resellers serve local or regional markets. Salespersons calling on such firms must be familiar with the economic, demographic, social, and political characteristics of the reseller's markets. Manufacturer's offerings must be aligned as closely as possible to local needs if they are to appeal to resellers. As an example of this, a national food processor may vary the blend of his branded coffee to meet taste differences peculiar to regional markets.

Importance of Promotion.   For most small resellers, the largest single-budget item is the promotional and sales effort. Because of this, several questions are crucial to the resellers in making buying decisions: How much of it will sell? How fast will it sell? What will it cost to sell? What help is being provided by the manufacturer to make it sell?

Buying and Selling Decisions.   These decisions are usually made by the same person or persons. Accordingly, the sales representative calling on such small business managers has as his objective to show them how to buy and sell their offerings at a profit. If a systems view is taken of the channel, the transaction between the manufacturer and the reseller, though important, is intermediate. The crucial transaction is between the reseller and his customers—the ultimate users. Consequently, the manufacturer's salespeople have done only half of the selling job when they induce the resellers to buy. They must be concerned with ways and means of assisting these middlemen to influence *their* customers and prospects to buy. To do this effectively, the salesperson must understand how resellers handle the selling-buying process in their markets.

SUMMARY

Large markets exist for goods and services in the government and nonprofit sectors. There are important differences in each sector that must be understood if suppliers are to be effective in their marketing and selling efforts. Especially important are the intricacies of the "who's who" groups, the relative rigidity of specifications and procedures, and the use of bidding for large expenditures.

Various kinds of resellers exist in all markets, and are crucial to full-market coverage for most manufacturers. Despite the diversity of resellers, they have many special characteristics in common. Most important, these organizations must buy and sell profitably. In addition, bilateral, rather than unilateral decision making is imperative in the selling-buying relationship.

PROBLEMS

1. Suppose you are a salesperson calling on accounts in the government sector. Which points made in the chapter would you consider most important as guides?
2. What do the government and nonprofit sectors have in common? How do they differ?
3. What points might a salesperson calling on retail stores use to help his customers sell his products?
4. What is the push-pull effect? How can a manufacturer's salesperson implement: push? pull?
5. What characteristics do most resellers have in common?

Exercise 19

SELLING TO NONPROFIT ORGANIZATIONS

Objective: To observe the selling-buying process at first hand.

Find out where purchasing is done at your college or university. Get permission to observe a sales call. Write up your observations covering:

1. Preparation of salesperson
2. Selling techniques displayed
3. Impact on the buyer
4. Effectiveness of the call

Case 19-1 Elite Printers and Engravers

Elite is a highly regarded wholesale house which provides a full line of printed and engraved products, ranging from business cards to wedding invitations. Elite has two broad categories of accounts—business and professional organizations, which are sold direct; gift and stationery shops and stationery departments in large stores. This latter category accounts for about 75% of total sales. Ina Kahn has a territory in which most of the potential is accounted for by retailers.

One of Ina's prospects is the Atkin Card and Gift Shop. At present Atkin does not offer such personalized items, and Ms. Elizabeth Atkin has been reluctant to put on such a line.

On previous calls Ms. Atkin told Ina that she has all she can handle now. She operates the store herself except at peak hours and in the holiday seasons, when she uses part-time help.

Ina feels the Elite line would do well with Atkin's. The store is in a shopping mall which serves a fairly affluent surrounding area. True, it is small and space is at a premium. However, the Elite catalog and sample books could be stored out of the way when not in use. Besides, Ina is sure that the limited variety of gift items doesn't add too much to profit. On her calls to Atkin's she noticed that most of the traffic is focused on cards. Atkin's carries the best label in that industry. Two barriers face Ina: (1) the store as it is now run provides Ms. Atkin an adequate livelihood, and (2) Ms. Atkin is change-resistant. On the positive side, Ina has overheard Ms. Atkin talking with her customers. Many patrons compliment Ms. Atkin on her excellent taste in the cards she stocks as well as the other items in the store. Ina has noticed how Ms. Atkin beams when complimented or when asked for advice. Ms. Atkin seems to be ideal for her job; she really loves people and has a wonderful way with them.

What type of strategy should Ina use in making her next call to Atkin's?

Case 19-2 Greenlawn Hospital

Greenlawn Hospital is a nonprofit, church-affiliated, general hospital with 220 beds. Jack Schiff, a salesperson for Morrow Pharmaceutical Products, calls there regularly and has been successful in getting most of Morrow's prescription products on the formulary (drugs approved for use by the medical staff). His relations with the attending physicians, the purchasing agent, and other personnel are good. However, he has been unable to place Morrow's nationally known mouth-wash, Thycol, in the kits of sundries furnished to each bed patient. We find him visiting Mr. Thomas, the senior pharmacist.

Mr. T.: We've talked about Thycol before. It's a good product. But why should we add one more item to the patient's bill? He's being charged $5 now for soap, toothpaste, and a few other things he doesn't need.

Jack: Well, I can't make a case for what's now in the kit. However, the purchasing department tells me you would have to approve any pharmaceutical product included. If you give the OK I think I'd have the sale.

Mr. T: I mix my own wash and furnish it in bulk to each nursing station. It's up to the nurses to furnish each patient a cup of it when he asks for it.

Jack: Knowing how busy those gals are I wonder how many even let their patients know it's available.

Mr. T: Well, it's there if it's needed.

What should Jack do next?

SUGGESTIONS FOR FURTHER READING

Coor, Paul W. Jr., "Fact and Fancy on Identical Bids," *Harvard Business Review*, Vol. 41 (January–February, 1963), pp. 67–72.

Kotler, Philip, *Marketing for Non-Profit Organizations* (Englewood Cliffs, N.J.: Prentice-Hall, 1975).

Kotler, Philip, and Sidney Levy, "Broadening the Marketing Concept," *Journal of Marketing*, Vol. 33 (January, 1969), pp. 10–15.

Kotler, Philip, and Gerald Zaltman, "Social Marketing: An Approach to Planned Social Change," *Journal of Marketing*, Vol. 35 (July, 1971), pp. 19–27.

Shapiro, Benson P., "Marketing for Non-Profit Organizations," *Harvard Business Review*, Vol. 51 (September–October, 1973), pp. 123–132.

20. Selling to Individuals and Organizations by Telephone

It is difficult to imagine what would happen if, suddenly, all telephone services stopped. It would pose a serious threat for those in immediate need of medical aid. Police and Fire Departments would be inaccessible for emergencies. Our social lives would be markedly impaired. Many businesses would come to a standstill. To get some idea of the pervasiveness of the telephone, consider these data: There are three telephones for every four Americans. There are five telephones for every four persons in our nation's capitol. There are about 400,000,000 telephones in service throughout the world.

Proper and effective use of the telephone in business, and especially in selling, is vital to the firm's success. The field salesperson, who is responsible for maintaining personal contact with the prospect or customer, relies on the telephone to follow up on earlier visits, to make appointments, and, in some cases, to close the sale. The in-house salesperson—the retail salesperson or the inside salesperson who handles his responsibilities from within the firm—uses the phone to generate new business. In addition, the inside salesperson plays an important intelligence and expediter role for the firm, by maintaining telephone contact with customers and prospects in between visits by the field sales representatives.

In this chapter we examine the effective use of telephone selling with special attention on pre-call planning and the unique applications of the telephone sales call for the field sales representative, and the in-house salesperson. We also discuss the differences between incoming calls and outgoing calls. As with any sales situation, there are certain strategic and tactical considerations that must be taken into account in using the telephone.

PRE-CALL PLANNING

It is fully as important to plan a telephone sales call as it is to plan a personal sales visit. All of the principles that apply to actual call planning apply here. A carefully outlined plan can be used as an agenda while the actual conversation with the customer or prospect is taking place. There are four unique concepts to telephone selling that should be taken into consideration when planning the call: (1) most telephone calls are an interruption to the party being called; (2) only the auditory channel can be used in telephone selling; (3) timing is important; and (4) courtesy on the telephone is necessary at all times.

The Telephone Call Is an Interruption

A telephone call almost always constitutes an interruption for the other person. Very rarely is the individual at the other end of the line just sitting at his or her desk waiting for the salesperson to call. As a result, what is said in the first few moments of the call can mean success or failure. The opening remark must immediately grab the attention and arouse the interest of the other person. It must have "you," not "I" appeal. Here is an example:

> Mr. Jones, this is Bill Smith at Hill's Clothing Store. We've just received some new sports jackets that I know you'll like. . . .

The other person's initial reactions are the best guide for determining whether an order can be completed on the phone or a personal visit will be required. In most types of businesses, a visit is necessary. Thus, the objective is to get a commitment for a follow-up in person. It is important that the salesperson not use all of his ammunition only to receive a turn down. Continuing the above example, assuming a favorable initial reaction:

Mr. Jones, you'll really have to see these jackets to appreciate their style and quality. Would it be more convenient for you to come in this afternoon or this evening? I'll be here ready to show them to you.

Auditory Channel

In telephone selling, only the auditory channel is available. From a perceptual standpoint, this puts a premium on the salesperson's *manner* of speaking as well as *what* he says. His enthusiasm and conviction must be reflected in how he conveys his sales message. Image-provoking language, examples, and illustrations are imperative. The salesperson must paint a picture in the mind of the prospect or customer. Contrast the impact of these statements:

It's small enough to fit in your pocket.
The dimensions are 2″ × 3″.

The salesperson cannot *obtain* manner cues except by full attention to what is said and how it is said. As a result, the salesperson must pay close attention to any innuendos, changes in pitch, side comments, or other cues the prospect may be saying between the lines.

The Importance of Timing

Time is of the essence. Rarely does a telephone sales call last longer than a few minutes, so the call must be well planned—every word must count. Far more can be sold by asking the right questions than by a lengthy discourse. A questioning approach also insures active participation on the part of the prospect or customer, whereas a monologue is usually ineffective.

It is easier to follow a call plan on the telephone than in a face-to-face situation, because the salesperson can write down his plan and use it as an agenda. As each point is made, it can be checked off, and if the customer provides any relevant information the salesperson can make a note of it.

The Importance of Courtesy

Courtesy is often lacking on the telephone. For some unknown and unjustifiable reason, many people are not as courteous on the telephone as they are in person. This may be because the two parties who are communicating with each other do not have eye-to-eye contact. Yet it is critical for the salesperson to remember that the individual he is talking with could represent a substantial potential profit for his firm, and therefore deserves to be treated respectfully.

The telephone conversation is sometimes the only contact the salesperson and customer have. In this situation, the customer must be made to trust the salesperson's judgment, and if the salesperson is not respectful to begin with, there is little chance that a positive seller-buyer relationship will develop.

Southern Bell Telephone Company suggests the test shown in Figure 20-1 as a good measure of telephone courtesy. Courtesy really costs the individual nothing. The only cost to the individual who scores 100 on the telephone courtesy test is that he or she is willing to take a few minutes to think of others. The salesperson who follows this philosophy is likely to find that he is treated much better by his customers in all aspects of their business relationship.

USES OF THE TELEPHONE BY FIELD SALES REPRESENTATIVES

Field salespeople use telephone calls to complement and increase the effectiveness of personal visits. The key psychological impact is that it aids in keeping the salesperson, his company, and his products and services in the *conscious awareness* of the prospect or customer. The longer the time span between field calls, the more necessary it is to fill in the gaps. Otherwise, a competitor might move in.

Figure 20-1 The Telephone Courtesy Test*

*For each "yes" you receive 4 points, for each "sometimes" you receive 2 points, and no points are given for a "no" answer. If you score over 85, you are a very courteous telephone user.

DO YOU?

	Yes	Sometimes	No
1. Answer promptly	_____	_____	_____
2. Greet the caller pleasantly	_____	_____	_____
3. Identify yourself properly	_____	_____	_____
4. Speak in a natural tone	_____	_____	_____
5. Say "Thank you" and "You're Welcome"	_____	_____	_____
6. Explain waits	_____	_____	_____
7. Leave word where you're going	_____	_____	_____
8. Check the number	_____	_____	_____
9. Apologize for mistakes	_____	_____	_____
10. Keep a pad near	_____	_____	_____
11. Stay on the line	_____	_____	_____
12. Take the message	_____	_____	_____
13. Signal the company operator slowly	_____	_____	_____
14. Allow time to answer	_____	_____	_____
15. Ask if it is convenient to talk	_____	_____	_____
16. Help the company operator	_____	_____	_____
17. End the call properly	_____	_____	_____
18. Replace receiver gently	_____	_____	_____
19. Listen attentively	_____	_____	_____
20. Ask questions tactfully	_____	_____	_____
21. "Space" your calls	_____	_____	_____
22. Make your call brief	_____	_____	_____
23. Listen for the dial tone	_____	_____	_____
24. Keep the cord free of kinks	_____	_____	_____
25. Plan your conversation	_____	_____	_____

A particular call may be made to achieve one or more of these recurrent objectives: to follow up on a previous visit, to arrange for the next visit, or to seek an order.

Follow-Up

Follow-up calls may cover many matters, depending on conditions in the account. It is always appropriate to thank the person for seeing you. Often a salesperson calls to furnish information that was not available at the time of his personal call, or he may call to make sure delivery was received. Here is an effective take off on this technique: When the shipping department notifies the salesperson that the customer's order should have been received, he calls the account to inquire about the status of the shipment. When the purchasing agent checks and finds that the order was received on time, the call serves as positive reinforcement for the buyer-seller relationship. This technique works particularly well if the buyer has requested that the order be expedited because of some problem the buyer is experiencing. The telephone call then serves to drive home the point that the salesperson and his company have been helpful to the buyer.

To Make an Appointment

If the primary objective is to set a time for the next visit, it is important for the salesperson to provide sufficient information to whet the interest of the prospect, but not enough so as to make the call unnecessary. It is better to offer a choice of two dates than to ask, "When may I see you?" Also, if the salesperson wishes to see other persons in the account, he should indicate this and, if appropriate, ask the customer to make such arrangements. In this regard, the salesperson should caution against making the customer feel like his private secretary. However, if a group meeting is to take place or if the salesperson and buyer have built up a solid relationship, it may make sense to ask the buyer to help with the arrangements.

To Close the Sale

The closing of a sale on the phone is more likely to occur with an established customer than with a prospect. The firm that has no prior buying experience with a salesperson is understandably reluctant to place an order on the basis of a telephone solicitation. Generally speaking, low volume and distant accounts are handled in this manner due to the high costs of personal calls. Of course, it sometimes happens that such a call is, in reality, a continuation of a personal visit. The salesperson may have been unable to close during the face-to-face discussions because the prospect wanted time to consider the proposal.

USES OF THE TELEPHONE BY IN-HOUSE SALES REPRESENTATIVES

The telephone can be used effectively by two types of in-house salespersons: retail salespersons who sell their merchandise to the final consumer, and inside industrial salespersons who sell their merchandise to other organizations.

Retail Salespersons

Retail salespeople have frequent opportunities to increase business by their effective use of the telephone. Periods of low store traffic can be used for phoning regular customers. The following circumstances might prompt such outgoing calls:

1. Receipt in the store of a special order
2. Advance announcement of a sale
3. Addition of a new line
4. Clearance of overstocked items
5. Setting a date and hour for delivery of goods already purchased
6. Arrival of new models
7. Invitation to a fashion show or other special event
8. Verification of delivery of goods previously ordered
9. Goodwill (e.g., calling a person who has not shopped in the store for a long time)

The alert retail salesperson keeps a card file on each customer containing dates of personal contacts plus telephone calls and other pertinent information. This system familiarizes the salesperson with his customers, and when the right situation develops, he will be aware of it. Figure 20-2 is a card that a salesperson in a men's clothing store keeps on each of his established customers. When a suit or sport coat arrives that he thinks the customer might like, he can check measurements against the data on the card and call the customer if it is right for him.

Inside Sales Representatives

An inside salesperson for an industrial firm sells some of the same products that his counterpart, the outside salesperson, sells. The major difference between these two individuals is that the inside man does all of his work from behind a telephone or a typewriter. We will examine the activities of an inside industrial salesperson along with his career mobility, his need for technical expertise, and his roles as intelligence gatherer and expediter.

Figure 20-2 Men's Store Card File

1. Suit
     Size
     Color preference
     Quality preference
2. Sport jacket
     Size
     Color preference
     Quality preference
3. Dress shirts
     Neck size
     Sleeve size
     Quality preference
     Color preference
4. Sport shirts
     Size
     Quality preference
     Color preference
5. Slacks
     Waist size
     Inseam Size
     Quality preference
6. Hat size
7. Shoe
     Size
     Quality preference
8. Formal wear
9. Marital status
10. Occupation
11. Address
12. Telephone Number

Activities of the Inside Salesperson.   The inside salesperson is not just a passive ordertaker. He is a full member of the sales team involved in the distribution of the firm's product. One study found that in metal service centers (wholesalers for 16 to 18 percent of the steel sold in the United States) 85 percent of the orders were received by telephone.[1] These inside salespersons function to keep their firm in conscious awareness and to provide and obtain information of mutual interest to the customer and prospect accounts.

Inside and outside sales representatives will frequently "team sell" an account. That is, the outside salesperson may call on an account once each month. At that time, he will demonstrate new products and try to sell as many of these and other products as the customer needs. When the outside salesperson has completed his call, he will send a note to the inside salesperson explaining

[1]Robert J. Boewadt, *An Analysis of the Internal Sales Force as a Factor in the Design of Total Sales Strategy* (Ph.D. dissertation, Michigan State University, 1970).

what occurred. Then, the inside salesperson follows up by telephone during the month to try to complete the sale or make new sales.

The Inside Salesperson's Career. The highly effective inside salesperson is frequently promoted to a field sales position, which has a higher salary and associated fringe benefits. For some, this move is beneficial. For others, promotion to the outside leads to dismal failure and personal defeat. In many instances, this failure is management's fault for not recognizing that inside and outside selling require differing skills and temperaments. In fact, the individual who is highly effective on the inside should probably remain there and be compensated, monetarily and psychologically, on a par with the equivalent field salesperson.

In order to maintain a strong, technically competent, and aggressive internal sales force in the years ahead, the firms will have to make this job as attractive as the field selling job—by revising their compensation scales significantly upward and creating new avenues of promotion for the inside people.

The Technical Competence of the Inside Salesperson. The inside salesperson is a technical advisor, and the level of his technical competence directly influences his selling effectiveness. An alert management will, therefore, encourage him to continually update his technical knowledge, possibly by participating in material and/or technology seminars or by making plant visits in order to more fully understand the exact nature of the problems confronting the customer. The inside salesperson should also be given time to read the current literature that pertains to his industry and his stake in it. In essence, management should realize that, to a large extent, the inside salesperson is only as effective as the customer's confidence in his technical ability. If he is not allowed proper time to develop and maintain his competence at a high level, the firm will ultimately suffer.

The Inside Salesperson's Intelligence Role. The inside salesperson is an important element in the firm's marketing intelligence system. He is uniquely able to furnish valuable information to both upper management and the field sales force. He can provide on-line reporting to upper management regarding new customers, changes in the order patterns of old customers, and special requests for items not carried in stock. This information may call for immediate tactical adjustments which could not have been accomplished if the same facts had been discovered via a monthly sales analysis report.

The inside salesperson may also be able to sense when certain customers are dissatisfied with specific aspects of a field salesperson; in such a situation, behavioral adjustments can be made and a potential crisis averted. Another intelligence function he can provide for the outside individual is to make note of any potential customer leads he uncovers in his many daily conversations.

The Inside Salesperson as an Expediter. Finally, the inside salesperson is an expediter. More than any other single individual, the inside salesperson translates his firm's commitments to the customer into tangible products delivered on time. In so doing, he has a unique opportunity to develop patronage motives on the part of the customer, and it is the repeat business engendered by these motives that assures the long-range success of the firm and its product offerings.

Let us underscore this interlocking nature of the inside-outside selling effort with an example. The prospective customer who calls the steel service center is often one or more steps away from an actual purchase. The outside salesperson has presumably performed his functions of supplying the customer with general product and service information, public relations activities, and extolling his firm's outstanding qualities. The stage has been set, but the action will not begin until the inside salesperson precisely relates his firm's offerings to the customer's needs.

INCOMING CALLS

If the selling effort is to be effective, the incoming calls must be courteously and competently handled. In many companies, full-time salespeople (inside sales representatives) exist to whom such calls can be channeled. In many companies, however, such inquiries are handled on a "who's available" basis. In this case, any and all employees who are likely to answer should be trained in telephone courtesy and should be able to switch each inquiry to the person best able to handle it. Often it is simply a matter of getting the caller's name, company, and telephone number so that a salesperson can call back.

Outcomes of Customer/Prospect-Initiated Calls

Customers and prospects initiating calls furnish prime evidence of interest, and if dealt with effectively, sales are likely to result. Attentive listening and skillful questioning can be used to help the caller to define his needs and wants. In the course of the conversation, additional requirements may be developed beyond those that prompted the inquiry. Five categories of positive outcomes are possible:

1. Order taken as specified by caller
2. "Trade-up" achieved—higher quality, greater quantity
3. "Tie-in"—additional items sold
4. Conversion of inquiry into "follow-up"
5. Substitute products sold—specified items unavailable

It is important to verify all details so that order processing or follow-up can be handled promptly and efficiently. Firms handling a large number of incoming calls often use a form to ensure that full and accurate information is obtained and recorded.

Handling Complaints

Every business, despite its best efforts, is likely to receive calls airing complaints. If goodwill and repeat business are to be sustained, such calls must be handled promptly and effectively. Switchboard operators must know where to channel each problem. They must quickly connect the person with someone capable of handling the complaint. Ineptness and delay only aggravate the situation.

The person handling the complaint should start by identifying himself by name and title, for example, "This is Bill Jones in the shipping department. May I help you?" Next, he should allow the other person to talk. This is a prime application of *catharsis*—the need when one is upset to tell someone else the problem. Warm and attentive listening is called for.

Even if the complaint seems trivial or unwarranted it should be handled with care. The matter is *real* and *important* in the customer's *mind* or he would not have called. Phrases that may reflect on the validity of the complaint, such as "You claim," should be avoided.

There is no substitute for honesty and forthrightness. It is generally better to incur what seems to be an unjustified settlement than to have a dissatisfied customer. A generous settlement may create an unpaid salesperson; a grudging settlement may result in losing repeat business from the account as well as potential business from those who are influenced by the unhappy customer.

An agreement should be reached before the customer hangs up. If it is not feasible to handle the matter immediately, a commitment should be made as to what steps will be taken and when they will occur. The longer the delay, the more aggravated the customer will become.

STRATEGIC AND TACTICAL CONSIDERATIONS IN THE USE OF THE TELEPHONE

Several strategic and tactical considerations apply to telephone selling. The most important of these is that the salesperson immediately establish with the customer that he is interested in satisfying the customer's problems. Other considerations include the "hinge" technique for opening a call, the effective use of long distance calls, telephone services that are useful in selling, and problems that can develop in using the telephone. Let us consider each of these key tactical concerns.

Establishing Customer Rapport

Throughout the text we emphasize the need to focus on the other person. This certainly applies to selling by telephone—a "you" attitude is a must. This is particularly important when the person reached has no advance knowledge of the call. Rapport must be established in the first few seconds.

One method to establish rapport is to use *praise* for the prospect or his company. All of us react to praise when it is appropriate and sincere. For example, opening a call by saying, "Mr. Jones, in view of your firm's number one position in the industry . . ." is very likely to be favorably received. In contrast, praise that is phony and is perceived that way by the customer will be very badly received. If the salesperson cannot think of any genuine praise to use, he should try other ways to gain acceptance.

Another technique takes into consideration the fact that few people can resist the opportunity to give advice. This might be capitalized on by saying, "Mr. Black, we need your help and advice in evaluating a new publication on miniaturization. May we send you a copy for review?"

The "Hinge" Technique

The term "hinge" is used to describe the way a telephone salesperson opens a call or links it to a previous occurrence in the selling-buying relationship.[2] As an example, a salesperson might telephone the customer to tell him that the merchandise he ordered is being packed today and that if he placed any additional orders at this time they would be subject to the firm's quantity discount. Another example would be the retail salesperson in a woman's clothing store who calls a customer to tell her that the coat she looked at during the previous month is now on sale. With the hinge technique the telephone salesperson is trying to tie himself and his product back to the customer. Twelve recurrent hinges are presented in Figure 20-3.

The Effective Use of Long-Distance Calls

Long-distance calls tend to have a greater impact than local calls. Switchboard operators and secretaries are more reluctant to screen out such calls than those where the caller is local. Some sales representatives take advantage of this by setting up appointments in the next city on their itinerary from the place in which they are working. Some firms do telephone selling on a national basis from a single location using WATS line (Wide Area Telecommunications Service). We will discuss these special telephone services for long-distance and other calls.

TELEPHONE SERVICES USEFUL IN SELLING

There are a number of telephone services that the salesperson can use. Some of the most important ones are WATS lines, 800 numbers, answering services, mobile telecommunications services, conference calls, and amplification.

[2]William A. Garrett, *Phonemanship–The Newest Concept of Marketing* (New York: Farrar, Strauss, 1959), pp. 139–142.

Figure 20-3 Twelve Recurrent "Hinges"

1. Thank-You Approach

   Salesperson: Mr. Customer, this is Mr. Telephone Salesperson of the Alpha Company. We received your order in the mail this morning and wish to thank you for it. Shipment will be made immediately. You should have it Wednesday. Will that meet your needs?

   Customer: Yes. Thank you.

   Salesperson: Mr. Customer, while I have you on the phone, I was wondering if you knew we could give you a quantity discount if your order was increased to. . . .

2. Inactive Account Approach

   Salesperson: Good morning, Mr. Customer. This is Mr. Telephone Salesperson of the Alpha Company. Our records show we haven't done business with you for two months, and I thought I'd call you to find out why. . . . (Settle any complaints at once before trying to sell.)

3. After-Mailing Approach

   Salesperson: Good morning, Mr. Customer. This is Mr. Telephone Salesperson of the Alpha Lumber Company. We mailed you a letter a few days ago telling you about a special offer we had in house siding. . . .

4. Advertising Tie-In Approach

   Salesperson: Good morning, Mr. Customer. This is Mr. Telephone Salesperson of the Alpha Machinery Company. Did you see our ad in the Trade Journal about cutting down stitching time? I would like the opportunity to discuss this new machine with you. . . .

5. Saving Freight Cost (Railroad and Truck)

   Salesperson: Good morning, Mr. Customer. This is Mr. Telephone Salesperson of the Alpha Can Company. We are loading your order and noticed that it is just short of a carload lot; we were wondering if you might not wish to increase your order to take advantage of this savings. . . .

6. The Service Approach

Salesperson: Mr. Customer, this is Mr. Telephone Salesperson of The Alpha Company. Our truck is leaving to deliver your order of February 15. Since several days have elapsed since then, I was wondering if there are any last minute items you may need. . . .

7. Special Sales or Bargain Approach

Salesperson: Good morning, Mr. Customer. This is Mr. Telephone Salesperson of the Alpha Auto Tire Store. We just received a new shipment of Wear Better Tires which we were able to obtain at a very low price. As a result, we are giving our better customers an opportunity to purchase before we start our big sales offering to the general public on Monday. . . .

8. Special Occasion Approach

Salesperson: Good morning, Mr. Customer. This is Mr. Salesperson of the Alpha Jewelry Company. Congratulations on your approaching first wedding anniversary. I was looking over my sale of wedding rings of a year ago and saw your name. I suppose you are thinking of some sort of anniversary present for your wife. . . .

9. Birthday Approach

Salesperson: Good morning, Mrs. Customer. This is Mr. Telephone Salesperson of the Alpha Boy's Store. I just happened to think that Johnny was having a birthday next Thursday (three days hence) and I was wondering if you had in mind buying any clothing as a present. I recall the nice overcoat you bought for him here last September, and he seemed to like it very much. Incidentally, if you can drop by we have a present for Johnny. . . .

10. Demonstration Approach

Salesperson: Good morning, Mr. Customer. This is Mr. Telephone Salesperson of your Alpha Automobile Company. We are calling some of our better customers to let them know we are having a special showing of the new model next Thursday. . . .

11. Inventory Approach
   Salesperson: Good morning, Mr. Customer. This is Mr. Telephone Sales-
                    person of the Alpha Oil Company. We are taking annual
                    inventory beginning next week and are offering the following
                    items at a special price to cut down on inventory cost. . . .

12. Inventory Control Approach
   Salesperson: Good morning, Mr. Customer. This is Mr. Telephone Sales-
                    person of the Alpha Wholesale Company. My purpose for
                    calling this morning is to make sure that you are not running
                    short of —. Due to change in (weather, demand, price, etc.)
                    we felt you might need an additional shipment. . . .

WATS Lines.   The purchase of a WATS line permits the caller to make an unlimited number of long-distance calls within a specified geographic area. The area may be as small as a state or as large as the entire continental United States. WATS lines can be purchased for as short a period of time as ten hours spread over thirty days or for as long as eight hours per day each day of the month. Companies that do a considerable amount of telephone selling may save thousands of dollars in toll charges by converting to WATS. In addition, since costs are fixed, more frequent contacts can be made than might not be affordable on a toll-charge basis.

800 Numbers.   Complementary to an outgoing WATS line is the payment of incoming calls by the firm through an 800 service. With this system, the customer or prospect may call in without incurring toll charges for himself. Perhaps the widest use of this method is by the motel chains. Firms whose incoming sales volume does not warrant such service may increase sales by encouraging incoming collect calls.

Answering Services.   Field sales representatives working without back-up office personnel may increase their effectiveness by using an answering service —either live or electronic. The live service has the advantage in that the salesperson can call in periodically and obtain messages, but many businesses use electronic answering devices to receive incoming calls placed after hours.

Mobile Telecommunications Services.   To eliminate time lag in receiving calls as well as answering them, some sales representatives have cars equipped with MTS (mobile telecommunications service). This may take the form of general service (a regular two-way telephone); a citizen band radio (limited service to and from the office); or signaling service (one-way signal alerting the salesperson to call in).

Conference Calls.   These have several uses in selling. A sales manager may establish a specific time each week to conduct a meeting with his sales representatives. Or a salesperson may use such a service to confer with several persons in various locations. For example he may wish to talk to his district sales manager, the credit manager at headquarters, and the plant that makes shipments to his customers. As another example, the salesperson may facilitate decision making in one of his accounts by conferring simultaneously with members of the buying "who's who" who may be scattered geographically.

Amplification.   The salesperson may also have occasion to use telephone amplifying equipment. For example, he may assemble several people in his organization prior to calling a customer. In this way, each member of the group can back up the salesperson's efforts without the time and expense of their making a joint call in the field.

CAUTION IN USING THE TELEPHONE

There are some cautions to be observed in using the telephone as a sales tool. First, sometimes the person called is interrupted *during* the salesperson's conversation with him. If this occurs, it is important for the salesperson to quickly recap the points that were covered prior to the interruption. It is unrealistic to expect the other person to remember what was said. This is critically important if a call back is necessary. Second, just as in face-to-face selling, the pace and tempo of coverage should be adequate for comprehension. Third, the other person must be a participant, not a passive listener; questions can help insure this. Fourth, in large organizations, it is important to determine that the right person is on the phone. Here, too, judicious use of questions can make sure of the proper contact.

SUMMARY

The telephone is an invaluable selling tool, but it must be used properly to be effective. Telephone sales calls must be planned with the same care as field calls. The call plan, once formulated, can be used as an agenda for note taking and questions. Courtesy is of paramount importance.

Field sales representatives have three recurrent objectives to achieve through telephone calls: follow-up on a previous visit, arrangement for next visit, and request for an order. In-house sales representatives have many reasons for making outgoing calls. However, they have a far larger number of incoming calls to handle. In many firms, they coordinate their efforts with the field sales representatives, and often play an important role in the total sales effort.

There are several guidelines for handling incoming calls, especially when handling complaints effectively. Suggestions were made in this regard.

Strategic and tactical aspects of telephone selling were highlighted, including twelve "hinges" for opening a telephone sales call. We also discussed the importance of establishing rapport with the customer and the effective use of long-distance calls.

We concluded with brief descriptions of a variety of telephone services useful in selling, including the WATS lines, 800 numbers, answering services, mobile telecommunications services, conference calls, and amplification. The telephone call has a special nature of its own and the salesperson should use it carefully.

PROBLEMS

1. Which items on the test of telephone manners do you think are violated most often? Which ones are most likely to "turn off" the other person?
2. Assume you are a salesperson in a local store. Outline a plan for a telephone sales call.
3. Why are sales calls by telephone more effective with a customer than with a prospect? How would the salesperson's call plans differ for each?
4. How can a complaint call be made a sales opportunity?
5. Which of the "hinges" have you experienced as the prospect or customer being called?

Exercise 20

SELLING TO INDIVIDUALS AND ORGANIZATIONS BY TELEPHONE

Objective: To learn more about using the telephone in selling.

1. Phone a local store requesting information of some kind. Note the manner in which your inquiry was handled by the salesperson.
2. Resume the role of a fashion salesperson. You are phoning ahead for an appointment. What do you say?
3. Use the test of telephone manners as a checklist, and note how many violations occur on calls you make or receive in the course of a week.

Case 20-1 Les Deux Soeurs

Les Deux Soeurs is an exclusive dress shop in West Palm Beach located on a shopping promenade. It is owned and operated by two sisters, Marie and Antoinette Bourjois, now in their sixties. The store carries the most costly clothes in the area, many of the selections being one-of-a-kind imports by name designers. Whenever the store is open one of the sisters is likely to be present. The sales force varies in size—six during the height of the winter season, two or three during the summer.

Customers include year-round residents, many of whom are retired, and affluent winter vacationers. Each sister, as well as the more experienced salesladies, has a personal following. Word of mouth is the strongest promotional force, although display ads are run from time to time in the local paper. Each saleslady is encouraged to keep a card file on her customers and to make phone calls to let them know of new arrivals.

Susan Baxter, a middle-age widow, has been with Les Deux Soeurs for 10 years and has developed a good following. One of her customers is Mrs. Thomas L. Green, owner of a sumptuous winter home and acknowledged to be one of *the* hostesses among the well to do.

Susan has selected a Christian Dior creation, a luscious, deep green caftan which she feels Mrs. Green will like. It is set off at the neckline with tiny sequins, and is priced at $575.00.

How should Susan handle this telephone sale?

Case 20-2 Gulden's Department Store

Gulden's is the largest of three department stores in a metropolitan shopping area—it has two suburban branches in addition to the main store downtown. Intensive advertising and direct mail are used to generate traffic to the stores. Sales personnel are encouraged to remind shoppers of specials and possible tie-in purchases. Gulden's has a large number of charge customers who are viewed as the "backbone" of the business. All transactions and other records are computerized and continuing sales analysis takes place.

Jack Bolton has just graduated from college and has been employed by Gulden's as a trainee. Mr. Thompson, the vice-president of marketing, is addressing Jack and the other trainees on the importance of Gulden maintaining a personal, "customer is right" image. He poses this assignment to each of them:

We have over 14,000 charge customers on the books. About 20% of them are inactive. We seldom hear from them. It costs Gulden's about $10 per year to maintain them in the files. How can we stimulate business from this group?

Jack decides a telephone campaign might be directed to the inactive group.

Outline a plan Jack could utilize effectively.

SUGGESTIONS FOR FURTHER READING

Bethards, H. Gordon, "The Telephone: Keep Those Calls Ringing," *Sales Management,* Vol. 106 (May 1, 1971), pp. 46–47.

Burstiner, Irving, "Improving the Productivity of a Telephone Sales Force," *Management Review,* Vol. 63 (November 1974), pp. 26–33.

Garett, William, *Phonemanship–The Newest Concept in Marketing* (New York, N.Y.: Farrar, Strauss, 1959), pp. 139–142.

Stores, "Tell and Sell—How Stores Are Using Telephone Selling," Vol. 50 (August 1968), p. 23.

Weiss, E. B., "Picturephone Will Reshape Tomorrow for Marketing," *Advertising Age,* Vol. 40 (Aug. 18, 1969), pp. 58–59.

Wulff, Peter, "Phone Orders Save $500/Month," *Purchasing,* Vol 64 (May 30, 1968), pp. 44–45.

SIX

Building the Sales Force

In Part Six of the text we are concerned with the managerial and legal aspects of personal selling. The chapters included in this part are entitled, "Selection and Development of Sales Personnel," "Marketing and Financial Aspects of Sales Management," and "Legal and Ethical Considerations in Selling."

In chapter 21 we focus on defining the selling job or jobs and the main qualities needed for successful performance. In addition, we examine the problems of recruiting, screening, and selecting new salespersons; and training and developing the entire sales force.

In Chapter 22 we analyze the marketing and financial aspects of sales management, such as marketing intelligence, sales forecasting, territory alignment, and quotas. We also examine budgeting as a planning and control tool, the concept of the contribution center, and three recurrently used analytical tools. Applications and examples are provided for the latter.

We discuss the legal and ethical aspects of personal selling in Chapter 23. Since the salesperson acts as the intermediary between the firm and its customers these are critical considerations for the salesperson. We detail the major process of anti-trust legislation along with the uniform commercial code and how these specific acts relate to the activities of the salesperson.

21. Selection and Development of Sales Personnel

IN THIS CHAPTER

Determining Manpower Requirements
The Recruiting Process
The Selection System
Hiring Decision
Developing Sales Representatives

Management of the sales force is one of the most critical aspects of marketing. Although no one component of marketing is truly more important than others, in that all must operate together in order to be effective, the firm will surely fail to achieve its objectives if it does not manage its sales force properly. In this chapter we center on the selection and development of sales representatives by examining these specific topics: determining manpower requirements, the recruiting process, the selection system, the hiring decision, the need for sales training, and developing a sales training program.

DETERMINING MANPOWER REQUIREMENTS

A time-honored rabbit stew recipe begins with the phrase, "First catch a rabbit." Similarly, the successful operation of a sales force begins with finding the right salespersons. The firm must examine its present and its future needs for sales representatives. This can be best accomplished by analyzing the present and contemplated selling job and then determining the qualifications needed for successful performance.

Present and Contemplated Selling Job

Examining the present and contemplated job is what is known as developing a *job description*. Unfortunately, most job descriptions are not detailed enough to permit management or the prospective employee to know whether or not he is "right" for the job. A job description should include title, organizational relationships, duties and responsibilities, technical requirements, and unusual demands.

Title of the Job.   The title must be sufficiently detailed so as not to be vague. This is especially important when the firm has several types of sales positions. Although many salespersons are called territory managers, this title can lead to unnecessary confusion because customers and prospects may not know what to anticipate when they are told that a "territory manager" who represents a supplier wishes to see them.

Organizational Relationships.   The job description should clearly state to whom the salesperson reports and whether or not he will be closely supervised. Some firms put the salesperson in almost daily contact with his superiors, whereas in others the salesperson may operate out of a branch office in which the only other company employee is a secretary. Some experienced, independent salespersons enjoy the freedom that goes along with operating an area branch office, but other individuals need more frequent contact with superiors.

Duties and Responsibilities.   The duties and responsibilities of the sales position must be clearly stated in the job description. Each job will vary in the amount of planning activities, actual selling activities, customer servicing tasks, and managerial functions required. As an example, a *missionary salesperson's* primary task is to work with his firm's distributors and their customers. Missionary sales representatives do relatively little selling; they spend most of their time helping distributor sales personnel to be more effective. The sale of photocopying equipment offers another example of different duties and responsibilities. Many of the manufacturers in this industry have two types of salespersons: new business and service. The new business salesperson sells the actual machine itself, and the service representative is responsible for selling service policies and maintaining the equipment when it breaks down. Each sales individual is important to the organization, yet each has vastly different responsibilities.

Technical Requirements.   How much product and service knowledge does the salesperson need to have? How much in the way of consulting services does he actually provide his customers? Some selling jobs require that the salesperson provide a significant amount of technical service to the customer before a sale is completed, whereas others do not require any of this type of activity.

Demands of the Job.   The final factor that must be spelled out in the job description is how demanding is the sales job. How much imagination and creative selling will be required? How tough is the competition? What management responsibilities will the salesperson have? And, finally, how is he or she to be compensated? The more creative the selling and the tougher the competition, the more difficult the job will be for the salesperson. In addition, if the salesperson has to spend a significant amount of his time managing office personnel or other sales representatives, it will be harder for him to succeed in his selling activities. Also, if the salesperson is paid in straight commission rather than some form of guaranteed salary, he may find that the job is more demanding because he must be very concerned with the outcome of each sale.

Both management and the firm's present sales representatives should play an important role in developing the job description. The salespersons are more aware of the daily problems and requirements of the job than management is; therefore, the salespersons can make a valuable contribution to writing an accurate job description. In contrast, management is aware of any impending changes that are planned for the sales operations. For example, it may be that management is considering asking its sales representatives to provide a higher level of technical assistance to its prospects. This new function would have to be incorporated into the technical requirement portion of the job description.

Qualifications Needed to Fill the Job

After the firm has developed a job description for the sales position, it is then in a position to determine what type of person it will need to fill the job.

Mental Requirements.   The mental requirements for a sales position may vary a great deal depending on the specific job. A position that involves selling highly sophisticated electronic equipment usually requires a rather bright individual. The man or woman in this position is likely to have a technical degree, or he may have received extensive on-the-job training. At any rate, in order to master the technology he must be above average in intelligence. However, there are many sales positions that require only average intelligence. In these cases, the following characteristics are more important in determining how successful the individual will be in a selling career.

Physical Requirements.   Several physical characteristics, such as health and appearance, are important to the sales position. As an example, a salesperson who is required to deliver merchandise may have to be physically capable of carrying a certain amount of weight. Most firms look on their salespersons as their link with the market, and they expect them to have a clean and neat appearance. An example of a firm that takes physical appearance very seriously is a major computer company which requires its sales personnel to maintain a very strict dress code. Each man is expected to wear conservative business suits and to look sharp! Only a few years ago the president of this company required all of the sales personnel to wear white shirts while on the job. The age and sex of the prospective employee used to be a critical factor in hiring salespeople, but the federal government now prohibits discrimination in hiring on the basis of age or sex.

Background.   This encompasses a large set of factors, including education, sales experience, marital status, and family and social background. The firm may feel that for its product the individual does not need a college degree but he must have a specified type of selling experience. In contrast, a person who is being considered to sell computers may not have to have any sales experience but probably he or she would need a college degree.

With regard to marital status, many employers prefer to hire someone who is married. This feeling stems from their belief that married individuals are more stable and thus are more likely to stay with the firm. The salesperson's family and social background also becomes important in some selling situations. As an example, if an insurance firm wants to hire an individual to represent it in a high-income area of the city, it may seek to employ someone who was raised in this type of environment. The presumption is that such an individual will find it much easier to sell to high-income clients because he will understand the types of insurance protection they need and will feel at ease mixing with them on a social and professional basis.[1]

Personality Characteristics.   Although personality variables are difficult to measure, the firm may wish to attract people who have certain characteristics such as ambition, enthusiasm, and resourcefulness. Some sales positions are perceived by the firm as entry points to management, in which case they would seek persons who have a long-run ambition for management. If a firm were looking for a salesperson to run a one-man district sales office, they would want a resourceful individual since he would solve most of his own problems. Or the firm may be looking for someone who is vivacious and enthusiastic and aspires to a life-long sales career, but has no immediate interest in management—an individual who would be happy to make a good living as a professional sales-

[1]Franklin B. Evans, "Selling As a Dyadic Relationship—A New Approach," *American Behavioral Scientist,* Vol. 6 (May 1963), pp. 76–79.

person, and yet have no interest in the pressure that a management position might bring.

Once the selling job is defined and the main qualities are specified the firm must consider recruiting persons who meet the requirements.

THE RECRUITING PROCESS

The recruiting process is one of the sales management team's most important efforts. It involves *finding* and *attracting* sales candidates. Many firms estimate that it takes two years or more before a salesperson begins to contribute significantly to the firm's profit. As a result, each time the firm recruits an individual who does not work out it loses a substantial investment of time and money.

In addition, the type of individual recruited will not only be a function of the job description and qualifications needed to fill the job but also of the amount of sales training a firm is able to provide him. If the firm needs salespersons who have technical understanding of its products, but is unable to provide the training, it will have to hire individuals who already possess this knowledge. In contrast, if the firm is equipped to provide this knowledge, it is in a better position to get the best person available and not just an individual who has a technical background. We will examine the sources for new sales representatives along with a check-up procedure to determine which sources are best for any particular firm.

Sources of Salespersons

Many firms want their sales managers to maintain an up-to-date file on potential salespersons, so that if an opening becomes available there is a talent pool available for consideration. Many possible sources of sales representatives are commonly used—for example, educational institutions, salespersons in the firm, other employees within the firm, other companies' sales representatives, and unemployed labor pools.

Educational Institutions.   When individuals graduate from an educational institution, they usually enter the labor market or another educational institution. Graduates from high schools, trade schools, and junior colleges represent potential salespersons in many areas. For example, many retail salespersons with only a high school education can be trained to be very effective in their work. Individuals who are hired for sales positions out of four year colleges and graduate programs frequently are looking for a path into management via the sales route.

One of the very serious obstacles that companies face in hiring salespersons out of colleges and universities is the low regard that both students and faculty have for salespeople. A study done several years ago indicated that only 1 student in 17 was considering sales as a career.[2] In addition, the survey found that both student and faculty understanding of selling was largely limited to retail and door-to-door selling. Finally, the study showed that selling had an image of low-status, job insecurity, and lack of creativity—a position in which a college education would be wasted.

Sales Staff.   The firm's present sales force can be a very important source for locating new salespersons. They have a good understanding of what it takes to sell successfully in the firm. As a result, they are in an excellent position to screen out individuals who might be successful with another company but for some reason would not fit in with their organization.

Salespersons also tend to know competitive as well as noncompetitive salespersons who sell in their territories. They meet these people in clubs, at customer's offices, at airports, and in hotels and restaurants. Since salespersons have one very important thing in common—their careers—they tend to talk more freely with each other than do most relative strangers.

Finally, salespersons come in contact with a large number of people on a daily basis, some of whom may want to enter selling as a career. A good example of this is with book salespersons. Many of these individuals were recruited by salespersons from college book stores or teaching positions.

Other Employees within the Firm.   Another potential source of new salespersons are employees who have other jobs in the firm who might like the opportunities that exist in selling. Production people or engineers have excellent knowledge of a firm and its products. If the firm is selling highly technical products, these people may be prime candidates for selling jobs.

Another group from which field sales personnel can be recruited are inside salespersons. An inside salesperson is someone who normally follows up on customers by telephoning them regularly to see if they need any more of the firm's merchandise. Where a field salesperson may be able to call on a customer only once a month, an inside salesperson can telephone him much more often. These individuals play an important role in following up on the customer, yet by virtue of their experience they are also excellent prospects to go into the field and call on customers face-to-face.

Competitors' Employees.   Management is normally reluctant to recruit employees of competitors to become salespersons for their organizations. This is often referred to as "pirating," and it has a very negative connotation. The major advantage of hiring someone from the competition is that he or she already has extensive experience in that industry. The individual will have a strong under-

---

[2]"Attitudes Toward Selling: A Survey Among a Thousand College Men," *Sales Management,* Part I, Vol. 89 (Oct. 5, 1962), p. 44; Part II, Vol. 89 (Oct. 19, 1962), p. 44; Part III, Vol. 89 (Nov. 2, 1962), p. 46.

standing of the products that are sold, the competition, and the needs of the various customers. It is also good for the firm from time to time to hire someone from the outside, just to get a different perspective on how to attack old problems. This helps to reduce inbreeding and tends to stimulate creativity on the part of the other employees. Finally, if the particular individual has already been selling, many of his customers may be loyal enough to him to switch over to his new employer. As a result, the firm not only gains a good person with new ideas but it may also acquire some valuable new accounts.

There are, however, several problems involved with hiring someone who has been working for a competitor. First, there is the ethical question which must be considered. This individual has been a trusted employee of the competition. He is aware of product and customer information that the firm may not know. It would seem to be unethical for the firm to hire an individual as an attempt to spy on its competition. A second problem is that a good person who is being hired away from competition will normally be paid substantially more than the average compensation for the firm's salespersons. This will upset some individuals who will resent the fact that a newcomer is being paid more than the firm's trusted long-term employees. Since there is no way to solve the salary problem, management simply must be aware of it before hiring such an individual and should be prepared to face the internal opposition if and when it occurs.

Unemployed Labor Pools.   The firm may at times be able to attract people from sectors of the economy that have a permanent or temporary oversupply of manpower. The classic example of this is high school teachers who do not teach in the summer. Frequently, these individuals would like a rewarding summer job. Many retail stores have traditionally hired these people to work in areas of their stores that experience a greater demand during the summer than during the rest of the year. This permits the teachers to make additional money, and the store is able to hire honest professional people on a short-term basis.

Contacting the Prospective Employee

If the individual to be hired is in the process of completing his education, the initial contact point may be through his campus placement service. On the other hand, if the individual is being recruited from within the firm or is a friend of a salesperson, the first formal contact point may be in the firm's personnel office. The individual under consideration will have talked at some length with a representative of management on an informal basis.

There are two other means that are frequently used to attract sales applicants: advertisements and employment agencies. A newspaper ad reaches a larger pool of manpower than can be reached in other ways. However, if the ad is not well thought out it will attract a great many people who do not qualify for the job. Employment agencies take a detailed job description of the sales position and then try to match it with people who are seeking employment through the agency's efforts. This technique has particular advantages for a small firm that does not do a great deal of hiring. In effect, the organization is "farming out" part of its personnel functions to the employment agencies. The small firm simply may not have the time or the money to establish its own sales recruiting operations. In contrast, most large firms would simply be duplicating their efforts if they were to use an employment agency for activities of this nature.

Evaluation of the Sources of Salespersons

Although it is critically important for management to know how and where it can attract good people, it is also important to evaluate its sources regularly. Most firms find that, because of their own unique situation, one or two sources work best for them in recruiting most of their sales force. There are five basic questions a sales manager should ask in evaluating his sources of manpower:

1. How many recruits did I get from each source?
2. How many recruits looked promising?
3. How many recruits were made offers?
4. How many recruits were hired?
5. How many recruits have become successful sales representatives?

THE SELECTION SYSTEM

Once a number of qualified applicants is recruited, the next stage is the selection process. This process normally takes several steps. First, the prospective candidates go through an initial screening process, usually consisting of a completed application form, reference checks, and an initial interview. Then, those individuals who pass over this first hurdle are asked to come in for a second series of in-depth interviews and tests.[3] The last step in the selection process is an actual hiring interview with the prospective supervisor.

Initial Screening

The initial interview is frequently done by the firm's personnel office. These people talk with candidates and ask them to fill out application forms. During this interview, objectives are to:

1. determine if the individual meets the general requirements.
2. furnish the candidate with information he or she needs for decision-making.
3. suggest next steps as appropriate.

[3]Many firms incorporate psychological testing in the selection process, but discussion of this complex technical tool is outside the scope of the book.

Some firms elect not to use personnel staff members for this initial interviewing. One very successful department store (Foley's of Houston) uses only operating managers to do their college recruiting. Their feeling is that the students want to talk with the people who are actually running the business.

From the perspective of the *individual being interviewed,* it is critically important that he or she understand that just as the firm is trying to make a sound hiring decision he or she is making a vocational decision. First impressions will count a great deal in this situation. Frequently, the first interview will take no more than 15 to 30 minutes. The interviewee should be neat and polite, but not bashful. Managers who are considering candidates for a sales position expect them to be well prepared, well groomed, and enthusiastic. The individual who is to be interviewed may wish to spend a few minutes in the library reading about the company.

In-Depth Interviews

Before a prospective employee is granted a job offer most firms require that he have several in-depth interviews with members of management. In addition, many firms will try to arrange a visit with one of their salespersons.

Interviews with Members of Management.   Most firms want the prospective employee to visit with several members of the company's management—usually the sales manager, his assistants, and possibly the director of marketing. These contacts are important because frequently more than one person in the organization will be involved in the final decision as to whether the individual should be offered a job. It may be that the sales manager is looking for a first-rate career salesperson, whereas the marketing manager wants someone who would only stay in sales for a few years and then move into product management or advertising. In addition, various members of the management team will have different slants on company needs, and this diversity will help the interviewee to understand the organizational dynamics of the firm.

Interviews with Sales Representatives.   No matter how hard management tries to give the prospective employee a good understanding of the sales position, no one can do it as well as an experienced sales representative. Many organizations will ask a prospective employee to spend two days visiting the firm. The first day involves meeting with management, and the second day is spent traveling with a salesperson. This system gives the prospective employee a good understanding of the job. Even if the individual does not accept the position, the day that he spends working with a salesperson will usually prove to be a very valuable experience.

From the Candidate's Perspective.   The prospective employee should understand that if a firm thinks enough of him to invite him for a second interview, his chances of getting the job are quite good. The firm normally pays the prospect's expenses on the interview trip. In addition, the firm will give up several members of its management and sales teams for one or two days. This total cost amounts to a substantial investment on the part of the firm. As a result, the prospect should relax and ask the types of questions that will get at the points he or she considers to be important for sound decision-making.

THE HIRING DECISION

The decision whether or not to hire a particular individual for a sales position should be made by a line manager—preferably the individual the new employee will be working for. If this procedure is not followed and the new employee is just sent to the sales manager by the personnel office, the manager will not feel the same level of interest or loyalty to the new employee as he would if he had hired the person himself. In addition, if the new employee does not work out, it is too easy for the line manager to blame the failure on personnel rather than work with the individual more closely to identify and resolve problem areas.

Another important reason why the sales manager should hire the new salesperson is that he knows a great deal more about the sales position and the types of individuals he can work with. A sales manager should interview several prospects that have gotten through all of the initial screening processes. He can then hire the individuals he feels will have the best chance of succeeding in the particular position.

DEVELOPING SALES REPRESENTATIVES

The common myth that "sales representatives are born and not made" has done more to hinder the acceptance of sales training than any other factor. Thus it should be stressed to the recruit that given the proper attitudes and qualifications he or she can be *made* into a first-rate salesperson.[4] In this section, we will consider who should be trained, the factors which influence sales training content, major sales training topics, and training methods.

Who Should Be Trained?

Should the firm concentrate its sales training programs on newly hired salespersons or on its well-established, experienced salespersons? In training mature salespersons, should the firm direct its efforts to its poorer salespersons or to the ones who exceed their quota month after month? These are important questions for the sales manager. Possible answers are suggested below.

---

[4]William J. Stanton and Richard H. Buskirk, *Management of the Sales Force,* 4th ed. (Homewood, Ill.: Richard D. Irwin, 1974), pp. 319–320.

Newly Hired or Experienced Salespersons.   There is no question that all sales recruits, no matter how much selling experience they have, must go through some training. If for no other reason, they need to learn about company policies and products. Those who have little or no selling experience may also be required to attend seminars and participate in role-playing sessions on selling.

The salesperson who has been with the firm for a number of years should also participate from time to time in sales training sessions. After all, forgetting is as active a process as learning. Normally, these training sessions are designed primarily to update the individual on new products the firm will be introducing. However, many firms also take time at such meetings to discuss new sales techniques that seem to have potential for the sales force.

The training session is, therefore, an important communication and educational experience for both the newly hired and the experienced salesperson. A wise management will develop special training programs geared to the unique needs of each of these elements in the sales force.

Below- or Above-Average Salespersons.   The firm will have many opportunities during the year to send members of its sales force to clinics on selling. Many sales managers feel that these clinics can accomplish something that they have not been able to do: make their below-average sales representatives into above-average sales representatives. Unfortunately, this rarely occurs, and the sales manager may become disillusioned with the concept of outside sales clinics.

Research shows that it is far more effective to focus on making good salespersons better than to try to bring the marginal salesperson up to above-average performance. The person who has taken the time to think about what makes a good salesperson and who is driven to learn more about selling will not only be among the company's best sales representatives, but will also get a great deal out of the formal class sessions and the discussions with fellow classmates in the sales clinic. One seminar requires that the sales manager certify that the people he is sending are in the top 25% of his sales force on overall performance.

Factors Which Influence Sales Training Content

Although there is no one set pattern for training content that works for all firms, there are three basic factors which influence what types of content a firm will offer its trainees.[5] We will analyze each of them below.

Experience Level of Trainees.   New employees who have no selling experience will need the most training. The firm will have to deal with a broad set of issues such as company history, the firm's organization, sales policies, products,

---

[5]Kenneth R. Davis and Frederick E. Webster, Jr., *Sales Force Management* (New York, N.Y.: Ronald Press, 1968) pp. 478–481.

markets, competition, selling techniques, and territory management. The amount of time given to each subject and the total time of the training program will of course vary with each firm. As an example, an individual who is to sell encyclopedias door to door may have only one week of training in total, whereas a sales engineer may spend up to two years in the factory learning the engineering aspects of the product before he makes his first sales call.

A new employee who has selling experience will usually need less formal training than does the inexperienced individual. Many firms will *custom design* a program to fit the experienced individual, because no two experienced sales-persons will have the same background. As a result the firm would be wasting a great deal of efforts by sending them through a standardized sales training program.

New Products and New Markets.   A firm that is continually offering new products will need to have frequent training sessions devoted to the new prod-ucts attributes and their buyer benefits. The sessions may be a part of another sales meeting or they may involve sending the salesperson back to the factory to obtain an in-depth understanding of the product.

In the same manner a firm that decides to extend its marketing operations may require extensive sales training programs to provide the salespersons with the knowledge they will need to sell to the new customers. As an example, if a firm that has been producing and selling industrial-strength detergents to cor-porations decides to market its product to the final consumer, it will have to spend substantial time training its sales people to sell these products if it plans on using the same sales force. Where the salesforce has been trained previously to call on purchasing agents or a firm they will now have to be trained to sell to supermarkets and convenience stores which in turn sell to the final consumer.

Changing Company Policies.   The third factor which greatly influences the content of the sales training program pertains to shifts which may take place in the firm's policies toward its employees—for example, changes in its compensa-tion plan. If a significant change were to take place in the sales compensation plan, management would no doubt hold a conference to explain the impending changes to the employees.

Major Sales Training Topics

There will be considerable differences in the content of different sales training programs, yet there are still five basic areas that most programs should cover: products, markets, sales policies, selling techniques and work patterns.[6]

Product Knowledge.   There is probably more emphasis on this than on any other aspect covered in most sales training programs. These sessions should

[6]Stanton and Buskirk, *op. cit.,* pp. 481–485.

cover features of the product as well as its application to the customers' problems. In addition, these sessions frequently review the competition's product offering. This knowledge helps the salesperson to emphasize areas in which his product has the greatest advantages. (This strategy of *differential competitive advantage* was discussed in Chapter 9.)

Market Knowledge.   Market knowledge is closely related to product knowledge. New salespersons have to be taught how to identify potential customers and evaluate their future buying potential. Experienced salespersons in the firm will need new training in this area as the firm branches into other markets.

Sales Policies.   Both the new salesperson and his experienced counterpart must be made aware of any company policies which affect them—this could range from the sales compensation plan to the firm's policy on cooperative advertising, shipping specifications, returns, or credit policies. If the salesperson is to be effective he must (1) understand the firm's policies which affect him directly, and (2) be able to explain the firm's policies to its customers.

Selling Skills.   A major portion of the training sessions is often spent on selling skills. Most firms provide the new recruit with some classroom experience and then send him into the field for some first-hand experience. After several months of training the salesperson is brought back for more intensive sales training. Regardless of the initial sales training, most sales executives believe that it is important to provide their salespersons with a way to periodically update and review their selling skills.

Effective Work Patterns.   Many sales training sessions are geared toward how the salesperson can use his time more efficiently. This is particularly important for salespersons who work alone most of the time with little or no direct supervision. Topics such as routing, preparation of report, call frequency, credit evaluation, and service responsibilities are discussed during these sessions devoted to work patterns.

Training Methods

There are three training methods a firm will normally employ in training its salespersons. These include lecture-discussion, role playing, and on-the-job training.

Lecture-Discussion.   The instructor using the lecture method must make sure that the sales representatives feel free to ask questions. This method works best for explaining such facts as company policy, or explaining new products that are being developed, assuming sufficient time is given for questions, or even to discuss new techniques that might improve effectiveness. It works badly when the lecturer is not attentive enough to the audience to realize when he has lost their interest. The salesperson must be given a chance to interact with the lecturer.

Role Playing.   With this approach, the individual acts out the part of a salesperson calling on a customer. The customer might be one of the other individuals in the class or the instructor. If possible these sessions should be videotaped and made to appear as real as possible—the videotape gives the salesperson a chance to review his own performance. The instructor and other sales representatives in the clinic should review and critique each of the role-playing sessions.

On-The-Job Training.   The third approach is performed by the sales manager. At least every two months, and more often for less-experienced salespeople, the sales manager should travel with his sales representatives. This gives him a chance to maintain contact with the market and to evaluate the individual salesperson's performance. As a result, the sales manager is in a better position to help the salesperson improve his effectiveness. If the sales manager is tactful in making suggestions, this type of situation can be a very useful experience for both parties.

SUMMARY

In this chapter we presented an overview of the selection and development process of salespeople. The first step is the development of a detailed job description, which answers the question: "What is expected?" This, in turn, leads to specifying personal qualifications, which answers the question: "What attributes are needed to do what is expected?"

The recruiting process itself consists of finding and attracting candidates. Sources of talent include educational institutions; referrals by the firm's salespersons; referrals from other employees in the company; competitor's salespersons; unemployed labor pools; advertising; and employment agencies.

The actual selection of prospective salespersons starts with a screening step —an initial interview, checking of references, and completion of an application form. For promising candidates the next step is to invite them in for additional detailed interviews. The final step is a hiring interview most likely conducted by the immediate superior.

The company must provide for the initial training of new recruits as well as the ongoing development of *all* sales personnel. Such efforts must be *learning* oriented and designed to meet learning needs. Key decisions involve who shall be trained, and content and methodology of the program.

PROBLEMS

1. Write a job description for a retail sales clerk in an open-stock furniture department.
2. If you were the sales manager for an automobile dealer, what would be your best source for new salespersons? Explain why you selected the source you did.
3. Do you feel there is an ethical problem in hiring a salesperson who works for a competitor? Explain.
4. What role should the personnel office play in hiring new salespersons?
5. What content is appropriate to a training program for new salespersons?
6. How would you feel about having the sales manager travel with you as a part of your regular evaluation? Do you feel the sales manager *personally* has anything to gain from such visits?

Exercise 21

SELECTION AND DEVELOPMENT OF SALESPERSONS

Objective: To increase our understanding of the selection and development of salespersons.

Interview a person in charge of sales (e.g. department head in a department store, automobile dealership, insurance agency, regional or district manager of a large firm). Use the following questions in your interview.*

1. What are the essential duties a salesperson must perform?
2. What qualities are needed to do the job effectively?
3. How do you recruit salespeople?
4. What are the best sources for such persons?
5. What steps do you take in screening and selecting candidates?
6. What follow-up training do you do?
7. How do you assess job performance?
8. How frequently do you go over each person's performance with him?
9. What are some of the points generally covered?

Case 21-1 Supreme Meat Products (A)

Supreme is a highly regarded brand in the meat products field with a significant market share throughout the country. The company sells direct to regional and national chains

*May be conducted in class.

and reaches smaller accounts through a network of food brokers. The sales force is organized by region, district, and territory as is shown below:

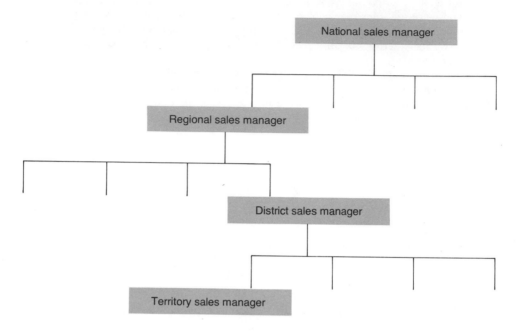

The company has a philosophy of decentralization, and personnel at all levels are expected to plan, decide, and act within the restraints of corporate policy and agreed-upon operating objectives.

Heavy consumer advertising plus a high-quality product line has established continuing demand for their packaged meats. In terms of marketing strategy they maintain a strong "pull" among consumers. Their "push" is mainly accomplished by the field sales force plus modest trade advertising.

Tom Watson is a district sales manager in the southwest region. He has five territory representatives reporting to him. One of them, Jack Young, has an above-average record with Supreme—he has the label in almost every chain in his territory; he has succeeded in getting a fair share of display space in the stores, and his loss of accounts has been minimal. Jack has had a great attitude—he's been constructively self-critical and is always trying to do better.

Tom is disturbed by the following note from Jack:

Dear Tom:

I'm really feeling "down." Despite my best efforts, I can't seem to crack the Alton account. The buyer, Ed Crawley, is adamant about not putting Supreme in his stores. He says all of our competitors are willing to share local advertising costs and unless we change our policy on this we'll never get in.

Tom, maybe we are out of line. This may be preventing us from getting other accounts. It also may be keeping us from getting a bigger share of business in some of our present accounts.

This business is getting tougher and tougher. Maybe it's time I quit.

Sorry to bother you with all this.

Sincerely,

Jack

Jack

What steps should Tom take?

Case 21-2 Lakeshore Steel Supply

Bill Mahoney, sales manager for Lakeshore, faces a real dilemma—what to do about filling Ed Norris's shoes.

Ed is about to retire after selling for Lakeshore for 27 years. He has built a strong personal following in just about all of his accounts. To them he *is* Lakeshore. Like most sales representatives, he has a possesiveness about his territory and his customers. He uses "my," not "Lakeshore," when referring to accounts or customers. With no malicious intent he has done his work in his own way and kept things pretty much to himself. Because of his age, his time with the company, and his evident good results, Bill has been reluctant to interfere with his operation.

Ed has a close friend, Bob Peters, who sells industrial paints and coatings. Ed is now pushing Bob as his successor. In fact Ed told Bill: "I've got the right man to take over my territory. Here's his business card. He's expecting a call from you. I told him I'd break him in once he's on the payroll. Of course he'll need to let his firm know he's quitting once you've settled things with him."

How should Bill proceed?

SUGGESTIONS FOR FURTHER READING

Boyd, Harper W., and Robert T. Davis, *Reading in Sales Management* (Homewod, Ill.: Richard D. Irwin, 1970).

Davis, Kenneth R., and Frederick E. Webster, Jr., *Sales Force Management* (New York, N.Y.: Roland Press, 1968).

Dawson, Leslie M., "Toward a New Concept of Sales Management," *Journal of Marketing*, Vol. 34 (April 1970), pp. 33–38.

Dodge, H. Robert, *Field Sales Management* (Dallas, Texas: Business Publications, 1973).

Donnelly, James H., Jr., and John M. Ivancevich, "Role Clarity and the Salesman," *Journal of Marketing,* Vol. 39 (January 1975), pp. 71–74.

Downing, George D., *Sales Management* (New York, N.Y.: John Wiley, 1969).

Ellman, Edgar S., "Nine Uncommon Ways to Recruit Salesmen," *Business Management,* Vol. 36 (May 1969), pp. 44–46, 60.

Ford, Charles H., "Recruiting by Introspection," *Sales Management,* Vol. 103 (Sept. 15, 1969), pp. 70–76.

Hall, William P., "Improving Sales Force Productivity," *Business Horizons,* Vol. 18 (August 1975), pp. 32–42.

MacDonald, Morgan B., Jr., and Earl L. Bailey, *Training Company Salesmen* (New York, N.Y.: National Industrial Conference Board, 1967).

Markin, Rom J., and Charles M. Lillis, "Sales Managers Get What They Expect," *Business Horizons,* Vol. 18 (June 1975), pp. 51–58.

Newton, Derek A., "Get the Most Out of Your Sales Force," *Harvard Business Review,* Vol. 47 (September–October, 1969), pp. 130–143.

Stanton, William J., and Richard H. Buskirk, *Management of the Sales Force,* 4th ed. (Homewood, Ill.: Richard D. Irwin, 1974).

Still, Richard R., Edward W. Cundiff, and Norman A. P. Govoni, *Sales Management Decisions, Policies and Cases,* 3rd ed. (Englewood Cliffs, N.J.: Prentice-Hall, 1976).

22. Marketing and Financial Aspects of Sales Management

The field-level sales manager has profit, growth, and perpetuity objectives for his district that parallel those of his company. Indeed, unless the units of the field sales organization perform successfully, the firm cannot survive. In the last chapter, we observed the many responsibilities and activities that comprise the "people" side of the field sales manager's assignment; in this chapter, we see that his "market" and "money" duties are also formidable.

In the market side of sales management we examine several of the manager's marketing and sales responsibilities, including marketing intelligence, sales forecasting, and personnel deployment.

Among his money duties, we look at the sales compensation plans and the sales manager's budgetary responsibilities. We examine three useful tools for evaluating financial performance: break-even analysis, incremental analysis, and return on assets managed. Finally, to give the salesperson a comprehensive picture of the relationship of his duties and responsibilities to the broad fiscal policies of the firm, we examine additional financial considerations.

MARKETING AND SALES RESPONSIBILITIES

One of the firm's objectives is to sell the full line of its products and services to the full marketplace. This objective must be tempered, though, because no company, however large, can do business with everybody. However versatile the firm's market offerings are, they will only be purchased by selected market segments. Thus, it may be better to rephrase this objective as: to determine the needs of various market segments and to sell to each segment those products which meet their needs. It is axiomatic to state that this central objective must be met at a profit if the firm is to continue to provide want-satisfying products to the respective market segments.

In order to translate this key business objective from a philosophy of management to a working plan each salesperson must accomplish it for his or her territory. To accomplish this objective, the sales manager must be concerned with several important tasks: marketing intelligence, short-term marketing and sales forecasting, and personnel deployment.

Marketing Intelligence

The field sales organization provides the primary informational input for such matters as changing needs and wants of market members; demographic shifts in local markets; reactions to the firm's other promotional efforts, such as advertising and direct mail; and data on competitive activities. In other words, the field sales force is the firm's means of monitoring all aspects of its markets. As important as staff-generated market research may be, at best it is a supplement to the steady flow of information from salespeople in the field.

Open Communication Between Headquarters and Salespersons.   To perform the marketing intelligence functions, the field sales executive must keep communication channels open between headquarters and the sales staff. He must know what information is needed by upper management and insure that it is obtained. This puts a premium on an effective reporting system. If such paperwork is to be done well, each salesperson must see uses and applications to his own work as well as how the data fits into the company's total marketing information system.

The field sales manager must in turn insure a *downward* flow of useful information from headquarters to the field. A recurring complaint by salespeople is that they don't hear how the information they provided is used; when this occurs, it is demotivating and is likely to cut off the flow of information *upward*.

Screening and Collating Information.   In handling information flows in both directions, the field manager has a screening and collating function. Data furnished by sales personnel must be aggregated and checked for reasonableness and completeness. Data from headquarters must be reviewed and summarized to be useful to the sales force. Sometimes sales representatives complain that they are deluged with information, much of which is not useful.

Assisting with Marketing Research.   Occasionally, the field sales executive becomes involved in the marketing research activities of the firm. For example, he may assist in designing the sample of market members to be included in a study. The salesperson may "open doors" for interviews with key personnel in selected accounts, but it is important to ensure that such assistance does not interfere with the ongoing selling effort and account relationships.

Aggregative Marketing and Sales Forecasting

Most businesses rely heavily on the field sales force to provide short-term marketing and sales projections. Periodically the salesperson reviews each customer and prospect in his territory, and then estimates the likely available business in the account and how much of the total he will obtain. This should be done in as specific terms as possible, and it often includes the identification of competitors who share the account. When the estimates are compared with past experience, trends can be established and, where warranted, the account can be reclassified. Let us consider the following example and then see how these data should be aggregated.

A Ladies-Wear Salesperson.   Jim Brown, a salesperson representing a ladies wear manufacturer, analyzes the Grand Mart specialty shop located in his territory (Table 22-1). In discussing the Fall season forecast with Jim, his supervisor felt the estimates were realistic. Jim explained: "Competitor A's entire line receives heavy national advertising. The buyer at Grand Mart rarely must put any of the line on sale to clean out end-of-season inventory. Competitor B is not too aggressive, and the buyer says she rarely sees the salesperson. The C items are likely to be kept for they are price-lined at the low end of Grand Mart's market. We can expect to increase our share across the board. The buyer is pleased with my personal sessions with the department salesgirls."

Level of Aggregation.   Presumably Jim's boss will hold similar reviews with the other members of the sales force in the district and then aggregate the data in district figures. In turn, the regional manager will aggregate the district figures. Finally, the regional data will be aggregated to provide the total market and sales forecast.

Obviously, decisions must be made regarding the detail required. In a highly segmented market, the data are likely to be aggregated by segment characteristics. In a firm with a varied product line, aggregation may be made by product or product group.

TABLE 22-1 ANALYSIS OF SALES AND MARKET SHARE PERFORMANCE FOR GRAND MART
LADIES WEAR SPECIALTY SHOP

	Dresses		Skirts		Blouses	
	Past Season	Next Season	Past Season	Next Season	Past Season	Next Season
Competitor A	8	8	12	13	18	19
Competitor B	5	4	3	2½	3	2
Competitor C	2	2	2	2½	3	4
Total competitors	15	14	17	18	24	25
Ours	4	5	8	9	12	14
Total	19	19	25	27	36	39
Our share	21%	26%	32%	33%	33%	36%

The advent of the computer has made more sophisticated forms of aggregation possible. If the data are collected in raw form from the customers—with such information as the size of the account, its location, the types of customers it serves, past sales of the firm's products and competitors' products—the sales manager can ask his computer department to analyze the data in just about any manner he wishes. As an example, the sales manager might request that a sales forecast be developed for his largest accounts by their territory. This type of analysis is both inexpensive and fast. The data it provides will help the sales manager to better allocate the efforts of his sales force by directing them to markets that seem to have the greatest potential.

Personnel Deployment

To achieve the basic objective of selling an optimum mix of products to an optimum mix of accounts, the sales manager has to ensure appropriate personal coverage of all customers and prospects. Although the computer can be a great asset in this task, the sales manager must make the final decisions as to how his sales force should be deployed throughout the region. Important concerns in this regard are territory alignment, territory realignment, and the special territory problems in the case of highly technical products.

Territory Alignment. The overall objective of territory alignment is to insure that each territory represents a reasonable work assignment for a salesperson. If a company enjoys a significant share of business and accounts are densely clustered, the size of the territory will be small. Where market share is small and accounts are scattered, the territory size will be large. For example, the sales territories of one office equipment firm range from twelve city blocks to four states! Let us examine nine factors which influence the salesperson's workload and therefore the design of his sales territory.[1]

1. *Nature of the job.* The more jobs the salesperson is asked to perform by his management, the smaller his territory must be. As an example, if a salesperson is asked to sell as well as service the products he sells or to train his distributor's salespersons, his territory must be smaller.

2. *Nature of the product.* A staple product which has a high turnover normally requires more frequent calls on the account than would an industrial product which has limited repeat business. As a result a salesperson who handles products in which there is not a substantial amount of repeat business can handle a larger sales territory than a salesperson who must continually take reorders from existing accounts.

3. *Channels of distribution.* If the salesperson's firm uses wholesalers to reach its retail accounts, the salesperson can have a much larger territory than if he had to sell directly to all of its retail accounts. An extreme example of this principle is a firm which sells merchandise on a door-to-door basis. These firms must have a great many salespersons all of whom have small sales territories.

4. *Stage of market development.* A firm entering a new business generally will assign larger territories to its salespersons than would a firm that has an established reputation. This occurs because a large geographic territory is needed to yield an adequate volume to support the salesperson. As the firm becomes more successful, it may have to reduce the size of its territories if it wants intensive coverage.

5. *Intensity of market coverage.* If a firm wants mass distribution it will have to reduce the size of its sales territories. In contrast, if a firm wishes to be selective in the accounts it calls on, it will have to assign each salesperson to a larger territory in order that he can have enough accounts to support himself.

6. *Competition.* It is difficult to make any generalizations about the role of competition on the size of the sales territory. However, it is evident that when a firm faces tough competition its first reaction is to reduce the size of its territories so as to provide better market coverage. In contrast, if the competition in a territory is so tough that the firm feels it can not make a profit, it may wish to merge that territory with another and simply call on those accounts in which the salesperson has a chance of receiving profitable orders. If this strategy is followed the firm, in effect, is abandoning the mass business while still trying to skim the cream off the top.

---

[1] William J. Stanton and Richard H. Buskirk, *Management of the Sales Force,* 4th ed. (Homewood, Ill.: Richard D. Irwin, 1974), pp. 597–601.

7. *Ability of salesperson.* Even if two districts are comparable in all factors the firm may have to modify the size of the district based on the salesperson's ability. As an example, some individuals are better able to manage their own time than others. In the same way, some individuals may have physical impairments which do not permit them to travel as much as other people and thus their territories must be smaller. In addition, some older salespersons may be very effective, but are no longer willing to spend many nights on the road as they did when they were younger. As a result their territories must be reduced in size.

8. *Ethnic factors.* The firm may adjust the size of its sales territories because of the ethnic make up of the market. As an example, in large urban areas such as New York and Chicago, separate territories may exist to cater to the Black, Italian, Polish, and Jewish markets. The firm which follows such a strategy feels that if it has a salesperson from each of these ethnic groups selling to each of these respective submarkets it will have a better chance of speaking their language, understanding their needs, and therefore getting their business.

9. *Sales potential.* The larger the sales potential, the smaller the geographic sales territory. As an example, a person who is selling Mexican lead crystal in the southwest may sell only retail to customers in Arizona and New Mexico, whereas his counterpart in the East may have an eight or nine states to sell to. The reason for this is that southwestern people realize that Mexican crystal is a good product for the dollar expenditure, whereas easterners are unaware of the value of Mexican crystal.

Territory Realignment.   As business grows, it becomes necessary to realign territories. For example, three territories might be created from two to keep up with increasing volume. This poses a serious "people" problem, because the two salespersons who are losing pieces of territory are likely to be upset. They must be convinced that their earnings will not be adversely affected. If there is a sound basis for the split, they will make more money in the long run because they will have more business concentrated in a smaller geographic area. Firms often cope with this problem by guaranteeing that there will be no loss of income for a short term—say, for a year after the split.

A similar problem exists when a business expands into new geographic areas. Often a seasoned salesperson will be asked to open up the potential business. Such missionary assignments require special financial incentives to make them attractive.

Territorial Allocation Problems of Technical Firms.   Industrial firms marketing a technical line of products and services may find it necessary to make a salesperson's assignments on the basis of product group and/or user categories.

As an example, General Electric may be promoting two product lines, such as highly sophisticated electronic switching gear and diamond-impregnated carbon cutting tools to the same company. Yet no salesperson could know enough about each product lines to represent the company adequately. As a result, General Electric must send two members of its sales force to call on the same account. This may result in widely varying territory sizes; and it almost inevitably results in large sales districts or regions. Districts or regions also vary greatly in what constitutes an optimum mix of accounts and an optimum mix of quotas.

SALES COMPENSATION PLANS

One of the field sales manager's "money" responsibilities is the compensation system of the sales force. There are a great many sales compensation plans, and we will examine the different objectives and types that exist, as well as the use of sales quotas.

Objectives of the Compensation Plan

Any sales compensation plan must have both *general* and *specific* objectives. It is important to be aware of both when considering a particular compensation scheme.

General Objectives.   The general objectives relate to the needs of the company, its sales force, and its customers. They are:

1. To attract and hold good salespersons.
2. To stimulate the sales organization to produce the maximum attainable volume of profitable sales.
3. To control selling expenses, especially where there are major fluctuations in sales volume.
4. To insure full attention to customer needs through complete performance of the sales job.[2]

The relative importance of these general objectives may vary over time and with each company. As an example, a new, undercapitalized company may be primarily interested in stimulating sales and controlling expenses. In contrast, a mature, profitable firm may be more interested in attracting and keeping good salespersons and providing excellent service to its customers.

Specific Objectives.   Specific sales compensation objectives relate to the company's own product and marketing objectives. They can be described as follows:

[2]Kenneth R. Davis and Frederick E. Webster Jr., *Sales Force Management* (New York, N.Y.: Ronald Press, 1968), p. 627.

1. To encourage solicitation of new accounts and development of new sources of revenue.
2. To encourage full-line selling.
3. To stimulate the sale of more profitable accounts.
4. To hold the salesperson responsible for contribution on sales where he can influence margins.
5. To encourage and reward team effort and cooperation.[3]

Again, depending on the market position, product line, and mission of the individual firm, the importance of each of these objectives may vary. Likewise, companies that have different general and specific compensation objectives will select different forms of compensation plans.

Types of Compensation Plans

There are three basic types of compensation plans: straight salary, straight commission, and combination. Each has its own unique set of advantages and disadvantages.

Straight Salary.   With a straight-salary plan, the salesperson is paid a regular wage which does not vary with the number of sales he makes. If the individual does a good job, he will be rewarded the next year by a raise in his salary level.

The major advantage of the straight-salary plan is that the salesperson is committed to following his supervisor's instructions. If the sales manager wants him to solicit new accounts that will not have an immediate payoff, but that should yield substantial long-term profits, the salaried salesperson will have no reservations about performing this function. In the same way, if the salaried salesperson is asked to help train his distributors and to install point-of-purchase displays, he has no reason to object.

The most significant limitation with a straight-salary approach is that many good salespersons are motivated by the commissions that they expect to make on their sales. A salesperson who receives only a straight salary does not have the direct motivation to sell more than he might have if he were paid on a commission.

Straight Commission.   With a straight commission, the salesperson is paid only if he sells. If he sells 20 units he gets twice as much as if he sold only 10 units. The distinct advantage of this system is that it provides substantial incentive for the salesperson to sell more merchandise.

There are, however, three important disadvantages to using a straight commission. First, it makes the salesperson almost an independent business-man. Since he is only paid if he sells—and therefore not compensated for any other type of activities—he feels that management does not have the right to tell him how or when to sell or what secondary activities to perform. Second, many salespersons like the motivation of a commission but do not like the insecurity that exists with such a system. If sales drop off for any reason, the straight-commission salesperson may find it hard to make ends meet.

Third, the salesperson may be tempted to take a short-term view in his dealing with his customer. That is, he may not be quite as interested in satisfying the customer's real needs as he is in getting a sale. This can cost the salesperson and his firm sales in the long run.

Many firms try to partially resolve this problem by providing their sales employees with a "draw." The draw is an amount of money the salesperson gets each payday regardless of how many units he sells. However, at the end of some period (at least once each year) the salesperson and the company settle up. If the company has paid the salesperson more money than he earned on his commissions, the salesperson must pay the company back. Usually, though, the company has paid less, and as a result, the salesperson is given a check that represents the difference between the amount drawn and the amount due. This system does provide some security while it also offers a monetary stimulus to sell.

Combination.   Combination salary plans are designed to have the advantages of both salary and commission plans, but without the limitations of each. Normally, a combination plan consists of salary plus commission or salary plus bonus.

With a *salary-plus-commission* plan, the salesperson is paid a flat rate. For this, he is expected to follow the directions of his sales manager. However, he is also paid a commission, which is expected to stimulate his sales efforts—the commission may begin with the first unit he sells or it may start after he has sold a predetermined quota.

Under the *salary-plus-bonus* plan, the salesperson is paid a straight salary, and then at the end of the year he receives an extra amount based on his performance. This system is much more subjective and flexible than the salary-plus-commission plan. As an example, a salesperson might be given a good bonus because he opened an unusually large number of new accounts and/or has solved several important problems for key customers. It would be very difficult under the salary-plus-commission plan to reward the salesperson for these activities, and as a result they have a smaller probability of being accomplished with the less flexible plan.

Sales Quotas

The salesperson's quota serves as his sales objective. Usually the quota is in dollars, but it could be stated in units. In addition, a salesperson might have different quotas for different products. As an example, a salesperson who represents a manufacturer of home appliances might have a quota of 1575 refrigerators and 1400 microwave ovens in his sales district.

The sales manager's usual starting point for developing quotas is last year's sales. This figure for a mature sales area and product represents the amount the firm can reasonably expect to sell in the forthcoming year. However, the sales manager will also want to consider such relevant factors as the marketing research his firm has developed and changes in future business conditions. As an example, prior to 1972, virtually all coffeemakers made for the home were percolators. However, beginning in that year, automatic drip coffeemakers began to take large portions of the coffee market, and today more than 50 percent of the coffeemakers made for home use are of the automatic drip variety. Thus a sales manager who made his quotas for percolators by simply looking at past sales would be very far off target because of these drastic shifts in the marketplace.

For incentive compensation, the firm as a matter of policy may use some percentage of quota as a base for salary or draw and provide commission on sales above that figure. The presumption is that salary or draw covers the sales up to the base. Some firms establish sales quotas arbitrarily as a percentage increase on the previous year's sales. This usually results in demotivating sales performance, because the salesperson perceives himself as being on a treadmill. The better he performs, the more he is expected to perform.

FINANCIAL RESPONSIBILITIES

More and more firms are decentralizing profit responsibility—that is, they are trying to disaggregate costs and revenues to as low a level as possible in order to know what segments (products, market groupings, territories, etc.) of the firm are profitable. The units to which cost and revenue responsibilities are assigned are called *contribution centers*. For instance, some companies consider each sales district a contribution center, whereas others decentralize the profit responsibility to the sales territory. This development points up the need for greater financial insight on the part of the field sales executive as well as each salesperson.

Constructing the Budget

If contribution centering is to work, budgets must be built aggregatively, commencing with the lowest center—that is, the sales territory or district. Just as forecasts must be adjusted at each level of aggregation, so too must proposed budget entries be carefully reviewed and amended by successive levels of management. The total sales budget becomes a part of the total marketing budget, which must be approved by top management before it is operational.

In a contribution-centered system, costs must be forecasted as carefully and in as much detail as revenues. In marketing generally, and in field sales particularly, contingencies are bound to arise; hence, allowable variation to projected expenditures must be provided so that unforeseen actions can be taken when and where needed. For example, a key competitor may mount an intensive advertising campaign in the local market or perhaps reduce his prices. Such moves may need to be offset by extra advertising and sales expenditures. Although sales budgeting is usually done on an annual basis, more frequent checkpoints—quarterly or even monthly—must be provided; otherwise, control of the field sales operation is difficult. Such reviews allow for replanning and shifting promotional emphasis where required.

Management's Responsibility in a Contribution-Centered System[4]

Management's responsibility should be fixed for each contribution center. For instance, if each sales territory is viewed as a center, then each salesperson is responsible for adhering to budget and for yielding the stipulated contribution to profit. If the sales district is the lowest center in the organization to be analyzed, then the district manager has the contribution responsibility. Naturally, at each higher level of aggregation the same responsibility exists. Thus, even where each salesperson is responsible, the district is viewed as a center. We will examine three analytical tools the salesperson can use to evaluate financial performance: break-even analysis, marginal analysis, and return on assets managed (ROAM).

BREAK-EVEN ANALYSIS

Break-even, in simple terms, means the point at which total revenues equal total costs. Profit occurs when revenues exceed costs; loss, when costs exceed revenues. In this section, we will discuss how to calculate break-even, the application of break-even to the sales territory, and the limitations of break-even analysis.

The Calculation of Break-Even

Three terms must be defined before we can calculate the break-even point. They are: fixed costs, variable costs, and unit price.

Fixed Costs.   Fixed costs do not vary with production; they are such costs as administrative overhead, salaries, accounting expenses, and depreciation. If a firm stopped producing products it would still have to pay these expenses.

Variable Costs.   These costs do vary with production. They consist of such items as the materials that go into the product and the commission that must be

[4]William E. Crissy, Frank Mossman, and Paul Fischer, "Segmental Analysis-Keys to Profit," *Business Topics,* Vol. 21 (Spring 1973), pp. 42–49.

paid on each unit sold. It is important to note that a commission is a variable expense to the firm because it is only paid if the product on which it is based is sold. However, a salary is a fixed cost because its payment is not tied directly to the salesperson's success in selling a product. If the firm were to cease production and stop selling its products, the variable costs would stop completely.

Unit Price.   This is the price that the customer is charged for the product.

How to Calculate Break-Even.   To calculate the break-even point divide the product's fixed cost by its price minus its variable cost. Therefore, if a product had fixed cost of $20,000, and a price of $10.00, and variable cost of $8.00, its break-even point in units would be 10,000 units. That is, since the firm receives $2.00 over its variable cost for each unit it sells, it will break-even when it sells 10,000 units.

Figure 22-1 presents a chart of break-even. Note that fixed costs do not vary with volume. Also, when the variable costs are added to the fixed costs, we have the total costs line. At the point where this line intersects the revenue line (price × quantity) the firm breaks even. Prior to this intersection it loses money, and after the intersection it makes a profit.

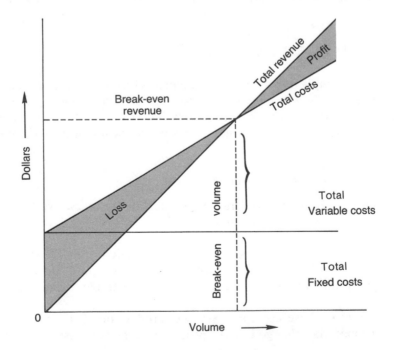

Figure 22-1 Break-Even Chart

Application to a Sales Territory

Management uses break-even analysis in a territory to determine if there is a reasonable opportunity that the territory will be profitable. Once the break-even point has been determined, management can use the information it has on the price structure, the competitive environment, and the size of the market to predict the territory's profitability.

To illustrate this process, assume that the firm has the following cost structure and that it charges $15.00 for each unit it sells. How many units would the firm have to sell to (1) break-even and (2) make a $10,000 profit?

Cost Structure

1. Fixed Costs (salesperson's salary, car, administrative overhead) = $12,000

2. Variable costs
   - (a) product at factory = $10.00
   - (b) handling and field storage = 1.00
   - (c) commission and expenses = 1.50
   - Total variable costs = $12.50

To break even:

$$x = \frac{\$12,000}{\$15.00 - \$12.50} = 4800 \text{ units}$$

To make a $10,000 profit, we add the required profit to the fixed cost

$$x = \frac{\text{fixed cost} + \text{profit}}{\text{price} - \text{variable cost}} = \frac{\$12000 + \$10000}{\$15.00 - \$12.50} = 8800 \text{ units}$$

Therefore, the firm must sell 8800 units to make a $10,000 profit. With this information, the firm is in a better position to determine the profit potential of the territory. If management feels that it must make at least $10,000 to warrant the investment in this territory, but does not think it will be able to sell 8800 units, it must either raise its price, lower its cost, or stop selling the product in this territory.

Limitations to the Use of Costs

There are four major limitations to break-even analysis: the time-period in which break-even occurs; the assumption that fixed costs do not change; the assumption of linear increases in variable costs; and the fact that there is a negative relationship between price and quantity demanded.

When Does Break-Even Occur?   Break-even analysis tells *how many* units it takes to break-even, but the question of *when* is critically important in opening a new territory. The length of time the firm will be forced to accept losses before it begins to generate a profit is an important question not covered by break-even analysis.

No Change in Fixed Costs.   Break-even analysis implicitly assumes that fixed costs will not increase with volume. Yet such costs are likely to increase in a step-ladder fashion. For example, as volume reaches a certain point, a firm may have to increase the number of managerial and technical personnel. It cannot buy one-tenth of a needed technical specialist!

Linear Increases in Variable Costs.   Break-even analysis assumes that variable costs increase in linear fashion. These costs, too, are more likely to change in steps. For example, once a firm reaches 100 percent of production capacity, it may have to pay time and a half for overtime to keep up with demand.

Demand-Price Relationship.   Break-even analysis does not attempt to deal with the relationship that exists between price and demand. Economics teaches us that most products face a downward sloping demand curve. This means that if a firm raises its price it can expect to sell fewer units than before. By raising the price of the product the number of units required to break-even will decrease. The problem is that the increase in price may cost the firm so many units in sales that it will not be as profitable as it was before the price increase. Thus, break-even analysis does not deal with the critical issue of the demand-price relationship.

INCREMENTAL ANALYSIS

Incremental analysis involves examining the extra profit (incremental profit) and the extra cost (incremental cost) of a proposed project. As long as incremental profit exceeds incremental cost, the project is commercially viable for the firm. We will discuss the use of incremental analysis in selling and the major problems incurred by its use.

An Example of Incremental Analysis

Incremental profits should equal or exceed incremental costs for all promotional efforts of the company, including selling. The following example illustrates this concept:

	Incremental Cost	Projected Extra Sales for Each New Salesperson	Incremental Profit
	Cost of New Salesperson		Increase in the Firm's Profit Before Considering Salesperson Expenses*
1.	$24,000	$225,000	$45,000
2.	26,000	190,000	38,000
3.	28,000	170,000	34,000
4.	30,000	155,000	31,000
5.	32,000	145,000	29,000
6.	34,000	135,000	27,000
7.	36,000	125,000	25,000

*Assume a 20% margin on sales.

Here, the first additional salesperson would cost $24,000 and the second additional salesperson $26,000, on up to where the seventh additional salesperson would cost $36,000. This higher incremental cost per salesperson is not because the firm must pay more money in either salary or fringe benefits to hire additional salespersons, but because as more salespersons are added to the payroll the firm will incur added overhead expenses, such as more secretarial services, and more heat, light, and office space. Eventually, the firm will have to add a new sales manager to administer the new salespersons.

The first additional salesperson, because he has almost a virgin territory to cover, would be able to generate $225,000 of additional revenue. Similarly the second salesperson would be able to generate $190,000 in extra revenues while the seventh salesperson would add only $125,000 to the firm's sales because there are now six additional salespersons selling in the field. The more salespersons the firm adds to the same territory the less sales per salesperson there will be even if the total sales of the firm rise.

The third column, incremental profit, represents the increase in profits as a result of each additional salesperson. In this example we assume that the firm has a 20 percent margin on sales. Margin is defined for this purpose as price-less-direct-costs, such as manufacturing expenditures. Therefore, the firm has a marginal profit of 45,000 ($225,000 × 20%) on the first salesperson and only $25,000 on the seventh salesperson ($125,000 × 20%).

Additional salespeople would be hired as long as they can generate incremental profits in excess of their incremental cost, thus adding to the total profit of the firm. In this example, it would be wise for the firm to add only four new salespersons, since the fifth would be added at a cost of $32,000 and would generate only $29,000 in extra profit.

Problems in Using Incremental Analysis

There are exceptions to the principle that the incremental profit of a project should always equal or exceed its incremental cost. For example, the promotional investment in establishing a position in a new market or the initial promotion of a new product may be included in the capital expense budget. The outlay is then viewed as an investment that will pay out beyond the current period.

Our example of incremental analysis was somewhat oversimplified, as it is difficult to forecast the extra sales dollars each additional salesperson can be expected to bring in for the company. In addition, it is difficult to estimate what the true extra cost is of each salesperson. The costs probably do not go up in such neat steps as shown in our example, but may rise very little for several salespeople as the firm uses its resources more efficiently, and then jump up when the firm makes substantial new investments in capital or manpower support.

RETURN ON ASSETS MANAGED (ROAM)

The return on assets managed (ROAM) plan was developed by Schiff and Schiff.[5] Marginal analysis resolves increases or decreases in field sales force personnel by determining if the marginal profit derived from the salesperson is greater than its extra cost, but the ROAM plan further takes into consideration the implications of the additional working capital required to support the salesperson, namely, for inventory and accounts receivable.

A Sales Territory Example of ROAM

Assume a company wants to know more about the profitability of its four sales territories than is revealed by total profit figures alone. Table 22-2 presents a set of accounting data for each of four territories. Note that, while each territory has the same total sales, territory D has the highest profit because it is apparently able to control its costs better.

Working capital consists of accounts receivable (line 4) and inventory (line 5). Territory A has the lowest total working capital investment, and territory D has the highest. Profit on sales (line 7) is calculated by dividing total profit by the amount of sales. Note that territory D has a significantly higher profit on sales than the other territories. The turnover on working capital investment is calculated by dividing sales by the total working capital. Territory D has a relatively low turnover because of a high total working capital investment.

ROAM is calculated by multiplying profit on sales by the turnover. This shows how much the territory has made on the investment involved, accounts receivable, and inventory. Note that even though territory D was first in profit, it

[5]J. S. Schiff and M. Schiff, "New Sales Management Tool: ROAM," *Harvard Business Review,* Vol. 45 (July–August 1967), pp. 59–67.

TABLE 22-2 RETURN ON ASSETS MANAGED

Accounting Variable	Territory A	B	C	D
1. Sales (1000 @ $15)	$15,000	$15,000	$15,000	$15,000
2. Total costs	13,130	12,670	12,200	11,730
3. Profit	$ 1,870	$ 2,330	$ 2,800	$ 3,270
4. Accounts receivable	$ 3,000	$ 3,250	$ 3,500	$ 5,000
5. Inventory	1,500	1,750	1,800	2,000
6. Total working capital investment	$ 4,500	$ 5,000	$ 5,300	$ 7,000
7. Profit on sales (3 ÷ 1)	12.5%	15.5%	18.7%	21.8%
8. Turnover on working capital investment (1 ÷ 6)	3.3	3.0	2.8	2.1
9. ROAM (7 × 8)	41.3%	46.5%	52.4%	45.8%

*Includes allocated fixed costs based on break-even volume.

is third in ROAM. Apparently territory D's customers are much slower in making payments than the customers in other territories (line 4) and require more inventory in the field to service their needs (line 5).

Primary Advantage of ROAM

The most significant advantage in using ROAM is that it permits the firm's management to evaluate performance in terms of the assets committed. A territory manager presumably can exercise control over receivables and inventory, as he is in the best position to know how much inventory he needs. Also, he is the one who determines how much credit each client should receive. If he makes bad decisions, inventory will pile up and the accounts receivable will increase faster than his sales increase. Thus, it is reasonable to evaluate him on the basis of how he uses his working capital, since this is an item over which he has primary control.

SUMMARY

In this chapter we examined selected aspects of sales management's marketing and financial responsibilities. The sales organization is seen as the prime marketing intelligence arm. In addition, the sales force collectively provides short-term sales forecasts. The salesperson provides the basic input by reviewing the customers and prospects in his territory and then estimating how much business will be available in each account and how much of it he expects to get.

Sales personnel deployment must insure optimum market coverage. We discussed nine factors which influence the salesperson's workload and the design of his territory. Also, several of the key problems in territory realignment were discussed. When a salesperson's territory is reduced, he must be assured that his earning will not be adversely affected.

Sales compensation plans were also discussed. The most common types of compensation plans are straight salary, straight commission, and combination plans. The most significant advantages of the straight-salary plan is that the salesperson should be willing to follow the sales manager's counsel; the most important advantage of the straight commission is that it provides a substantial incentive for the salesperson to sell his merchandise. The various types of combination plans try to combine the advantages of both the straight salary and commission plans.

We examined the sales manager's financial responsibilities within the mode of a contribution-center system. This type of system permits the firm to determine which segments of its organization are profitable and which are not. Since the sales manager is one of the key centers in this type of a system, it is important that he be aware of how to measure financial effectiveness.

We highlighted three analytical tools and provided applications and examples: break-even, incremental analysis, and return on assets managed (ROAM). Break-even analysis permits the firm to determine how many units must he sold for the firm to cover all of its expenses. Incremental analysis is a technique for determining how to optimize promotional effort. Applied to selling, the general rule is that the firm should hire salespeople until the added incremental profit generated by the salesperson is no longer more than the added cost of hiring the extra salesperson. ROAM takes into consideration the extra working capital needed to support a project. In selling, ROAM can be used to demonstrate that one territory might not be as profitable as it first appears because of the large amount of working capital required to support the territory.

PROBLEMS

1. What role does the salesperson play in marketing intelligence?
2. Which of the nine factors related to territory alignment do you feel are most important? Explain.
3. What are the advantages and disadvantages of straight-salary and straight-commission compensation plans? Which would tend to motivate you the most? Explain.
4. What is meant by a contribution-centered system?
5. Which of the three financial techniques examined (break-even analysis, incremental analysis, or ROAM) do you feel is most applicable in analyzing sales problems? Explain.

Exercise 22

MARKETING AND FINANCIAL ASPECTS OF
FIELD SALES MANAGEMENT

Objective: To learn by example applications in selling of break-even and ROAM.

A. Break-Even   A. BREAK-EVEN

1. Application to territory:

   (a) Fixed costs   = $15,000
   (b) Unit variable costs
       product at factory   = $150.00
       handling and storage   = $ 12.50
       commission & selling expenses   = $ 17.50
   (c) Unit price   = $ 200

   What volume must be sold to break even? To make $9000 profit for the firm?

2. Application to account:

   The same company (in 1 above) has an average of 150 accounts in each territory and it has a profit objective of at least $7500 per territory.

   What is the breakeven volume for an average account? What volume in an account is needed to meet the profit objective?

3. Application to new product:

   A company makes these assumptions in pricing new products. (1) Life expectancy—three years. (2) Break-even to be achieved in one and one-half years. In the case of its latest new product it has these costs and cost projections:

   (a) Development costs   = $100,000
   (b) Allocated administrative burden
       per annum   = $ 10,000
   (c) Introductory promotion and expenses   = $ 10,000

(d) Unit variable costs at plant assuming
400 minimum annual volume = $ 90.00
(e) Unit variable costs (marketing and
distribution) = $ 30.00

What price must be set to reach break-even in 18 months, assuming a minimum lot is manufactured and marketed? (Answer to nearest $10.)

What profit will be realized by the end of the third year, assuming a constant rate of sales?

B. Return on Assets Managed

The figures set forth below are hypothetical data on three territories.

	Territory I	Territory II	Territory III
1. Annual sales	$70,000	$75,000	$80,000
2. Total costs	55,000	57,500	59,000
3. Accounts receivable	15,500	16,000	20,000
4. Inventory	5,500	5,000	5,000

What is ROAM for each territory?

Case 22-1 Supreme Meat Products (B)*

Tom Watson breathes a sign of relief. "Thank goodness Jack Young is back on track. You don't find salespeople like Jack very often."

Tom turns to the financial review of his five territories. He peruses the following summary printout of first-quarter results from headquarters:

REVENUE	A	B	C	D	E	DISTRICT TOTAL
Direct Accounts	$152,250	$140,300	$145,200	$ 90,000	$129,370	$657,120
Broker Accounts	38,900	31,120	22,460	50,320	46,310	189,110
TOTAL	$191,150	$171,420	$167,660	$140,320	$175,680	$846,230
EXPENSES						
Cost of Goods	$167,918	$151,105	$149,350	$124,100	$153,410	$745,883
Selling Costs	8,260	8,090	7,990	6,110	7,790	38,240
TOTAL	$176,178	$159,195	$157,340	$130,210	$161,200	$784,123

Examine Case 21-1, Supreme Meat Products (A) before analyzing this case.

Gross Contribution	$ 14,972	$ 12,225	$ 10,320	$ 10,110	$ 14,480	$ 62,107
Gross Contribution %	7.8%	7.1%	6.2%	7.2%	8.2%	7.3%
Annual Quota %	26%	25%	24%	26%	27%	26%
New Accounts	2	1	0	2	3	8
Lost Accounts	1	1	0	1	0	3

Tom smiles. "I wonder how many districts can match that record," he thinks. "What a performer Jack Young is!" Ed Fox is doing a great job out in the boondocks. But what about Bill McMann? He's up in years and coasting. His territory would have real potential for a guy like Tom."

1. Match up territories and men with reasons for your answer.

2. What can a manager do to motivate an older man who is coasting?

3. What factors might account for the relatively small percentage of sales to brokers in C? The higher percentage in D?

Case 22-2* Bulls and Bahrs

Mr. Roberts, sales manager for Bulls and Bahrs, a moderate-sized brokerage firm, put aside his copy of the day's "Wall Street Journal" after reading a front-page article about the difficulties brokerage firms were having in encouraging their better people to take managerial jobs. The article hit home hard because Mr. Roberts was encountering precisely the same problem in staffing his firm's 40 branch offices.

The article quoted various security salespersons as saying, "I can earn a six-figure income working simply as a broker; I don't need the aggravation of managing six to a dozen salespeople." "Last year I earned more than $200,000 in commissions by bringing in more than $400,000 brokerage fees, but I'll do even better this year because we're opening a plush uptown office where I'm going to be free from management chores that would only hinder my selling efforts."

The brokerage commission paid to sales representatives ranges between 25 and 50 percent of the fee the customer pays on a stock transaction. The total fee generally averages about 1 percent of the value of the transaction. Branch managers, themselves, usually handle some customers directly, and they also earn a 1 or 2 percent share of the office's gross commissions. Their total income, however, is usually about half of the potential income of a top salesperson. Some brokerages pay their managers a salary, plus a percentage of the office's profits, plus the commissions the managers earn on transactions with their own accounts. Unfortunately, the manager's job conflicts with his handling of his own customers to the detriment of his total income.

The basic problem is caused by the changing times in the stock market. Broker's commissions have been more or less standardized throughout the industry. The level of

*Adopted from William J. Stanton and Richard H. Buskirk, *Management of the Sales Force,* 3rd ed. (Homewood, Ill.: Richard Irwin, 1969), pp. 348–349.

commissions is set in relation to the level of total market activity—the average number of stock shares traded daily on the New York Stock Exchange. Present-day commission rates are based on a relatively low level of total market activity—2 to 4 million shares traded daily. During those less active times, sales commissions must be set sufficiently high so that the marginal salespersons can earn sufficient income to live on. With the advent of a much higher rate of stock market activity in which trading has increased up to 38 million shares a day, along with higher securities prices, the salespersons' commissions have increased considerably. This has resulted in substantially increased earnings for many sales representatives.

This high income has created problems, however. Many managers claim that their salespeople became prima donnas when their earnings approached the $100,000 level; they requested gold-plated telephones and private secretaries. "One salesperson would never report to work before noon. His conduct was ruining the morale of the rest of the office. I played up to him, pleaded with him, threatened him, but to no avail. He knew his sales performance was so great that he could take any advice with a grain of salt."

Mr. Roberts had been instructed by his top management to prepare a report on what the company should do about the situation. He realized that it was an extremely complex problem not readily solvable by lowering commissions, because his company had to be able to attract salespeople. In addition, he realized that these commission rates, while providing a few top men with handsome incomes, still left a number of salespersons earning only a fair income. He wondered if the basic problem was in the fundamental compensation structure in the industry. Questions that occurred to him included: Is it wise to pay the sales representatives on a straight commission basis at all? Is it really important to have top-notch salespersons in the industry? Why not put a lid on earnings? Unfortunately, the answers to these questions did not come easily to Mr. Roberts, for he saw all sorts of problems connected with every alternative.

1. What, if anything, should be done about the situation?
2. Should the compensation plan be changed to encourage salespersons to move into managerial positions? If so, what do you recommend?

SUGGESTIONS FOR FURTHER READING

Brice, M. A., "The Art of Dividing Sales Territories," *Dun's Review*, Vol. 89 (May 1967), pp. 47, 93–96, 98.

Cotham, James C., III, and David W. Cravens, "Improving Measurement of Salesman's Performance," *Business Horizons*, Vol. 12 (June 1969), pp. 79–83.

Herzog, Donald R., "Setting Sales Quotas," *California Management Review*, Vol. 3 (Winter 1961), pp. 47–52.

Mossman, Frank H., Paul M. Fisher, and William J. E. Crissy, "New Approaches to Analyzing Marketing Profitability," *Journal of Marketing*, Vol. 38 (April 1974), pp. 113–118.

Risley, George, "A Basic Guide to Setting Quotas," *Industrial Marketing,* Vol. 46 (July 1961), pp. 88–93.

Sales Management, "Using Sales Expense Ratio Reporting to Influence Profitability," Vol. 114 (May 19, 1975), p. 11.

Scanlon, Sally, "A New Role for Incentives," *Sales Management,* Vol. 114 (April 7, 1975), pp. 41–44.

Schiff, Michael, "The Use of ROI in Sales Management," *Journal of Marketing,* Vol. 27 (July 1963), pp. 70–73.

Smith, C. W., "Gearing Salesmen's Efforts to Corporate Profit Objectives," *Harvard Business Review,* Vol. 53 (July–August, 1975), pp. 8, 12, 14, 16.

Smyth, Richard, "Financial Incentives for Salesmen," *Harvard Business Review,* Vol. 46 (January–February 1968), pp. 109–117.

Winer, Leon, "The Effect of Product Sales Quotas on Sales Force Productivity," *Journal of Marketing Research,* Vol. 10 (May 1973), pp. 180–183.

23. Legal and Ethical Aspects of Selling

Popular culture is full of humorous stories about skillful con artists who are able to sell streetcars and monuments to trusting tourists. The stories may be funny, but their underlying concepts are very serious. Why does society typify the salesperson as an individual who will deceive in order to make a sale? Is the popular image of the salesperson based on observed behavior, or is it just an unfounded stereotype?

In this chapter we are concerned with the legal and ethical aspects of the sales function. In the United States, legal provisions in the field of sales are primarily concerned with maintaining competition and protecting consumers' rights from abusive trade practices. The dynamic character of our economy and our culture is reflected in the principles and regulations established by our federal, state, and local governments. It is essential that those responsible for the sales function understand these principles and regulations, since their relationship with customers, dealers, and their own firm is continually affected by the government's action. We will examine the many laws that regulate selling and then look at the ethical aspects of the sales function.

THE SHERMAN ACT

After the Civil War, the rapid growth of many industries (particularly of a few firms within those industries) increasingly threatened competitive activities in the United States. Although monopolization was illegal prior to 1890, it was controllable only through common or case law. This meant that every case involving alleged monopoly practices had to be compared with similar precedent-setting cases to determine whether it could be prosecuted. In addition, most of the common law principles dealt only with the monopoly condition itself, not with the practices that would lead to a monopoly. And most of the preceding cases were only statewide in scope, ruling out action by the federal government. As a result, few firms were ever convicted of monopoly practices.

The First American Antitrust Law

The Sherman Antitrust Act of 1890 was the first federal statute designed to prevent restraint of trade in interstate and foreign commerce. It stated that, "every *contract, combination,* in the form of trust or otherwise, or *conspiracy,* in restraint of trade or commerce, is illegal among the several states." In addition, anyone found guilty of violating the Sherman Act would be guilty of a misdemeanor, and subject to fine, or imprisonment, or both, as stated in section 2 of the Act. The Sherman Act was essentially a positive pronouncement of the intentions of the American government to preserve the philosophy of capitalism as it had been adopted in this country.

An important interpretation of the Sherman Act was made in 1911 in the Standard Oil case. In its decision in that case, the Supreme Court introduced the "rule of reason."[1] According to this rule, for an action to constitute a violation of the Sherman Antitrust Act, it must be deemed an *unreasonable* restraint of competition. This implies that each case must be judged individually. As a result, it became much more difficult to obtain a conviction based on the Sherman Act because the defense was permitted to argue that although certain actions might involve a conspiracy in restraint of trade, they may not constitute an *unreasonable* restraint of competition. The Supreme Court has held that certain combinations and agreements in restraint of trade are *per se* antitrust violations. They do not therefore have to be proven unreasonable. Some of those

[1]*Standard Oil Company of New Jersey v. United States,* 221. U.S. 1 S.Ct.502 (1911).

are: (1) territorial allocation of markets, (2) horizontal price-fixing, and (3) the sale of an unpatented product tied to a patented article.

Implications of the Sherman Act

Specific sales practices that are illegal in interstate commerce under the Sherman Act are (1) the dividing up of markets by agreement of competing firms, and (2) the fixing of prices either horizontally (between competing firms) or vertically (between members of the same channel of distribution).

A classic case of restraint of trade was the great electrical conspiracy of 1960, in which salespersons and executives of the electrical industry met regularly to decide on pricing and trade policies. The companies and individuals involved were found to be in violation of a number of laws, including the Sherman Act.

THE CLAYTON ACT

Partially as a result of the "rule of reason" interpretation, the Sherman Act was not sufficient to stop trade abuses. In order to strengthen and complement it Congress passed the Clayton Act, in 1914.

The major modification introduced by the Clayton Act was that it was no longer necessary to produce proof of conspiracy or actual monopoly as had been required under the Sherman Act. The Clayton Act states that certain practices are illegal, where the effects "may be to substantially lessen competition or tend to create a monopoly. . . ." The government did, however, have to prove to the court that the defendant did indeed "substantially lessen competition." Sections 2 and 3 of the Clayton Act have provisions that apply directly to selling.

Section 2

This section of the Clayton Act states that it is generally illegal for a seller to sell the same merchandise to two different buyers at different prices. Price discrimination had to be based on different marketing and distribution costs or on variations in grade, quality, or quantity of the product. Differences in price could also be justified by the need to meet competitive practices. This section of the Clayton Act was subsequently amended by the Robinson-Patman Act, which we will discuss later.

Section 3

This portion of the Clayton Act prohibits *exclusive dealing* and *tying contracts* when they substantially lessen competition. Exclusive dealing contracts are those agreements that force a middleman to handle the products of only one manufacturer. Tying contracts are those whereby a buyer is forced to purchase unwanted products in order to obtain a desired item. Violations occur only when the agreement substantially affects competition. There is no definite general standard that can be applied to all firms, because several factors are considered, such as sales volume, and the location of competitors. Defining "competition" and "substantially lessen" is the task of the enforcement agencies in each case. A specialized agency was created in 1914 to handle economic and technical questions in antitrust cases: the Federal Trade Commission.

THE FEDERAL TRADE COMMISSION ACT

In 1914, during Woodrow Wilson's presidency, the Federal Trade Commission (FTC) Act was passed. With this act, a new commission of specialists was established and given the power to investigate any business practices that might represent "unfair methods of competition." If the Commission feels that an improper act that falls within its jurisdiction is being committed, it can issue a cease and disist order. If the firm in question refuses to accept the order, the FTC is empowered to take the firm to federal court to have its order enforced. The theory behind the creation of the FTC was that it would be a body that could investigate potentially monopolistic practices and stop them faster and on a more informal basis than the courts could.

The Wheeler-Lea Act

In 1931, the courts determined that the FTC only had power over cases involving injury to one firm by another and not over cases involving damages by a firm to the final consumer. As a result, in 1938 Congress passed the Wheeler-Lea Act, which amended Section 5 of the FTC Act to declare unlawful, "unfair methods of competition in commerce and unfair to deceptive acts or practices. . . ." This extended the FTC's power to include the investigation and prohibition of unfair or deceptive practices involving the *final consumer*.

Although there have been many cases where the FTC has acted to protect the final consumer, one of the most significant was the FTC's move against "games" that were being played at many retail establishments, particularly gasoline stations. After a through investigation, which found many abuses of "games," the FTC passed the following rules:

1. A company can not continue to give away tickets or play the game after it has expired. That is, many firms continued the games after there was *no* chance the customer could win.
2. The company must state the odds of winning. In most games the *odds against* winning a significant prize were much higher than any one realized.
3. The company can not direct tickets to particular market areas. That is, many firms would push their *winning* tickets to the area in which they had the most competition.

4. The firm must give away all of the prizes that it advertises. Many games would state that they had a certain amount of prizes. But if a person who drew a winning ticket did not play the game or lost his or her ticket, the prize went *unclaimed*. Since this happened to many of the tickets the firms had to give away only small portions of their prizes.

Implications of the FTC for Selling

The FTC investigates all selling practices that may be deemed unfair. Acts ranging from collusion in pricing between supposed competitors to false statements by a salesperson are legitimate concerns for the FTC. In addition, the FTC is concerned with all sales practices that attempt to deceive and mislead customers, such as dissemination of false advertising for foods, drugs, and cosmetics. Since the Wheeler-Lea Amendment does not specify the "unfair trade practices," the FTC can dynamically adapt to changes and determine what it may consider unfair according to each specific case. The sales force should be kept informed of the decisions of the courts in FTC cases, as well as the regulatory activities of the Commission itself, in order to be aware of legal trends in this field.

THE ROBINSON-PATMAN ACT

The economic depression that followed the collapse of the stock market in 1929 led to the growth of chain and vertically integrated discount organizations. These organizations sought to eliminate middleman costs by acquiring large quantities of goods at discount prices, and they in turn passed those savings on to the consumers. Chain-store organizations became so powerful that they threatened the survival of small, independent businesses. The lobbying efforts at the federal level of small retailers resulted in several pieces of regulatory legislation of which the Robinson-Patman Act of 1936 was the most important. This act was designed to take away many of the buying power advantages of large chain stores by putting further restrictions on price discrimination.

An Amendment to the Clayton Act

The Robinson-Patman Act amended Section 2 of the Clayton Act. It made unlawful in interstate commerce any price discrimination between different purchasers of goods of "like grade and quality" that may tend to "injure destroy, or prevent competition." It was, therefore, no longer necessary to show that competition had been substantially lessened—the *injury* to competition was sufficient cause to bring action. The Robinson-Patman Act also included regulation against such discriminating practices as advertising allowances which are not available to all customers on "proportionately equal terms." This means that if a manufacturer wishes to give a large chain store assistance in designing a full-page newspaper to promote its products, it has to offer the same type of service to the small retailer in a manner that would be useful to him.

Exceptions to the Clayton Act

Another important change brought about by the Robinson-Patman Act was that price discrimination was no longer considered unlawful per se. Two important defenses to price discrimination were identified. First, if a seller could prove that it cost less to sell to one firm than to another, it could pass the cost reduction on to the firm that made the saving possible. As an example, if a manufacturer ships a few packages by parcel post to a small retailer and a full truck load to a large department store, there will be substantial per-unit transportation cost differences between the two customers. This cost saving can be passed along in whole or in part to the large buyer.

The second exception to price discrimination is that a firm could discriminate in price between two customers if it was doing so to meet the lower price of competition. Therefore, if a manufacturer has two customers in one market area and one of the customers is considering buying the product from another manufacturer, the firm can reduce its price to meet that of its competitor. These defenses were also identified in Section 2 of the Clayton Act, but they had been *narrowed* under the Robinson-Patman Act by limiting discounts to the cost savings actually realized by the seller.

The Robinson-Patman Act was intended to assure a competitive framework and the elimination of unfair and discriminatory practices in price setting. Over the years, the courts' interpretations of the act have not always been clear. Some commentators argue that it promotes inefficiencies by sustaining small, nongrowth businesses.

Implications of the Robinson-Patman Act For Selling

The Robinson-Patman Act and the subsequent court decisions make it very clear that the salesperson must be cautious in giving preferential treatment to any of his customers. If a salesperson grants a price break or extra cooperative advertising expenditures to one customer, he must be prepared to offer the same types of programs to each of his customers unless he can justify them by (1) the fact that it costs less to do business with one customer, or (2) the fact that he is meeting the practices of his competition. In addition, the salesperson must resist temptation to get speedier delivery or better service arrangements for his larger customers, for if he offers one customer these incentives and not others he will find himself in violation of the law.

FEDERAL CONSUMER PROTECTION LEGISLATURE

Since the early 1900s, several laws and regulations have been passed to protect consumers from trade abuses by overly aggressive merchants and salespersons. Although the American capitalistic system provides the highest standard of living in the world, numerous complaints have been brought against it. Such complaints have led more recently to a movement called "consumerism," which attempts to achieve organized reaction to abuse, fraud, deception, and misrepresentation in marketing.

The federal legislation protecting consumers covers a variety of specialized issues dealing with product content, packaging, labeling, and several informational points about contractual agreements, such as credit and lending. Following are some of the laws passed by Congress that concern sales and marketing activities:

The Pure Food and Drug Act (1906) made the misbranding of food and drugs at the interstate level illegal.

The Tariff Act (1930) regulates imported goods packaging or imported goods, and requires the indication of their country of origin.

The Food, Drug and Cosmetics Act (1938) establishes quality standards for canned foods, drugs, and cosmetics.

The Wool Products Labeling Act (1939) and the *Fur Products Labeling Act* (1951) require information disclosure to the consumer regarding contents, specifications of product quality and origin, as well as care for the product.

The Automobile Information Disclosure Act (1958) requires all automobile manufacturers to display on the windows of new cars the list price.

The Harzardous Substances Labeling Act (1960) concerns labels of hazardous household products and requires that warnings be given on the label to customers.

Public Health Cigarette Smoking Act (1965) forbids the advertising of cigarettes on television.

The Consumer Credit Protection Act (1968), or "Truth in Lending Law," requires that true interest rates and transaction costs be clearly disclosed to consumers.

The Consumer Product Safety Act (1972) protects consumers against unreasonable risks of injury associated with consumer products; assists consumer in evaluation of the safety of such products; develops uniform safety standards, and promotes research and investigation into the causes and prevention of product-related deaths, illnesses, and injuries.

Real Estate Settlement Procedures Act (1974) protects real estate buyers by providing detailed disclosure of each change arising in connection with the settlement to be made to designated persons and federal officers or agents.

The consumer protection laws enable a salesperson to emphasize product quality and reliability and to use compliance with federal regulation as a competitive advantage, when it is the case. At the same time, since oral agreements between the salesperson and his customers are often a very important part of the sales contract, the salesperson must be aware of the legal requirements and disclose the appropriate information to his customers. This is a complicated area of the law, but one that is critical to the salesperson who deals with final consumers. (Later in the chapter we will discuss state consumer protection laws.) To better understand the contractual agreements between salesperson and buyer, consideration must be given to the Uniform Commercial Code.

THE UNIFORM COMMERCIAL CODE

The Uniform Commercial Code (UCC) and its chief predecessor, the Uniform Sales Act, comprise the legal guide to commercial practice in the United States (Louisiana excepted). The code was drafted by the National conference of commissioners on Uniform State Laws and the American Law Institute over a period of ten years. The initial draft was completed in 1952, and the final edition, which has since been accepted by 49 states, appeared in 1958. The provisions of the UCC bear directly on the salesperson's relations with his customers. In each, the salesperson faces *must and must-not* actions and decisions. He is the firm's agent under the law. Let us consider some of the implications of the UCC.

The Definition of a Sale

The Uniform Commercial Code defines a *sale* as "The transfer of title to goods by the seller to the buyer for a consideration known as the price."[2] The code introduces a number of separate rules which apply to sales between merchants or involving merchants as a party. Fifteen sections of the UCC are concerned with sales between merchants, and cover such items as the need for written contracts, warranty of goods sold by merchants, delivery agreements, commission, reimbursements, and many others.

Oral agreements between sellers and buyers are considered as binding as are written contracts; special consideration is given in some cases to the Statute of Frauds, in order to enforce the sales contract. It is important that the salesperson be aware of such provisions since he is the spokesperson and legal representative of his company in its relations with buyers and potential buyers.

[2] Len Young Smith and G. Gale Robertson, *Business Law–Uniform Commercial Code Edition* Third edition, (St. Paul, Minnesota: West Publishing, 1971), pp. 497–498.

The salesperson must be *informed* on all details of the contracts of sale he negotiates for his firm. This is a particularly important consideration if the unit order is large, or if durable goods with warranties or guarantees covering the purchase are involved, or where stipulated services are included in the sale. The salesperson has the power to legally obligate the company he represents.

The Salesperson and the Reseller

Where the salesperson has resellers as customers and prospects, he must know the details of the contractual relationships between his firm and the reseller. In particular, he must note the *obligations of his firm to the reseller* and the *expectations his employer has of the reseller*. A recurrent problem area is the stipulated marketing and sales performance of the intermediary with respect to the manufacturer's product line. Another potential source of difficulty is where the relationship stipulated is vendor and purchaser, but the reseller deliberately or inadvertently holds himself forth as agent for the manufacturer. This may occur in the reseller's advertising, use of trademarks, and other promotional efforts.

Warranties and Guarantees

The Uniform Commercial Code distinguishes between express warranties and implied warranties. Express warranties under the Sales Act are those found only in express language of the seller. Implied warranties are obligations imposed by law upon the seller which he has not assumed in express language.[3]

Statements or promises made by the seller a long time prior to the sale or subsequent to the contract of sale may be express warranties. The Code also states that manufacturers and sellers of goods may be liable to users and consumers on the basis of (1) negligence, (2) fraud or misrepresentation, and (3) express or implied warranty. Salespersons handling durables covered by warranties and guarantees must be aware of the extent of the coverage. The problems associated with this coverage become acute when the goods move through indirect channels. The ultimate user complains to the reseller, and the reseller in turn attempts to shift the burden to the manufacturer. The manufacturer is one step removed from the situation and must rely on his salesperson to be an able investigator and arbitrator.

Financing

Another legal aspect of customer relations involves financing. The salesperson often faces situations in which his firm is directly involved in financing the items purchased or in arranging such financing from outside sources. Under the UCC, claims against products being financed are treated by reserving a security inter-

---

[3]*Ibid.*, p. 414.

est in the seller (referred to as a lien in earlier legislation). If repossession becomes necessary, the salesperson must know the legal restraints under which this action can be accomplished.

Consignment

There is another legal factor peculiar to some sales operations—namely, the handling of goods on consignment, where title remains with the seller. This becomes complicated if the goods involved have a finite shelf life and depreciation occurs with time. In the event that repossession is necessary, the salesperson must know the legal restraints on accomplishing this as well as his company's rights with respect to depreciated value. In most states, for example, it is a criminal offense for a reseller to sell consigned goods and not immediately pay the consignor the monies owed.

The provisions in the UCC regulate business transactions and cover in detail those involving the sale of goods and services. Because the UCC is so widely adopted, it is important that salespeople be aware of its implications in regulating their activity.

THE COOLING-OFF RULE OF THE FEDERAL TRADE COMMISSION

The Federal Trade Commission has adopted a Trade Regulation Rule which deals directly with sales practices. This rule, effective since 1974, established a cooling-off period for door-to-door sales.

The basic purpose of this rule is to allow consumers to review buying decisions which have been made during a sales presentation or under the persuasive influences of a salesperson who has called on them at their home. Under this rule, the consumer may cancel a business transaction during the three working days subsequent to the time at which the transaction was originally made.

The Notice of Cancellation

The cooling-off rule specifies the form in which this information must be given to the buyer. Along with the requirement to present the buyer with a complete contract and/or receipt of the transaction, in the same language as that principally used in the sales presentation, the seller must include in this contract on the first page, or in the space next to the buyer signature, the following statement:

> You, the buyer, may cancel this transaction at any time prior to midnight of the third business day after the date of this transaction. See the attached notice of cancellation form for an explanation of this right.

In addition the seller must furnish the buyer with a notice of cancellation stated as follows:

Notice of Cancellation
(enter date of transaction)
(Date)

You may cancel this transaction, without any penalty or obligation, within three business days from the above date.

If you cancel, any property traded in, any payments made by you under the contract or sale, and any negotiable instrument executed by you will be returned within 10 business days following receipt by the seller of your cancellation notice, and any security interest arising out of the transaction will be cancelled.

If you cancel, you must make available to the seller at your residence, in substantially as good condition as when received, any goods delivered to you under this contract or sale; or you may if you wish, comply with the instructions of the seller regarding the return shipment of the goods at the seller's expense and risk. If you do make the goods available to the seller and the seller does not pick them up within 20 days of the date of your notice of cancellation, you may retain or dispose of the goods without any further obligation. If you fail to make the goods available to the seller, or if you agree to return the goods to the seller and fail to do so, then you remain liable for performance of all obligations under the contract.

To cancel this transaction, mail or deliver a signed and dated copy of this cancellation notice or any other written notice, or send a telegram, to *(Name of seller),* at *(address of seller's place of business)* no later than midnight of _____

(date)

I hereby cancel this transaction.

_____
(date)

_____
(buyer's signature)

Failure to provide these two items is considered an *unfair* or *deceptive practice*.

Where Does the Rule Apply?

The cooling-off rule applies to any door-to-door transaction of goods with a price of $25.00 or more, whether this is done under single or multiple contracts.

The FTC rule does not annul or exempt any seller from complying with the laws of any state, or with municipal ordinances regulating door-to-door sales. An exemption is made, however, when such state laws or ordinances are considered directly inconsistent with the rule. State laws could be tougher, but not more lenient than the Federal rule.

The FTC's concern with unfair or deceptive trade practices is exemplified by this rule. The federal government through its agencies and other regulatory bodies has had an increasingly important role in trading practices and activities; and this greater concern with the intent of the consumer has been extended to most states. It is important, therefore, to examine the role of state legislation as it affects the selling-buying relationship.

STATE CONSUMER PROTECTION LAWS

In addition to the fair trade laws and the Uniform Commercial Code, state legislation is a more recent development resulting from consumers' reactions to deceptive trade practices. Several states have passed consumer protection laws, also called "little FTC laws," which are aimed at preventing and prosecuting abuses and deceit by salespersons and merchants at the local level. The "little FTC laws" are in many cases more specific than their federal counterparts, and they are usually enforced through the attorney general's office at the state level.

An excellent example of a "little FTC law" is the Texas Deceptive Trade Practices and Consumer Protection Act. This law was passed to give the Texas Attorney General the power to prosecute "false, misleading, or deceptive acts or practices in the conduct of trade or commerce." The law is relevant to all salespersons whether they are dealing directly with the final consumer or with a firm. Several acts singled out as deceptive which apply to salespersons are the following:

1. Passing off goods or services as those of another.
2. Causing confusion or misunderstandings as to the source, sponsorship, approval or certification of goods or services.
3. Using deceptive representations or designations of geographic origin in connection with goods or services.
4. Representing that goods or services have sponsorship, approval, characteristics, uses, or benefits which they do not have.
5. Representing that goods are original or new if they are deteriorated, reconditioned, reclaimed, used, or second hand.
6. Representing that goods are of a particular standard, quality or style if they are not.
7. Disparaging the goods, services, or business of another by false or misleading representation of facts.
8. Making false or misleading statements concerning the reasons for, the existence of, or the amount of price reductions.

Although most, if not all, of these acts would also be deceptive under the Federal Trade Commission Act, it is impossible for the FTC to monitor all markets. This law gives the Texas Attorney General the right to take action against deceptive practices which would easily slip by the Federal Trade Commission. There is a wide variation in the content and severity of state consumer protection laws, and salespersons should become familiar with the statutes that affect their own sales territories because more and more states are adopting laws such as Texas' "little FTC Act."

Although it is necessary that the sales activity be performed within legal boundaries at the federal, state, and local levels, it is also important that the individual performance of salespersons follow a set of ethical and moral standards acceptable in our culture. Since morals and ethics have often been considered differently, we will examine some aspects of what we consider to be a general code of ethics for salespersons.

A CODE OF ETHICS FOR THE SALESPERSON

To be effective in his position, a salesperson must first of all be trusted and respected by his customers. People evaluate others by comparing their behavior with a set of standards. Morality and ethics have, however, abstract standards, and as such they will vary from individual to individual.

A persons' judgment of what is ethical behavior is usually based on two concepts: the generally accepted social standards of ethics, and the individual's acceptance of specific behavior according to his personal ethical judgment. The question of what is ethical and moral for salespersons must conform to the generally accepted social standards, and since salespersons are exposed to many individuals, their actions must be acceptable to the majority rather than the minority.

Some companies may require their employees to obey more rigid standards of behavior than those generally acceptable to society. When this is not the case, however, the salesperson must at least conform to general rules of ethics. We will examine some general rules of business ethics and then describe specific professional standards relating to the salesperson's customers.

The Salesperson and Business Ethics

One definition of ethics is: "a set of moral principles or values." Companies do not have ethics, people do. However, each firm's policies as written and as practiced comprise the *ought/ought-not system* of the company, just as the individual's life values as verbalized and manifest in his behavior are his *ought/ought-not system*. When plans, action, and decisions of the individual company reach the ethical level, they are, at a minimum, defensible in terms of morals and mores.

Critics of business are cynical with regard to the ethics which guide those who pursue business careers. To illustrate this, one writer has this to say:

> Mass production and mass consumption have also transformed the ego into an instrument of salesmanship. Personality has become a means of manipulation. The successful person makes an instrument of his own appearance and personality. The smile becomes a commercialized lure. Kindness and friendliness are devices to disarm the unwary. Sincerity is detrimental to one's job, until the rules of salesmanship and business become a genuine aspect of oneself. Tact is a series of little lies about one's own feelings, until one is emptied of such feelings. Each person needs to become a quick character analyst. If the other individual is phlegmatic, he should be handled deliberately; if he is sensitive, he should be handled with directness; if opinionated, with deference; if openminded, with frankness; if cautious, handle him with proof.[4]

These observations notwithstanding, it seems unlikely that a sustained favorable interpersonal relationship can be maintained without truthfulness, honesty, trustworthiness, and sincerity on the part of all parties. It is extremely difficult to be what one is not over the long run. Each person is best at being himself.

Throughout this text we stress that the way the salesperson conducts the affairs of the firm with customers and prospects directly affects profits and growth and, in the extreme case, the firm's very survival. Any order obtained by dishonest or "shady" methods can be costly. False claims or questionable deals cannot contribute to sustained, mutually profitable selling-buying relationships.

To the extent that the salesperson fulfills his obligations as a good citizen and actively participates in community groups, he assists his firm in operating at an ethical level. Often, because of the overlap among the firm's various publics, the salesperson's conduct in the community as an individual citizen may contribute favorably or adversely to increased business. By the nature of his assignment, the salesperson can claim little privacy.

If a firm is to achieve leadership status, those who represent it must work at a level that will be appreciated by others. Their conduct must be defensible and considered worthy of emulation. The salesperson has the challenge of meeting this rigid standard. If he does, he is likely to have an important competitive advantage. People will take pride in doing business with him. Those who adjust at the aesthetic level do things for the other fellow that are beyond reasonable expectation. Their plans, decisions, and actions are considered exemplary. The salesperson who views his work professionally is unwilling to settle for a lesser standard by which to govern his conduct.

---

[4]C. Wright Mills, as quoted in *Ethics in Business,* edited by Robert Bartles ed. (Columbus, Ohio: Bureau of Business Research, Ohio State University, 1963), pp. 65–66.

Professional Standards

The behavior of a salesperson directly affects his customers; it may influence the customer's decision to buy as well as his recommendations to other customers. For these reasons, a salesperson should establish standards of behavior to follow when in contact with customers and with his company.

Ethics Toward The Client.   A salesperson gains his customers' confidence and thereby acquires the responsibility of satisfying their needs. His persuasive contact with the consumer must always be realistic and truthful. No use of deceitful means to make a sale is acceptable. Truth and honesty are essential if he is to maintain the confidence of his customers.

Discretion is also an important requirement of a sales relationship. Often salespersons are exposed to confidential competitive information that has no bearing on their product or their firm. Such confidences must be kept private and should not be used in gossip with others. The greater knowledge of his customers and their problems must be used by the salesperson only to allow him to better satisfy their needs—not as a conversation topic with other clients or colleagues.

One last, very delicate topic is that of gifts or other inducements given by salespersons to clients. Traditionally the salesperson's activity has included lavishly entertaining clients in order to obtain orders from them. Although entertainment is considered more acceptable than gift giving, both activities could easily be exaggerated to the point where they may be considered a form of commercial bribery.

Discussing business at lunch or dinner may be a very wise sales practice, since the customer may be more attentive to the salesperson's considerations in a relaxed atmosphere than he would be during his own hectic business schedule. A simple promotional gift sent to all customers at Christmas could serve the purpose of reminding them of the firm's products and services. It is essential, however, that neither of these activities exceed their business purpose and that they both be kept within standards of good taste.

Ethics Toward the Company.   The salesperson faces ethical questions in his relationships with his own firm. He is on his own much of the time. No one is present to check the hours he works or the effort he expends. Furthermore, he often has discriminative judgment over expenditures of funds for traveling and entertainment. It is up to him to determine whether the dollars are invested or wasted or used for personal matters. In fulfilling his important marketing intelligence function, his reports should be objective and honest even if the content does not reflect favorably on his own performance.

In addition, the salesperson must feel and show loyalty for his company. If he becomes critical of some of his company's personnel or its performance, this criticism should not be passed on to clients or competitors. Such behavior would only draw negative reaction from outsiders, which would ultimately be reflected in the salesperson's own performance. The salesperson should, however, feel free to constructively criticize his company's operations to its management. This is one of the best ways the company has for identifying and correcting its legitimate problems.

The individual's participation in formal and informal company activities is very important for the firm's human relations and the cohesiveness of its personnel. The salesperson should participate in meetings and share his experiences with his colleagues so that all can benefit from his acquired knowledge of the field. An organization will always improve when joint efforts are realized.

The Professional Salesperson

Business historians, when looking back at the twentieth century, may see the first half of the century as a period of great technological advance. It is possible that they will view the second half of the century as a time of professionalization in business. The American Marketing Association and Sales and Marketing Executives International are two groups concerned with professionalizing careers in marketing and sales. Less formally, however, the individual salesperson acquires the benchmarks of the professional through his mode of adjustment, his attitude, and his approach to work.

The professional salesperson adjusts at the aesthetic level. He handles all aspects of his work in good taste. The values he manifests in interpersonal relationships are worthy of emulation. He has an attitude of continuing self-improvement. He seeks to master the relevant bodies of knowledge associated with his work and to achieve excellence in his performance. As a professional, he shares information with his colleagues in the firm, knowing that the person who shares is helped by others. As a professional he is innovative, seeking new and better ways to do old jobs. In fact, this is one of the key distinctions between the professional and the technician in any field. The technician masters prescribed ways and uses them effectively, but he makes no significant contribution to the body of knowledge. In contrast, the professional seeks the new and is creative in his work. He uses the relevant bodies of knowledge, but he also contributes to them.

SUMMARY

Sales activity is regulated by federal, state, and local laws aimed at protecting competitive efforts and consumers' rights. This legal framework directly and indirectly affects the activities of salespersons who should be aware and knowledgeable about their effects and consequences.

Government regulation of business activities increased greatly since 1900. As an example, the Sherman Act (1890) states that, ''Every contract, combination in the form of trust or otherwise, or conspiracy, in restraint of trade or commerce . . .'' is illegal. In contrast, the Robinson-Patman Act (1936) indicates that a person or company is guilty of price discrimination if the effects of such an act may be to *substantially lessen* competition or *tend to create* a monopoly in any line of commerce.

In addition, many more recent laws have been passed to further protect the final consumer. It is important for the salesperson to be aware of certain types of activities that have become illegal.

We discussed a number of ethical questions for the salesperson, as well. The salesperson has ethical responsibilities toward his customers and firm, and if he does not act in a professional, ethical manner, his short-term success will inevitably result in long-term failure.

The salesperson, like his company, can survive and succeed only by maintaining standards above the legal (must/must-not) and the ethical (ought/ought not) levels. The implication is that the salesperson must be a professional. His conduct must be worthy of emulation.

PROBLEMS

1. Outline a speech entitled, "The Legal Responsibilities of the Salesperson."
2. How does federal legislation affect pricing practices by salespersons?
3. What aspects of the relationship of the salesperson with his customers are affected by the Uniform Commercial Code?
4. Why is ethical behavior especially important for salespersons?
5. What are some of the ethical responsibilities a salesperson has toward his customers?
6. Is selling a profession? Explain your answer.

Exercise 23

LEGAL AND ETHICAL ASPECTS OF SELLING

Objective: To gain increased insight regarding ethics.

A. Self-Analysis

Set forth in "ought/ought not" form your own code of personal ethics. Do these contrast with the normally accepted code of ethics that most business persons have adopted for themselves? If there are differences between the two sets of ethics explain why you feel they exist.

B. Salesperson Analysis

Make arrangements to interview a salesperson in your community. Try to determine the following:

1. What does he know about the federal and state laws that govern his behavior.

2. Does the salesperson feel that new laws should be passed to regulate selling? If so, what would these laws cover.

3. Does the salesperson feel that some of the existing laws which govern salespersons should be eliminated? If so, which laws would the salesperson like to eliminate, and why?

4. Does the salesperson feel that *other* salespersons are at times unethical? What does he feel can be done about such practices if they occur.

5. Does the salesperson feel that customers are at times unethical? Ask him to explain.

   Be very careful when holding this interview, as many of these matters are quite delicate.

Case 23-1 The Singing Cow Dairy Co.

The Singing Cow Dairy Co., located in Jollyville, Texas, was founded in 1949 by Sam Fulcher, the owner of the Blue Ribbon Ranch. The company started as a family operation and sold a small line of dairy products to local retail stores. When Sam Fulcher died, in 1968, his son, David, inherited the factory, and decided to initiate an expansion program.

The Singing Cow Dairy products were well known within a 100-mile radius immediately surrounding Jollyville. The quality of the products and the reputation of the Fulcher family granted Singing Cow a stable market in that area. The same was not true, however, of the rest of the state, because Sam Fulcher had never believed in advertising; he relied solely on word-of-mouth communication to establish his demand.

David felt that his father's traditional business approach had limited the expansion of the firm. He felt that two major steps had to be taken in order to expand sales: (1) a major advertising campaign through the whole state of Texas, in order to familiarize consumers with the Singing Cow Dairy products; and (2) an intensive sales effort with retailers of major outlets in all large cities in Texas in order to gain their support and secure shelf space for the firm's products.

An advertising agency, McDaniel Advertising, was hired and given the contract for statewide advertising during the 1969–70 period. The agency was very modern and managed by young, dynamic, and experienced people.

In order to accomplish his second objective, David hired Thomas Achabal, an ambitious young man with a master's degree and five years' sales experience in the grocery business. Tom was given the responsibility of motivating the existing salespeople to aggressively pursue the major retail supermarket outlets in the state and secure their orders as well as good shelf space for Smiling Cow products. He was also told to hire additional salespersons to cover the rest of the Texas territory. Tom's title was Assistant to the President in Charge of Sales, but he felt that if he could show results he would have a good chance to be promoted to Sales Manager.

The Smiling Cow products were priced slightly above the average, and quantity discounts were granted. The product lines were available to any retailer in the state for the same price. The firm calculated a uniform markup for all their products which allowed them to absorb freight and shipping charges regardless of the distance covered. A computer simulation projected sales and shipping costs for the next five years, and included an average as a percentage of total markup.

Approximately two months after he had started the new sales program, Tom Achabal received a long-distance call from one of his more ambitious salespeople, Katherine Bentley. Ms. Bentley had been assigned the Lake Jackson territory and had already been successful in selling the firm's product line to several small retailers in the area.

Ms. Bentley was calling to obtain Mr. Achabal's permission to grant a special price reduction to a chain of food stores in that area. According to Ms. Bentley, the manager of the stores was willing to "deal" and to give Smiling Cow products a very desirable shelf location, provided that he could have a special price on the products. Tom had been hoping to get a chance to obtain this support of a major retail chain in Southeast Texas, and the proposition seemed appealing. The discount would probably allow the chain to compete in price with the small retail stores in the area, but Achabal was more interested in the retail chain's support than in the potential sales to small retailers in the area. For all these reasons, he told Ms. Bentley to accept the proposition and grant the new customer a special discount of 15%.

Two weeks later, Tom Achabal met with David Fulcher to give him a first progress report on his activities. At that time, he was very proud to be able to report that the cooperation of a major food retail chain had been secured, and he explained the special conditions of the sale. He was very careful to mention, however, that the discount granted was a unique case, and a similar situation would not occur in the future. Fulcher was furious when he heard the story and fired Achabal on the spot.

1. What was wrong with Achabal's decision?

2. Is it an unethical practice to allow large store chains to sell products at lower prices than the small competitors?

Case 23-2* The Great Electrical Conspiracy

Flint Fletcherson was a senior salesperson for General Electric. He had been with the company for 10 years; prior to this he had been an honor engineering student at the University of Michigan. Flint had worked hard and was recognized as one of the company's "coming young men." He had sold for several General Electric Divisions, but was currently selling their switch gear.

Flint was asked to attend a conference at which some very delicate matters would be discussed. After being sworn to secrecy Flint was briefed by an aide to the sales manager's boss, Chuck Lewis. The conversation was as follows:

Chuck: As you know business has been very hard these last few months. Prices have fallen a great deal. If we had not decided to take rather bold action, the firm's profits would have dropped, and that $8000 bonus you received last year would have been in jeopardy.

Flint: I am aware of the very tough competition we have faced. It seems that everyone wants too big a piece of the action.

Chuck: Yes, this is correct. As a result we have contacted Westinghouse, Allis-Chalmers, and Federal Pacific and have asked them to meet with us in Portland next week. At that time we will try to reactivate a plan which gives us 45% of the business, Westinghouse 35%, and Allis-Chalmers and Federal Pacific 10% each. As you may know we have had this arrangement now for several years.

Flint: I really did not know, Chuck; I had heard rumors like everyone else but I really did not believe it.

Chuck: When the plan is working, every ten days to two weeks a meeting is called to decide who gets the next order. Turns are decided by the ledger list, and the only decision that has to be made is the price the firm that is to "win" should submit.

Flint: Is this not illegal? What happens if you are caught?

Chuck: First, you will never be caught, and second, it may be illegal but it certainly is not unethical. This all began during World War II when the government asked all manufacturers to meet and discuss mutual problems so as to maximize our country's efforts over the war.

Flint: Yes, but. . . .

Chuck: Well, the government people insisted that we increase plant capacity so as to meet the nation's demand. That was well and good until after the war was over. Then, beginning in 1950, the bottom fell out of our industry because we had so much excess capacity and besides, as you know, we are all gentlemen and we certainly have never charged an unfairly high price for our product.

Flint: Why are you telling me all of this?

Chuck: It should be obvious to you by now. We have decided to make you our representative to the weekly meetings where this actual price is set for the next contract. Of course, you will still be expected to handle your day-to-day sales activities but you will receive a substantial salary adjustment at the end of the year. Also, if you carry out this job effectively, I feel you will receive a promotion fairly quickly.

Flint: How much of this is going on in the company now?

Chuck: It is really difficult to say. It is not the type of thing we talk about regularly at staff meetings but it certainly is quite pervasive in the industry.

Flint: Well, I will have to think about it.

Chuck: I understand; but whatever you decide do not mention any of this to anyone.

Flint: OK.

1. Is the plan that has been discussed illegal? If so under what statutes?

2. Is this plan unethical? Explain.

3. What should Flint do?

SUGGESTIONS FOR FURTHER READING

Cunningham, William H., and Isabella C. M. Cunningham, "Consumer Protection: More Information or More Regulation," *Journal of Marketing,* Vol. 40 (April, 1976).

Jackson, John D., "Here's What You Must Know about Purchasing Law," *Purchasing,* Vol. 68 (April 2, 1970), pp. 53–60.

Levitt, Theodore, "Ambivalence and Affluence in Consumerland," *Sales Management,* Vol. 103 (Nov. 1, 1969), pp. 43–50.

Levy, Sidney, and Gerald Zaltman, *Marketing, Society and Conflict,* (Englewood Cliffs, N.J.: Prentice-Hall, 1975).

*This case is taken in part from "The Incredible Electrical Conspiracy" by Richard A. Smith, published in *Fortune,* April 1961; and May 1961.

Mayer, Ramond R., "Management's Responsibility for Purchasing Ethics," *Journal of Purchasing,* Vol. 6 (November 1970), pp. 13–20.

Russell, Frederic A., Frank H. Beach, and Richard A. Buskirk, *Textbook of Salesmanship,* 9th ed. (New York, N.Y.: McGraw-Hill, 1974) Chapters 18, 21.

Schutte, Thomas F., and Laurence W. Jacobs, "Business Ethical Dilemmas: An Analysis of Conflict," *Journal of Purchasing,* Vol. 4 (November 1968), pp. 23–30.

Schwartz, David J., "Salesmanship and Professional Standards," *Atlanta Economic Review* (September 1961), pp. 15–19.

Tootelian, Dennis H., "Attitudinal and Cognitive Readiness: Key Dimensions for Consumer Legislation," *Journal of Marketing,* Vol. 39 (July 1975), pp. 61–64.

Werner, Ray O., "Marketing and the United States Supreme Court, 1956–1968," *Journal of Marketing,* Vol. 33 (January, 1969), pp. 16–23.

EPILOG
The Future of Selling

The various trends alluded to in this book are likely to continue—namely, the salesperson's increasing professionalization, his widening marketing responsibilities, and his recognized managerial status.

Evidence of professionalization includes: certification and licensure such as has already occurred in insurance, securities, and real estate; general upgrading of educational requirements for entry; systematic training in selling concepts, methods, and techniques; and efforts to improve the image of selling by such groups as Sales and Marketing Executives International.

More and more firms are recognizing the sales organization as the prime tactical force in the total marketing effort. Each salesperson focuses the firm's promotional effort and customizes the firm's offerings on a one-to-one basis. It is the salesperson who adjusts to the unforeseen and unexpected whether this be a change in an account or a move on the part of the competitor. The very tempo of business dictates placing responsibility for many marketing decisions in the hands of the salesperson.

As companies adopt segmental analysis and contribution centers as a way of financial life, the salesperson becomes crucial to the fiscal soundness of the operation. After all, he manages the "bricks" (accounts) out of which is built a profitable enterprise. In addition, increasingly it is he who must commit scarce and costly resources in managing the sales effort—for example, supportive personnel, samples, trial use of equipment. It is obviously imperative that the salesperson use sound commercial judgment in these decisions.

There are also a number of general business trends that will have an indirect impact on selling: increased social demands on the private sector; shift in values from possession to use; pervasive impact of systems thinking; the knowledge explosion; and growth in demand for services.

Society is likely to assess each firm's contribution on the basis of social as well as economic criteria, taking up such issues as use of scarce resources, especially energy; protection of the environment; safety; equal employment opportunities; and service to the community. Inasmuch as the salesperson *is* the company to many people, he will have to be sophisticated in these matters. In addition, his personal example as a participating citizen will be an important factor in his credibility.

As a people, we are placing more importance on availability and use than on personal possession. One of the impacts of this trend is the increasing importance of renting and leasing as alternatives to purchase. The salesperson handling big-ticket items will need to understand the implications of renting and leasing in order to best match his offerings with the needs and wants of the market members in his assigned territory.

In our discussion of industrial selling we mentioned the impact of systems thinking. This concept is becoming more widespread in all sectors of the economy. Thus, the salesperson must be competent to help the customer optimize each man-machine system where his products and services are a part. Sales representatives handling products which in themselves do not constitute a full system will need to stress their compatibility with other products. This in turn means a broader base of technical knowledge.

One impact of the knowledge explosion is the increased sophistication of those with whom the salesperson must deal. While his personal charm may add a plus in the selling-buying relationship, the salesperson has to be a "knower" if he is to influence increasingly knowledgeable purchasers. Even consumers are engaging in value analysis as they weigh the merits of competing products. Also, more of them are consulting such evaluative sources as *Consumer Reports*.

Some writers call our present state of the economy postindustrial. Putting this in historical perspective, we might refer to the first part of the twentieth century as the age of mass production. The next part might be considered as mass promotion and distribution. The period following World War II might be designated an era of technological development and innovation. Now, we are moving into the period of quality of life and the quest for knowledge and services. Note, that although these developments continue, they are not self-replacing—all of them are still evident. Rather, it is a matter of emphasis. Thus the salesperson must be prepared to provide knowledge, advice, and service in ever-increasing amounts. This is bound to make selling, more than ever, a team operation.

All of these developments suggest that personal selling—far from lessening in importance in the face of increased automation of production and mass promotional efforts—is going to be a critically important business activity in the years ahead. The challenges will be many, but the rewards will be great. No other vocational field will be more intellectually challenging.

SUGGESTIONS FOR FURTHER READING

Dawson, Leslie M., "Toward a New Concept of Sales Management," *Journal of Marketing,* Vol. 34 (April 1970), pp. 33–38.

Frank, Paul, "Selling the Professional Buyer," *Sales/Marketing Today,* Vol. 15, No. 8 (August–September, 1969), pp. 12–13.

Holloway, Robert J., "The Hallmark of a Profession," *Journal of Marketing,* Vol. 33 (January 1969), pp. 90–95.

Nation's Business, "Birth of a Salesman," Vol. 58 (August, 1970), pp. 31–34.

Nekvasil, C. A., "Do Sales Careers still Turn People on?" *Industry Week* (Dec. 23, 1974), pp. 24–29.

Reuschling, Thomas, "Black and White in Personal Selling," *Akron Business and Economic Review,* Vol. 4 (Fall 1973), pp. 9–13.

Sales Management, "For Selling: There's No Shortage of Challenges," Vol. 112 (Jan. 21, 1974), pp. 16–17.

Sales Management, "Should a Top Salesman Go into Management," Vol. 105 (Dec. 1, 1970), pp. 31–32.

Van, Karl, and John Hahn, "Professionalism in Selling," *Sales Management,* Vol. 107 (August 15, 1971), pp. 38–39.

Wheatley, Edward W., "Glimpses of Tomorrow," *Sales Management,* Vol. 104 (May 1, 1970), p. 41.

Wilsman, Leo G., "What a Salesman Should Be," *Sales/Marketing Today,* Vol. XV, No. 11 (December 1969), p. 15.

Glossary

Accountability. To be answerable for carrying out a given task, assignment, or responsibility.

Achievement. Knowledge or skill that has been learned or acquired.

Active Listening. Consciously paying attention to what someone is saying or to other audible stimuli.

Adoption Process. Process through which an innovation is adopted by a social system.

Advertising. Any paid form of nonpersonal presentation and promotion of ideas, goods, or services by an identified sponsor.

Advertising Campaign. A program or series of planned advertisements carried on through mass media. The coordinated employment of various media and methods of advertising to gain acceptance for a certain idea or product, or to increase the sales of a particular product or service. The placement of isolated and uncoordinated advertisements does not comprise a campaign.

Aggregate Sales Forecasting. Developing an estimate or forecast of what total sales will be in some future period by adding up the forecasts or projections of each of the subparts. For example, estimating the total sales for a company for the new year by adding together the sales projections for each of the sales territories.

Apathy. Lack of interest, indifference.

Aptitude. The capacity to acquire knowledge or skill.

Aspiration, Level of. The standard by which a person judges his own performance as being up to what he expects of himself; hoped for or sought after performance versus actual performance.

Association. The process of tying present messages with past experiences.

Attention Span. The number of distinct objects or other stimuli that can be perceived in a single momentary presentation.

Attitude. An enduring, learned predisposition to behave in a consistent way toward a given class of objects, people, or institutions as the individual perceives them to be.

Authority. Power to act, especially on behalf of the company.

Awareness. The cognizance, or consciousness of products, services, and ideas.

Branching. A characteristic of the creative thought process which refers to the way ideas lead to other related ideas.

Brand. A name, term, sign, symbol, or design, or a combination of them that is intended to identify the goods or services of one seller or group of sellers and to differentiate them from those of competitors.

Break-Even.   The level of production and/or sales volume in a business at which operations are neither profitable nor unprofitable (i.e., that volume at which all costs or outflows of funds are exactly equaled by the inflow from sales).

Broker.   An agent who does not have direct physical control of the goods in which he deals but represents either buyer or seller in negotiating purchases or sales for his principal.

Buygrid.   A matrix diagram of the decision areas involved in an industrial sale and of the types of reasons for purchasing a product.

"Canned" Sales Presentation.   Standard, prepared sales presentation used by some salespersons in their contacts with all customers.

Canvass.   Sales coverage of an area in door-to-door fashion.

Capital Goods.   The machinery installations and other goods needed for production which are not consumed within the manufacturing process.

Change Agent.   A professional (i.e., someone who is paid) who attempts to influence adoption decisions in a direction that he feels desirable.

Channel(s) of Distribution.   The structure of intracompany organization units and extracompany agents and dealers, wholesale and retail, through which a commodity, product, or service is marketed.

Clayton Act.   Federal legislation passed in 1914 and amended by the Robinson-Patman Act in 1936 that prohibits price discrimination and other forms of discrimination in restraint of trade.

Close.   Agreement of minds between buyer and seller; the inducement of purchase or acceptance of the proposition.

Closure.   A phenomenon of visual perception whereby certain stimuli are selectively attended to and the remainder become background; irregularities are smoothed out.

Cognition.   (See Thinking)

Cognitive Dissonance.   The posttransactional perceived difference toward the product or the purchase decision by the customer.

Cold Call.   The sales call directed to a prospective account, without being solicited by the potential customer.

Cold Canvassing.   To call on people who may or may not be potential users of the salesperson's product or service.

Communicability.   The degree to which the results of new products can be easily transmitted to others.

Compatibility.   The degree to which a new product or service is in accordance with existing norms and products.

Compensatory Adjustment.   A personality adjustment mechanism whereby an individual attempts to offset (compensate for) real or imagined personal shortcomings.

Competitive Structure.   The complex of direct and indirect competitors a firm has which share its common market.

Complexity.   The degree to which a new product is hard to use or understand.

Conditioning.   A basic method of learning by which responses are linked to stimuli that initially did not elicit them.

Consumer Goods.   Those products purchased and consumed by individuals or families.

Convenience Goods (Services). Those consumers' goods that the customer usually purchases frequently and immediately, with a minimum of effort and with little or no comparison shopping.

Counter-Selling. Common retail sales practice where salespeople help consumers from sales counters located in the store.

Cue. Secondary stimuli which guide individual behavior in order to achieve drive satisfaction. (Relates to learning theory.)

Culture. The concepts, habits, skills, arts, instruments, and institutions of a given people in a given period.

Customer. An individual who has purchased merchandise from a specific company previously.

Customer Orientation. The implementation of the marketing concept with regard to a firm's customers. The main focus of a firm's activities is the satisfaction of customers' needs.

Customer-Prospect Mix. The combination of customers and/or potential customers for a product or service of a specific company or industry.

Customer Representative. A salesperson whose general duties are to handle customer complaints and explain to them a firm's rate structure and marketing policies. These are generally salespeople of public utility companies.

Decentralization. The downward placement of authority in the firm (e.g., allowing the salesperson to commit to a delivery schedule without clearing with his superior).

Deductive Reasoning. Reasoning from the general to the particular; in purest form, syllogistic reasoning.

Derived Demand. The amount or quantity of the goods or services that will be required, based on the amount of some other goods or service required, (e.g., the amount of demand for automobile steering wheels is derived from the demand for autos).

Differential Competitive Advantage. Advantage enjoyed by one firm's marketing offering vis-a-vis direct and indirect competitors.

Diffusion of Innovation. The way in which new ideas are communicated to the members of a social system.

Diminishing Returns (Law of). The principle which states that the utility of each additional unit of the same product decreases as more units are consumed.

Direct Channel. The process whereby the firm responsible for production sells to the user, ultimate consumer, or retailer without intervening middlemen.

Distribution Mix. The combination of channels of distribution that a firm uses to get its product from the producer to user. One firm may use a number of different channels for different market segments or geographical areas (e.g., direct sales to firms close by, agents in outlying areas, and wholesalers or distributors in foreign states or countries).

Diversified Company. A corporation composed of different companies in different industry classifications.

Divisibility. The degree to which a new product can be used on a small scale for trial purposes.

Dominance. An attitude of control and authority; the exercise of influence of a person.

Drive.   The basic needs, urges, and motives felt by individuals which provide stimuli for action. (Relates to learning theory.)

Economy of Scale.   Refers to the cost or other savings associated with a larger size of operations (e.g., as a firm produces more goods, the cost per unit generally is reduced, as a firm markets a wider product line, unit costs of marketing and distribution are generally reduced).

Empathy.   The projection of one's own personality into the personality of another; the ability to see through another individual's eyes.

Environmental factors.   Factors which are extraneous to the firm and which can not be controlled by manipulating the firm's resources.

Euphoria.   A feeling of well-being, of buoyancy.

Evaluation.   The process through which the advantages and disadvantages of a decision are weighed.

Exclusive Dealing and Tying Contracts.   The contract or agreement by which a buyer agrees to purchase a certain product or product line only from a specific seller, or vice-versa.

Expendable Supplies.   Products which are completely consumed while producing other goods, in the performance of organization or administrative activities by the firm.

Extrinsic Interest.   Interest in something derived from an external consideration (e.g., the consequences of not being interested, the necessity of being interested, etc.) (See also Intrinsic interest)

Fact.   Any information, the reality of which is independent from the reporting source.

Family Life Cycle.   The different stages a family unit goes through during its life. The cycle runs through marriage, the children coming into the family, the growing up of the children, their leaving the home, and the old-age period of the parents. During each stage of the cycle, the needs for goods and services change.

Feedback.   A direct and immediate reaction to a message or observation.

Field Selling.   The activity of selling performed outside the firm, at the customers' place of business.

Forecast.   A prediction of the future or an estimate of the future based on reasonable assumptions, past experience, and current values (e.g., forecast of future sales, income, costs, etc.)

Goal Gradient.   The tendency toward increased efficiency and attention as the goal is approached—an individual well on the way to completing a task is virtually uninterruptible.

Gross National Product (GNP).   The total market value of all the goods and services produced in the country in a certain period of time (usually in one year).

Habit.   Modes or patterns of response that have become overlearned and occur without conscious effort.

Heterogeneous Product Line.   A set of products which are not related as to their use, type of customer, or buying characteristics.

Heterophyly.   The quality of two people having dissimilar qualities or characteristics.

Hierarchy of Needs.   Maslow's theory of motivation which postulates an ordering or ranking of human needs from biological to self-actualization.

"Hinge." A telephone selling technique by which a salesperson links his call to a customer to a previous occurrence in the buying-selling relationship.

Homeostasis. See "Need Homeostasis."

Homophyly. The phenomenon by which two individuals have similar qualities or characteristics.

Ideation. A stage of creative thinking when ideas flow and branch.

Image. A composite of concepts, judgments, preferences, and attitudes held by an individual or group with respect to an object, person, or institution.

Impulsiveness. A tendency to act suddenly, without conscious thought.

Incentive. An object or external condition having motivational value to the individual.

Incremental Analysis. The examination of the extra profit and extra cost involved by a proposed project or sale.

Incubation. A stage of creative thinking not in conscious awareness.

Indirect Channel. Refers to the use of middlemen in the sale and distribution of goods (as opposed to direct channel which means the manufacturer sells and distributes the goods directly to the user).

Indirect Representation. Selling to final users or consumers through wholesalers or dealers, rather than directly.

Inductive Reasoning. Reasoning from the particular to the general; deriving generalizations from particular happenings.

Industrial Goods. Those products purchased and consumed by industrial users.

Inner Direction. The personality characteristic of people primarily self-oriented and not particularly responsive to other people's feelings and attitudes.

Innovation. A new product or a new idea.

Inside Ordertaker. The salesperson whose major task is to fill orders telephoned in by customers. This individual does not call on clients, he remains at the firm to provide immediate response for repeat and routine orders.

Intangible Products. Goods or services which are nonmaterial in nature, such as insurance, security services, etc.

Integrated Marketing. The organized and combined efforts of all a firm's marketing resources in order to satisfy its customers' needs. Includes the coordination of such elements as advertising, distribution, and selling.

Interaction. Action on each other; reciprocal action or effect.

Interpersonal Communication. The communication occurring between two individuals.

Intrinsic Interest. Interest in something in and of itself.

Learned Drives. The basic urges or impulses identified with specific goods or products which different cultures have traditionally used to satisfy physiological or psychological needs.

Limited-Function Wholesaler. A wholesaler that buys and resells merchandise to retailers and other merchants and/or industrial, institutional, and commercial uses but that does not offer significant amounts of associate services.

Line. Two uses: (1) A group or family of products that have common characteristics or qualities. (2) The decision-making, action-taking management group of a firm (as contrasted with staff).

Low-Pressure Selling. A technique by which the salesperson lets the customer initiate his decision making without attempting to dominate him during the sales presentation.

Macro. Term used in economics to refer to the economy as a whole, as opposed to micro which refers to the units (i.e., the firms comprising the whole).

Manner Cues. The style of behavior which reveals specific traits or personality characteristics.

Manufacturer's Agent (Representative). An individual who generally operates on an extended contractual basis; often sells within an exclusive territory; handles noncompeting but related lines of goods, and possesses limited authority with regard to prices and terms of sales. The manufacturer's agent is paid by the firm only if he sells its products.

Marketing Concept. The philosophy that the satisfaction of customers' needs and wants at a profit should be the main objective of a business.

Marketing Information (Intelligence). Types of data or facts about the marketplace useful to marketing management in planning, deciding, and acting; derived mainly from marketing research and from the field sales force.

Marketing Research. The process of gathering and analyzing marketing information relevant to the sale of products or the establishment of a firm's marketing policies.

Market Segmentation. A division of a market according to product uses, characteristics of purchasers, or other relevant dimensions of concern to the marketer.

Markup. The difference between the cost and selling price of the goods being sold by reseller; generally refers to the dollar differential, but it can be expressed as a percent of the cost or selling price, in which case the terms "markup on cost" or "markup on retail" are used.

Matrix. A diagram or schematic used to differentiate parts of a larger entity to show the interrelationships of the various parts. Usually a two-dimensional diagram using the horizontal axis for one set of parameters and the vertical axis for another set.

Matter Cues. Information generated by inquiry about a person's personality and motivational characteristics.

Media. Vehicles of communication (e.g., advertising, personal selling) and the specific institutions involved (e.g., radio, TV, a particular salesperson).

Merchandising. The planning and supervision involved in marketing the particular product or service at the places, times, prices, and in the quantities which will best serve to realize the marketing objectives of the business. All that is done to make the product or service attractive and differentiable.

Merchant (Full-Service) Wholesalers. A wholesaler that buys, resells, and provides a variety of associated services along with the goods. (See also Limited-Function Wholesaler)

Message. The ingredient of the signal that has meaning.

Micro. A term used in economics that refers to the study or analysis of specific business entities as opposed to the overall economy; related to or of concern to the individual business enterprise.

Middleman. A business concern that specializes in performing operations or rendering services directly involved in the purchase and/or sale of goods in the process of flow from producer to consumer.

Missionary Salesperson. A salesperson whose task is to promote the institutional image of a company or organization rather than to sell products as such. He frequently helps his firm's distributor salesperson to be more effective by making joint calls on the distributor's customers.

Mood. A particular state of mind or feeling, humor or temper.

Motivation. The "why" of behavior; purposefulness; includes motives (inside the individual) and incentives (aspects of the environment).

Motives. Forces within the individual underlying his behavior.

Multiple Sourcing. The practice by the customer or prospect of purchasing a product from more than one firm. (See also Sole Sourcing)

Need Homeostasis. A state balance of needs characterized by satisfaction with the status quo.

Noise. A term used in communication theory which refers to the distortion of the signals transmitted and received, thereby impeding the message ingredient of the signal.

Nonverbal Communication. The sending and receiving of messages which do not utilize spoken language.

Off-the shelf. Standard items produced by a company and not modified to the customer's desires.

One-Way Communication. The form of communication that terminates with the message reaching the receiver. No feedback is allowed from the receiver to the sender.

Open-Stock Selling. A retail practice used in selling large items. The items are located on the sales floor rather than behind the counter.

Operational Buying Motives. The reasons for purchase which are directly related to the anticipated performance of a product.

Opinion. Any information, the worth of which is dependent on the reporting source.

Original Equipment Manufacturer (OEM). Manufacturers or producers of products (e.g., television tubes sold to Philco versus those sold to television repairmen for replacement usage).

Outer Direction. The personality characteristic of people who are very responsive to other people's attitudes and reactions.

Overlearning. Learning in which practice proceeds beyond the point where the act can just be performed with the required degree of excellence, thus making for reinforcement and lessening the forgetting process.

Participation. The customer or prospect's involvement with the sales presentation.

"Party" Selling. A sales practice by which a prospective customer invites guests to a party so the salesperson can present the product line.

Passive Listening. Making no effort to attend to incoming auditory stimuli; "sensing" but not "perceiving."

Perception. The process of attaching meaning to stimuli received through the various senses.

Perceptual Constancy. A characteristic of perception by which objects and other stimuli retain their relative size, color, and form even when presented otherwise.

Personality. The distinguishing qualities of an individual; the style or "how" of his behavior; his uniqueness.

Persuasion.   To cause someone to do or to change his attitudes about something or some idea by reasoning, urging, or inducement.

Physical Distribution.   The management of the movement and handling of goods from the point of production to the point of consumption or use.

Positioning.   A marketing strategy designed to establish a product or a line of products in a specific niche in the marketplace so as to differentiate it from competitive offerings.

Posttransactional.   Refers to the period of time after the sale or transaction has taken place; it encompasses the numerous follow-up activities of the salesperson and other personnel.

Product Line.   A group of products that are closely related either because they satisfy a class of need, are used together, are sold to the same customer group, are marketed through the same type of outlets, or fall within given price ranges.

Product Orientation.   The business philosophy based on the concept that the main goal of the marketing activities of a firm is to sell the goods the firm produces. (See also Marketing Concept)

Product-Service Mix.   The combination of products and services a company offers for sale.

Profit.   That portion of income remaining after all expenses are paid, or the excess of business income over business expenses or costs.

Promotional Mix.   The combination of marketing forces and tools used by a company to cultivate or sustain market demand for their product(s) (e.g., advertising, personal selling, merchandising, and sales promotion).

Prospect.   Technically an individual who has not previously purchased merchandise from a specific company.

Prospecting.   The activity of looking for new customers by canvassing door-to-door, or following other types of leads.

Prospective Account.   A potential customer for a firm's products or services.

Psychological Moment.   The "optimum time" during a sales call to ask for the order. (We do not believe that this concept has a great deal of usefulness in selling.)

Publicity.   Any information which brings a person, place, thing, or cause to the notice or attention of the public. Unlike advertising publicity, it is not paid for.

Public Sector.   The portion of the market for goods and services that is made up of government entities (e.g., the armed forces, the national space program, the federal penitentiaries, etc.).

Purchasing Agent.   The individual in charge of purchasing goods and services for others or for business organizations.

Push-Pull.   This concept refers to two different marketing strategies. The "push" strategy refers to the process whereby a company tries to gain the assistance of the marketing intermediaries to help push the sale of a product. (This might be done by giving larger than normal trade discounts, spiffs, or other incentives.) The "pull" strategy refers to the method of creating the demand for the product and then having the consumers request the product from the middleman. Normally a "pull" strategy costs the firm more in advertising than does a "push" strategy, but the margin to the dealer is higher with a "push" strategy. An example of product that is pushed through this channel would be furniture, whereas cigarettes are pulled through the channel.

"Pyramiding." The sales practice by which companies enlist each of their customers to recruit their own sales force and set up their own business. This practice is now considered a violation of Federal Trade Commission's regulations.

Quota. A goal established for a sales territory, a product group, or a category of customers, usually in terms of revenue but sometimes in terms of units to be sold.

Rapport. A close and sympathetic relationship.

Rationalization. The process of justifying by reasoning after the event, as, for example, an act after it has been performed; often a defense mechanism against self-accusation, or a feeling of guilt.

Receive. In communication theory, the individual's role as a receiver of signals through the various sensory channels.

Receiver-Sender. In communication theory the individual's simultaneous role as both receiver and sender, as in two-way communication.

Reciprocity. An agreement under which one company favors another in purchasing, or the understanding that it will receive the same preference from the other.

Reference Groups. Formal or informal social groups which influence individual behavior directly or indirectly. Directly, they set standards of behavior which are to be followed by all those who belong to the group.

Relative Advantage. The degree to which one product is considered superior to competing products.

Repeat Sales. The continuous process of selling specific goods to one customer at regular intervals. The number of repeat sales reflects a customer's loyalty to the firm and/or to the product.

Reseller. A company or business concern that buys products from one company and offers them for sale to other companies or individuals (e.g., a retailer, a wholesaler).

Response. Each individual's reaction to cues.

Responsibility. A stage of obligation or accountability in a business. The chief executive officer is ultimately responsible for all that happens in the firm; other employees have intermediate responsibility through delegation.

ROAM (Return on Assets Managed). An evaluation of profit in terms of the assets managed or available.

Robinson-Patman Act. The federal law passed in 1936, and since amended, that further extends the coverage of the antitrust laws. The price sections of the act prohibit price discrimination between customers, unequal advertising and promotion allowances, price reductions, or concessions not justified by costs, etc.

ROI (Return on Investment). In general, the profit earned in relation to the value of the capital required to produce the profit.

Role Consensus. The degree of agreement between two individuals regarding behavior in a particular situation.

Routing. The formal procedure used to determine which customers and prospects the salesperson should call on during a particular time period.

Sales Bonus. A one-time reward given to salespeople for efficient performance. Bonuses are usually awarded on an annual basis or as a prize for reaching specific sales goals.

Sales Clinics. The training of salespeople to perform specific activities or to familiarize themselves with new products or lines of products.

Sales Commission.   A compensation proportional to the amount of sales made by a salesperson. A commission frequently is based on a percentage of the total sales amount.

Sales Forecasting.   The estimating of sales in dollars or physical units for a specified future period under a proposed marketing plan or program and under an assumed set of economic conditions and other forces.

Sales Pressure.   The use of aggressive and "pushy" sales tactics.

Sales Promotion.   (1) In a specific sense, those marketing activities, other than personal selling, advertising, and publicity, that stimulate consumer purchasing and dealer effectiveness—such as displays, shows and exhibitions, demonstrations, and various nonrecurring selling efforts not in the ordinary routing. (2) In retailing, all methods of stimulating customer purchasing, including personal selling, advertising, and publicity.

Sales Quota.   The minimum amount of sales to be made in a specific territory or by a specific salesperson during a certain established period of time.

Sales Representative.   A salesperson.

Sales Resistance.   Any objection or opposition to the arguments used by the salesperson in his presentation.

Sales Territory.   The geographical boundaries within which a salesperson or a group of salespeople operate.

Search.   The process of gathering information on all available alternative solutions for a need or problem.

Selective Perception.   The phenomenon by which only a portion of the signals received by one person is actually converted into messages.

Selectivity.   The perception of only specified characteristics of messages by the customer or prospect.

Self-actualization.   The highest form of need, according to Maslow's theory of motivation.

Sender.   In communication theory, the individual's role as a transmitter of signals by voice, gesture, or other means.

Sherman Act.   The federal law passed in 1890 and widely known as the Anti-Trust Law. It provided for the outlawing of trusts, as such, and made illegal a variety of practices leading to the monopolization of any line of business by one or a group of companies. This law provided imprisonment and fines for violators, as well as triple-damage lawsuits for authorized persons injured by the monopolistic practices of others.

Shopping Goods (Services).   Those consumer items that the customer, in the process of selection and purchase, characteristically evaluates on a comparative basis as to suitability, quality, price, and style.

Signal.   In communication theory, the unit of transmission; includes message and noise.

Single-Industry Segments.   All the firms classified as belonging to a specific industry group (such as defined by the SIC codes, for example).

Skill.   Ability to perform complex motor acts with ease, precision, and adaptability.

Sociopsychological Buying Motives.   The purchase motivation based on social attributes or psychological attributes perceived to be attached to the product, rather than the product performance.

Specialty Goods (Services). Those consumer items with unique characteristics and/or brand identification for which a significant group of buyers are habitually willing to make a special purchasing effort.

Spiff. A bonus or incentive offered the retail salesperson for selling a specific product or item; sometimes referred to as PM.

Staff. Management personnel who render a combination of advice and service to those who decide and act. (See also Line)

Status. The individual's standing in a role relationship with others as he or she perceives it.

Strategy. An overall plan of action. In a selling situation a strategy would consist of such things as who an individual plans on visiting and what approaches will be used to sell the merchandise.

Subconscious. The portion of mental activity of which the individual has little or no conscious perception.

Subculture. The unique cultural characteristics pertaining only to a segment of society which shares general common institutions, language, and other traits.

Subjective Perception. The ability of each individual to perceive the same message differently, according to his personality characteristics.

Suggestions. The process through which an idea is brought to the mind because of its connection or association with an idea already in the mind.

Summation. A characteristic of perception; temporal summation refers to the effect of successive stimuli finally eliciting a response; spatial summation, to the impact of stimuli reaching two senses or more simultaneously and hence eliciting a response that neither stimulus would have caused singly.

Summative Perception. The cumulative effect of signals which are converted into a message.

System. A complex, unitary whole set of connected parts or members that operate as an entity.

Tactics. The adjustments required in a plan or strategy as the actual event unfolds.

Tangible Products. Those goods which are material in nature, such as food, furniture, etc.

Target markets. Those specific market segments whose needs are best matched by a firm's product offerings.

Team Selling (and Buying). The industrial practice by which special teams are in charge of buying and/or selling activities (e.g., an industrial salesperson may ask his firm to provide him with a technical specialist and a plant engineer to help sell a product).

Technology. The science or study of the practical or industrial arts.

Terms of Trade. In general, the terms or conditions under which a sale is made or will be made, including the period allowed for payment, insurance, transportation, provision of charges, discounts allowed, etc. In common use it refers specifically to the period allowed for payment and to any discount allowed for prompt or early payment.

Territory Alignment. The establishment of sales territories based on work assignment criteria.

Thinking (Cognition). Mental process; has memory and perception as inputs.

Tie-in Sales. The practice by which a salesperson induces a customer to purchase additional items somewhat related to his initial purchase, such as accessories, etc.

Trading-up. The practice by which a salesperson may be instrumental in inducing a customer to purchase higher quality or bigger quantities of products.

Trait. Any enduring or persistent characteristic of a person by means of which he can be described or distinguished.

Transfer. A psychological term referring to the degree to which the learner can apply what he has learned; in general it is a function of common elements in the learning and application situations.

Two-Way Communication. The form of communication which includes a circular flow of information, therefore providing feedback from the receiver to the sender.

Type. A class of individuals having a characteristic or a pattern of characteristics in common.

Typecasting. The description of people with reference to an *a priori* classification system.

Uniform Commercial Code. A codification and combination of the uniform laws affecting business activities. It includes such uniform laws as the uniform bill of lading act, uniform negotiable instrument act, uniform sales act, uniform stock transfer act, uniform trust receipts act, and the uniform warehouse receipts act.

Value(s). The core of personality; the ought/ought-not, right-wrong, and beautiful-ugly standards underlying the individual's choices and attitudes.

Value Analysis. A systematic method developed by professional purchasing executives for evaluating products and services offered by sellers.

Verbal Communication. The sending and receiving of messages which utilize language as the code.

Want Book. A book kept by reseller in which items to be ordered are noted.

Weber's Law. A classical psychological theorem which states that the least-added difference of stimulus that can be noticed is a constant proportional part of the original stimulus. The unit of change is referred to as a just-noticeable difference.

Index